# The Civil War on the Rio Grande, 1846–1876

*Publication of this book was supported by a gift from the Texas Historical Foundation.*

NUMBER FORTY-SIX
Elma Dill Russell Spencer Series in the West and Southwest

Ranches and Ferry Landings
of Civil War Era Hidalgo County

**Map Legend**

Ferry Landing

Battle

Trail

The Military Telegraph Road

# *The Civil War on the Rio Grande, 1846–1876*

*Edited by*

ROSEANN BACHA-GARZA
CHRISTOPHER L. MILLER
RUSSELL K. SKOWRONEK

*Foreword by Gary W. Gallagher*

*Texas A&M University Press • College Station*

Second printing, 2020

This paper meets the requirements of ANSI/NISO Z39.48–1992 (Permanence of Paper).
Binding materials have been chosen for durability.
Manufactured in the United States of America

LIBRARY OF CONGRESS CATALOGING-IN-PUBLICATION DATA

Names: Bacha-Garza, Roseann, author, editor. | Miller, Christopher L., 1950– author, editor. | Skowronek, Russell K., author, editor. | Gallagher, Gary W., writer of foreword. | Miller, Christopher L., 1950— Prelude.
Title: The Civil War on the Rio Grande, 1846–1876 / edited by Roseann Bacha-Garza, Christopher L. Miller, Russell K. Skowronek ; foreword by Gary W. Gallagher.
Other titles: Elma Dill Russell Spencer series in the West and Southwest ; no. 46.
Description: First edition. | College Station : Texas A&M University Press, [2019] | Series: Elma Dill Russell Spencer series in the West and Southwest ; number forty-six | Includes bibliographical references and index.
Identifiers: LCCN 2018039740| ISBN 9781623497194 (book/hardcover (printed case) : alk. paper) | ISBN 9781623497200 (ebook)| ISBN 978162349961-7 (paperback)
Subjects: LCSH: United States--History--Civil War, 1861–1865. | Lower Rio Grande Valley (Tex.)—History, Military—19th century. | Texas—History—Civil War, 1861–1865 — Biography. | United States—History—Civil War, 1861–1865—Biography.
Classification: LCC F392.R5 C58 2019 | DDC 973.7—dc23 LC record available at https://lccn.loc.gov/2018039740

A list of titles in this series is available at the end of the book.

*This book is dedicated to the forty-three members of the Contributors Committee who took the bold step on May 22, 2014, to endorse the creation of the Rio Grande Valley Civil War Trail.*

*And to the memory of our colleague and friend, Bobbie L. Lovett, one of the founders of the CHAPS Program, whose support will never be forgotten.*

# Contents

# *Foreword*

The invitation to write a brief foreword for this book of essays brought back many memories of my years as a resident of Austin. I left southern Colorado in 1973 to study southern history at the University of Texas. As I drove southward through New Mexico in January, my route paralleled that of Brig. Gen. Henry Hopkins Sibley's 2,500 Texans when they moved up the Rio Grande Valley in the winter and early spring of 1862. I thought about how those Texans must have reacted to the sight of the imposing Sangre de Cristo Mountains, to the effects of altitude as they approached Santa Fe, and to the cold weather (the night before I left Colorado, the temperature dropped to twenty-two degrees below zero in Alamosa, my hometown). Sibley's grand hopes to establish a long-term Confederate presence in New Mexico, gain access to Colorado's mineral wealth, and if all went well, push on toward California came to nothing, but his operation, including the climactic engagement at Glorieta Pass on March 26, had interested me since I read Martin Hardwick Hall's account of the campaign as a boy. Other than Sibley's quixotic foray, which brought the Civil War's military action closest to where I grew up, I knew relatively little about Texas and its residents during the conflict, except that the state had contributed soldiers to the Confederacy—most obviously the famous brigade that fought in the Army of Northern Virginia—and shared a long international border with the Republic of Mexico untouched by United States military forces. Beyond those facts, and knowledge of a few episodes along the Gulf Coast involving land and naval forces, my principal engagement with Texas during the war came from my close, and appreciative, reading of Arthur James Lyon Fremantle's *Three Months in the Southern States: April–June 1863* (published in 1863), which includes a long section on the British officer's travels from the mouth of the Rio Grande through much of the state.

My years in Austin revealed how the war's impact remained visible in Texas. I quickly grasped the dominance of the Lost Cause memorial landscape. The capitol grounds feature the massive Confederate Soldier's Monument (dedicated in 1903), which offers Jefferson Davis as its central figure; a large tribute in stone and bronze to Terry's Texas Rangers (1906); and a tall obelisk, topped by a bronze common soldier, commemorating Hood's Texas Brigade (1910). Various other portraits, plaques, and architectural details in and on the capitol also recall the Confederacy. In the State Cemetery, I encountered Elisabet Ney's recumbent statue of Albert Sidney Johnston, whose remains had been moved from New Orleans to Austin in 1867, as well as the graves of several other Confederate generals and a large number of veterans. On the UT campus, the South Mall included statues of Jefferson Davis, Robert E. Lee, Albert Sidney Johnston, and John H. Reagan (all four removed from campus in the summer of 2017). To my surprise, the state also observed Confederate Heroes Day—some called it Confederate Memorial Day—on January 19, Robert E. Lee's birthday.

I also discovered evidence of the war in Texas beyond what the Lost Cause chose to emphasize. Before moving to Austin, I had never heard of Juneteenth, which commemorates the reaction of African Americans in Galveston to the arrival of Maj. Gen. Gordon Granger's federal troops on June 19, 1865. A striking example of the Emancipation Cause memory of the conflict, it became a Texas state holiday in 1980 and has since spread to many other parts of the United States. I also found an echo of the Union Cause stream of Civil War memory southwest of Austin in Comfort, where the Treue der Union Monument, erected in 1866, honors thirty-four men killed as they attempted to escape Confederate conscription in August 1862. The State Cemetery, though in some ways dominated by Lost Cause memorialization, also contains an imposing monument over the grave of Edmund J. Davis, a unionist who joined Gov. Sam Houston in opposing secession in 1861, fought for the United States as a brigadier general during the war, and served as the Republican governor of Texas from 1870 to 1874. When I first glimpsed the monument, I wondered how its prominence in the cemetery must have struck ex-Confederates who loathed Davis for, among other things, his strong support for expanding the rights of black Texans. I often visited bookstores and publishers in Austin, and in 1976 a talk with Jay Matthews at Presidial Press introduced me to another facet of Texas during the war. I bought a copy of Jerry Thompson's *Vaqueros in Blue and Gray*, just published by Presidial, a pioneering study that dealt with the participation of nearly ten thousand Tejanos in the conflict.

I left Austin in the mid-1980s but have maintained an interest in the developing literature on Texas during the Civil War era. The expansion, both in size and breadth of topics, has been very impressive. The bookshelves in my study include volumes by, among others, James Marten, David Pickering and Judy Falls, Dale Baum, Richard B. McCaslin, Richard Lowe, David Paul Smith, James W. Daddysman, Ralph A. Wooster, Carl H. Moneyhon, Donald S. Frazier, John P. Wilson, Clayton E. Jewett, Charles D. Grear, and Don E. Alberts. These authors examine politics, dissent, economics, military affairs, and other elements of the state's wartime experience. Talented editors have annotated a number of primary accounts, including the letters of Dr. Gideon Lincecum, Theophilus and Harriet Perry, Joseph Rafael de la Garza and Manuel Yturri, and Louis Lehmann, and the diaries and journals of Lucy Pier Stevens, Sallie McNeill, Henrietta Baker Embree, Tennessee Keys Embree, Elizabeth Scott Neblett, A. B. Peticolas, and William Randolph Howell.

*Civil War on the Rio Grande, 1846–1876* is a welcome addition to this literature. Its eleven essays traverse a great deal of ground, addressing ethnicity and race, military action, transnational relationships, and how material culture can inform understanding of historic episodes and groups. The focus on the Rio Grande Valley gives the collection an interpretive cohesion often absent in volumes of essays. Beyond expanding what we know about the war in that region, this book should inspire additional scholarship on how Texas shaped, and was shaped by, the most disruptive event in American history.

—Gary W. Gallagher
John L. Nau III Professor in the History of the American Civil War
University of Virginia

# *Preface*

This book is about a specific era in a particular place. The era is that of the Civil War in the United States. The place is the Rio Grande Valley. To most readers, that would seem to announce that this book is very limited in scope and parochial in focus—that this is not only *local history* in its narrowest sense, but also *micro history* in its circumscribed chronological coverage. While the chronological limitation might be forgiven—after all, the Civil War era is the most written about period in US history—there can be no excuse for dedicating an entire volume to a geographical area that clearly was less than even tangential to the *real* Civil War. We believe, however, that readers who exercise the patience to wade into the pages that follow will be pleasantly surprised.

Even before dealing with the broad historical significance that the essays in this book represent, we must first deal with the complexity inherent in just defining the time and place that these essays deal with. The *Civil War era* and the *Rio Grande Valley* sound quite concrete and easily delimited; however, readers will find as they go further into these pages that neither is as definite as it may seem.

Looking first at the era, no right-thinking historian would say that the Civil War era started precisely on April 12, 1861, with the shelling of Fort Sumter, nor that it ended with the stroke of a pen on April 9, 1865, at Appomattox Court House. It is, of course, a matter of some argumentation among historians exactly when the critical moment was that the Civil War era began. It may be even more controversial to assert a definitive ending date: for most people in the Union states, the Appomattox Court House date may seem right; for more, perhaps, the burial of Abraham Lincoln; or the final surrender of the last Confederate holdout, Brig. Gen. Stand Watie of the 1st Cherokee Mounted Rifles, more than a month after Lincoln was interred. But for those in the former Confederate states, formal military occupation and martial law extended for more than a decade after Robert E. Lee's surrender. As German historical theorist Reinhart Koselleck has noted, chronology for historians is determined by the stories they wish to tell, and that has certainly been the case in telling of the Civil War.[1]

In the case of this book and the story it is telling, the Civil War era begins in 1846 and ends in 1876. These dates are not arbitrary. The first marks the entry of US troops for the first time into the territory of the Rio Grande Valley and the firing of the first shots in the war between that country and Mexico. In that place and on that occasion, not only were many of the officers who would later lead the armies on both sides in the Civil War present, but in firing those shots and eventually winning that war, they grafted that place onto the United States. The closing date is also significant to the story. Having been a declared member of the Confederacy, Texas—the entire state, not just those who actively took up arms against the Union—was placed under military authority and occupied by federal troops. Along the Rio Grande, a string of military posts stretching inland from the Gulf of Mexico were reinforced and manned by predominantly African American soldiers—initially members of the United States Colored Troops (USCT)—until Reconstruction came to an end in 1877. After that, the posts remained, their attention focused primarily southward, but the African American occupiers—now known as Buffalo Soldiers—were moved into the Great Plains to round up the last of the resistant Native American peoples in that region.

As for the place, it is no more set in stone than the era, but no more arbitrary either. There are two sticking points to the name Rio Grande Valley. The first of these is geological: the fact is that the area discussed in this book is not a "valley" at all. As described by Paul Horgan:

> [A]t last the river comes to the coastal plain where an ancient sea floor reaching deep inland is overlaid by ancient river deposits. After turbulence in the mountains, bafflement in canyons, and exhaustion in deserts, the river finds peaceful delivery into the sea, winding its last miles slowly through marshy bends, having come nearly one thousand nine hundred miles from mountains nearly three miles high.[2]

Thus it is not a "valley" but a coastal plain. This also reveals the second sticking point, which is geographical: it is only that last leg in this nearly two thousand mile course of the river—of its "valley" so to speak—with which this book is concerned. Where, specifically, this part of the river starts is as controversial a question as when the Civil War era began.

For some it begins at Eagle Pass at the southeastern end of the Big Bend in the Rio Grande, the location of Fort Duncan, the northwestern most of the USCT-occupied forts during Reconstruction. Others claim that it does not begin until the town of Roma, several hundred miles farther downstream, the point farthest inland that steam navigation could reach on the river. But here again, as Koselleck might say, just as the story creates its own chronology, it also must define its geography. In this case, the place farthest inland that is meaningful to the narrative is just about halfway between these two points: at Laredo. Here multiple skirmishes and one major battle between contending Union and Confederate forces took place, and here too much of the wheeling and dealing that characterized the Civil War economy in the region and the rivalries that animated both the trading and the fighting took place.

At this juncture, readers may be wondering how a book that consists of eleven essays written by a variety of authors from disparate disciplines could possibly constitute a narrative coherent enough to define anything. Here we turn back to our opening point in this preface, the issue of marginality. Some years ago, historian Elliott West found himself facing a similar dilemma: how to discuss events taking place in the American West during the era of Civil War and Reconstruction without loss of coherent focus. As he pointed out, "It's as if there are two independent historical narratives, and because the one that is set in the East and centered on the Civil War has been tapped as the defining story of its time, the one that is set out West seems peripheral, even largely irrelevant, to explaining America during a critical time in its history."[3] In order to bridge this gap, West conceived the idea of the "Greater Reconstruction," a theoretical construct predicated on the realization that we cannot understand "Reconstruction" as it is usually defined (i.e., the dozen-year period of political reunification of the nation following the Civil War) without understanding "Construction," that "burst of territorial growth that increased the size of the nation by roughly 70 percent."[4] Hence the seemingly marginal American West is, in fact, integral to understanding the bigger picture of the United States' mid-century crisis. In this book, author James Leiker twists West's conception slightly by phrasing the process the "Greater Consolidation," a formulation that more clearly gets at the process not of "reconstructing" a broken nation, but which views events from 1845 through 1877 as integral steps in the formation of a consolidated nation, or as another author in this book has phrased it elsewhere, a consolidated empire.[5]

The eleven chapters in this volume narratively tell the story of that process of consolidation through a unique lens and over a much longer period of time; the story told here actually begins in the 1700s and extends to the present. In a very real sense, the lower Rio Grande Valley is a microcosm not only of the process of formation for the United States as a nation (or empire) but of the globalization that seems to have caught the twenty-first century off guard, but which was a matter of everyday common sense to residents in that seemingly out-of-the-way corner of the North American continent. The intersections of races, cultures, economic forces, historical dynamics, and individual destinies that made the unique world of the Rio Grande Valley are the same as those that made the contemporary United States and the increasingly interconnected and messy world in which we now live. That is what unifies the chapters that follow and what, we believe, makes this volume a significant contribution to historical scholarship.

Roseann Bacha Garza
Christopher L. Miller
Russell K. Skowronek
Edinburg, Texas

## Notes

1. Reinhart Koselleck, "Time and History," in *The Practice of Conceptual History: Timing History, Spacing Concepts*, trans. Kerstin Behnke (Stanford, CA: Stanford University Press, 2002), 100–114.

2. Paul Horgan, *Great River: The Rio Grande in North American History*, 2 vols. (New York: Holt, Rinehart and Winston, 1960), I:5.

3. Elliott West, *The Last Indian War: The Nez Perce Story* (New York: Oxford University Press, 2009), xviii.

4. Ibid.

5. Leiker, this volume; Christopher L. Miller, "Prelude to Rivalry: The Frontier Foundations of Two Global Empires," in *The Soviet Union and the United States: Rivals of the Twentieth-Century: Coexistence and Competition*, ed. Eva-Maria Stolberg (Frankfurt am Main: Peter Lang, 2013), 11–31

# *Acknowledgments*

The Community Historical Archaeology Projects with School (CHAPS) Program at the University of Texas Rio Grande Valley would like to thank all of the regional community partners who have played an integral role in this project. Their thoughts, input, and participation have helped lay the foundation for the Rio Grande Valley Civil War Trail. Without their assistance, this book would not have come to fruition. On May 22, 2014, forty-three members of the Contributors Committee took the bold step to endorse the creation of the Rio Grande Valley Civil War Trail. They are (front row from left to right) Russell Skowronek, UTRGV CHAPS Director and Professor of History/Anthropology; Valerie Ramirez, Hidalgo County Historical Commission/Juneteenth Coordinator; Amparo Montes-Gutierrez, Curator Zapata County Museum of History; Virginia Gause, UTRGV Media and Marketing Librarian (retired); Karen Fort, RGV Author/ Museum Exhibit Designer; Lendon Gilpin, Texas State University; Mark Allen, UTRGV graduate student; Roseann Bacha-Garza, UTRGV CHAPS Program Manager; Maria Elia Ramos, Starr County Historical Museum; Nancy Deviney, Texas Tropical Trails Executive Director; (second row from left to right) Stephen Walker, TXDOT District Landscape Architect; Robert Ramirez, Nuevo Santander Press; Christopher L. Miller, UTRGV Professor of History and Co-director of the CHAPS Program; Manuel Hinojosa, Port Isabel Preservation Architect; Rolando Garza, National Park Service Resource Manager Palo Alto Battlefield; George Gause, UTRGV Special Collections Librarian (retired); Tom Fort, Museum of South Texas History Senior Historian; Mark Spier, National Park Service Superintendent Palo Alto Battlefield/Padre Island; James Leiker, Johnson County Community College and Kansas Studies Institute Director; Elisa Flores, UTRGV, The Studio Marketing Services Account Services Manager; Samuel Ramos, Starr County Historical Museum; Wilson Bourgeois, Brownsville Civil War Sesquicentennial Chairman; Eran Garza, Peñitas Historical Society; (back row from left to right) Noel Benavides, Starr County Historian; Jerry Thompson, Civil War historian/author and Texas A&M International Regents Professor; Bryan Winton, Santa Ana Wildlife Refuge Manager; James Mills, UTRGV Lecturer in History; Anthony Zavaleta, Professor of Anthropology (retired); Jeff Cortinas Walker, RGV writer/columnist; Scot Edler, LRGV National Wildlife Refuge Assistant Manager; W. Stephen McBride, Camp Nelson Civil War Heritage Park Director of Archaeology; Daniel Cardenas, UTRGV, The Studio Marketing Services Graphic Designer; Doug Murphy, National Park Service Chief of Interpretation Palo Alto Battlefield; Norman Rozeff, Cameron County Historical Commission Secretary; Jack Ayoub, Texas Heritage and Independence Celebration Association; Craig Stone, Brownsville Historical Association/Sons of Confederate Veterans Commander Camp 2216.

Missing from photo are Hidegardo Flores, Zapata County Museum of History Director; William McWhorter, Texas Historical Commission, Coordinator Military Sites Program; Alonzo Alvarez, Starr County Historical Commission President; Jeanie Flores, Port Isabel Museum Director; Elisa Beas, Rio Grande City Deputy City Manager; Toni Nagel, King Ranch Museum Director; and Frances Isbel, Hidalgo County Historical Commission.

Thanks to President Guy Bailey, Provost Havídan Rodriguez (now president University at Albany–SUNY), Deputy Provost Cynthia Brown (retired), Executive Vice President for Academic Affairs Patricia Alvarez McHatton, and Executive Vice President for Research Parwinder Grewal of the University Texas Rio Grande Valley for their support of our work. Also, thanks are due to Dean Walter Diaz and Assistant Dean Monica Denny of the College of Liberal Arts; Kimberly Selber, Elisa Flores, and

Daniel Cardenas of The Studio Marketing Services; Velinda Reyes, Felipe Salinas, Cecilia Johnson, Kathryn O'Neil, and Madahy Romero of the Division of Institutional Advancement; George Gause, UTRGV Special Collections Librarian (retired); and Perla Pequeno and Russell Dove of Information Technology Services.

Thanks also to Executive Director Shan Rankin, Curator of Collections and Registrar Dr. Lisa Kay Adam, and Archivist Phyllis Kinnison of the Museum of South Texas History. MOSTHistory houses primary source materials, photographs, and documents that have truly enhanced the research for this book.

We are eternally grateful to our sponsors for their continued support of the Rio Grande Valley Civil War Trail. We offer our gratitude to John Crain of the Summerlee Foundation of Dallas, David D. Jackson of the Summerfield G. Roberts Foundation of Dallas, Cori Pena of the Brownsville Community Improvement Corporation, Bobby Salinas of the City of Roma, and Elisa Beas of the Rio Grande City Economic Development Corporation for their financial contributions that have assisted in the development, enhancement, and sustainability of this project. Special thanks are due to Gene Krane and The Texas Historical Foundation for funds to cover the expenses associated with the many illustrations that appear in this book,

We would like to thank Mr. John Nau, III, Chairman of the Texas Historical Commission, for touting our program's community engagement activities and the positive impact that our educational projects have had on the regional, state, and national communities.

We also recognize Dr. Rolando Avila, Jose R. Perez, and Megan Birk as the authors of the lesson plans that pertain to this project. Mark Spier, Douglas Murphy, Rolando Garza, Karen Weaver, Daniel Ibarra, and Ruben Reyna of the National Park Service have contributed greatly to the reproduction of material items that pertain to the education of our regional K–12 students.

Thanks to the many organizations throughout the Rio Grande Valley that have invited us to speak to their groups and promote awareness of the Rio Grande Valley Civil War Trail. They are the US Department of Veterans Affairs, Texas Historical Commission's Texas Tropical Trails, Las Porciones Society of Edinburg, Daughters of the American Revolution, United Daughters of the Confederacy, Sons of Confederate

Veterans, Nuevo Santander Genealogical Society, McAllen Public Library, McAllen Old Timers Club, and Annual Juneteenth Observances–Restlawn Cemetery of Edinburg, Texas.

Many thanks to Elizabeth O. Skowronek of North Carolina State University for her help with some of the graphics in this volume.

# The Civil War on the Rio Grande, 1846–1876

# I

# *Prelude*

## From the Seno Mexicano Frontier to the Nueces Strip Borderland

CHRISTOPHER L. MILLER

Ever since the days of Herbert Eugene Bolton, the region in which the Rio Grande Valley is situated has been spoken of as the "Borderlands."[1] But as indicated in the preface to this book, the contours of a story must determine the time and space in which that story is told, and in this case both time and space bring into question the applicability of the Borderlands paradigm to at least the opening phases of our narrative. A major contention in this chapter is that the Rio Grande Valley, as it is defined by this story, did not constitute a "Borderland" until the very end of the time period covered by it. That is to say that a subtheme in this story is the role played by events during the Civil War era in the transformation of a frontier into a borderland and then finally into a border.[2]

For the first two centuries of Spanish colonization in North America, the Rio Grande Valley was not even a frontier; rather it was a total wilderness—that which, in Frederick Jackson Turner's monumental thesis, lays beyond the "frontier."[3] From the time of Hernán Cortés's conquest of Mexico in the 1520s, the Spanish frontier along the Gulf of Mexico stopped at the Pánuco River, the site of the modern-day city of Tampico.[4] What lay beyond was truly a no man's land called *Seno Mexicano* (Mexico Bay).[5]

As it came to be defined, Seno Mexicano was bordered by the Gulf of Mexico on the east, the Pánuco River on the south, and the Sierra Madre Oriental mountain range in the west.[6] The northern boundary was less well defined: lack of systematic exploration much farther south than the presidio at La Bahía on the Guadalupe River in the province of Tejas left questions as to whether the Nueces River or the Río Bravo del Norte was its northern terminus.[7]

Lack of interest in settling this region stemmed from a number of causes. First and foremost among these was the geophysical nature of the area itself. Largely a flat coastal plain, the region was extremely arid and largely inhospitable for human life, or at least for human life as Spaniards defined it. Native American groups, most prominently Coahuiltecans—but by the time of Spanish colonization in Mexico, Apaches and Comanches as well—roamed across the land in either nomadic or seminomadic fashion, harvesting wild plants and animals.[8] In addition, many Indian groups from the colonized parts of Mexico took advantage of the lack of a Spanish presence in the area, fleeing into the region to escape from the missions and *congregas* (secular Indian hamlets) and the forced labor associated with them.[9] The presence of these so-called *indios bárbaros* (wild Indians) and runaway apostates constituted another reason for the lack of concerted colonization efforts. As noted by historian Lawrence F. Hill:

> During the century and a half preceding 1747 many attempts had been made to pacify Seno Mexicano. Many expeditions, punitive as well as pacific, had been made into the region for this purpose, but none had achieved the desired end. The usual experience was that the forces were out fifteen or twenty days and then returned home to wait a few months before repeating the fruitless experiment. Not only did these efforts fail to settle the Indian problem, but they also failed to produce extensive information on the nature of the country.[10]

Adding to these drawbacks was what appeared to be a total lack of exploitable resources. The area was remarkably poor in mineral wealth—gold and silver were virtually nonexistent—with the single exception of salt, which was overabundant to the point of making much of the water in the region undrinkable and much of the soil unplantable. With neither souls nor fortunes to be won without a struggle, Spaniards looked elsewhere for new lands to conquer.

However, Spanish indifference to the region came to an end late in the seventeenth century. In 1685, while war raged between Spain and France in Europe and on the high seas, a French party under the command of René-Robert Cavelier, Sieur de La Salle, came ashore within the confines of Seno Mexicano in the vicinity of what is now known as

Matagorda Bay. Ill-fated from the beginning—two ships in the expedition were lost to the shifting currents and sandbars that characterized the coastline of Seno Mexicano—a colony was eventually established on Garcitas Creek near the place where the Spanish would later establish the presidio of Nuestra Señora de Loreto de la Bahía.[11] Loss of their ships and the uncompromising struggle against the harsh conditions in the area led to considerable suffering and ill feeling; La Salle was killed in a mutiny against his authority, and then the last survivors were themselves killed by Karankawa Indians.[12] Unaware of the French colony's precarious and doomed condition, however, the Spanish sent an expedition under command of Alonso DeLeón to seek and root out the French settlement in July 1686, but it failed to find La Salle's location.[13]

This failed counterinsurgency expedition was made necessary, despite Spain's own indifference toward settling in the region, by a quirk in international law and practice. In a legal tradition dating back to Roman times, title to land could only be claimed legitimately through occupation and cultivation; unoccupied and unworked land was considered *terra nullus*, Latin for literally "no man's land," and as such subject to seizure by any sovereign power that would occupy and change its condition from a state of *vacuum domicilium* (lack of domestic order) to one of *dominium* (domestic rule).[14] Were he and his party to map and cultivate the land, La Salle's entry into the terra nullus of Seno Mexicano would have given legal title to France and put a huge block of foreign territory between Nuevo España and Spanish territories in Tejas. This could have threatened the whole of Mexico and its frontier provinces in the north. The end of the war between Spain and France, along with La Salle's failure to institute dominium, brought an end to the immediate threat, allowing authorities in Mexico City to again neglect the territory. However, war with England, beginning in 1739, restored the fear that a foreign power might declare the area terra nullus and seek to implement dominium.[15]

Even before war broke out with England, the royal government had put out a call for plans to conquer and colonize Seno Mexicano. Two plans came forward in 1736—one from Narciso Barquín de Montecuesta of Santiago de los Valles near Tampico and another from José Antonio Fernández de Jáuregui y Utrrutia, governor of Nuevo León. Both called for direct support from the royal treasury and extensive privileges for the colonists and even more extensive rewards for the proposers.[16] A third plan came forward in 1738 from Antonio Ladrón de Guevara, a large-scale rancher from Nuevo León. The plan put forward by this *hacendado* had more promise than the previous ones, largely because of Ladrón de Guevara's proven rapport with the Indians in Nuevo León, which promised that he might enjoy some success in pacifying the indios bárbaros in Seno Mexicano.[17] Like the other two plans, Ladrón de Guevara's called for significant financial support from the crown, but more controversial than that was his intent to utilize the congregas system as the primary means for taming the Indians. As historian Hubert J. Miller has pointed out, the congregas system was largely responsible for the hostility that Indians in Seno Mexicano felt toward the Spaniards, which not only made the territory dangerous to settle, but also spurred Indians from there and the adjoining *Sierra Gorda* to make raids into settled areas to steal livestock and take revenge on their former masters.[18] This feature of the plan and the extensive cost that it projected for the royal treasury ill-disposed the *Junta General de Guerra* (war council) that had been convened to manage the project. Leading the opposition was Juan Rodríguez de Albuerne, Marquis of Altamira, who had already begun to form an alternative plan with a very different leader in mind.[19]

The leader that Altamira had in mind was a military man who had come to prominence for his service in North America, José de Escandón. Born in Soto la Marina, Santander, Spain, in 1700, Escandón had migrated to Mexico at the age of fifteen to serve as a cadet in a mounted company in Yucatán. By 1727 he had risen in rank to sergeant major and was serving in the garrison at Querétaro, near the frontier with the dreaded Sierra Gorda.[20] Here he proved successful in pacifying the local Indians, leading to his being made lieutenant captain general of the Sierra Gorda district in 1741. He led four expeditions into the most dangerous enclaves of indios bárbaros and hostile runaways, successfully coercing agreements with the Indians to stop their raids into neighboring provinces. This achievement was made all the more impressive—especially to Altamira and the Junta—by the fact that it was done at no cost to the treasury: Escandón had paid for the enterprise out of his own pocket. In the following year he came to prominence again when he volunteered his regiment's service to fend off a threatened English attack on Veracruz, again at his own expense. The attack never actually came, but his offer was seen as a grand gesture and, like the expeditions

*José de Escandón*
*Arriving in Mexico as a military cadet in 1715 at the age of fifteen, José de Escandón rose through the ranks to become Lieutenant Captain General of Sierra Gorda at the age of forty-one and the founder of the new province of Nuevo Santander in 1747. Sculpture of José de Escandón, University of Texas Rio Grande Valley, by Roberto Garcia Jr.; photo by the author.*

into the Sierra Gorda, earned him a solid reputation with the Junta de Guerra.[21]

While Escandón was busy polishing his military reputation, the Junta was bogged down in its deliberations over which plan to recognize for the colonization of Seno Mexicano. Finally, in August 1746, after enduring mounting pressure from both Ladrón de Guevara and Viceroy Francisco de Güemes y Horcasitas, the Junta decided to bring in Escandón as a consultant, hoping to draw upon his extensive experience with Indian pacification. Within a matter of weeks the Junta decided to dispense with the other proposals and recommended Escandón to lead the exploration and settlement of Seno Mexicano.[22]

Escandón immediately began planning for a massive entrada (exploring expedition). Drawing on his experience in Sierra Gorda, he decided that only an overwhelming Spanish force would have any chance of penetrating the wilderness.[23] In light of the danger and the vast extent of the territory to be explored, he hit upon a novel approach. In the lyric words of Paul Horgan:

> [I]n January, 1747, from seven different posts on the outlying perimeter of the arc of Mexico Bay seven different armed detachments began to move simultaneously toward the mouth of the Rio Grande, which required about a thirty-day march for each. In one great, co-ordinated movement, Escandón brought all of Mexico Bay under comprehensive examination, which, he said, would "cause great wonder to the natives to see Spanish soldiers entering from all directions, before the news of their presence can be transmitted by smoke signals." There were seven hundred sixty-five soldiers in his seven divisions. They reconnoitered a region of almost a hundred and twenty thousand miles, which Escandón described as "a sort of bag lying between Tampico, Pánuco, Villa de Valles, Custodia de Rio Verde, Nuevo Reyno de León and the Bahía del Espirtu Santo," where stood the farthest Spanish fort of coastal Texas.[24]

And as with his earlier expeditions in Sierra Gorda, no cost was to accrue to the crown from the entrada: Escandón bore most of the cost personally, while asking the commanders of each contingent as well as the individual soldiers to bear their own personal expenses.[25]

In just over a month, from late January to early March, the seven divisions of the grand exploring expedition had finished their work. Not only had the entirety of Seno Mexicano been mapped and settlement sites surveyed, but miraculously, given the severity of the land and the hostility of its inhabitants (human, plant, and animal alike), not a single life had been lost.[26] Escandón disbanded his force, sending each detachment back to its point of origin, while he returned to Querétaro to write up his final report to the Junta and craft a formal plan for colonization of the region that he decided should be called *Nuevo Santander*, named after his home province in Spain.[27]

The plan that Escandón crafted was unlike any that had been employed in the entire course of Spanish colonization in North America. First off, he insisted that the settlement be done under civilian rather than either church or military authority: no presidios were to be established and church involvement was to be limited to the founding of missions at the outer edge of the secular communities.[28] Missionaries were to minister to both the Spanish population and any Indians in the immediate area. Indians were not to be collected at the missions, nor were the settlers to be allowed to establish congregas in order to exploit native labor.[29] Military burdens were to be borne by the colonists themselves, to which end Escandón encouraged military veterans to become colonists, especially those who had participated in the entrada and spent their own money in the process.[30]

What was more radical was the plan for governing Nuevo Santander. Central to Escandón's plan was his rabid insistence that the *villas* he was to establish be granted self-rule: "the new settlements were to be independent of the officials of the older establishments."[31] While ostensibly the colony came under the overarching authority of *Audiencia* of Mexico, Escandón, who established himself as captain general in a provincial capital on the Santander River (now the Soto la Marina) at the very geographical center of Nuevo Santander, situated himself between any external authority and the colonists. As Lawrence F. Hill noted: "The villa, or town, the local unit of government, was under the control of a captain, who possessed both civil and military authority. He secured his appointment from Escandón, might be removed by him, and exercised his power without the interference of the customary *ayuntamiento* [town council]."[32]

Hence Escandón and his handpicked captains governed affairs in the new province with no interference from either above or below. As a result, from the very beginning, the region failed to develop any meaningful ties with the bureaucracy and authorities outside the province. This institutional autonomy established a pattern of independence and self-reliance that would have an impact on the character of the region for a long time to come.

The captain general also planned to make the various settlements in the province as mutually dependent on each other as possible. To this end, he planned to place the villas in such a way that communication and commerce between them could be maintained easily. Hubert Miller describes the system as follows:

> One of the main transportation routes left Laredo to Reynosa and from here it passed south and southeast, connecting San Fernando, Santander, Padilla, Güemes, Aguayo, Jaumave, Palmillas and Tula. From Tula the route continued southeastward to San

> Luis Potosí. From this main artery there were branch routes to the Real de Borbón, Hoyos, Llera, Escandón, Horcasitas and Altimira. A look at the current map of the state of Tamaulipas shows that Escandón had planned his road system well since the routes are similar to the state's present highway system.[33]

This not only simplified the task of ruling the province and allowed for mutual protection from marauding Indians, but also recognized an important economic reality.[34] The northern portion of Nuevo Santander was a dry grassland with few sources of fresh water, whereas the southern interior was well suited for agriculture. It was clear that settlements in the north would have difficulty producing sufficient crops to sustain themselves, but could produce large quantities of beef, tallow, and leather as well as salt, which could be traded for corn, beans, and other commodities produced in the interior.[35] In addition, Escandón founded and maintained a two-masted cargo ship (a *goleta*), which carried "fish, salt, beef, mutton, hides, and tallow" from the Bay of Santander to the export hub in Veracruz, an enterprise that, in addition to his textile mills, mines, ranches, and other enterprises, added greatly to the captain general's personal fortune.[36] Again, this mutual dependency within the province and relative independence from other provinces in Mexico gave the region a highly autonomous quality.

Another radical innovation was not actually put forward in the plan—in fact, Escandón kept it to himself—but it was central to his actual intent. As a matter of long tradition and at the heart of Spanish colonial conceptions of citizenship and manhood, colonists expected that land in new colonial settlements would be granted to each individual male head of household in severalty. As noted by Ana Maria Alonzo, "Possession of and property in land, as well as the right to freely alienate or acquire the means of production, were privileges accorded to the *gente de razón*, signs of civilization and of the mastery integral to the honor of men."[37] And Escandón's plan called for such grants. However, when the settlements were actually planted, Escandón did not issue individual titles. As reported by Bolton:

> At the first foundation of the pueblos, the lands were not definitely assigned nor granted in severalty. A large grant was made

> in common, sufficient to satisfy the needs of the original settlers in the near future, estimating for each family two *sitios de ganado menor* and six *caballerías*; for the captains two *sitios de ganado mayor* and twelve *caballerías*; and for common use, four *sitios de ganado mayor* as *ejidos*, besides lands for the missions. Escandón was authorized on his first expedition to make these divisions, but he considered it unwise to do so, thinking that if the settlers held the lands in common they would stay closer together and be safer against Indian attacks.[38]

Several years later, Escandón explained and justified his decision to the viceroy, citing reasons quite different from those asserted by Bolton:

> I was advised to make the said individual [distributions] of land but I have not done it for three reasons; first, for as good as the place is for habitation, there is not room for all and because of this there will be disputes over the preferred places; second, that from time to time better and more useful settlers are coming into the communities than those who comprised the first settlers and it has seemed best for me to assign them that which they can enjoy in common, irrigation, pastures, fields, all of this would not take place in a harmonious way if the best sites had fallen as they were supposed . . . to half a dozen settlers; third, there has not been sufficient time at the exact moment to dispose of this and other happenings as they occurred and it was not possible for me to engage in this difficult business; furthermore, there is not in all of these surroundings an intelligent person to whom I could confide and particularly so, since a person of high integrity is needed to execute justice and leave all who are interested contented, so that each one will get his preference.[39]

Read cynically, one might conclude from this that, as with his power to appoint and remove captains at will, Escandón wished to exercise a great deal of discretion over who in each settlement got access to what resources, an extraordinary degree of power for any provincial governor to possess. Not surprisingly, there was a great deal of uncertainty among colonists concerning the permanence of their tenure, and one might surmise a good degree of anxiety about actual or potential threats to one's livelihood which, following Alonzo's reasoning, also meant anxiety about one's manhood. While this situation was eventually rectified by a viceregal commission in 1767, it nonetheless set a pattern for insecurity about land that would persist in the region for generations, setting the tone for many of the squabbles to be discussed in later chapters.[40]

Escandón envisioned an initial planting of fourteen settlements in Nuevo Santander. To populate these villas he advertised for settlers, giving priority to those from the seven posts that had provided men for the 1747 entrada. In addition to soldiers, he specified that he wanted colonists with frontier living experience and specific skills, including ranching and farming as well as building crafts and even maritime skills, as he envisioned the establishment of some harbors in the new territory.[41] Initially he called for five hundred families to be spread between the proposed settlements; however, by the time the colonizing expedition came together late in 1748, nearly seven hundred showed up to make the trek into the new territory.[42] As described by Herbert Bolton:

> At the end of December 1748, Escandón left Querétaro with what was probably the largest caravan that ever went into the interior provinces to found a colony. In his train were seven hundred and fifty soldiers, and more than twenty-five hundred settlers, Spaniards and Christianized Indians, while others joined him on the march. The families had their household and agricultural equipments, and they drove before them many thousand head of horses, cattle, burros, sheep and goats.[43]

By the end of the year, thirteen of the fourteen settlements had been established.[44] The vast majority of the settlements established in 1749 were not in what we are calling the Rio Grande Valley; most were far to the south, though two were placed along the Rio Grande in the initial planting and several more came later in Escandón's governorship. The first of the river villas was actually begun before Escandón arrived. A party of forty families from Nuevo León led by Blas María de la Garza Falcón had already begun building a site called Camargo near the junction of the San Juan River and the Rio Grande. By the

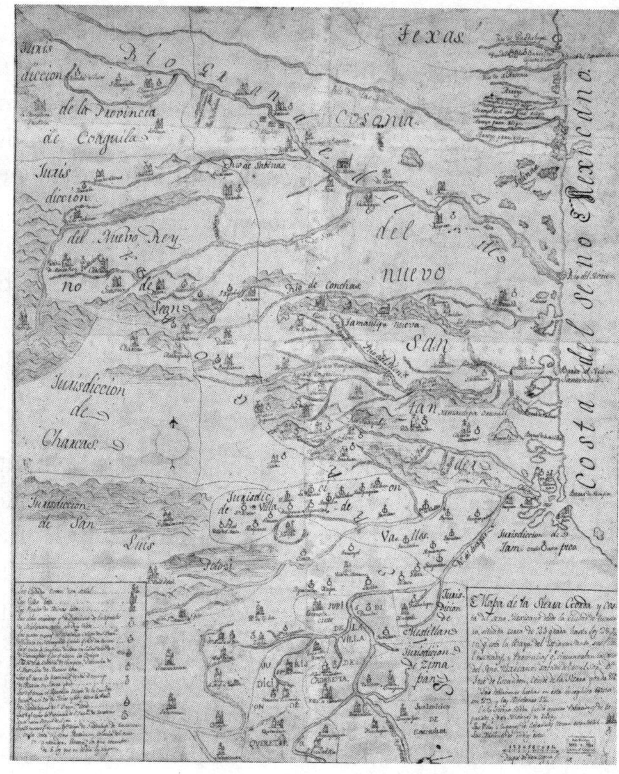


*Though this map is dated as 1747 by the Library of Congress, the fact that Laredo and Mier appear on it means that it cannot date from before 1755 and most likely is related to the inspection tour made by José Tienda de Cuervo in 1757. "Mapa de la Sierra Gorda y Costa del Seno Mexicano desde la Cuidad de Queretaro, circa 1747," Library of Congress, Geography and Map Division, 2007632265.*

time Escandón found them, the settlers had already begun building houses and digging irrigation canals while they waited for his arrival and official recognition. On March 5, a mass was held and the community received the blessing not only from the church but from the captain general as well.[45] Escandón then traveled east down the river for some twelve leagues to the site he had designated for the villa of Reinosa. Here, too, he found that forty families had already begun to settle the place under the leadership of Carlos Cantú, an experienced frontiersman who spoke some of the local Indian languages. Escandón delivered relief supplies of corn, tools, oxen, and clothing, and officially dedicated the town site.[46] With these two settlements established, the captain general turned his attention northward, where two detachments were to converge on the Nueces River to form a villa to be called Vedoya.[47] Friar Simón del Hierro, who was accompanying Escandón, noted that this would be far more difficult than Escandón had supposed because of the harsh conditions between the Rio Grande and the Nueces.[48] This proved prophetic: Escandón later learned that the military and civilian parties had found the site uninhabitable and had gone back to Nuevo León.[49] Escandón then began heading southward toward his capital with no developments moving forward north of the Rio Grande.

In the following year, however, Escandón returned to the river to start two new settlements. The first, Revilla, on the south side of the river, was to house a group of settlers from Coahuila under the leadership of Vincente Guerra. The other was to be on the north side, across from Revilla, and was granted to a wealthy Coahuila hacendado, Juan José Vázquez Borrego, who formed the community of Rancho de Dolores.[50] Two years after that, Escandón founded a small settlement between Revilla and Reinosa called Mier, with nineteen families recruited from Camargo. Two years after that he commissioned another wealthy rancher, Tomás Sánchez, to start a community on the north side of the river, where Sánchez wished to settle a party of pioneers at his own expense. This would become the villa of Laredo. Before approving Sánchez's request, however, Escandón urged the hacendado to explore for an alternative site somewhere on the Nueces; like the would-be settlers for Vedoya, however, he reported that there was no suitable place there for a settlement.[51] Thus by the end of 1755, six settlements had been established along the Rio Grande: Reinosa, Revilla, Mier, and Camargo on the south side and Dolores and Laredo on the north side, but still no communities had been formed at the far northern end of Nuevo Santander; as Friar Simón del Hierro had predicted, the strip between the Rio Grande and the Nueces remained impenetrable to civilization.

Despite Escandón's apparent desire to keep Mexico City and the Spanish bureaucracy as distant as possible from his domain, two viceregal inquiries intruded into Nuevo Santander—one in 1757 and another in 1767. The first, led by José Tienda de Cuervo and Agustín López de la Cámara Alta, was concerned primarily with conducting a census of the province and also to inspect the villas for their conformity with Spanish colonial town planning. An engineer by training, López de la Cámara Alta recommended redesigning or moving some of the sites, especially those on the Rio Grande, because of issues with flooding and difficulties in engineering irrigation systems.[52] They reported that the province had experienced amazing growth during its short existence:

> In the eight-year period ending with the Cuervo inspection, about eight thousand colonists had been settled in two dozen communities. As proof that these settlements were not temporary in character is the incontestable evidence that all are on the map today, some still small to be sure, but most of them towns ranging in population from five to fifteen thousand. While many of the inhabitants were poor in earthly possessions, not all could be placed in this class, for belonging to the citizens of the province were approximately eighty thousand cattle, horses, and mules and nearly a third of a million sheep. Furthermore, the future seemed to hold out even greater possibilities in ranching inasmuch as *hacendados* from the outside sent their shepherds and servants into the province to find pasture during a large part of the year for a million of the fleecy animals. It is true that livestock constituted the principal source of wealth, but certain settlements, particularly those in the highlands, produced large quantities of beans, maize, and vegetables. And in spite of the discouraging outlook for a port on the Bay of Santander, commerce in salt, fish, beef, veal, mutton, hides, and tallow was assuming an important place among the occupations.[53]

The one disturbing thing noted by the inspectors was the lack of individual land titles among the settlers, and they recommended that this situation be rectified.[54] By the time of the second inspection, by Don Juan Fernando de Palacio and Don José de Osorio y Llamas, ten years later, the land tenure issue still had not been addressed. Osorio y Llamas, an attorney by trade, used his royal commission to survey the lands held by each of the villas and divide it into individual *porciones*, as had been called for in the original plan, with the requirement that all colonists build houses on their assigned plots or risk confiscation.[55] The commissioners also ordered that town councils be elected by the landholders "by a simple plurality of votes" and that an *alcalde mayor* (civilian mayor) be placed in charge, replacing Escandón's appointed captains.[56] Not surprisingly, such rapid and radical change caused a great deal of insecurity about land holding, and despite the precaution of allowing settlers to select the surveyors and appraisers who would mete out the porciones, disputes were inevitable, again foreshadowing conflicts that would arise later.[57] Appeals to Escandón for mediation were made impossible: he was removed as captain general and called to Mexico City to face charges of maladministration.[58]

The removal of Escandón and privatizing of land marked a pivotal change in the history of Nuevo Santander generally, and in the Rio Grande Valley in particular. Miller notes that after 1767, land grants became much more common and that a great many new settlers moved into the region, especially that portion bordering on the Rio Grande. He also notes that a great many more were made between 1767 and 1810 on the north side of the river, and that these tended to be much larger than those originally specified in Escandón's plan.[59] For the most part, the newcomers tended to live on the south side, but ran herds of goats, sheep, and cattle on their holdings to the north, placing ranch hands on site to watch the animals and defend them from predatory

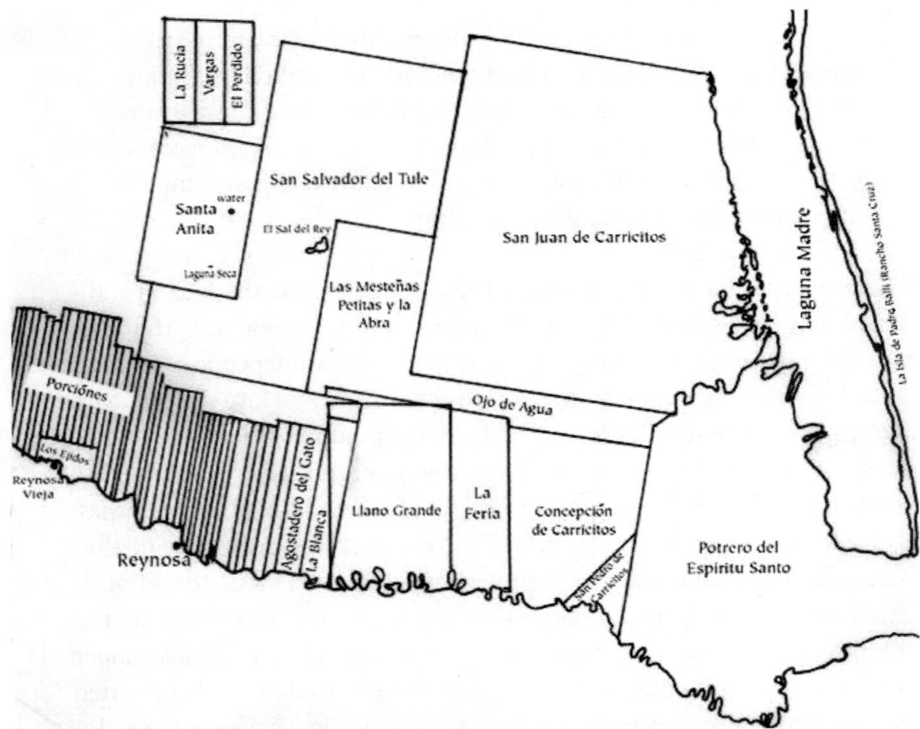


*The eighteenth-century Spanish land grants along the north bank of the Rio Grande, called porciones, were fairly uniform in size and shape. Later grants, especially in the Mexican era, tended to be much larger and intended primarily for animal grazing. Courtesy of Mary Margaret McAllen.*

animals and equally predatory Indians and rustlers.[60] Their lives were lived, as anthropologist Mary Jo Galindo has described it, "*con un pie en cada lado,*" literally "with one foot on each side of the river."[61]

While the population of the Rio Grande Valley changed dramatically between 1767 and the end of Spanish rule with the Mexican Revolution (1821), the character of life changed very little. One significant change though was the opening of lands and peopling of the river between Reinosa (eventually to be respelled Reynosa) and the Gulf of Mexico. Escandón had not seen that region as being particularly attractive for settlement, noting that the twenty-five leagues of open plain extending to the coast was inhabited by many Indians and that Reynosa would constitute the frontier outpost that would shield settlements farther upstream.[62] In a process repeated throughout the colonization of the Americas, however, the Indians soon began to disappear: European-borne diseases killed many, Comanche and Apache raiders claimed a share, and others were either absorbed into missions bordering the region or into the ranching population itself through intermarriage.[63] In 1774, the ranchers who had gotten grants downriver from Reynosa banded together to establish a villa near the mouth of the river, a community initially called San Juan de los Esteros Hermosos and then redubbed Refugio.[64]

Despite its proximity to the Gulf of Mexico and the potential for trade in goods that could flow downriver from the prosperous settlements upstream, Refugio did not immediately become a commercial center. Dating back to the days of Cortés's rule, Spanish policy in Mexico designated Veracruz as Mexico's exclusive international Gulf port. Although efforts were made as early as 1795 to obtain royal approval to open a port in Refugio, no official approval came until 1820, when King Ferdinand VII sent instructions to alcalde Juan José Chapa to open Puerto del Refugio.[65] Following Mexican independence, the government sought to raise money to pay off the soaring debt incurred during its war with Spain by establishing a customs house in Refugio and encouraging trade in order to generate customs income. In 1824, Nuevo Santander was reconstituted as the free state of Tamaulipas, and two years later Refugio was renamed Matamoros in honor of revolutionary hero Mariano Matamoros and was constituted as an international maritime port.[66] As Craig H. Roell explains: "Recognizing its commercial potential, merchants—Mexican, European, and North American—flocked to the town, which blossomed to 7,000 residents by 1830. The town's increase in trade was quickly reflected in monthly tax revenues through the customs house, which in 1826 reached 51,000 pesos, and exceeded 100,000 pesos by 1832, making Matamoros the largest town on Mexico's northern frontier."[67]

Although settlements along the Rio Grande began prospering after the 1767 reforms, prosperity that continued in the wake of Mexican independence, the area to the north, now also part of Tamaulipas, continued to live up to Friar Simón del Hierro's expectation that the harsh conditions between the Rio Grande and Nueces would be prohibitive to settlement. Early travelers making their way overland to the now booming city of Matamoros gave ample testimony to the still frontier-like conditions and its continuing status as terra nullus. Roell notes that the

*Matamoros, circa 1843*
*Established in 1774 as San Juan de los Esteros Hermosos, after Mexican independence, this community was renamed Matamoros in honor of revolutionary hero Mariano Matamoros, and in 1824 was established as Mexico's northernmost international port. This color lithograph was published in John Phillips's* Mexico Illustrated in Twenty-Six Drawings by John Phillips and A. Rider, with Descriptive Letterpress in English and Spanish (London: n.p., 1848, plate 26) *and is believed to be based on sketches made before a hurricane hit the city in 1844. Courtesy of Dorothy Sloan, Rare Books Inc., Austin, Texas.*

Spanish called the area *El Desierto Muerto* (the dead desert). Swiss-born naturalist Jean Louis Berlandier, who settled in Matamoros in 1829, described it as "almost deserted," noting only miserable huts being occupied by transient stock hands.[68] Frederick Law Olmstead characterized it as being "abandoned to hopeless chaparral."[69] In a colorful account by one of the soldiers who accompanied Zachary Taylor on his march from Corpus Christi Bay to Matamoros in 1846, George C. Furber put it plainly: "[T]hose extensive prairies . . . never can, or will be settled; for there is a great scarcity of water;—in one place over which we came, four or five days since, there was a tract of thirty miles, without a drop;—more than that, there is a total want of timber; nothing of that description growing, save thickets here and there, or musquit bushes."[70]

The single exception to its abandoned character was the remarkable number of wild horses that resided along the coastal plain. Roell quotes one early observer who noted "a drove of mustangs so large as it took us fully an hour to pass it, although they were traveling at a rapid rate in a direction nearly opposite to ours. As far as the eye could extend on a dead level prairie, nothing was visible except a dense mass of horses, and the trampling of their hoofs sounded like the roar of the surf on a rocky coast."[71]

The presence of these animals led Americans, especially those who risked both natural and bureaucratic threats by entering Mexican territory to round up these broncos, to call the region the "Wild Horse Desert."

Following Mexican independence, the area to the north of El Desierto Muerto, the province of Coahuila y Tejas, became a popular destination for settlers from the United States. In an effort to put a barrier between hostile Comanche and Apache Indians and the productive settlements along the Rio Grande and farther inland, the Mexican government allowed so-called *empresarios* such as Stephen F. Austin, Samuel May Williams, Green DeWitt, and Martín De León to bring in migrants, many of whom were from the American South and had been bankrupted by the Panic of 1819.[72] In a story far too familiar to bear re-telling here, these foreign settlers grew increasingly restive under Mexican rule, often ignoring Mexican laws and customs altogether. Finally, in 1835, a mostly Anglo American group began a revolution against Mexican authority, fighting a war for independence that lasted until April 1836, when, in the Battle of San Jacinto, Mexican President

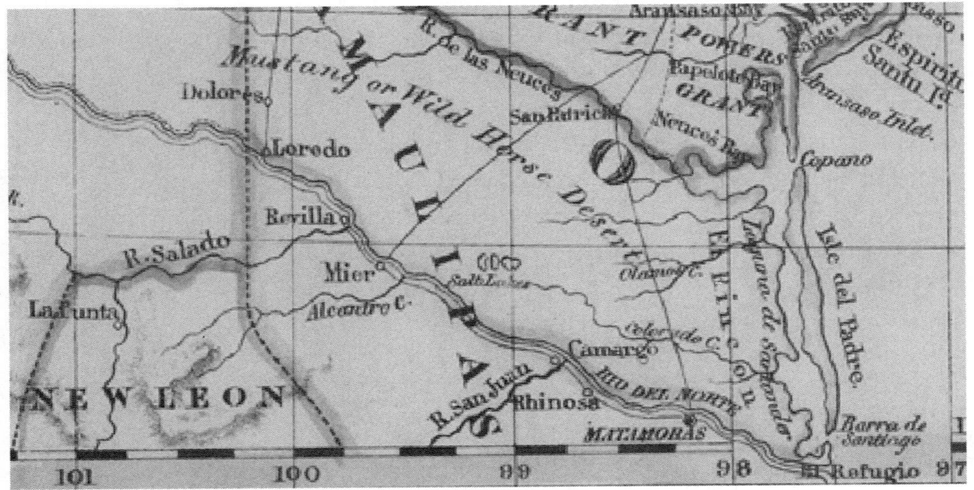


*The Wild Horse Desert*
*This detail from "Map of the Republic of Texas and the Adjacent Territories, Indicating the Grants of Land Conceded under the Empresario System of Mexico / 1841," Map Number 1594, shows the area of the Nueces Strip between the time of Texas independence and the Mexican-American War. Note the description of the region as "Mustang or Wild Horse Desert" and the utter lack of settlement north of the Rio del Norte. Courtesy of the Texas State Library and Archives Commission.*

Antonio Lopez de Santa Anna was captured by Texas troops.[73] Santa Anna signed two treaties: one public and one private. The public Treaty of Velasco specified that "Texas independence was recognized, hostilities were ended, the Mexican army was retired beyond the Rio Grande, confiscated property would be restored, and prisoners would be exchanged."[74] But the private treaty only assured that Santa Anna would do his best to convince the Mexican government that it should honor the public treaty; there were no guarantees that its provisions would be honored. In fact, Mexico repudiated the treaty, and officially it never went into effect.[75]

One point of contention between Texans and the Mexican government that helped lead to the independence movement had been Santa Anna's seizure of power in 1835 and his suspension of the Federalist Constitution of 1824.[76] This was the cause of much dissension throughout Northern Mexico, but especially in the highly independently minded former Nuevo Santander. As noted by Craig Roell, political officials in Tamaulipas were at first sympathetic to Texas and sought to collaborate as long as they believed that the Texans wanted only the restoration of the Constitution and not independence.[77] Texas' eventual success in attaining independence left Tamaulipans without support in their struggles against the centralizing tendencies of Mexican Conservatives. This led to another independence movement in the Rio Grande Valley: the establishment of the Republic of the Rio Grande. A number of long-time Rio Grande political actors, including Jesús de Cárdenas, Antonio Canales Rosillo, Antonio Zapata, José María Jesús Carbajal, and possibly Laredo mayor Basilio Benavides, the uncle of later Confederate commander Santos Benavides, led the movement.[78] They held an independence convention in January 1840 at which they "declared independence from Mexico and claimed for its territory the areas of Tamaulipas and Coahuila north to the Nueces and Medina rivers, respectively, and Nuevo León, Zacatecas, Durango, Chihuahua, and New Mexico" and set their capital at Benavides's town of Laredo.[79] Although the republic survived only until November, when it was crushed by the Mexican Army, its brief existence demonstrates the persistence of independent-mindedness after the separation of Texas from Mexico and the emergence of the Rio Grande Valley as a true frontier.[80]

In the course of the struggle between the Republic of the Rio Grande and Mexico, insurrectionist leaders sought and received help from Texans. Canales Rosillo personally met with Texas president Mirabeau Buonaparte Lamar to secure Texan collaboration. As noted by history writer Mike Coppock: "Lamar was certainly a gambler and an aggressive one . . . a Republic of the Rio Grande offered a fallback plan against possible Mexican aggression. For Texas' long-term benefit, the river republic could be absorbed later. Lamar officially declared Texan neutrality in the enterprise while privately either giving an approving word or turning a blind eye to Texans joining Canales' cause."

He goes on to note that at the time of this meeting, "the river was not generally considered the boundary between Texas and Mexico" and would not assume that role until after Lamar's presidency.[81] It is true that Lamar used the Rio Grande boundary as an excuse for his 1841 military expedition to seize Santa Fe, which lay to the east of the river and so might have been thought to be in Texas territory.[82] But it seems fairly safe to say that no one thought or cared about the godforsaken wilderness—that "d-v-l-sh chapparal," as Furber called it[83]—that lay below the Nueces River to the south, except those borderland politicians who launched the struggle for the Republic of Rio Grande, for whom the principle of Mexican federalism was more important than the actuality of real estate.

Nonetheless, the boundary between Texas and Mexico became a matter of great significance when annexation negotiations between the Republic of Texas and the United States of America began.[84] Now, despite its condition as virtual terra nullus, the strip between the Nueces and Rio Grande had truly become a borderland, a place of contest between contending parties and national cultures. In April 1846, at a site near Matamoros called Palo Alto, that contestation would escalate into all-out war when troops under Gen. Zachary Taylor, sent by the US government to patrol the region between the two rivers, were attacked by Mexican forces. Shortly thereafter, the US Congress declared war.[85]

*Taylor's Army, 1845*
*This lithograph depicts Gen. Zachary Taylor's army encamped near Corpus Christi prior to the march southward to the Rio Grande. Taylor's march would lead to the engagements with Mexican forces at Palo Alto and Resaca de la Palma, starting the Mexican-American War. "Birds-eye view of the camp of the army of occupation, commanded by Genl. Taylor, near Corpus Christi, Texas (from the North), Oct. 1845, D. P. Whiting, Capt. 7th Inf. del."; on stone by C. Parsons. Library of Congress Prints and Photographs Division, LC-DIG-pga-06205.*

Just more than seventeen months later, Mexico City fell to an American army and the war came to an end with an all-out victory for the United States. In the treaty that finally ended the conflict, the 1848 Treaty of Guadalupe Hidalgo, the United States acquired Alta California (i.e., the modern state of California) and nearly all of the present American Southwest between California and Texas. And for the purposes of this story, most importantly it finally set the southern boundary of Texas at the Rio Grande.[86] Diplomatically it could now be said that the Rio Grande Valley had made the transition from having been a frontier—terra nullus—to a borderland, and finally to a border. But as the rest of this story unfolds, it will become clear that this was true only in a strictly legal sense. For those living on the river, this change in official status presented only further complication in an already complicated existence. The treaty did nothing to change the fact that the people were still *con un pie en cada lado.* It would take the Civil War and the changes it wrought in the region to truly form the old Río Bravo del Norte into a border.

## *Notes*

1. This usage was coined by Bolton in his classic *The Spanish Borderlands: A Chronicle of Old Florida and the Southwest* (New Haven, CT: Yale University Press, 1921) and was then carried through in dozens of books and articles throughout his professional life. For an assessment of Bolton's work and influence, see Albert L. Hurtado, *Herbert Eugene Bolton: Historian of the American Borderlands* (Berkeley: University of California Press, 2012). It was then picked up by generations of acolytes, perhaps most prominently John Francis Bannon, S. J., whose *The Spanish Borderlands Frontier, 1513–1821* (New York: Holt, Rinehart and Winston, 1970) was perhaps the most successful synthesis of Bolton's work. A new generation of historians led by David J. Weber has brought greater clarity and depth to the concept. See, for example, David J. Weber, *The Spanish Frontier in North America* (New Haven: Yale University Press, 1992). An interesting review of Weber's work in contrast to Bolton's may be found in James A. Sandos, "From 'Boltonlands' to 'Weberlands'; The Borderlands Enter American History," *American Quarterly* 46, no. 4 (1994): 595–604.

2. The theoretical foundation for this transition from frontier, to borderland, to border, or "bordered land," is derived from Jeremy Adelman and Stephen Aron, "From Borderlands to Borders: Empires, Nation-States, and the Peoples in between in North American History," *American Historical Review* 104, no. 3 (1999): 814–41.

3. As Turner characterizes it, the "frontier" is defined as "the meeting point between savagery and civilization," with "savagery" being the characterization of wilderness. Frederick Jackson Turner, "The Significance of the Frontier in American

History," in *The Annual Report of the American Historical Association* (1894), 119–227. I should note that I am not advocating Turner's view—especially with respect to the erasure of Native American civilizations that were present in the region; citation of Turner's thesis is simply to make a point. I should also note that this region would constitute a "frontier" in the sense described by Adelman and Aron who, as noted, this analysis follows theoretically.

4. Oakah L. Jones, *Los Paisanos: Spanish Settlers on the Northern Frontier of New Spain* (Norman: University of Oklahoma Press, 1996), 19. Tampico was originally founded on the north side of the Pánuco River in 1554 by Andrés de Olmos as a mission called San Luis de Tampico de Alto but was abandoned in 1684 due largely to pirate depredations; after that time there was no permanent settlement north of the river for almost another hundred years. Edward Burian, *The Architecture and Cities of Northern Mexico from Independence to the Present* (Austin: University of Texas Press, 2015), 43–44.

5. Herbert Eugene Bolton, *Texas in the Middle Eighteenth Century; Studies in Spanish Colonial History and Administration* (1918; reprint, Austin: University of Texas Press, 1970), 57.

6. Hubert J. Miller, *José de Escandón: Colonizer of Nuevo Santander* (Edinburg, TX: New Santander Press, 1980), 1–2.

7. Prior to the first systematic exploration of the entire Seno Mexicano in 1746, it was believed that the Nueces flowed into the Río Bravo somewhere northeast of the its entry into the Gulf of Mexico. While this confusion was eventually cleared up, as this and later chapters will show, the question of whether the Nueces or Rio Grande was the natural boundary for this territory remained controversial for at least another century. See Bolton, *Texas in the Middle Eighteenth Century*, 293.

8. The most authoritative and complete discussion of the prehistoric population in this region may be found in Thomas R. Hester, "The Prehistory of South Texas," chapter 4 in *The Prehistory of Texas*, ed. Timothy K. Perttula (College Station: Texas A&M University Press, 2004). For a briefer overview, see Bobbie L. Lovett et al., eds., *Native American Peoples of South Texas* (Edinburg, TX: Community Historical Archaeology Project with Schools Program, 2014).

9. *Congregas* were the descendants of the earlier colonial encomienda system, through which Indian people were assigned to Spanish overlords and compelled to provide labor in exchange for learning Spanish, Catholicism, and "civilized" trades. See Miller, *José de Escandón*, 6; Bolton, *Texas in the Middle Eighteenth Century*, 288.

10. Lawrence F. Hill, *José De Escandón and the Founding of Nuevo Santander, a Study in Spanish Colonization* (Columbus: Ohio State University Press, 1926), 58–59.

11. Robert S. Weddle, "La Salle Expedition," *Handbook of Texas Online*, http://www.tshaonline.org/handbook/online/articles/up101 (accessed July 24, 2016).

12. Ibid.

13. Paul Horgan, *Great River: The Rio Grande in North American History*, 2 vols., 4th ed. (Hanover, NH: Wesleyan University Press, 1991), I: 302.

14. David Armitage, *The Ideological Origins of the British Empire* (Cambridge; New York: Cambridge University Press, 2000), 96–97. These Latin principles governed rules of colonization and land tenure throughout the colonial period, stemming

largely from the pioneering legal writings of Francesco de Vitoria (1485–1546), and were used primarily to justify the seizure of Native American land on the premise that they were not making productive use of it. In addition to Armitage's work, see also Anthony Pagden, *Lords of All the World: Ideologies of Empire in Spain, Britain and France 1500–C. 1800* (New Haven, CT: Yale University Press, 1995).

15. Bolton, *Texas in the Middle Eighteenth Century*, 57.

16. Miller, *José de Escandón*, 6.

17. Ibid., 7.

18. Ibid., 6. For more about the Sierra Gorda region and the persistent threat that Indians there posed to Spanish settlement, see Bolton, *Texas in the Middle Eighteenth Century*, 56–57. Lawrence F. Hill goes so far as to say that the Sierra Gorda was the key to the eventual conquest of Seno Mexicano; Hill, *José De Escandón*, 2, 18.

19. Miller, *José de Escandón*, 7.

20. Clotilde P. García, "Escandon, Jose De," *Handbook of Texas Online*, http://www.tshaonline.org/handbook/online/articles/fes01 (accessed July 25, 2016).

21. Miller, *José de Escandón*, 5.

22. Ibid., 7.

23. Ibid., 9.

24. Horgan, *Great River*, I:342.

25. Hill, *José De Escandón*, 65.

26. Ibid., 13.

27. Ibid.

28. Hill, José De Escandón, 66.

29. Debbie S. Cunningham concludes that Escandón's plan was "explicitly exclusionary of the natives," though it is unclear as to his motive. His experience in the Sierra Gorda and observations elsewhere in Mexico had demonstrated that congregas were unsuccessful and that the resentment they caused among the Indians was unnecessarily disruptive—Miller reports that the governor of Nuevo León had banned them (Miller, *José de Escandón*, 6). Escandón repeatedly said that he wanted the missions to be founded, but that getting the civilian settlements firmly rooted was a higher priority. See Debbie S. Cunningham, "The Natives of the Seno Mexicano as Documented in the Escandón and Hierro Manuscripts from 1747–1749," *Southern Quarterly* 51, no. 4 (2014): 55–71 (quotation from page 58), and Debbie S. Cunningham, "Friar Simón Del Hierro's Diary of the Preliminary Colonization of Nuevo Santander, 1749: An Annotated Translation," *Catholic Southwest* 23 (2012): 36–55.

30. Miller, *José de Escandón*, 13; Horgan, *Great River*, I:343.

31. Hill, *José De Escandón*, 66.

32. Ibid., 11.

33. Miller, *José de Escandón*, 27.

34. On the placement of settlements with respect to protection from Indians, see Miller, *José de Escandón*, 13.

35. Craig H. Roell, *Matamoros and the Texas Revolution* (Denton: Texas State Historical Association, 2013), 28–29.

36. Hill, *José De Escandón*, 10; Miller, *José de Escandón*, 5–6.

37. The term *gente de razón* is a somewhat fluid term that is usually applied to Spanish colonists who were of mixed racial or ethnic background but who had been fully acclimated to Spanish civilization. Alonzo argues that on the northern frontiers of New Spain this term was also applied to Indians who had made a full transition to a Spanish lifestyle. See Ana María Alonso, *Thread of Blood: Colonialism, Revolution, and Gender on Mexico's Northern Frontier* (Tucson: University of Arizona Press, 1995), quote from page 106.

38. Bolton, *Texas in the Middle Eighteenth Century*, 299. A *sitio de ganado mayor*, lot for grazing large animals (i.e., cattle, horses, etc.), was one square league, or approximately 1,373 acres. A *sitio de ganado menor*, lot for grazing small animals (i.e., sheep, goats, etc.), was half the size of a sitio de ganado mayor, and hence approximately 685 acres. A *caballeria*, a unit of measure based on a medieval knight's allocation, is usually given as approximately 103 acres; however, Hubert Miller has it as 125 acres specifically in Nuevo Santander. It should be noted that none of these measures were standardized and varied widely throughout the Spanish empire. University of Michigan anthropologist David L. Frye provides a table of equivalencies on his website: http://www-personal.umich.edu/~dfrye/fanega.htm, accessed July 26, 2016. An *ejido* is land set aside for public and/or communal use, like a village commons. Miller, *José de Escandón*, ii.

39. Quoted in Miller, *José de Escandón*, 25.

40. Bolton, *Texas in the Middle Eighteenth Century*, 299.

41. Ibid.

42. Hill, *José De Escandón*, 6.

43. Bolton, *Texas in the Middle Eighteenth Century*, 294.

44. Miller, *José de Escandón*, 16.

45. Hill, *José De Escandón*, 77.

46. Miller, *José de Escandón*, 18.

47. Ibid.

48. Cunningham, "Friar Simón Del Hierro's Diary," 44–45.

49. Bolton, *Texas in the Middle Eighteenth Century*, 296.

50. Ibid., 297.

51. Ibid., 297–98.

52. Hill, *José De Escandón*, 128.

53. Ibid., 139.

54. Miller, *José de Escandón*, 28.

55. Jones, *Los Paisanos*, 72–73.

56. Ibid., 73.

57. Miller describes this process in detail in *José de Escandón*, 33–35.

58. Miller, *José de Escandón*, 5–6, 36–38. Escandón died before his case had been decided. Miller suggests that because his sequestered lands and businesses were eventually awarded to his son, José de Escandón de Llera, the royal government had determined that his conduct had been legal.

59. Miller, *José de Escandón*, 36.

60. Ibid., 35.

61. Mary Jo Galindo, "*Con Un Pie En Cada Lado*: Ethnicities and the Archaeology

of Spanish Colonial Ranching Communities along the Lower Rio Grande Valley" (PhD diss., University of Texas at Austin, 2003), ix.

62. Hill, *José De Escandón*, 78.

63. Russell K. Skowronek and Bobbie L. Lovett, "Coahuiltecans of the Rio Grande Region," in *Native American Peoples of South Texas* (Edinburg, TX: Community Historical Archaeology Project with Schools Program, 2014), 18–19.

64. Roell, *Matamoros*, 7–9.

65. Ibid., 29–30. Note that this was very near the end of the Mexican War for Independence and probably was intended to curry support for the royalists in the highly independent state of Nuevo Sandander. Oakah L. Jones notes that during the revolution, the residents of the region remained loyal to the crown. The *alcalde* of Laredo went so far as to prescribe the death penalty for anyone who dealt with traitors, insurgents, or Indian allies of those in revolt against royal authority in 1813. Jones, *Los Paisanos*, 78.

66. Roell, *Matamoros*, 31–32.

67. Ibid., 32. It should be noted that among those who arrived during these years was Charles Stillman, who came to Matamoros in 1828, just as the port began to take off as a center for international trade and profit. See John Mason Hart, "Stillman, Charles," *Handbook of Texas Online*, http://www.tshaonline.org/handbook/online/articles/fst57 (accessed July 30, 2016). It is also interesting to note that Stillman's father, Captain Francis Stillman, died in Matamoros in 1838, suggesting that there may have been a Stillman enterprise in the city from very early on. Francis D. Stillman, *The Stillman Family: Descendants of Mr. George Stillman of Wethersfield, Connecticut and Dr. George Stillman of Westerly, Rhode Island* (Greensburg, PA: F. D. Stillman, 1989), 48.

68. Jean Louis Berlandier, *Journey to Mexico during the Years 1826 to 1834* (Austin: Texas State Historical Association in cooperation with the Center for Studies in Texas History, University of Texas at Austin, 1980), II:542.

69. Quoted in Roell, *Matamoros*, 20.

70. George C. Furber, *The Twelve Months Volunteer; Or, Journal of a Private, in the Tennessee Regiment of Cavalry, in the Campaign, in Mexico, 1846–7* (Cincinnati, J. A. & U. P. James, 1849), 165.

71. Quoted in Roell, *Matamoros*, 22.

72. "Empresario," *Handbook of Texas Online*, http://www.tshaonline.org/handbook/online/articles/pfe01 (accessed July 30, 2016). For more details on the empresario system, see Mary Virginia Henderson, "Minor Empresario Contracts for the Colonization of Texas, 1825–1834," *The Southwestern Historical Quarterly* 31, no. 4 (1928): 295–324.

73. One of the best short accounts of the entire revolutionary struggle is Eugene C. Barker and James W. Pohl, "Texas Revolution," *Handbook of Texas Online*, http://www.tshaonline.org/handbook/online/articles/qdt01 (accessed July 30, 2016).

74. Ibid.

75. Ibid.

76. It should be noted that political labels in Mexico were almost exactly

opposites of those in the contemporary United States. In Mexico, Federalists were decentralists, believers in states' rights. Santa Anna, on the other hand, represented Centralists, who wanted greater power for the national government and reduction of states' rights. On Federalism in Mexico, see J. Lloyd Mecham, "The Origins of Federalism in Mexico," *The Hispanic American Historical Review* 18, no. 2 (1938): 164–82.

77. Roell, *Matamoros*, 38–40.

78. David M. Vigness, "Republic of the Rio Grande," *Handbook of Texas Online*, http://www.tshaonline.org/handbook/online/articles/ngr01 (accessed July 31, 2016). Surmising participation by Benavides is premised upon his personal and political significance in Laredo, the selection of that town as the republic's capital, and by personal communication with Laredo scholar Jerry D. Thompson.

79. Vigness, "Republic of the Rio Grande."

80. Mike Coppock, "The Republic of the Rio Grande," HistoryNet, http://www.historynet.com/the-republic-of-the-rio-grande.htm (accessed June 26, 2016).

81. Ibid.

82. H. Bailey Carroll, "Texan Santa Fe Expedition," *Handbook of Texas Online*, http://www.tshaonline.org/handbook/online/articles/qyt03 (accessed July 30, 2016).

83. Furber, *The Twelve Months Volunteer*, 184.

84. C. T. Neu, "Annexation," *Handbook of Texas Online*, http://www.tshaonline.org/handbook/online/articles/mga02 (accessed July 30, 2016).

85. See Douglas A. Murphy, *Two Armies on the Rio Grande: The First Campaign of the US-Mexican War* (College Station: Texas A&M University Press, 2014).

86. David M. Pletcher, "Treaty of Guadalupe Hidalgo," *Handbook of Texas Online*, http://www.tshaonline.org/handbook/online/articles/nbt01 (accessed July 31, 2016).

# 2

# *To Occupy and Possess Our Own*

## The Mexican War, the Civil War, and the Fight for the Rio Grande Valley

DOUGLAS A. MURPHY

"The war news from Charleston has produced a thrilling excitement throughout the entire country," the editors of the *Baltimore Sun* announced in the aftermath of the Confederate bombardment of Fort Sumter in April 1861. "Nothing that occurred during the Mexican war equaled it. It was then a battle with a foreign enemy. Now it is brother in deadly, hostile array against brother—the beginning, perhaps, of a long and bloody civil war."[1]

The newspaper was correct on several points. The fighting in South Carolina did represent the first shots of a prolonged civil war and the confrontation produced considerable excitement in both the Northern and Southern states. But it was incorrect to claim that nothing during the Mexican War had equaled it. Enthusiasm about the battles of that earlier conflict had swept the nation in 1846, causing Americans to clamor for details of clashes, to make heroes of the men who fought them, and to enlist by the thousands to participate in the war effort. Moreover—as demonstrated by the reference in the *Sun*—the Mexican War continued to resonate strongly almost two decades later in the aftermath of Fort Sumter.

Indeed, for many Americans on either side of the growing civil divide, the conflict with Mexico gave special meaning to the looming fight. At a speech given in his home state of New Hampshire immediately following the Fort Sumter clash, former president Franklin Pierce—himself a Mexican War veteran—looked to the earlier conflict to illustrate the tragedy of disunion and rebellion on display in Charleston. After proudly recalling the many glorious American victories at Palo Alto,

Buena Vista, Veracruz, and Mexico City, he assured his audience that the foundation of those successes was national unity: "Never can we forget that the gallant men of the North and of the South moved together like a band of brothers, and mingled their blood on many a field in the common cause." To retain this greatness, however, citizens would have to fight for preservation of the Union, and he encouraged his listeners "to stand together and uphold the flag to the last."[2] Meanwhile, south of the Mason-Dixon line, one of the many wartime ballads inspired by recent events recalled notable Southerners who had fought for freedom—a list that ended with the Mexican War general Zachary Taylor,

*Who on Palo Alto's day, Mid fire and hail at Monterey,*
*At Buena Vista led the way, "Rough and Ready."*

But instead of echoing Pierce's call for unity, this song built toward a final, dramatic plea for rebellion.

*Southerns all, at freedom's call, For our homes united all.*
*Freemen live, or freemen fall! "Death or liberty."*

In both instances, the events of the war with Mexico justified men taking up arms to fight each other in civil war.[3]

This rhetoric was especially evident in discussions of and activities in the Rio Grande delta of Texas, the region at the heart of the territorial dispute with Mexico so many years before. In the spring of 1846, an American army under the command of Zachary Taylor marched to the area, built a fort, and raised the stars and stripes to claim the Rio Grande as the national boundary. Mexican forces contested this by crossing the river, besieging the American fort—later known as Fort Brown—and engaging the US Army on the battlefields of Palo Alto and Resaca de la Palma. US troops prevailed in these clashes, forced the Mexican Army back across the Rio Grande, and then pressed onward into the heart of Mexico with a series of campaigns and battles that culminated with the occupation of Mexico City in September 1847. When Mexican leaders finally accepted a peace treaty in February 1848, they surrendered claims to a huge expanse of territory extending from Texas to the Pacific coast. That vast land included very few battlefields from the war, but did contain the three initial venues of conflict near the Rio Grande. This small collection of sites, therefore, assumed a special importance for Americans from all sections, a quality that did not diminish over the years. Decades later, the strategically important Rio Grande delta once again became a place of military conflict. But, just as significantly, this home to treasured battlefields also emerged as an ideological arena, where Unionists and Confederates would vie over the legacy of the Mexican War.

Fittingly, the Civil War saga in the region began with the actions of a veteran of the Mexican War. In 1846, Col. David Twiggs served as brigade commander under Zachary Taylor. As a member of that force—known first as the "Army of Observation" and later as the "Army of Occupation"—he marched to the Rio Grande and participated in construction of the earthen fieldwork on the bank of that river. When fighting erupted and Mexican troops commenced a bombardment of that fort, he was one of the 2,300 soldiers who rushed to break the siege and assist the garrison trapped within. On May 8, 1846, Twiggs directed the right wing of the American forces in the battle of Palo Alto, a prolonged exchange in which US cannon pounded Mexican lines on a broad open prairie. The following day, he and Taylor's army engaged the Mexicans once again in the dense brush of Resaca de la Palma, where the Mexican force had taken refuge from the withering artillery fire. This time, infantry troops relied on fierce hand-to-hand combat to drive their foes from the position and forced them to retreat across the Rio Grande. At the time, Twiggs expressed pride at the role he and his troops played in winning the clash and ending the siege of the US fort. "The enemy having been routed with great loss, this day's action closed with much honor to the American army," he wrote in his official report of the battle. "In this action every officer and man performed his duty most gallantly."[4]

He displayed much less gallantry as commander of the US Military District of Texas in 1861. In February, a state secession committee made the decision to leave the Union and called for the United States to cede control of all army facilities and bases as well as all weapons, munitions, and equipment contained within them. Twiggs, now a general and one of the highest ranking officers of the US Army, found himself in a difficult position. He had loyally served the United States for decades and did not wish to violate any orders to protect military property, but he was also a Southerner and a strong advocate of states' rights who

*Gen. David Twiggs tarnished a reputation earned in battles with Mexico in 1846 when he surrendered US forts and forces in Texas to secessionists in 1861. Library of Congress.*

had no desire to wage war on the citizens of his homeland. To escape this dilemma, he requested that his superiors send a replacement to deal with the secession issue, but events forced his hand. When Texan troops surrounded his headquarters in San Antonio on March 16, 1861, and demanded compliance with their resolutions, Twiggs capitulated without a fight. Though he refused to require his troops to surrender their weapons, he agreed to turn over all public property and forts within the state and issued orders for his subordinates to comply.[5]

Twiggs's reputation became the first real battleground of a building propaganda war. Shortly after he surrendered his command in Texas, US officials dismissed him from the army, bringing to a close his distinguished forty-nine year career in that institution. Residents of Georgia welcomed him home to assume command of that state's militia troops in the coming rebellion. But Unionists derided him for his choice. Editors of the *Virginia Free Press* called his actions "Treachery of the basest sort" and noted that "what faith the government of Georgia can put in the traitor Twiggs after the violation of his oath and trust remains to be seen." Others agreed and found the betrayal all the more hurtful because the general had provided such valuable service to the nation in the past. Many Northern newspapers provided an extensive review of his record, giving considerable attention and praise to his accomplishments in the war with Mexico. Nevertheless, they found the surrender of Texas to be unforgiveable. The *Daily Cleveland Herald*, for example, stated that Twiggs, "whose name in the Mexican war calls up memories of Palo Alto, Resaca de la Palma, Monterey, and Veracruz, has by one act dashed out the long record of his valuable services, and, among a horde of traitors, proved himself the most infamous of them all." The Southern press, by contrast, believed that the vilified Twiggs had followed a "sensible and manly course" and dismissed the criticism as little more than "the inane twaddle and vague denunciations of Northern fanatics."[6]

As this debate raged on, Unionists found a counterpoint to this treason at Fort Brown, Texas—a place where Twiggs had previously distinguished himself. By 1861, the fort was no longer just the hastily constructed earthwork of 1846, but a full-fledged military base that provided protection to Brownsville, a thriving community that had grown up alongside it. And the officer in charge of that post was not a blind follower of Twiggs, but a loyal US soldier who took a much more active stand against the secessionists. As General Twiggs negotiated terms for transfer of government property, Capt. Bennett Hill hurriedly gathered artillery and attempted to transport it safely out of Texas. That effort failed, and Texan military units captured the guns before they could be smuggled out via the Gulf. The fort, however, remained in Union hands, and when Col. John S. Ford, commander of the Texas Rio Grande Military District, arrived in Brownsville in late February to take possession of the fort, Hill refused to abandon his post or turn over any property. Even when shown a copy of the order from General Twiggs, he refused to abide by the terms until he had received confirmation from the US War Department.[7]

The stance infuriated Colonel Ford, who had hoped to quickly seize control of Brownsville, but it pleased Americans in the North. Many of these citizens still remembered the story of Maj. Jacob Brown, the namesake of the fort, who had commanded the site during the Mexican siege of 1846. In charge of a small garrison of troops, surrounded by Mexican forces, and with limited ammunition with which to return fire, Brown had bravely held his post and urged his soldiers to remain positive as artillery shots rained down upon them. Even a direct strike to his leg failed to sway his determination. He endured a painful amputation, suffered from gangrene and fever, and slowly deteriorated in health, but maintained a defiant spirit until the moment of his death, just hours before General Taylor's army triumphed at Resaca de la Palma and liberated the fort. For those Americans of 1861 who may have forgotten this tale, newspapers like the New York *Commercial Herald* retold it in extensive detail, drawing parallels between Jacob Brown and Bennett Hill. Hill, in direct contrast to the traitorous Twiggs, Ford, and other Texans, upheld the spirit of patriotism established fifteen years before, and the newspaper praised his vow to defend the fort against a Texan attack. "We believe that Lieutenant Hill will do what he says he will," cheered the editors of the *Herald*. "If the fort is assaulted, the spirit of the honored Major Brown will cry out from his grave for Lieutenant Hill not to ignominiously tear down that flag that he once so gloriously defended against such odds." By emulating Jacob Brown, the newspaper suggested, Hill would also serve as an inspiration for similarly beleaguered Union troops ensconced in Fort Sumter, South Carolina, and Fort Pickens, Florida, as well.[8]

Southerners, however, saw the confrontation over the fort as a matter of principle and believed that theirs was the just cause. In a fiery speech to the committee charged with drafting a constitution for the new Southern government, delegate James Chestnut of South Carolina declared that the Confederate states had every justification to claim properties like Fort Brown as their own:

> If the theory of secession be true, upon which we have put this government in motion we have not lost our rights in the public lands of the United States. And, sir, never, with my consent, while this Confederacy has an arm to defend its rights, shall the Confederate States give up their interest in the public domain. Never, sir, and more especially as a Southern man, will I consent to relinquish those rights.

And though Chestnut did not go so far as to speak the name of the beloved Jacob Brown—who had hailed from Vermont and not from the South—he did invoke the war with Mexico to explain why seceding states had a legitimate claim to federal lands within their borders. These properties, he insisted, "were emphatically the purchase of Southern treasure and Southern blood."

> It is true, sir, the expenses of the Mexican war were borne out of the national treasury, but, if we are correct in our opinion, the greatest amount of revenue received by that government, is directly and indirectly contributed by the South. Upon the other point there can be no doubt. So far as the sacrifice of human life is concerned, the largest portion of those lands belong to us. It was Southern blood and valor that won the principle laurels in the Mexican war.[9]

Northerners like Jacob Brown certainly played heroic roles in the conflict with Mexico, and that past service was appreciated. But in the view of Chestnut and his peers, men like David Twiggs—supported by thousands of Southern volunteers who turned out to fight in the aftermath of Palo Alto and Resaca de la Palma—had truly decided the conflict in Mexico. Now the time had come for the Confederacy to appropriate the spoils of that war.

Even some in the North conceded that Southerners had contributed more than their fair share in the war with Mexico and other conflicts. The Columbus, Ohio, newspaper *The Crisis* challenged Unionists who seemed to claim that the patriotism and sacrifice of men like Jacob Brown or Bennett Hill were traits exhibited only by citizens of the free states. According to editor Samuel Medary, "Official records exhibit the utter falsity of the pretention, and establish the fact that in the Mexican war, as in every other conflict of arms, the South gives up the best blood of her citizens for the maintenance of national honor and right with a prodigality that stands in marked contrast to the volunteer forces contributed by the free labor states." To support this assertion, Medary included statistics showing that Southern states had provided 45,630 troops to fight the war with Mexico, while Northern states offered only 23,064 volunteers to the cause. The states of Maine, New Hampshire, Vermont, Connecticut, and Rhode Island failed to provide a single volunteer in the aftermath of Palo Alto and Resaca de la Palma.[10]

*The Crisis* was a newspaper for the Peace Democrats, or "Copperheads," who sided with the South, so this type of analysis was expected in its pages, but other journals provided similar information. The *Baltimore Sun*, for example, confessed that Maryland had a dismal record in providing troops in the nation's various conflicts and expressed surprise that the state leaders had responded quickly to events and immediately equipped a volunteer unit, "showing more alacrity than was displayed during the Mexican War." The *New York Herald* agreed with Medary's figures, noting that the Northern states had twice the population of the South but had contributed half as many soldiers to the war with Mexico. Moreover, Northern soldiers had made minimal sacrifice in the conflict. Massachusetts, the only New England state to provide a regiment for Mexico, assembled only 1,047 troops for combat, and of those, only two died during the war. Unlike *The Crisis*, these two papers were not seeking to endorse the Southern cause. Instead they eyed the growing tension in Texas at Fort Brown and feared that the Union would not be able raise troops and sustain a fight with the Confederacy if war erupted.[11]

Despite the concern and the rhetoric, Fort Brown would not become the starting point of a second war. As the Northern and Southern press wrangled over which region had the better claim to the success and spoils of the Mexican War, the second siege of Fort Brown ended without the dramatic fighting that occurred in 1846. Captain Hill had originally strengthened his hold on the site by calling in reinforcements from Fort Ringgold, about 80 miles upstream on the Rio Grande. This placed more than four hundred troops at his disposal. Moreover, he had retained thirty cannons for the fort's defenses, reportedly including a light artillery battery famously used by Capt. Braxton Bragg in the Mexican War battle of Buena Vista. Those same guns had been commanded by then lieutenant Bragg to fend off the 1846 siege of Fort Brown. Symbolism and numbers originally gave Captain Hill confidence that he could hold off a new assault by the secessionist forces of Colonel Ford. But as more and more Texan troops poured into the Rio Grande delta, topping a thousand men at arms, Hill saw the advantage turn significantly in favor of the Confederates. His supplies also dwindled, further reducing his options for resistance. For this reason, he welcomed the arrival of Maj. Fitz-John Porter in early March. Porter, a representative of authorities in Washington, had been allowed to pass into Brownsville by Colonel Ford and finally provided Hill with official authorization to comply with the agreement signed by General Twiggs weeks before. On May 4, Hill subsequently notified Ford that he would surrender his post without a fight. Eight days later, the captain and his men, carrying nothing but their side arms and escorting a single battery of light artillery (perhaps the guns once used by Bragg), boarded a ship at the nearby Brazos Santiago depot and left Texas behind.[12]

It was a decision that frustrated many of those who had recently celebrated Hill's boldness. Editors of the *Philadelphia Inquirer*, for example, had previously viewed Captain Hill as the new incarnation of Jacob Brown and praised his "valorous defiance of the rebels at the outset of the difficulties." Now they stopped short of branding Hill a traitor in the mold of General Twiggs, but expressed disappointment that the soldier "seems to have repented of his determination." In fairness, circumstances dictated the captain's decision. In 1846, Major Brown resisted the Mexican siege with the knowledge that assistance was on the way in the form of General Taylor's army. Hill knew that no reinforcements were marching to the Rio Grande to rescue him and had little choice but to surrender.[13]

Colonel Ford's troops assumed control of the Fort Brown and the city of Brownsville, and immediately began preparations for their own Jacob Brown moment. Despite the peaceful evacuation of the US troops, the secessionists were convinced that some sort of US attack was being planned. To guard against this they needed protective fortifications, and they found them already in place at the original 1846 site. That fort—a large six-sided structure composed almost entirely of packed earth—had effectively shielded Jacob Brown's troops from artillery fire during the original Mexican bombardment and remained far more secure than the collection of buildings and parade grounds that had since sprung up to its west. Hill and his troops had made little use of the overgrown and eroding structure as they waited for an assault by the Texans, but Colonel Ford was eager to make it battle-ready. Just days after the Union departure, a force of Texas soldiers, Brownsville civilians, and a team of eighty hired Mexicans converged upon the site with picks and axes to clear the walls of trees and weeds and to restore ditches and bastions. Additional workers cleared the land around the fort for five hundred yards in all directions, to ensure an enemy could not approach unseen.[14]

As the famous earthworks rapidly returned to their original form, other soldiers planted artillery pieces in the bastions, supplied the magazines with ammunitions, and secured enough food to sustain defenders during a prolonged siege. By early April, those working on the project felt confident that their efforts would be sufficient to ensure "that the reception of Lincoln's troops might be a warm one." "We have a

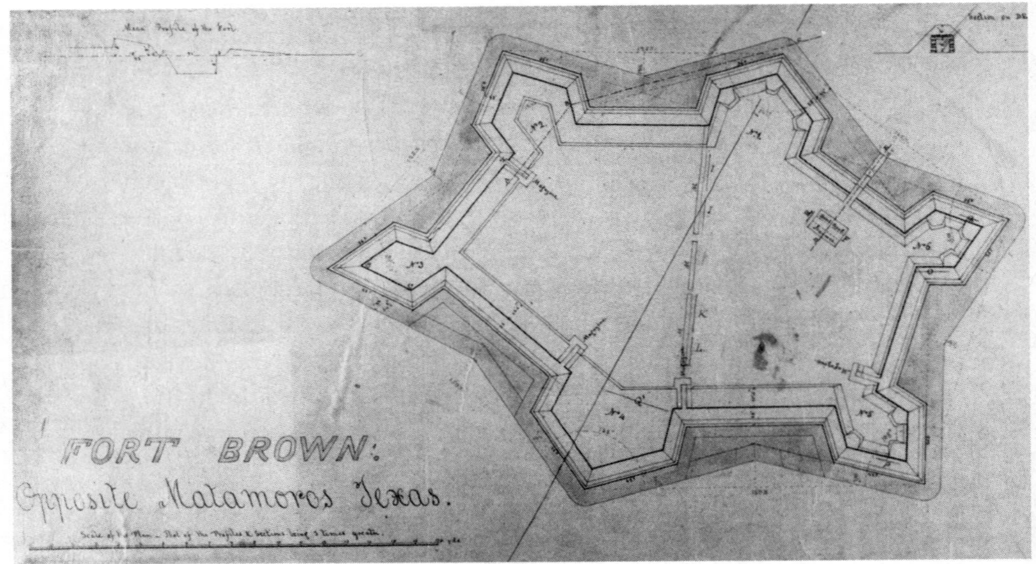


*Plan of the 1846 Fort Brown. The old earthworks became a centerpiece for strategy and interest in the Civil War campaigns in South Texas. US National Archives.*

large number of guns of various sizes and do not fear a dozen ship-loads of abolition soldiers," wrote one of the men at work on the project. "Our boys are anxious that they should come, and but one opinion is expressed, and that is, that they will never have the privilege of retreating from our shores. We will send them to the place where sulphur smells, and to a hotter climate than Texas."[15]

These preparations were not entirely without foundation. A large Union military force had assembled near the harbor at New York City in late March and early April. No one in the public at large knew the intended destination of this growing force, but rumors abounded that the combination of army and navy troops would be directed to the Gulf Coast of Texas, with the ultimate goal of retaking Fort Brown.[16]

As they completed their preparations for an invasion from the North, Ford's troops suddenly found themselves confronting a possible threat from the south. In late March, rumors began to circulate that Mexican general Pedro de Ampudia had assembled a force of three thousand soldiers and had commenced a march toward the Rio Grande and Brownsville. Initial accounts portrayed the advance as a sort of bandit raid, with Ampudia intent on pillaging towns on both sides of the river. But as the general reportedly moved to within sixty miles of Fort Brown, he appeared to have accumulated a thousand additional troops and a much more specific purpose. "Texas rightfully belonged to Mexico," Ampudia reportedly proclaimed as he resumed his advance. "She has declared that she will no longer support the Federal Government and now it is time to retake her." Ampudia had briefly been the general in chief of the Mexican force that had confronted Zachary Taylor's Army of Occupation in 1846 and served as second in command in the battles of Palo Alto and Resaca de la Palma and the siege of Fort Brown. At that time, he vehemently defended Mexico's territorial claims and even demanded the US withdrawal from all of Texas. He also had supervised a large portion of the troops besieging Fort Brown and had even advocated for a headlong assault on the earthworks. Now, at a time when so much of the dispute between Unionists and secessionists harkened back to incidents of 1846, Ampudia seemed determined to turn back the clock as well. With US troops finally out of Texas and the secessionists still settling in, it appeared that he would try to avenge his previous defeat. The next round of reports asserted that the general had planted cannons on the bank of the Rio Grande directly across from the fort, ready to bombard and capture the post that had eluded him so many years before.[17]

Ultimately the threatening advance of Ampudia proved to be a hoax. Journalists who delved into the story could find nothing to support the claims that the Mexican general had designs on Fort Brown, Brownsville, and Texas. To the contrary, all evidence suggested that the entire narrative had been fabricated. Subsequent stories on the subject reported that Ampudia had retired from active service, was living far away in the interior of Mexico, had no plans or means to attack Texas, and could not expect the cooperation of the Mexican government if he did. Later still, it became clear that there was an ulterior motive behind the invasion story. It appeared that Republicans, who had been frustrated by the surrender of Fort Brown, had propagated the tale to generate a response, not from the secessionists occupying the fort but by the Union army that had abandoned it. US military leaders appeared unwilling to risk warfare with their Southern brethren, but would, perhaps, prove to be more willing against a former foe. The perpetrators of this fictional invasion believed that the threat of a Mexican attack on the very spot where the 1846 siege had unfolded would spur the US Army to reoccupy the Rio Grande delta and reclaim Fort Brown. Once they returned to Brownsville in force, the Union troops could use this historically important region as a beachhead to reclaim the rest of Texas. The plan was far-fetched and doomed to fail, but the rumor had remarkable staying power. Even as some journals assured readers that no invasion was afoot, others continued to insist that an attack was imminent—now claiming that it would come from Mexican general Ignacio Zaragosa at the head of an even larger force.[18]

For the moment, no attack was coming from either the north or south, and the initial blows of the war would instead erupt in Charleston harbor. Maj. Robert Anderson, the Union commander of Fort Sumter, found himself in a similar situation to Captain Hill at Fort Brown, confronted by secessionist troops and resistant to surrender. Gen. P. G. T. Beauregard of the newly established Confederate army took on the role recently occupied by Colonel Ford, positioning an army around a US fort and demanding capitulation. This time the dispute escalated. On April 12, 1861, the Confederates opened fire and maintained a cannon barrage upon the US garrison until April 14, when the overmatched and undersupplied Major Anderson agreed to abandon the post. The dramatic outbreak of warfare caused all attention to shift to South Carolina and away from Texas and the Rio Grande. For the moment, thoughts about retaking Fort Brown were discarded, and Sumter took its place as the source of Northern outrage and Southern pride. But the incidents surrounding the fall of Fort Brown had pulled the Mexican War back into public awareness. And since the primary protagonists in the South Carolina confrontation were both respected Mexican War veterans, memories of the previous war were now being analyzed for indications of which side would measure up in the present one.[19]

With hostilities a reality, the question of who had fought past wars and who would fight the next took on new significance. Stung by recent criticisms about their failure to bear their fair share in Mexico, citizens of the Union were determined to show that they had the will to fight when the cause was just. The past war, they argued, had primarily been a southern initiative, designed to spread slavery and its influence into the westernmost reaches of the continent. A large segment of the northern population had found that cause to be distasteful. Some went so far as to label it as wicked and immoral. At the very least, many Northerners had viewed the conflict with Mexico to be "unnecessary, uncalled for, and impolitic." This array of concerns helped explain why that section of the country had lagged behind the south when the calls for enlistments sounded in 1846. "But it is very different now," wrote the editors of Ohio's *Scioto Gazette*, explaining why the Union would respond with enthusiasm in 1861. "The people of the free States are united as one man in favor of the immediate and decisive crushing out of the rebellion. Never before in this country—perhaps never in any country—was there such unanimity of feeling as to the necessity and justice of a war as there is in the Free States at this time." In other words, the residents of the northern United States struggled to find motivation to unite against Mexico following the bombardment of Fort Brown and the battles of Palo Alto and Resaca de la Palma in 1846, but—responding to the pleas of men like Franklin Pierce to defend the Union—they would rally to arms to defeat the traitorous attackers of Fort Sumter.[20]

Evidence of this came when Abraham Lincoln requested volunteers to help crush the rebellion that had commenced in Charleston. On April 15, the US president stated his intention to develop a 75,000 man militia force for this purpose and called for each of the remaining states of the Union to contribute a portion of that number. Slave states reacted negatively, and the presidential order helped push Arkansas, North Carolina, Tennessee, and Virginia to cast their lot with the Confederacy of Alabama, Florida, Georgia, Louisiana, Mississippi, South Carolina, and Texas. Northern states, however, answered the call with an enthusiasm not seen during the Mexican War and quickly provided a force that surpassed Lincoln's expectation.[21]

Curiously, this rush to preserve the Union also took on a distinct Mexican War theme. Northerners may have disapproved of the reasons behind the 1846 conflict, but they recognized its importance. First and foremost, those clashes had produced a generation of military veterans, many of whom answered the call to the colors after Fort Sumter. Some actively organized Lincoln's new regiments. Others assumed roles as officers of the new units. All provided a level of experience and knowledge that seemed vital for regiments that intended to confront their more militaristic brothers of the South. But the Mexican War also held important symbolic importance for the nation—one that became apparent as soldiers selected names for their units. Citizens of Reading, Pennsylvania, organized the Ringgold Light Artillery. That company, which was one of the first to respond to Lincoln's request for troops, took its name in honor of Maj. Samuel Ringgold, an artillery commander who had played an instrumental role in the battle of Palo Alto and was generally recognized as the first US officer to die in the conflict with Mexico. Other Pennsylvania cities and towns banded together to form the Scott Legion, named in recognition of Winfield Scott, leader of the Mexico City campaign in 1847 and still commander of Union troops in 1861. Meanwhile, in New York City, Mexican War veterans celebrated their own service in Mexico by forming the Montezuma Battalion. Their call for enlistments proved so successful that they quickly expanded their organization into the Montezuma Regiment. These units were not necessarily better than other units in leadership and ability, but the choice of names demonstrated the determination of Northerners to claim the events and heroes of the Mexican War as triumphs of the Union, not just of the secessionist South.[22]

Confederates scoffed at such ideals. Once again, Southerners recalled that their region had far greater numbers of Mexican war veterans than the North and these men were organizing their own companies for a fight. "In a great emergency," noted Tennessee's *Fayetteville Observer*, "the Southern States could place in the field a million of men—the greater part of them being such men as won the battles of Buena Vista and New Orleans." Moreover, these soldiers had no fear about confronting their units forming in New York, Pennsylvania, and elsewhere in the Union. The day after the battle of Fort Sumter, for example, a South Carolinian, signing himself only as "On Behalf of the South Carolina Volunteers," dared the governor of Massachusetts to send troops to the rebellious state. "We number about ten thousand men, well armed and accoutered and anxious for a fight," he wrote, "and cordially invite any number from your section to give us a meeting." The author also mocked the pretentions of the Northerners who claimed credit for old victories in Mexico. "Send all Massachusetts men," he warned, "none from Pennsylvania, for the regiment of that State flunked at Cerro Gordo; nor from New York, for at Cherubusco (although they claimed and received the right from the Palmetto Regiment), at the first fire the gallant New Yorkers fell back and hid behind a barn; nor from Indiana, for at Palo Alto, the nimble regiment from that State fled in inglorious confusion." The letter was riddled with errors—in spelling, grammar, and facts about the battles—but its message was unmistakable: the North contributed little to the victory in 1846–48.[23]

Conversely, the South had displayed great "military spirit and genius" during that period. As proof, the Macon, Georgia, *Daily Telegraph* listed numerous Southerners who had excelled in that conflict, Gens. Zachary Taylor and Winfield Scott, Chief of Engineers Robert E. Lee, and numerous others:

> The light batteries of Artillery which did such wonderful execution at Palo Alto, Resaca de la Palma, Monterey, Buena Vista, and in the valley of Mexico were generally under the command of Southern men, Ringgold, Ridgeley, Bragg, Washington, Steptoe, and Magruder. The heavy ordinance was under the control of Huger, of S.C. and Laidley of Virginia. The battery of mountain howitzers, was directed by Reno, of Virginia. The dashing charge of cavalry at Resaca de la Palma, which has a world-wide reputation, was made by May, of Washington city.

Some of those men were long dead, and some remained loyal to the Union, but the military tradition remained strong, and this, Southerclaimed, would ensure victory over the Union in 1861.[24]

Despite their bravado, many Southerners had grave concerns about their rebellion and focused on the Mexican War as a source of reassurance. The public displays of arrogance infuriated Northerners when they read these statements in the newspapers, but the proud words disguised deep-seated insecurities of the Confederates. Confederate leaders were fully aware of the weaknesses of their position with regard to the Union; they had a much smaller population, limited manufacturing capabilities, tenuous control of shipping and coastlines, and longstanding concerns about their ability to maintain control of the enslaved population. Confronted with these challenges and many more, the prospects of victory in the war seemed remote. But memories of the war with Mexico offered hope. In that conflict, the Southern population had mobilized in numbers, performed admirably in battle, and achieved success in the face of difficult challenges. If that behavior could be replicated for the current dispute, the South might triumph by force of will alone. In this environment, the arrogant assertion of Southern superiority in Mexico really served as an appeal to the population, calling men to arms and encouraging them to live up to the example of their forebears.

This sentiment was clearly captured in a popular poem titled "The Sword of Harry Lee." In this ballad, James Dabney McCabe tells the tale of an aging Southern gentleman displaying a sword to his young grandson. The weapon, according to the tale, had been presented to the man by Henry "Light Horse Harry" Lee during the American Revolution, a reward for saving the general's life in battle. The blade saw use throughout that conflict and then had been entrusted to the boy's father in the war with Mexico. There, according to the verse,

*He bore it manfully and well, In regions far away*
*It flashed o'er Palo Alto's plains, And sunny Monterey*

And the grandfather expressed pride that

*It never was laid down in shame, God grant I ne'er may see.*
*One base, foul blot upon the blade, Of dear old Harry Lee!*

Having explained the noble history of the sword, the elderly veteran next presented it to the boy for use in the current trouble, stating sadly,

*Now, boy I draw this sword again, Alas! That it must be,*
*That I must count as foes the sons, Of those who fought with me*
*My limbs are old and feeble now, And silv'ry is my hair;*
*I cannot wield this sword, and so, I give it to your care.*

In a close to the account, the man exhorts the grandson to uphold the honor of the family and to trust in his general. That leader, of course, was Robert E. Lee—the son of Light Horse Harry and an experienced veteran of the Mexican campaigns.

*I'm thankful, boy, he'll lead you on, To the wild battle field,*
*For his father's heart within him beats, And he will never yield.*
*Stand by your Gen'ral to the last, Obey his every word.*
*And yield your life before you dare, To yield his father's sword.*

Nowhere in the poem did the old man guarantee success. But he did make clear that victory was attainable only if the youth fought for liberty with the ferocity of his grandfather and battled for glory with the same determination of his father.[25]

The role of Robert E. Lee in the tale was equally significant and hinted at the importance that residents of both the Union and Confederacy placed on the combat experience of their leaders. Modern historians, acting with the benefit of hindsight, have detailed how the battles of the war with Mexico—from the opening battles to the final conquest of Mexico City—served as a training ground for famed Civil War leaders. In 1861, many of those leaders remained obscure and unproven. Nevertheless, residents of both sections sensed that experience in the last major war was necessary to successfully execute the current one. In the absence of other information, involvement in the Mexican campaigns became a measure of an officer's qualifications to lead troops into battle, and the Confederacy claimed a lion's share of these leaders. Newspapers throughout the South heralded the defection of former US Army officers like David Twiggs, James Longstreet, and Braxton Bragg, not only because they had demonstrated their loyalty to their Southern homeland, but also because these men could trace their military pedigree back to the battles of Palo Alto, Resaca de la Palma, and Fort Brown. Robert E. Lee was not in those battles, but stood out as a greater asset. His family tree, combined with his role as one of the primary architects of the Mexico City campaign, made him the preferred choice of two governments to lead military operations. His ultimate decision to cast his lot with his home state of Virginia and to serve as chief of Confederate forces gave the secessionists confidence that they could survive and even thrive in an armed conflict with their former countrymen.

Residents of the North countered by cheering the loyalty of another high-profile Mexican War veteran. As the roster of defectors to the Confederacy grew, many Unionists expressed concern that the South had lured a lion's share of experienced officers and would hold a tactical edge on battlefields of the conflict. Then came the alarming news that Gen. Winfield Scott had joined the exodus and would serve his native Virginia in the fray. Scott, the highest ranking officer of the US Army and the tactician who had orchestrated the campaign to capture Mexico City in 1847, was aged and infirm in 1861, but he remained a military genius and Southerners were thrilled to hear that "the conqueror of Mexico refused to be Chief Constable to lead bayonets against his mother state." But Scott assuaged Northern concerns by quickly and emphatically denying the rumor. "I have not changed," he wrote to Sen. John J. Crittendon. "I have not thought of changing. Always a Union man." This simple and direct statement crushed spirits throughout the South and generated a fierce backlash from secessionists who vowed that "the curses of unborn millions will damn him to the lowest depth of human degradation." By contrast, Northerners cheered that the "Hero of Mexico" remained true to the flag that he had advanced in 1847 and expressed relief that at least one great strategist still served the US cause.[26]

Other experienced veterans of Mexico also remained, and their virtues were touted at various points during the war. As it became clear that General Scott was in no condition to lead the armies of the North in the field, Gen. George B. McClellan was selected as his replacement. The *Philadelphia Inquirer* praised McClellan's qualifications for the job, insisting that "the memories of the Mexican campaigns and the example of his old commander stimulated him on to glory." When George Meade assumed control of the Army of the Potomac in 1863, the *New York Herald* similarly focused on his service in Mexico, noting that it "was marked by determination and bravery, and at the battle of Palo Alto he was particularly distinguished." And when Ulysses S. Grant attained the rank of Brigadier General in 1862, the *Boston Daily Advertiser* glossed over his more recent achievements, but remarked that "he was twice brevetted for gallant and meritorious conduct in the Mexican war, and was in every principal battle in which it was possible for any one man to be." Similar biographies appeared for dozens of other high-ranking Union officers during the course of the war, offering the population reassurance that commanders had proved their mettle in the previous war and would do so again in the current one.[27]

One of these men would ultimately carry the fighting back to the birthplace of the Mexican conflict. In May 1846, Napoleon J. T. Dana had endured the six-day siege of Fort Brown as a lieutenant in the US 7th Infantry. In 1863, he returned to the Rio Grande delta as a general, commanding the US Army XIII Corps—the vanguard force in Gen. Nathaniel Banks's invasion of Texas. Banks had initiated that assault with two objectives in mind. The first objective was to establish a presence that would prevent France from interfering in Texas. In 1863, Mexico was embroiled in its own civil war, and French forces had occupied that country to support one of the factions in the dispute. That presence was especially notable in Northern Mexico, and US officials wanted to dissuade the French forces south of the Rio Grande from setting their sights on lands to the north. The second objective was to halt the movement of Confederate cotton in the other direction. Union naval ships had sealed off most of the Southern coastline, preventing the export of the Confederacy's primary cash crop and hindering Southern efforts to fund the war. But scores of wagons filled with cotton rolled through Texas toward Brownsville and other border towns. From there, this "White Gold" could be ferried across the river, loaded onto ships bearing the flag of Mexico—officially a neutral power in this fight—and sailed past federal boats in the Gulf without interference. If Banks could wrest control of southern Texas towns and forts, this trade route would close, increasing stress on the faltering Confederate economy. The key to both goals was control of the familiar outpost—Fort

*Gen. Napoleon T. Dana, who endured the Mexican siege of Fort Brown in 1846, led the US invasion force that retook the post from Confederates in 1861. US National Archives.*

Brown in Brownsville. And on November 2, 1863, General Dana and six thousand Union troops occupied Point Isabel on the Texas coast and prepared to fight their way toward that destination.

Northern newspapers did not fail to recall the historical significance of the location. The *Philadelphia Inquirer* reacted with enthusiasm that Generals Banks and Dana would march from the same place that General Taylor had launched his campaign to rescue Fort Brown in 1846. The editors announced:

> There can be no better point for effective operations in that whole country. It is near the mouth of the Rio Grande. It is within short reach of Brownsville, where the Rebels exchange their cotton for arms, and between the two places lie Palo Alto and Resaca de la Palma, of glorious history in the Mexican war. But a little way beyond, to the west and north, is a country full of Unionists, anxiously waiting the advent of the old flag. With such surroundings, this expedition should be fruitful of grand results.[28]

A correspondent to the *New York Herald* who had observed the landing was somewhat more philosophical about the moment and its historical roots:

> Again an army of American soldiers is on Texas soil, and once more in the neighborhood of the almost sacred battle fields of Palo Alto and Resaca de la Palma. When these battles were fought the North and South were one, their sons nobly fighting side by side, "shoulder to shoulder." Now the enmity between them is far more bitter that that which existed between the contending parties on those fields, and the force which has just landed in Texas is indeed the long talked of Army of Occupation and Observation on the Rio Grande, and is there for the double purpose of watching the movements of the army of a foreign power in Mexico, which by its presence alone, already threatens our border, and even the very existence of the nation itself.[29]

These commentators focused on the battlefields of 1846 to offer a touch of poignancy to their explanations of the reasons behind the

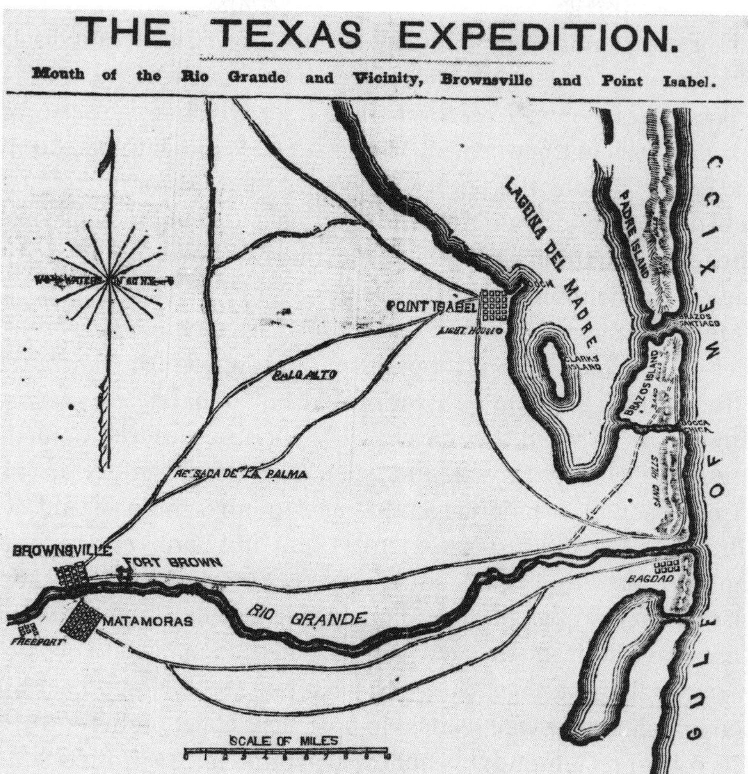


*A map of the region targeted by the 1863 US invasion of South Texas uses the well-known battlefields of 1846 as reference points.* New York Herald, *November 17, 1863.*

present campaign. But others viewed the grounds as an additional motive for the invasion. One anonymous US soldier who passed over the battlefields of Palo Alto and Resaca de la Palma en route to Brownsville suggested that the Confederates had mistreated these significant sites of the nation's history. "I rested long enough to view these historic plains," he wrote. "The secesh [secessionists] had displayed their vandalism here by overturning and breaking the stone that marked the place where the gallant Ringgold fell; and other small and mean displays of Confederate chivalry were scattered about." It is questionable whether any monument had ever been placed to commemorate Ringgold's death at Palo Alto, but the soldier nevertheless believed that defeat of the secessionists would help ensure that the battlegrounds received proper treatment.[30]

Maj. Augustus Pettibone of the 20th Wisconsin Volunteers took a much firmer stand, suggesting that the invasion itself was a display of respect and reconquest. "We have come," he wrote to a friend, "to 'occupy and possess' our own. To recover the soil for which our elder brothers fought and bled in the war with Mexico; to once more unfurl the ensign of the Republic along this Southwest border, made historic ground for all time by the battles of Palo Alto and Resaca de la Palma." In his opinion, the invasion and the expected battle for control of Brownsville was a continuation and culmination of the events of 1846.[31]

Major Pettibone, however, would not have a chance to reprise the battles of 1846. As Union troops advanced toward Fort Brown, retracing the path that Zachary Taylor had taken so many years before, no enemy troops opposed the march. Only about a hundred Confederate troops occupied Fort Brown, and when Gen. Hamilton Bee learned of the Union advance, he ordered the men to burn the post and evacuate Brownsville. As a result, Generals Dana and Banks entered the city without incident and claimed the fort once more for the United States. "Our white tents now glimmer along the left bank of the Rio Grande," Pettibone wrote from the newly established camp. "Old Fort Brown, grown over with weeds and bushes, lies a half mile below." The absence of combat along the way seemed to have little effect on his enthusiasm for his role in reclaiming this hallowed ground for the United States. "I little thought when, a boy, I read of General Taylor's deeds in the Mexican War, that I should one day march over the same road—at the head of a regiment of war-worn veterans. I went over the ground where the battle was hottest and found still the evidence of that old strife!"[32]

Others shared this passion. In the days following the occupation of Brownsville, rumors surfaced that Gen. John Bankhead Magruder, the Confederate commander of the District of Texas, New Mexico, and Arizona, was devising a plan to retake Fort Brown. According to columns in the Northern press, Magruder had expected the Union forces to land far to the north near the Sabine Pass and had been taken by surprise by the activity on the Rio Grande. Now, it was said, he had assembled a substantial army, which he planned to march across the state to confront the occupying army. These reports were overstated. Magruder had been aware of the Union move to the Rio Grande, but lacked the troops needed to resist it. He remained undermanned as 1863 came to a close. And with General Banks extending his conquest northward to Corpus Christi and General Dana improving the defenses and placing artillery around Fort Brown, a long campaign to try to retake Brownsville would have been foolhardy at best. The papers appeared to have created the scenario solely as a means to reestablish once again the link to the battles of 1846. "Magruder may, after he recovers from his surprise, attempt to drive back our forces," wrote the editors of the *Philadelphia Inquirer*. "He should beware how he attacks the soldiers of the Union near the memorable battle fields of Palo Alto and Resaca de la Palma."[33] Such wording suggested that US forces were the true heirs to the legacy of these Mexican War battlefields, and that this connection would empower them in any fight in their vicinity. In making this case, the *Inquirer* neglected to mention that General Magruder himself had served at Palo Alto and Resaca de la Palma as a lieutenant of the US 1st Artillery and could justifiably claim those battles as part of his own heritage.

Despite this emphasis on reconquering "almost sacred" ground, US military leaders displayed limited commitment to maintaining their hold on the area. Following the capture of Brownsville and throughout the winter of 1863–64, Union troops advanced as far north as Indianola, on the Gulf coast of Texas and Laredo on the Rio Grande. Soon, however, momentum slowed dramatically. As early as December 1863, General Dana had started pulling troops out of South Texas and redeploying them to the eastern part of the state to take part in the Red River Campaign. By March 1864, so many men had been withdrawn that Union troops ceased to advance and, in some cases, began to surrender previous gains. Sensing an opportunity, General Magruder now decided to launch the offensive that had been predicted immediately after the Union invasion. He selected Col. John Ford, who had accepted the surrender of Fort Brown in 1861, to lead the advance. Ford organized an army and departed San Antonio in March 1864, reached Laredo by mid-April, and then moved steadily southeastward toward the Rio Grande delta. On June 25, 1864, in a clash at Las Rucias, twenty-one miles west of Brownsville, Ford's troops defeated a Union cavalry force, opening the way for a Confederate return to Fort Brown. Even before Ford could summon supplies for a final assault, US general Edward Canby ordered the evacuation of Brownsville. On the morning of July 28, the last Union forces, under the command of Gen. Francis Herron, departed the town, allowing Confederate troops to reclaim it that same afternoon. By August, the only US troops to remain in the area were a small force quartered at the Brazos Santiago depot, on the northern end of the desolate barrier island known as Brazos Island. Confederate troops once again held Fort Brown and occupied the Palo Alto battlefield as they monitored the Union force on the coast.[34]

Earlier in the war, this shift of fortunes might have spawned celebration by Confederates and concern on the part of the Unionists, each using the Mexican War as a reference point. But on this occasion, both sides were largely silent. The Confederates of Texas did rejoice at the recapture of Fort Brown. The *Houston Telegraph*, for example, printed a letter in which an observer boasted that "our victorious little army marched into the city of Brownsville, that had been so long under Union control, with joyful shouts and exaltation, and the 'stars and bars' once more floats triumphantly over the rescued city." This time, however, the focus was not on reclaiming land won in 1846, but on avenging the loss of that area in 1863. "The Rio Grande," cheered the *Telegraph*, "is now free from the polluting tread of base and treacherous Yankees, who have long degraded our soil with the nauseous presence."[35]

Newspapers of the United States seemed to accept the events near the old Mexican War battlefields as an unfortunate reversal in a war that had turned sharply in favor of the Union. Most reported the evacuation of the area briefly, though with obvious disappointment. "Nothing remains now at Brownsville but desolation," reported the *New York Herald* in conclusion to its summary of events.[36] But unlike the traumatic surrender of 1861, this now appeared as a temporary setback. With federal troops waging an all-out assault on Virginia and others advancing on Atlanta, it was apparent that Union forces were now on the offensive and determined to retake all of the South, including the Rio Grande delta. The continued US presence at Brazos Santiago and occasional skirmishes between Union and Confederate forces on the coastal plains east of Brownsville also lent credence to official statements that the withdrawal was temporary in nature. For the most part, the US population appeared to be preoccupied with the larger course of the conflict and saw no need to fret over the loss of the historical battlefields that would be reclaimed in due time.[37]

In fact, by some accounts the land had already been placed back in US hands and by a most unlikely source. In September 1864, newspapers around the Northern states printed a detailed description of the latest fall of Brownsville. According to these persistent reports, Mexican general Juan Cortina, who had been fighting the French near Matamoros, had crossed the Rio Grande and fought his way to the old Resaca de la Palma battlefield, from which point he launched an assault against Colonel Ford and the Confederate troops at Fort Brown. In an ironic turn of events, Cortina, who had fought for the Mexican Army in the 1846 battles at Palo Alto and Resaca de la Palma, was reported to have declared his allegiance to the United States and seized Brownsville in the name of the Union. "The rebels retreated so hastily they left their 'rags' floating on the Court House and other public buildings," the Trenton, New Jersey, *Daily State Gazette* described, "but they were soon torn down and the Stars and Stripes hoisted amid the shouts of citizens and Mexican soldiers who were almost as proud of the 'starry banner' as our brave boys." The story had some pieces of truth—Cortina had briefly crossed the Rio Grande, declared common cause with US forces, and skirmished with Confederate troops. But the assault on Brownsville had never occurred, and Fort Brown remained firmly in Confederate hands.[38] Nevertheless, the story was never directly repudiated, and as 1864 approached its close, many Americans could easily have believed that a former foe had restored the historic battlefields to their rightful owner.

The true story was that US and Confederate forces settled into an extended period of stalemate in the region. Throughout 1864, Confederate troops from Fort Brown occasionally clashed with Union forces from Brazos Santiago when they journeyed to the Texas mainland on foraging expeditions. But as Confederate forces fell back on all fronts of the war, soldiers in both outposts realized that the conflict was approaching an end and their skirmishes gradually decreased in frequency and intensity. US general Lew Wallace recognized the declining desire to fight among the Confederates of Fort Brown, and in January 1865, he wrote a letter to Gen. Ulysses S. Grant in which he proposed to "invite the commandant of Brownsville to an interview on the old battle-field of Palo Alto." In that historic setting, he felt the soldiers of opposing armies would recognize common cause and reach agreement on differences in Texas. "You know how to get me there," he added, "an order to make an inspection of affairs on the Rio Grande will do so." Shortly afterwards he received that assignment. And in March he met with Gen. James Slaughter and Col. John Ford, the Confederate commanders at Fort Brown. The gathering occurred at Point Isabel rather than Palo Alto, but the men did reach an agreement as Wallace had expected. Unfortunately, proposals for an official cease fire ran afoul of Gen. John Walker, the current commander of the Confederate District of Texas, New Mexico, and Arizona. Walker rebuffed efforts at a cease fire or surrender, and his blunt response prompted US officials to dispatch additional troops to Brazos Island. This, in turn, led to several additional skirmishes in the area. Nevertheless, Wallace, Slaughter, and Ford had established a rapport, and an informal truce generally reigned in the region as the war drew to a close.[39]

That period of peace ended abruptly a month later. On May 11, 1865, Col. Theodore Barrett, the Union commander at Brazos Island, ordered troops to cross to the mainland and march in the direction of Brownsville. The reason for that command remains unclear. Some researchers argue that Barrett had simply sent his men to gather forage for horses. Others suggest that Barrett sought to earn glory by seizing Fort Brown before the war ended. The second motive gains credibility when one considers the importance that Northerners placed upon the fort: Barrett would not only capture a military objective; he would reclaim a revered piece of heritage from the war with Mexico. Whatever the motive, the results proved to be costly for a number of Union

COMPLETE.

"IT IS FINISHED."

Surrender of Kirby Smith and the Last Army of the Rebels.

General Canby's Official Announcement.

THE REBELLION ENTIRELY OVER.

THE LAST BATTLE OF THE WAR.

Details of the Engagement Between the Union and Rebel Forces on the Old Field of Palo Alto.

*Headlines about the last battle of the Civil War mistakenly noted that the clash occurred on the same field as the 1846 battle of Palo Alto.* New York Herald, *May 28, 1846.*

soldiers. After skirmishing with small parties of Confederate horsemen on May 12, the US column came under heavier fire the following morning. The afternoon arrival of Col. John Ford's cavalry decided the fight. Union troops fled for the coast with the Confederate horsemen in pursuit, leaving behind two men dead and six wounded.[40]

The *Washington Evening Star* summarized the event in a pair of sentences printed more than a month after the clash: "The last battle of the war was fought on Friday the 12th of May, on the shores of the Rio Grande not far from Pala [*sic*] Alto. It was fought near the old battlefield of Palo Alto, some two thousand miles from Bull Run." The brevity of this account summed up the significance that the American public placed on the distant clash that became known as the battle of Palmito Ranch. As a military action it was insignificant, involving limited numbers of troops and casualties. Strategically the encounter was also of little consequence. The major Confederate commands had already surrendered at Appomattox Court House, Virginia; Durham, North Carolina; and Mobile, Alabama, and forces in Texas were on the verge of collapse. Nevertheless, it merited some attention simply because it was the final land battle of the great war. Perhaps more significantly, it sparked a level of interest because it had occurred within miles of the noted Mexican War battlefields. Indeed, many newspapers mistakenly printed that the confrontation had occurred directly on one of those sites. "Old Palo Alto yesterday became again a battlefield," wrote a correspondent to the *Caledonian* newspaper in Vermont. "But alas it was not a second time a scene of glory to the Union arms."[41]

Such a symbolic defeat might have been viewed as a crushing blow by the Northern press at an earlier date, but now stirred little real concern. It was inevitable that some in the press refused to accept the truth. The *Philadelphia Inquirer*, for example, which had placed great emphasis on the legacy of the Mexican War since before the start of hostilities stated that the battle had unfolded "on a part of the field on which Taylor fought the battle of Palo Alto," and insisted that "our side was victorious although the Rebel strength was much superior." Other tabloids offered similar reports of Union triumph. Most, however, followed the example of the *Caledonian* and treated the loss as a slight blemish on an otherwise acceptable close to the war.[42]

After all, by the time the reports reached the majority of the public, events had progressed rapidly. On May 29, 1865, Gen. Edmund Kirby-Smith, unable to prevent the mass desertion of troops in Texas, declared his intention to surrender the Confederacy's Trans-Mississippi Department. Lamenting that he was "a commander without an army—a general without troops," the veteran of the battles of Palo Alto and Resaca de la Palma turned over the last major command of the Confederacy—including Fort Brown, the post he had fought to rescue in 1846. That same day, Union troops at Brazos Santiago once again marched toward Brownsville. This time there was no fight. Confederate troops had abandoned Fort Brown once again, and the US Army reoccupied the site and the entire Rio Grande delta without contest. Recalling the words of Maj. Augustus Pettibone, the Union had occupied and possessed its own, and US troops recovered the soil for which their elder brothers had fought almost two decades prior. The Northern states had asserted their claim to the heritage of the Mexican War, and even a final defeat on that sacred ground would not diminish the accomplishment.[43]

Curiously, the defeat of the Confederacy and the end of the fighting seemed to reduce interest in the Mexican War and the sites from that war in the Rio Grande delta. Dramatic and bloody Civil War battles at places

*Gen. Edmund Kirby Smith, a veteran of the 1846 Rio Grande campaign, refused to surrender his forces in Texas until long after other major Confederate had accepted terms. Library of Congress.*

like Gettysburg, Antietam, and dozens of other fields had become the new measure for service and valor in both the North and South, replacing familiar Mexican War clashes like Palo Alto and Resaca de la Palma. As respected Civil War leaders recorded their lives in memoirs or had them recorded by others in obituaries, it was their exploits from 1861 to 1865 that now demanded attention; their actions from 1846 to 1848 often became reduced to anecdotes or footnotes in advance of the main story. For some Americans, the Mexican War came to be seen as a training ground for Confederate leaders, further reducing the appeal of that conflict. In the early days of the Civil War, Southerners had bragged that they were primarily responsible for the victories in Mexico. Afterwards, many in the North now saw no need to celebrate or commemorate an event that involved the service of traitors and turncoats like Robert E. Lee, David Twiggs, Jefferson Davis, and dozens of others Confederate officers. In this atmosphere, the Mexican War sites that the Confederates had once been accused of defiling now suffered from neglect. As states and veterans' groups rushed to place markers and monuments on Civil War fields, not a single plaque recalled the 1846 actions at Palo Alto, Resaca de la Palma, or Fort Brown. None would appear for decades. By the 1870s, many US citizens had only a hazy memory of the Mexican War and its sites. "There was a time when the 8th of May was suggestive of Palo Alto," the editors of the Cincinnati *Daily Gazette* wrote in 1879, noting that the thirty-third anniversary of that battle had passed without comment, "but history soon gets old and to many of our readers this battle is barely known."[44] Most Americans did not care to know. Time had passed, the "sacred soil" of the Rio Grande delta was securely back under the protection of the Union, and a new war and battlefields now defined the nation. It was time to move on.

## *Notes*

1. "The Civil War," *The Baltimore Sun*, April 14, 1861, 1.

2. Henry McFarland, *Sixty Years in Concord and Elsewhere: Personal Recollections 1831–1891* (Concord, NH: Henry McFarland, 1899), 228–29.

3. "Southern War-Cry," *Shreveport Weekly News*, June 3, 1861, 4.

4. Senate, "Report of Colonel Twiggs to General Taylor: Message of the President of the United States Relative to the Operations and Recent Engagements on the Mexican Frontier," 29 Cong., 1st Sess., S. Doc. 388 (Washington, DC: May 11, 1846), 15.

5. Jeanne T. Heidler, "'Embarrassing Situation': David E. Twiggs and the Surrender of United States Forces in Texas, 1861," in *Lone Star Blue and Grey: Essays on Texas and the Civil War*, ed. Ralph A. Wooster (Austin: Texas State Historical Association, 1996), 29–44; "The Revolution in Texas: Gen. Twiggs' Place in History, How He Surrendered the Arsenal at San Antonio," *New-York Times*, March 21, 1861.

6. "Gen. Twiggs Dismissed from the Army," *New York Herald*, March 3, 1861; "The Commander of the Georgia Troops," *New York Herald*, March 2, 1861, 10; "The Disgrace of Gen. Twiggs," *The Ripley Bee* (Ripley, OH), Thursday, March 14, 1861; "A Second Benedict Arnold," *Daily Cleveland Herald*, March 1, 1861; "Twiggs' Expulsion," *The Wisconsin State Register* (Portage, WI), Saturday, March 16, 1861; "Treachery of the Basest Sort." *Virginia Free Press* (Charlestown, WV), February 28, 1861, 1.

7. "Look to the Army," *New York Times*, March 7, 1861, 1; "Important from Texas: Captain Hill Refuses to Surrender Fort Brown," *Philadelphia Inquirer*, March 2, 1861, 1.

8. *Commercial Herald* cited in "Fort Brown," *The Farmers' Cabinet* (Amherst, NH), March 15, 1861, 2.

9. "Thirty-Second Day," *The Macon Daily Telegraph*, March 14, 1861, 2.

10. "Who Have Fought the Battles of the Union?" *The Crisis* (Columbus, OH), February 28, 1861, 3.

11. Reed Williams Smith, *Samuel Medary and the Crisis: Testing the Limits of Press Freedom* (Columbus: Ohio State University Press, 1995), 3–6; "The National Crisis," *Baltimore Sun*, February 8, 1861, 1; "Invasion of the South and Invasion of the North," *New York Herald*, February 15, 1861, 4.

12. "Hostilities on the Rio Grande," *Philadelphia Inquirer*, March 11, 1861, 5; "Surrender of Fort Brown to the Secessionists," *New York Herald*, March 15, 1861, 1; "From Texas," *Pittsfield Sun* (Pittsfield: MA), March 21, 1861, 3; "From Texas," *Wisconsin Daily Patriot*, March 18, 1861, 3; "Matters at Washington, the South, &c.," *Daily Picayune* (New Orleans), March 20, 1861, 6.

13. "Affairs in Texas," *Philadelphia Inquirer*, March 27, 1861, 2.

14. Douglas Murphy, *Two Armies on the Rio Grande: The First Campaign of the U.S.-Mexican War* (College Station: Texas A&M University Press, 2015), 103–4; "Later from Texas," *Daily True Delta*, April 10, 1861, 1; "Later from the Rio Grande," *Daily True Delta*, April 5, 1861, 2.

15. "Later from Texas," *Daily True Delta*, April 10, 1861, 1; "Later from the Rio Grande," *Daily True Delta*, April 5, 1861, 2.

16. "A Conjecture as to the Destination of the Naval and Military Forces in the New York Harbor," *Fayetteville Observer* (North Carolina), April 11, 1861, 2.

17. "Threatened Invasion of Texas by Mexicans," *New York Herald*, April 3, 1861, 3; "The News," *New York Herald*, April 3, 1861, 6; "General Ampudia Marching on Brownsville," *Philadelphia Inquirer*, April 3, 1861, 1; "3000 Mexicans Marching on Brownsville," *Daily Picayune*, April 2, 1861, 1; "Mexicans Preparing for an Attack on Texas," *New York Herald*, April 23, 1846, 1; "More Trouble for Texas," *New Hampshire Sentinel*, April 4, 1861, 2.

18. "Refusal of General Houston to Cooperate with the Administration," *New York Herald*, April 11, 1861, 1; "Another Rumor of the Day Denied," *Philadelphia Inquirer*, April 11, 1861, 1; "The General Ampudia Ruse," *The Baltimore Sun*, April 10, 1861, 4; "Confirmed Rumor: Zaragosa Bringing Troops," *Daily True Delta*, April 16, 1861, 1.

19. James McPherson, *Battle Cry of Freedom: The Civil War Era* (New York: Oxford University Press, 1988), 268–73.

20. "United We Stand," *The Scioto Gazette* (Chillicothe, OH), May 7, 1861, 2.

21. McPherson, *Battle Cry of Freedom*, 274–81.

22. "Military Affairs at Baltimore," *Daily National Intelligencer*, May 17, 1861, 2; "Pennsylvania Troops," *New York Herald*, May 1, 1861, 4; "The Anniversary of the Battle of Cerro Gordo," *Philadelphia Inquirer*, April 11, 1861; "The Montezuma Regiment," *New York Herald*, May 5, 1861, 5; "Military Movements in New York," *New York Herald*, April 20, 1861, 2.

23. "The 'Weakness' of the South," *Fayetteville Observer*, June 6, 1861, 2; "South Carolina Arrogance in 1861," *Wisconsin State Register*, February 11, 1865, 2; "South Carolina to Massachusetts," *New York Times*, April 29, 1861, 1.

24. "The 'Weakness' of the South," *Fayetteville Observer*, June 6, 1861, 2; "Military Genius of the South," *Macon Daily Telegraph*, April 4, 1861, 2.

25. James Dabney McCabe, "The Sword of Harry Lee," *Charleston Courier, Tri-Weekly*, January 18, 1862, 3; *Daily Morning News* (Savannah, GA), January 18, 1862, 1.

26. "Scott on Our Side," *Boston Daily Advertiser*, April 29, 1861, 1; "General Scott and His Enemies," *Fayetteville Observer*, March 7, 1861, 2; "General Scott Is the Best Abused Man in the Country at the Present Time," *The Liberator* (Boston), March 22, 1861, 1; "The Public Career of Winfield Scott," *Daily Picayune* (New Orleans), January 16, 1861, 2; "General Scott for the Union," *New York Herald*, April 27, 1861, 1.

27. "Gen McClellan, the Napoleon of the Present War," *Philadelphia Inquirer*, July 18, 1861, 6; "The New Commander," New York Herald, June 29, 1863; "Brig. Gen Ulysses S. Grant, *Boston Daily Advertiser*, February 19, 1862.

28. "Banks on the Rio Grande," *Philadelphia Inquirer*, October 23, 1863, 1.

29. "Mr. Henry Thompson's Despatch," *New York Herald*, November 16, 1863, 1.

30. "Life on the Rio Grande," *New Haven Daily Palladium*, January 27, 1864, 1.

31. H. Pettibone, Maj. 20th Winsconsin Volunteers, to "Friend Lockwood," November 12, 1863, printed in *Cleveland Morning Leader*, December 26, 1863.

32. A. H. Pettibone to "Albert," December 2, 1863, printed in *Cleveland Morning Leader*, January 1, 1864.

33. "War Matters," *Lowell Daily Citizen and News* (Lowell, MA), November 17, 1863, 1; "Telegraphic," *Cleveland Daily Herald*, November 17, 1863, n.p.; "General Banks in Texas," *Philadelphia Inquirer*, November 17, 1863, 4; Stephen A. Townshend, *The Yankee Invasion of Texas* (College Station: Texas A&M University Press, 2006), 46–53.

34. Townsend, *The Yankee Invasion of Texas*, 69–89; "The War News," *Richmond Dispatch*, October 4, 1864.

35. "From New Orleans," *Baltimore Sun*, August 15, 1864, 1; "Important from Texas," *Daily True Delta*, August 2, 1864, 1; "Recapture of Brownsville-Victorious Entry of Col. Ford and Command," *Houston Daily Telegraph*, August 17, 1864, 2.

36. "Evacuation of Brownsville: Refugees Abandoning the Town," *New York Herald*, August 6, 1864, 8.

37. "Eastern News by Overland Stage," *Idaho Tri-Weekly Statesman*, August 25, 1864; "Very Latest News," *Philadelphia Inquirer*, August 1, 1864, 1.

38. "Capture of Brownsville by the Mexican General Cortinas," *Philadelphia Inquirer*, September 20, 1864, 1; "Further Particulars of the Capture of Brownsville," *Daily Ohio Statesman*, September 22, 1864, 3; "The War News," *Pittsfield Sun*, September 22, 1864, 2; "The Eastern News," *Daily Evening Bulletin* (San Francisco), September 21, 1864, 2; "Very Important from the Rio Grande: Mexican and Union Soldiers Fraternizing," *Trenton State Gazette*, September 20, 1864, 2; "The War News," *Baltimore Sun*, September 20, 1864, 2; "Cortina," *Daily Picayune*, September 19, 1864, 5; Jerry D. Thompson, *Cortina: Defending the Mexican Name in Texas* (College Station: Texas A&M University Press, 2007), 140–45.

39. Lew Wallace, *Lew Wallace: An Autobiography* (New York: Harper and Brothers, 1902), II: 813, 830–42.

40. Townsend, *The Yankee Invasion of Texas*, 125–33; Jeffrey Hunt, *The Last Battle of the Civil War: Palmetto Ranch* (Austin: University of Texas Press, 2002), 51–67, 80–116.

41. "The Last Battle of the War," *Washington Evening Star*, June 27, 1865, 1; "Army News," *Ashtabula Weekly Telegraph*, June 3, 1865, 2; "A Second Battle of Palo Alto," *The Caledonian* (St. Johnsbury, VT), June 16, 1865, 2.

42. "From Texas," *Philadelphia Inquirer*, May 27, 1865, 4; "Epitome of the News," *Weekly Perrysburg Journal* (Perrysburg, OH), May 31, 1865, 1; "Last Battle of the War," *St. Cloud Democrat*, June 8, 1865: 1.

43. Townsend, *Yankee Invasion of Texas*, 138; "Kirby Smith's Farewell to His Troops," *Daily Cleveland Herald*, June 20, 1865, 1.

44. "The Anniversary of Palo Alto," *Cincinnati Daily Gazette*, May 10, 1879, 1.

# 3
# *Life Lived along the Lower Rio Grande during the Civil War*

M. M. McALLEN

In January 1860, Brownsville and Matamoros finally quieted after six months of chronic violence known as the Cortina Wars, orchestrated by area *caudillo* (strongman) Juan Nepomuceno Cortina. The threats and mayhem had paralyzed the two sister communities. Brownsville's population, which stood at four thousand people in 1852, had dwindled to 2,734. The majority of the inhabitants were families composed of naturalized citizens or Mexicans, but a large coterie remained European, especially French, Spanish, Italian, German, and English. These families spoke more than one language, and up to four languages could be heard on the street on a regular basis: Spanish, French, German, and English. Regional newspapers were published in English and French, English and Spanish, and sometimes in all three languages. As transplanted citizens arrived in the region to work in this port of trade or to join family, they absorbed and were assimilated by the surrounding settlers to create a cosmopolitan culture. While ranchers in outlying areas remained cautious, hiring private managers and security to maintain their herds and properties, the merchants in the towns welcomed the brief modicum of peace.[1]

As Mexico began to emerge from its own civilian disturbances, the Matamoros economy, interdependent with Brownsville's, had dwindled. The population fell from twenty-five thousand to five thousand people. Most of its houses stood vacant or could be rented for low rates; a fine brick home could be had for as little as ten dollars a month. The small settlement of Bagdad on the Mexican side of the Rio Grande near the Boca del Rio languished as a miserable fishing village. However, this quiet spell would not last.[2]

The secession of the Lone Star State came only after difficult deliberation, and in Brownsville the political debate caused a factional split. Red Party members were generally Democrats and supported secession. In Austin, at the state convention in January 1861, Charles Stillman, Mifflin Kenedy, Richard King, Francisco Yturria, James Walworth, and Frank Cummings served as the local Red Party's delegates and supported Governor Edward Clark when Sam Houston refused to take the oath to the Confederacy. Brownsville's Blue Party members generally sided against secession, aligning themselves with the Union.[3]

When Texas seceded and joined with the Confederate States of America, Fort Brown fell under control of the Confederacy's Trans-Mississippi Department. On February 21, 1861, Col. John Salmon "Rip" Ford reached Brazos Santiago to assume command of the fort with the Texas Commissioners of Public Safety when the post was relinquished by federal brigadier general David E. Twiggs. As the federal officers prepared to hand over Fort Brown and Brazos Santiago, commanders ordered their supplies destroyed, the cannon spiked, and trunnions broken. However, six hundred Confederate soldiers arrived by steamer and saved the guns and supplies for the Confederacy. Within a month, by March 21, Ford, with the 2nd Texas Cavalry, and Col. Philip N. Luckett occupied all the former federal posts along the lower Rio Grande. The troops of mostly volunteers numbered twelve hundred, many of them Tejanos.[4]

*John McAllen, born in Londonderry, Ireland, immigrated to Texas by way of Boston. After being captured in the Merchant's War, he remained in the Brownsville/Matamoros region to become a merchant. He married Salomé Ballí McAllen in 1861. Courtesy of the McAllen Ranch Archives.*

During the spring of 1861, many Union supporters moved to Matamoros, by force or by choice. Foreign residents, like John McAllen, who remained a British citizen, generally maintained neutrality on the issues, focusing instead on making war profits. Most foreigners took a position only when their personal property was at stake. As it was, many Europeans living along the border were not totally conversant with the issues that led to the Civil War. Slave ownership was not common in Cameron or Hidalgo Counties; most of the farm labor was performed by workers from Mexico who sought a better life in Texas under a seemingly more stable government. Although independently minded, most people along the border generally supported Texas' decision to secede from the Union. Free from the pressure to take a side in the issue, the foreigners rode out the shifting control of Brownsville and Matamoros, to their considerable profit.[5]

The Confederacy was fully cognizant of its economic dependence on cotton, and shortly after the declaration of war came to understand that continued exports of the fiber would be necessary to finance its operations. Cotton was economically paramount; the bulk of it was shipped to New England and to the textile mills of Europe. In particular, the English regarded cotton as the substance that fueled Britain's industrial revolution, where four million people in the textile industry depended on cotton for their livelihoods. Another six hundred thousand in France also relied on cotton. Its trade had been the mainstay of Southern commerce for the previous fifty years. The English, who consumed 90 percent of America's raw cotton, paid top dollar, compelling merchants to ship it in any way possible. Throughout the war, British ships were the most frequent callers at Matamoros. From 1859 through 1869, the production of cotton in Texas rose from approximately 58,000 bales to more than 430,000, raising it to fifth place among cotton growing states.[6]

Federal officials quickly foresaw that the cash-poor South would have to make every attempt to ship cotton to England and France. As a result, in July 1861, President Lincoln gave the order to blockade all seaports, including Brazos Santiago, though this was largely ignored there until the end of 1861. When war was declared, the US Navy had only forty steamers and fifty sailing vessels, or one ship for every sixty-six miles of blockaded coastline. After acquiring faster steam-powered ships by the end of 1861, the navy had nearly doubled its supply of steamers and the blockades of the Texas coast began to make an impact. Cotton shipments at Galveston, Corpus Christi, and other Texas ports were interdicted, so the government of Texas decreed all cotton to be kept away from the coast. This shifted the trade south to the Rio Grande. International commercial interests carefully followed the flow of the precious fiber; when word of the whereabouts of cotton reached international markets, merchants followed, and despite federal search-and-seizure operations, officials could not stop cotton from leaving the mouth of the Rio Grande from the Mexican shore, especially at Bagdad.[7]

While the commencement of the Civil War did not immediately impact this insular region, merchants maintained established trade routes, sending and receiving goods through Brazos Santiago at the mouth of the Rio Grande. They issued their own tokens and accepted scrip, as well as Mexican eagle dollars and US greenbacks, when presented with them. A merchant's tokens could be used to pay for goods or services, including meals, haircuts, tailoring, and dressmaking. Store owners could also pay a customer's debt at other mercantiles. Commercial stores in Brownsville and Matamoros were often two-story buildings, with the owner and his family living on the second floor. One account describes the typical Brownsville store as "dark and uninviting . . . frequently during the morning [the merchant] would sell to his . . . customer from across the river a bill amounting to a hundred thousand dollars, receiving his pay in gold and silver, which he placed for safekeeping in his iron chest, for banks were unknown, and regarding paper money [as worthless].[8]

Merchants also acted as private bankers for their customers, there being no organized banking in the region until after the Civil War. Most stores' safes served as a depository for currency people wished to secure. The lawlessness on the frontier made people very cautious with even small amounts of money. This in turn gave merchants the ability to control credit and trade. Charles Stillman, José San Román, Humphrey E. Woodhouse, John Young, John McAllen, Jeremiah Galvan, Richard King, Mifflin Kenedy, and Francisco Yturria all operated their own banks—giving loans and charging interest. Merchants found it most advantageous to attract gold and silver coinage, and thereby gave discounts when it was used as payment. In 1861, John McAllen paid the going rate, a premium of about 3 percent for receiving American gold and Mexican eagle dollars as payment for goods or debt. This coinage would then be used

*The ferry boat, known as a chalan, which crossed people, animals, and carriages between Brownsville and Matamoros. Steamboats can be seen in the background, circa 1865. Courtesy of the McAllen Ranch Archives.*

to purchase goods or it was sent to bank accounts out of Texas, often to New Orleans, New York, England, or elsewhere in Europe.[9]

John McAllen sent specie to New Orleans, New York, and after the Civil War, to Ireland. It was sent either to pay for fine goods he had on order for his store or for deposit. His bank account in Ireland went to support his family in Londonderry—kinfolk who had paid his passage to America. Nearly every ship leaving Brazos Santiago, on the American side of the mouth of the Rio Grande, carried specie—on rare occasion up to nearly one million dollars. This practice of sending specie abroad continued until about 1898 when the First National Bank of Brownsville was organized.[10]

Making money, although highly important, was not the only reason merchants enjoyed life on the border. The excitement of a new place in its earliest stages of development also appealed to them. As an observer identified only as "a correspondent for the *New York Herald* at Brownsville" noted: "The . . . excitements of border life . . . among a population of antagonistical races, [no] restraints of law . . . the rights of property little respected, and . . . small value placed upon human life . . . prompted [the merchant] to depend much on his shrewdness and physical strength for protection."[11]

Despite the incipient justice system, people continued to take the law into their own hands. In Cameron County, around 1862, Judge E. P. McLane arrested a Mexican shoemaker who had just murdered his wife. While he was conducting the prisoner to the Market House, the shoemaker turned on McLane and plunged a long knife into his chest. McLane died within half an hour. The shoemaker was captured by a mob, rushed to the old tree in front of the McAllen home on Levee Street, and strung up. Frank Cushman Pierce, the son of Matamoros-based US consul Leonard Pierce Jr., reported that "the leaders of the mob compelled every American present to participate in the hanging. While hanging, but just before his pulse had ceased to beat, a stranger with flowing cape and slouched hat embraced the body and lifting his own feet from the ground so as to throw greater weight on the murderer, mustered, 'That's the way we used to do them in Californy.'"[12]

Downriver at Bagdad, new shanties sprang up overnight as hundreds of men descended on the town to operate lighters, shallow-draft boats able to shuttle the cotton over the river's sandbar to schooners waiting in the bay. The *New York Herald* described Bagdad as "an excrescence of the war, . . . full of blockade runners, desperadoes, and the vile of both sexes." Within a year, with seven hundred thousand bales of cotton in Texas, Gov. Francis R. Lubbock prohibited cotton from being brought within fifty miles of the Gulf Coast, exempting the line of the Rio Grande, giving the planters the right to export cotton across the river into Mexico. Traders therefore established powerful alliances with Mexican merchants and manufacturers who also supplied the French army, then in occupation of Mexico.[13]

The arrival of French forces under Emperor Napoleon III, who soon placed Maximilian von Habsburg of Austria as emperor of Mexico, caused unrest throughout the nation. As a result, the people along the lower Rio Grande again began to feel the effects of skirmishes for power by local caudillos. Gen. José María Jesús Carbajal, American educated and well-known on both sides of the border, attacked Matamoros and shut down trade as he forced loans from area merchants. Forcing loans was a device employed by various caudillos to fund personal wars. Though prohibited by the constitution of Mexico, it was routinely practiced. A revolutionary would take possession of a town, but often had no money. He would proclaim a *prestamo* and force merchants and citizens to hand over their quota. The leader would convene the authorities of the town, state his purposes, the amount needed, and assess every man. The loans were often enforced by the bayonet. If a merchant refused, the caudillo would take control of his business and sell his goods to raise cash. Some who refused to pay suffered worse fates—a few were killed. These seizures gripped the people of Matamoros and the merchants who had businesses on both sides of the Rio Grande.[14]

In the spring of 1862, Confederate officers finally controlled these attacks when martial law went into effect. Trade began to accelerate. Area caudillos in Mexico agreed to protect the cotton flow into Mexico, allowing Texas merchants to take cotton down the Rio Grande or store it in Matamoros, Bagdad, or even Monterrey, with no collection of import duty. The flow of cotton became immense. At least seventy vessels waited at anchor near Bagdad. At one point, Theodorus Bailey, the acting US rear admiral, counted between 180 and 200 ships from various nations at the mouth of the Rio Grande. By March 1862, Matamoros had attracted thousands of American and European settlers.[15]

Soon contraband supplies from Europe or the US eastern shore began arriving at Brazos Santiago. Cases of Enfield rifles arrived marked as "hollow ware" and gunpowder in barrels labeled "bean flour." Cargoes of percussion caps were sometimes labeled "canned goods," and munitions loaded in barrels marked "fish." At the height of the war, the Rio Grande remained the only reliable channel through which the Confederacy could obtain dry goods, hardware, foodstuffs, tobacco, military supplies, liquor, and drugs.[16]

By 1863, Bagdad had grown into a rough town of two thousand rowdy souls. As Father Pierre Fourrier Parisot put it, Bagdad was a "veritable Babel, a Babylon." The average man made between five dollars and six dollars a day, and a man with a lighter or skiff could earn twenty to forty dollars. Clarksville, the small town across the river from Bagdad, had the same reputation.[17]

Despite the advent of war, and its attendant hardships, life continued in the little towns along the lower Rio Grande. On July 19, 1861, María Salomé Ballí de Young, age thirty-two, married John McAllen, age thirty-five, in the Immaculate Conception Catholic Church in Brownsville. Father Parisot officiated at the ceremony, with Charles Stillman and Simon Celaya as witnesses. The wedding celebration at the Miller Hotel was a grand party followed by a shivaree. John McAllen purchased a thousand cigars from Salomé's store five days earlier, no doubt to distribute at the reception. Reportedly, McAllen presented a fine carriage and a team of black horses to Salomé as a wedding gift.[18]

Their home in Brownsville was located on Levee Street and was a Matamoros-style two-story brick and stucco house with a decorative iron railing on the upper balcony. The house fronted the street with only a narrow walk, typical of pre-1821 Matamoros architecture. It is thought that the couple operated their Brownsville store from the lower floor of this building while beginning their new family. Perhaps more importantly, John McAllen became a stepfather to seven-year-old John J. Young, Salomé's son by her first marriage to John Young.[19]

On September 12, 1862, Salomé gave birth to John's son, James Ballí McAllen, in Brownsville. Soon after, they bought a home in Matamoros on Garita de Reynosa and moved their primary wholesale and retail operation across the river. Most merchants in Brownsville made the same move. Much of the business activity in the once bustling town of Brownsville had shifted to Matamoros by the end of 1861. What made Brownsville's depopulation worse was the Confederacy's insistence in May 1861 that people take a "citizenship oath," in which they swore loyalty to the Confederacy. Though all but two Cameron County

*Salomé Ballí McAllen, who with husband John McAllen pieced back together the Santa Anita land grant buying rights from relatives, circa 1865. Courtesy of the McAllen Ranch Archives.*

officials signed the oath, the citizens responded only reluctantly. Many objectors moved across the river.[20]

With the wartime trade frenzy, the nature of John McAllen's business changed in Matamoros. Daily transactions increased, with even larger purchase by customers—mostly other merchants and suppliers. He bought cotton in increasing quantities, sometimes up to sixteen thousand pounds a day, baled or not. He also bought and sold hides and wool on a daily basis. McAllen sold supplies to the Confederate army and the Mexican military, as well as guns and ammunition. Like other merchants, McAllen also sold goods from his own farms located upriver from Brownsville and cattle and horses from Rancho Santa Anita. He grew cane and processed sugar. He also grew cotton, pressed it, and sold it on the open market with no middlemen. This vertical integration maximized profits.[21]

McAllen expanded his cotton farming on the river at La Blanca and the neighboring two and a half leagues (11,000 acres) of land that he called La Hacienda. He made the first large-scale effort to farm Sea Island cotton, a variety favored by Gulf Coast farmers for its long staple or fiber. The cotton was relatively easy to grow, planted in February and harvested in July. It required little water, and along the river he used small pumps powered by windmills to irrigate.[22]

McAllen ordered the loose cotton he purchased or grew bailed by a company called H. Jken. By 1864, a local Spanish-owned cotton-pressing service had developed in Matamoros. Another service inked the bales with brands, like <W> or E<A>B, representing the owner of the cotton. The inking ensured that when the bales reached their destination, the proper merchant would be billed for duties and paid. His sugar mill produced hundreds of hogsheads of brown sugar, formed into *piloncillo* (cones), and shipped to Europe along with the cotton.[23] The goods were shipped with agents, paid by commission, and dispatched by McAllen to their final destinations. McAllen relied on Angel de la Vega, Salomé's brother-in-law, to supervise the transportation of cotton from Matamoros to Boca del Rio. McAllen also relied on his other brothers-in-law Emilio and Francisco Ballí, as well as their father Francisco, as agents. He hired W. B. and John O. Thompson to escort goods to New Orleans, New York, or England, and return with purchased goods or specie in gold or British sterling. They brought stock to the store, including laces, fabrics, shoes, fine furniture, cigars, liquors, wines, champagne, lobsters, vegetables, guns, ammunition, glass, and lumber. Each arrival of goods would be advertised in the newspaper and sold at a profit.[24]

With the additional income, Salomé and John McAllen augmented the offerings from their store in Matamoros, aided by Salomé's father, Francisco. They also continued with Salomé's long-dreamed project of purchasing portions of the Santa Anita land grant. She bought additional *derechos* (land rights) from her Domínguez relatives over the next decades.[25]

Despite the regular skirmishing between caudillos looking to control the flow of cotton in Mexico through 1862 and 1863, merchants plied their wares and shipped cotton, prepared for the chronic outbursts of violence. Using a sophisticated broken-voyage system and shipping cotton through a circuitous route, trade with the Confederates or the Union army could be disguised. This, however, did not stop the armies from complaining about rampant inflation and the monopoly of commerce by the numerous speculators attracted to the war trade.[26]

Deserters and Union sympathizers arrived in Matamoros on a regular basis. Often the US consul, Leonard Pierce Jr., welcomed the hungry and forlorn refugees and supplied them with funds from his own personal accounts. The newly provisioned arrivals then often shipped out to New Orleans.[27]

The Civil War along the Rio Grande served to overshadow local disputes and differences between Mexicans, Europeans, and Americans living there. The thousands of strangers attracted by the cotton boom paid little attention to local prejudices or feuds. Their main concern was making money. In January 1863, when Confederate Brig. Gen. Hamilton Prioleau Bee, a former lawyer from Corpus Christi, took command of Fort Brown, he saw the benefit of finessing and wooing traders. Under his command, fandangos and formal dinners preceded by cocktails were common, especially when the army entertained English or European guests with whom they wished to do business. A number of the consuls in Matamoros operated side businesses to trade with the Confederates. Rebel and merchant liaison José Agustín Quintero summed up the disorder within the ranks of the Confederate command at Fort Brown and unscrupulous speculators: no unity, little cooperation, waste, inefficiency, and competition.[28]

On November 2, 1863, six thousand Union troops under the command of Gen. Nathaniel P. Banks arrived in the stormy and turbid port of Brazos Santiago. Bee soon realized that his Confederate troops at Fort Brown were grossly outnumbered by General Banks's division. His scouts reported that Brazos Island was covered with Union tents. In the face of this juggernaut in blue, he panicked and made plans to evacuate. As one of his last acts, General Bee had dinner at the Miller Hotel and paid the bill by giving his host permission to loot Fort Brown. The next day, Bee, in his drunken departure, ordered Fort Brown torched, along with one thousand bales of Confederate cotton to keep them out of Union hands. What could not be burned was shoved into the river, along with arms and munitions.[29]

The fort, and more importantly, Brownsville, erupted into chaos. The wind blew sparks from the burning fort and cotton over the town, igniting buildings. The fire quickly spread over two blocks. Frightened townsfolk poured into the streets, mixing with the fleeing solders. Mayor George Dye, Israel Bigelow, and other town leaders helped residents evacuate. People dashed to the river onto ferries and boats, but there was not enough room for their possessions. William Neale used a shotgun to hold back men, while allowing women and children to board. Then, in one of the burning buildings, eight thousand pounds of gunpowder exploded, violently shaking the town in a blast that could be heard for miles. The blast imploded a *garita* (sentry house) in the wall of Matamoros across the river. Smoke billowed about the streets. People jumped into the river and some drowned. Mayor Dye ordered a bucket brigade from the river, which saved the remainder of the city from burning, but looters were already at work stripping stores and buildings.[30]

A band of mounted Tejanos galloped through the streets shouting "¡*Mueren los gringos*!" ("Death to the *gringos*!"). Brownsville leaders appealed to Juan Nepomuceno Cortina to bring his band of soldiers across the river to restore peace, but Cortina declined. However, José María Cobos, a Spanish-born caudillo at Matamoros, responded quickly by recruiting two hundred men to control the panic and prevent people from crossing the river. The rioters were driven out, and Brownsville finally quieted.[31]

By then General Bee was well out of town, leading a wagon train north toward the Nueces River, by way of the King Ranch, with ammunition

*The* Andrew Ackley, *a steamboat loaded with wood, passengers, and cargo on the lower Rio Grande, circa 1865. Steamboats shuttled cargo and passengers to waiting schooners anchored at the mouth of the Rio Grande. Courtesy of the McAllen Ranch Archives.*

worth more than a million dollars that he hoped to keep out of Union hands. Although Bee's method of leaving Brownsville was universally condemned, there is evidence that some Brownsville merchants aided the Confederate evacuation and benefitted in some way. Bee later blamed his failure to raise and maintain an army at Fort Brown on many causes, including John McAllen, who was a conscription agent and whom Bee accused of failing to enroll enough soldiers for a home guard.[32]

As a British subject, McAllen remained exempt from the conscription law. Being from a neutral country, he was not forced to swear the oath of allegiance required of citizens of Brownsville, and he likely disagreed with conscription polices. Even though he remained relatively neutral, he dealt with leaders on all sides—Confederate, Union, Juarista, and Imperialista—and his help was requested by all officials during the war. By this time, McAllen was totally engulfed in the expanding Matamoros economy. He participated in the rapid trade in cotton, hides, wool, munitions, and other goods.[33]

After General Banks and the Union army moved into Fort Brown, hundreds of Brownsville citizens took an oath of allegiance to the Union through the efforts of Judge Israel B. Bigelow. Ever adaptable, Bigelow and other merchants made friends with the Union administrators, just as they had done with the Confederate troops. Pro-Unionists, like Gilbert Kingsbury, returned to Brownsville to reclaim their confiscated and abandoned properties. Kingsbury then set himself up as a merchant, cattle broker, and speculator, at one point investing in a load of shoes and boots to sell to Matamoros merchants.[34]

Gen. Napoleon J. T. Dana assumed command of Fort Brown when General Banks departed for New Orleans. Union officers proceeded to confiscate Texas properties of pro-Confederates and Red Party members who lived in Matamoros. Every citizen in Brownsville was affected. Prominent business owners such as Charles Stillman, Mifflin Kenedy, Richard King, Adolphus Glaevecke, Edward and James Dougherty, and William Neale all lost property.[35] Almost simultaneously, Union sympathizing Tejano and Mexican troops of the 2nd Texas Cavalry under Col. E. J. Davis captured a Confederate steamboat and raided Ringgold Barracks. They then rode north twenty-five miles to La Sal del Rey where they destroyed the salt works. The salt lakes of Texas had taken on even greater importance since Union gunboats destroyed other Southern salt stores; the Confederacy needed six million bushels of salt per year for food preservation.[36]

A portion of Davis's cavalry then ransacked Richard King's Santa Gertrudis ranch headquarters, after which King moved his family to San Antonio. William Neale was arrested as he crossed from Matamoros to visit his sick wife. His property was confiscated, and he was put in jail. Not until he took the oath of allegiance was he released. Brownsville mayor and merchant George Dye maintained his loyalty to the Union, but his family members did not. His wife and daughters were "strong Secesh [secessionist] and did not strive to hide their feelings but . . . made their sentiments public, anxious to show every Union soldier a Secesh lady. They refused to take the oath of allegiance and their impudence became intolerable—so that Gen. [Dana] issued an order banishing them into Mexico." A squad of Union soldiers escorted the ladies to the river's edge, and they were conveyed across the muddy waters to Matamoros.[37]

Although the Union army hoped to stem the flow of Southern cotton through Brownsville to Matamoros, trade only slowed. Merchants continued to triple their money on bales sometimes shipped from upstream at Laredo or Eagle Pass. Given the tremendous amounts of cotton that continued to flow to the border, comparatively little fell into the hands of the federal officers. The Union army captured only about eight hundred bales during its first month of occupation, an immaterial amount compared to the broad expectations of the Union government. Regulations permitting the Union to sell captured goods to support immediate needs made it probable that seized goods were sold to area merchants anyway, who then began to refuse to trade with either army in anything other than gold or cotton.[38]

Tensions between Union forces at Fort Brown and the military officials in Matamoros surged in early 1864 when Maj. Gen. Francis Jay Herron took command over the fort's 6,500 troops. On January 12, Juan Nepomuceno Cortina awarded himself the governorship of Tamaulipas, and factional fighting erupted. The sitting governor, Albino López, was shot by his own assistant as he took the ferry to Brownsville. The assistant, who wished to curry favor with Cortina by killing

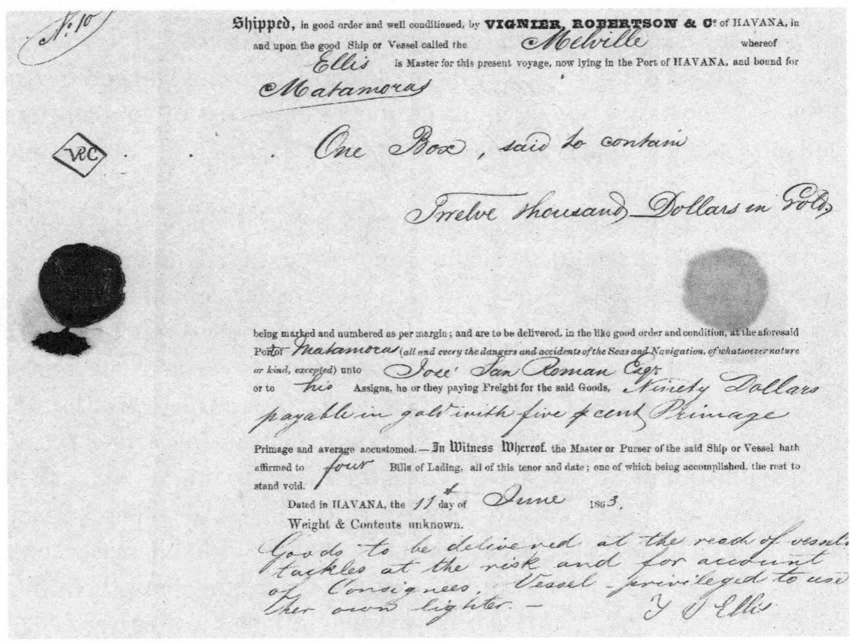

N.º 10

VRC

Shipped, in good order and well conditioned, by VIGNIER, ROBERTSON & Cº of HAVANA, in and upon the good Ship or Vessel called the Melville whereof Ellis is Master for this present voyage, now lying in the Port of HAVANA, and bound for Matamoras

One Box, said to contain

Twelve thousand Dollars in Gold

being marked and numbered as per margin; and are to be delivered, in the like good order and condition, at the aforesaid Port of Matamoras (all and every the dangers and accidents of the Seas and Navigation, of whatsoever nature or kind, excepted) unto José San Roman Esqr or to his Assigns, he or they paying Freight for the said Goods, Ninety Dollars payable in gold with five per cent Primage

Primage and average accustomed.—In Witness Whereof, the Master or Purser of the said Ship or Vessel hath affirmed to four Bills of Lading, all of this tenor and date; one of which being accomplished, the rest to stand void.

Dated in HAVANA, the 11th day of June 1863.

Weight & Contents unknown.

Goods to be delivered at the reach of vessel tackles at the risk and for account of Consignees, Vessel privileged to use their own lighter. —

J. Ellis

*Bill of lading for the mercantile establishment of José San Roman. Courtesy of the McAllen Ranch Archives.*

López, was instead ordered shot by Cortina. In the midst of the fighting, US consul Leonard Pierce sent a distress message to Herron. Pierce had about a million dollars in specie in collected duties at the consulate. He urged for protection from the chaos. Herron sent four companies of soldiers to protect the consulate until the monies could be transferred to Brownsville. Pierce wrote:

> What is to become of this country is a problem that can only lie solved by truce. The people are fighting among themselves not only in this state but also in states of the interior. President Juárez . . . is on his way and will establish his headquarters in this city, hoping for and expecting protection from the United States. All the better class of Mexicans are looking forward to the time when the French will be ordered from Mexico by the United States, and the [Union] occupation of the Rio Grande has encouraged them in their belief.[39]

As the violence on both sides of the Rio Grande intensified through 1864, John McAllen grew concerned about the serious threat to his family; he took Salomé and their two children to a home she owned in Brooklyn, New York. Other merchants had done the same. In the case of Charles Stillman, his wife and children remained with his family in Hartford, Connecticut. He only saw them in the summers when he traveled north. While McAllen wanted his family away from the fighting and danger, he returned immediately to operate his business.[40]

Since the flight of General Bee from Fort Brown, commanders of the Confederacy's Department of Texas had been mulling over strategies to restore Confederate control along the lower Rio Grande. Under Herron, 6,500 troops remained in the Valley, including 4,400 at Fort Brown. Col. John Salmon "Rip" Ford accepted the assignment to recapture Fort Brown for the Confederacy and soon sent out a call for recruits. His handbill made his opinions of the Union solders explicit and plain. He wanted men who would be "defending their own homes . . . [against] a mongrel force of Abolitionists, negroes, plundering Mexicans, and perfidious renegades . . . [who had] been allowed to murder and rob us." He challenged the "Texians" to fight for their honor.[41]

In view of one of the worst droughts on record, Ford mapped his strategy to march south to the lower Rio Grande, making use of the ranchlands' water wells. He knew he could cross the parched chaparral to Fort Brown by way of Goliad and south to Richard King's Santa Gertrudis ranch, from which King offered supplies, foodstuffs, and forage.[42]

By January 1864, Ford had raised a force of a thousand men, who were busy gathering provisions and drying beef. Scouts looked for enemy maneuvers, and by February 7, Ford planned to move more westerly toward Fort Ewell, Los Angeles, and San Antonio Viejo. However, simultaneous to his march, an order transferring Union forces from Brownsville to New Orleans commenced, leaving only about two thousand soldiers on duty.[43]

After finding a cache of weapons and supplies at Ringgold Barracks in Rio Grande City, Ford reconnoitered for six weeks, hesitating to move on Fort Brown due to the drought and varying reports on soldier activity. On June 16, Ford decided to move on Edinburgh and then downriver. Ford rode directly by the river road to the ranch of Salomé and John McAllen astride his new war horse "Bravo," which had previously belonged to the Union commander, General Herron. The horse had been given to him by friends in Matamoros. Transcending politics, many people in the region welcomed Ford, who managed to make tough decisions while keeping the citizens happy. He remained a popular man with many locals—especially because he facilitated the cotton and mercantile trade during the war.[44]

After some weeks of watching General Herron and Union troops transferring into and out of Fort Brown, Ford learned that Herron would soon be transferred and replaced by Brig. Gen. Fitz Henry Warren, "an old man and no account," according to Ford. Ford had his men, especially Col. Santos Benavides, prepare to attack. On July 5, Ford wrote, "Brownsville has been reinforced with one regiment of Iowa Infantry and about 200 cavalry. The whole force . . . is about 2,500 men. They had a happy time yesterday christening a new flag and flag staff in old Fort Brown. All hands drunk—Herron very drunk."

On July 17, Ford suspected that a portion of Herron's army planned to evacuate, but urged his colonels to make it appear that his army had effected the withdrawal. He wrote, "The General has told some of his intimate friends that they will leave a small force at Brazos [Santiago], with one gun boat in the harbor and one outside. Pardon me for the suggestion, but don't let them leave without some demonstration against them."[45]

Four days later, Ford and his troops camped a mile outside Brownsville. When his men encountered a group of Union soldiers and prepared a stealth attack, they miscalculated and let out a Texas war call too soon, and the Union troops fled. Ford, with eight hundred of his men, immediately pursued them toward Brownsville, but remained in the chaparral on the outskirts of town. On July 28, Ford learned that the last Union soldiers had evacuated Fort Brown. He followed his plan and ordered his men to find and harass the withdrawing Union soldiers. They found them eighteen miles downriver from Brownsville, and on August 4 attacked their rear guard, killing two and capturing two. Ford had chased them as far as Clarksville and eastward. As he likely concluded, he drove Herron and the Union army out of Brownsville with the help of Herron's horse.[46]

Brownsville welcomed Ford with fanfare. His wife, who had been in Matamoros for several months, had given birth to a baby girl on July 14, and Ford rushed to join his family. The Confederate forces reoccupied Fort Brown on July 30, 1864. Peace prevailed for the time being, in large part because citizens who had sworn allegiance to the Blue Party or Union fled to Matamoros and New Orleans. The Red Party Confederates returned to Brownsville. Under Ford's administration, traditional trade routes for cotton, cattle, hides, and wool through Matamoros resumed. The price of goods fell by half. The Union army remained at Brazos Island for the duration of the war. In August 1864, Henry Martyn Day at Brazos Santiago commanded a large number of black troops who camped near their remaining eleven artillery pieces, seldom venturing far. Both sides remained in their camps, patrolling their perimeters.[47]

Cortina, who typically favored the victor in most military struggles, became cordial with the Confederate troops, even paying a formal visit to the Matamoros home of Ford's wife, offering her assistance in any way. While Cortina made no interference in the cotton trade, for most of 1864, Texan ranchers accused him of running a huge rustling operation. He faced the daily encroachment of the French-dominated Imperialista army under Gen. Tomás Mejía, who camped at Bagdad and drew closer to Matamoros every day. Cortina's army also suffered at the hands of the Confederates, who he accused of sniping across the river, picking off Mexican soldiers. Feeling pressure as his enemies closed in, he declared a forced loan on the merchants of Matamoros. John McAllen paid his quota of two hundred dollars on May 31, 1864, and on July 31, he loaned his brother-in-law Emilio Ballí's company two hundred dollars to pay its forced loan. Ford wrote to Benavides, "I am just informed there will be another forced loan this morning. *Quien sabe*. They only ask for the small sum of $80,000." The merchants knew they had to pay or risk the torching of their businesses or the torture of their families.[48]

Like many working within the chaos along the lower Rio Grande, Consul Leonard Pierce also worried about his family and had requested to resign from his post. He wrote General Herron:

> It is now nearly six weeks since you left us, and . . . we have not heard one word from any one, not even a line from my wife. We have had stirring times among the heroic inhabitants since you left. The French landed 400 sailors at Bagdad and they hold that place now. Cortina came in from the interior with all his forces, bringing some twenty or more pieces of artillery with him and 1,500 men. Finding that the French were on all sides of them, the Mexicans held a meeting and determined upon crossing everything over the river and deliver all their arms, artillery and ammunition to the custody of the United States. . . . How this matter will end no one can tell at present, but a little responsibility will clear up everything. Please write and let me know how my family got through.[49]

Ford wrote of the wily Cortina, who engaged assistance from the Union soldiers at Brazos Santiago to escape the French, "He hates Americans; particularly Texans. He has an old and deep-seated grudge against Brownsville. He knows his career is nearly closed. If he could force his way through our lines, plunder our people, and get within the Yankee lines, it would [be] a finale he would delight in."[50]

Ford treated Cortina with equal measures diplomatic courtesy and steadfast resolve. One historian recalled the atmosphere in the lower Rio Grande at this time, "where men sworn to kill one another on one side of the Rio Grande could, if they chanced to meet on the opposite bank, share a convivial drink before returning home to take up the business of mayhem . . . in this era death was as common as dirt in the brush country of South Texas."[51]

The surrender of Robert E. Lee in Virginia on April 9, 1865, no doubt had great impact on the Confederates of the Trans-Mississippi Department, but they showed little evidence of it. The officers maintained their posts, despite rampant desertion. Brig. Gen. James Edwin Slaughter, who had been assigned to Fort Brown and served over Ford, declined to surrender when approached by Union major general Lewis "Lew" Wallace on March 11, 1865. The war was winding down in the South, but with the cotton trade still flowing, Slaughter and Ford refused to surrender.[52]

On the morning of May 13, Ford assembled three hundred cavalrymen and marched out of Fort Brown with six pieces of artillery. They meant to attack Union soldiers advancing from Brazos Santiago and met at Palmito Ranch. At the end of the day of skirmishing, the Confederates won the battle, with between 20 and 30 men killed and 113 taken prisoner. It was a hollow victory. Soon Slaughter and thousands of other former Confederate soldiers fled into Mexico to make a new life, away from their defeat and the US reconstructing government.[53]

By November 1865, John McAllen began to shut down his business in Matamoros and shift operations back to Brownsville. He resumed trading from his store on Levee Street, closed his cotton gin, and began to concentrate on selling beef and goods to the general public. He helped Confederate and Union soldiers leaving the area by buying their horses, saddles, and other property. His business shifted away from receiving gold and silver specie to accepting US currency, which he noted in his ledgers as "greenbacks."[54]

In all, about 320,000 bales of cotton had passed through the Brownsville to Matamoros route—an astonishing amount of commerce for such a tiny port.[55] The American citizens who had moved to Matamoros and engaged in the wartime cotton trade were forced to apply for a presidential pardon, required of former Confederate sympathizers who owned more than twenty thousand dollars in property. Richard King, Charles Stillman, and Mifflin Kenedy were forced to deal in their own ways with federal government officials.[56]

In 1866, John McAllen became a citizen, renouncing all ties to England. He legalized his relationship with his twelve-year-old stepson, John

J. Young, and he and Salomé continued to trade along the Rio Grande. As the decade closed, much of their economic efforts shifted to ranching and cattle drives to Kansas. Many of the other Civil War merchants made the same move, plowing their profits into land and cattle. Others, like Charles Stillman, returned to their native homes and invested in banking and infrastructures that would propel their families into new entrepreneurial prospects leading up to the turn to the twentieth century.[57]

## *Notes*

1. James H. Thompson, "A Nineteenth Century History of Cameron County, Texas" (master's thesis, University of Texas at Austin, 1966), 50–53, 66–75; Ronnie C. Tyler, "Cotton on the Border," *Southwestern Historical Quarterly* 73 (April 1970): 466; *Rio Grande Courier* (Brownsville, May 19, 1866); Rev. P. F. Parisot, *Reminiscences of a Texas Missionary* (San Antonio: St. Mary's Church, 1899), 55.

2. James A. Irby, *Backdoor at Bagdad: The Civil War on the Rio Grande* (El Paso: Texas Western Press, 1977), 5; Milo Kearney and Anthony Knopp, *Boom and Bust: The Historical Cycles of Matamoros and Brownsville* (Austin: Eakin Press, 1991), 117

3. Irby, *Backdoor at Bagdad*, 5; Kearney and Knopp, *Boom and Bust*, 117.

4. James E. Slaughter, correspondence, 1864–1865, Letter Copy Book, Fort Brown, 1865, Civil War papers, John McAllen Papers, McAllen Ranch Archives, Linn, TX (hereafter cited as MRA); Thompson, "A Nineteenth Century History of Cameron County, Texas," 87.

5. Thompson, "A Nineteenth Century History of Cameron County, Texas," 85–87; Johnathan Bardon, *A History of Ulster* (Northern Ireland: Blackstaff Press, 1992), 125; Kearney and Knopp, *Boom and Bust*, 118–21.

6. James W. Daddysman, *The Matamoros Trade: Confederate Commerce, Diplomacy and Intrigue* (Norwalk: University of Delaware Press, 1984), 29–30, 38.

7. Ibid., 32–34, 151–152.

8. Thompson, "A Nineteenth Century History of Cameron County, Texas," 66–75; Hidalgo County Commissioners Court minutes (Hidalgo County, TX: 1871), 111; *New York Herald*, July 29, 1965.

9. McAllen store ledger, 1861–70 (MRA); Thompson, "A Nineteenth Century History of Cameron County, Texas," 60; Santos Domínguez to John Young, December 18, 1856, Young Papers (MRA).

10. McAllen store ledger, 1861–70 (MRA); Thompson, "A Nineteenth Century History of Cameron County, Texas," 60.

11. *New York Herald*, July 29, 1865.

12. Frank C. Pierce, *A Brief History of the Lower Rio Grande Valley* (Menasha, WI: George Banta Publishing Company, 1917), 117.

13. *New York Herald*, March 28, 1863, July 29, 1865; Tyler, *Cotton on the Border*, 460; Daddysman, *The Matamoros Trade*, 31–34, 38, 50–52, 62.

14. Juan Fidel Zorrilla, Maribel Miró Flaquer, and Octavio Herrera Pérez, *Tamaulipas: Una Historia Compartida, 1810–1921*, 2 vols. (San Juan Mixcoac, Mexico:

Universidad Autónoma de Tamaulipas, 1993), II:13–16; Ronnie C. Tyler, *Santiago Vidaurri and the Southern Confederacy* (Austin: Texas State Historical Association, 1973), 61–63; John Salmon Ford, Memoirs (7 vols.) VI, John Salmon Ford Papers, Briscoe Center for American History (hereafter cited as BCAH), 1125; House report and accompanying documents of the Committee on Foreign Affairs on the Relations of the United States with Mexico, Part II, "Texas Frontier Troubles," John S. Ford to Mr. Schleicher, H. Exec. Doc. 701, 45th Cong., 2nd Sess., 1878, 67.

15. Kearney and Knopp, *Boom and Bust*, 123–24; Tyler, "Cotton on the Border," 466–67; *Rio Grande Courier* (Brownsville) May 19, 1866; Parisot, *Reminiscences of a Texas Missionary*, 55.

16. Tom Lea, *The King Ranch* (Boston: Little, Brown and Company, 1957) I: 193; Tyler, "Cotton on the Border," 477; D. G. Farragut to Commander French, August 25, 1862, *Official Records of the Union and Confederate Navies in the War of the Rebellion*, series I, XIX, 168 (hereafter cited as OR).

17. Parisot, *Reminiscences of a Texas Missionary*, 56.

18. Marriage record of John McAllen and Salomé Ballí Young (MRA); J. L. Allhands, *Gringo Builders* (Dallas: privately printed, 1931), 128; McAllen family oral tradition.

19. Photo: home of Salomé and John McAllen, Brownsville, ca. 1880.

20. John McAllen, store ledger, Matamoros, September 12, 1862 (MRA); title to home in Matamoros, purchase and sell agreements, Guillermo Hernandez to John McAllen, March 20, 1866 (MRA); Daddysman, *The Matamoros Trade*, 61, 83.

21. John McAllen, store ledgers, 1862–65 (MRA).

22. *Daily Ranchero*, October 10, 18, 1866.

23. McAllen store ledger, 1864, Matamoros (MRA); Frank H. Dugan, "Hidalgo County Grows Up," *Hidalgo County Centennial*, 1852–1952, December 7–13, 1952, 14.

24. McAllen store ledger, 1862, Brownsville (MRA); McAllen store ledger, December 11, 1860–February 5, 1866, 1866–67, Brownsville and Matamoros; Cameron County Census of 1860 (Microfilm Roll 1289, San Antonio Public Library).

25. *Centinela del Rio Grande* (Brownsville), June 26, 1861; abstract, *Western Part of the Santa Anita Grant*, 130–41, 188; Starr County Deed Records Book, 1861, 111.

26. Irby, *Backdoor at Bagdad*, 9–10; Charles Stillman, ledger, January 1862, Charles Stillman papers (Houghton Library, Harvard University); Daddysman, *The Matamoros Trade*, 117.

27. Irby, *Backdoor at Bagdad*, 25; Leonard Pierce Jr. to William Seward, December 8, 1864, Dispatches from US Consuls in Matamoros, 1826–1906 (Microfilm M281, Roll 3, National Archives, College Park, MD).

28. Irby, *Backdoor at Bagdad*, 6–7, 52; Arthur James Lyon Fremantle, *The Fremantle Diary: Being the Journal of Lt. Col. Fremantle, Coldstream Guards on His Three Months in the Southern States* (Boston: Little, Brown and Company, 1954), 13–15; Tyler, "Cotton on the Border," 467–68; Robert W. Delaney, "Matamoros, Port for Texas during the Civil War," *Southwestern Historical Quarterly* 58 (1955): 473.

29. Tyler, "Cotton on the Border," 462; Thompson, "A Nineteenth Century

History of Cameron County, Texas," 95; Richard Fitzpatrick to J. P. Benjamin, March 8, 1864 (OR), Ser. I, XXXIV, Part II, 1031; Thompson "A Nineteenth Century History of Cameron County, Texas," 95.

30. Richard Fitzpatrick to J. P. Benjamin, March 8, 1864 (OR), Ser. I, XXXIV, Part II, 1031; Thompson "A Nineteenth Century History of Cameron County, Texas," 95.

31. Maj. Gen. N. P. Banks to Maj. Gen. H. W. Halleck, November 6, 1863 (OR), Series I, XXVI, Part I, 399.

32. J. A. Quintero to J. P. Benjamin, November 26, 1863, Davenport (ed.), CSA 80–84 (quotation); Richard Fitzpatrick to J. P. Benjamin, March 8, 1864 (OR), Ser. I, XXXIV, Part II, 1031; H. P. Bee to W. R. Boggs, December 4, 1863 (OR), Ser. I, XXVI, Part II, 479.

33. McAllen store ledger, 1860–67, Matamoros (MRA).

34. Kearney and Knopp, *Boom and Bust*, 129; Daddysman, *The Matamoros Trade*, 119.

35. Kearney and Knopp, *Boom and Bust*, 130.

36. Jerry D. Thompson, *Mexican Texans in the Union Army*, Southwestern Studies no. 78 (El Paso: Texas Western Press, 1986), 15, 31; *New York Herald*, March 28, 1863.

37. Thompson, *Mexican Texans*, 15, 21; Margery Wentworth Petrovich, "The Civil War Career of Colonel John Salmon 'Rip' Ford" (master's thesis, Stephen F. Austin College, 1961), 76–77; Kearney and Knopp, *Boom and Bust*, 131–32; Nannie M. Tilley, *Federals on the Frontier: The Diary of Benjamin F. McIntyre* (Austin: University of Texas Press, 1961), 336–37, n. 148.

38. *New York Tribune*, December 16, 1863; McAllen store ledger, 1864, Brownsville (MRA); Daddysman, *The Brownsville Trade*, 119; Marilyn McAdams Sibley, "Charles Stillman: A Case Study of Entrepreneurship on the Rio Grande, 1861–1865," *Southwestern Historical Quarterly* 77 (1973): 237.

39. Richard T. Marcum, "Fort Brown, Texas: The History of a Border Post" (master's thesis, Texas Technical College, 1964), 168; Leonard Pierce Jr. to Francis J. Herron, January 16, 1864, Dispatches from US Consulate in Matamoros, 1826–1906, M281, Roll 3 (Microfilm Dept., N.A., C.P.).

40. Inventory of Properties, John and Salomé Young, December 31, 1873, Young Papers (MRA); McAllen store ledger, 1866–80 (MRA); Chauncey D. Stillman, *Charles Stillman, 1810–1875* (New York: privately published, 1956), 14–15.

41. Tilley, *Federals on the Frontier*, 285–309; Marcum, "Fort Brown, Texas," 169; John Salmon Ford, Memoirs, 1864, John Salmon Ford Papers, Box 20155 (BCAH); T. R. Feherenbach, *Lone Star* (New York: Wings Books, 1991), 373.

42. Petrovich, "The Civil War Career of John Salmon 'Rip' Ford," 71–90; Irby, *Backdoor at Bagdad*, 30–31.

43. Petrovich, "The Civil War Career of John Salmon 'Rip' Ford," 71–90; Irby, *Backdoor at Bagdad*, 30–31; Thompson, *Mexican Texans*, 27; John S. Ford to E. P. Turner, May 5, 1864 (OR), Ser. I, XXXIV, Part III, 807–8.

44. S. E. McClellan, John W. Lang, H. Seeligson, D. L. Angier, Joseph Kleiber to John S. Ford, "Presentation of a Horse to Gen. Ford," May 29, 1864, Ford Papers,

Military Correspondence and Papers, 1861–65 (Texas State Archives, Austin, TX, hereafter cited as TSA); Irby, *Backdoor at Bagdad*, 33; Petrovich, "The Civil War Career of John Salmon 'Rip' Ford," 90–106, 116; Marcum, "Fort Brown, Texas," 131.

45. John S. Ford to unknown, thought to be Showalter, July 15, 1864, Ford Papers, Military Correspondence (TSA).

46. Petrovich, "The Civil War Career of Colonel John Salmon 'Rip' Ford," 113–16; Francis J. Herron to Wm. Dwight, June 26, 1864 (OR), Ser. I, XXXIV, Part IV, 559–60.

47. Petrovich, "The Civil War Career of Colonel John Salmon 'Rip' Ford," 115–18; Thompson, "A Nineteenth Century History of Cameron County, Texas," 98.

48. Jerry Thompson, *Juan Cortina and the Texas Mexican Frontier, 1859–1877* (El Paso: Texas Western Press, 1994), 43–48, 67–69; Tyler, "Cotton on the Border," 466; Lyman L. Woodman, *Cortina: Rogue of the Rio Grande* (San Antonio: Naylor Company, 1950), 79; F. J. Herron to Wm. Dwight, June 26, 1864 (OR), Ser. I, XXXIV, Part IV, 560; John S. Ford to Santos Benavides, July 5, 1864 (quotation), Ford papers, Military Correspondence, Folder: Scout and Secret Service (TSA); McAllen store ledger, 1864, Matamoros (MRA).

49. L. Pierce Jr. to F. J. Herron, September 8, 1864 (OR), Series I, XLI, Part III, 101.

50. J. S. Ford to J. E. Dwyer, September 3, 1864 (OR), Series I, XLI, Part III, 909.

51. Bruce Cheeseman, "'Let Us Have 500 Good Determined Texans': Richard King's Account of the Union Invasion of South Texas, November 12, 1863, to January 20, 1864," *Southwestern Historical Quarterly* 101 (1997): 87, n. 38.

52. Petrovich, "The Civil War Career of Colonel John Salmon 'Rip' Ford," 138–40; James E. Slaughter to Thomas M. Jack, May 7, 1865, Slaughter Letter Copy Book, 280 (MRA); John Salmon Ford, *Rip Ford's Texas*, ed. Stephen B. Oates (Austin: University of Texas Press, 1963), 396, n. 4.

53. As noted in other chapters in this volume, the precise number of casualties suffered in the battle is not known and is a matter of some controversy. Ford, *Rip Ford's Texas*, 394–95; Irby, *Backdoor at Bagdad*, 47–50; James E. Slaughter to Thomas M. Jack, May 18, 1865, Slaughter Letter Copy Book, 305 (MRA); James E. Slaughter to Mifflin Kenedy, May 15, 1865, Slaughter Letter Copy Book, 299 (MRA); *Daily Ranchero* (Brownsville), May 31, 1865; Thomas Corwin to William H. Seward, May 19, 1865, Dispatches from US Ministers in Mexico, 1823–1906, Roll 31 (Microfilm Dept., N.A., C.P.).

54. McAllen store ledger, 1865, Brownsville (MRA).

55. Daddysman, *The Matamoros Trade*, 143.

56. Lea, *The King Ranch*, I:238–48; Stillman, *Charles Stillman*, 31; G. Weilzet to General Streeter, November 29, 1865, James B. Wells Papers, General Correspondence, 1850–1865, Box 2H349, and 1870–1871, Box 2H239 (BCAH).

57. Interview, Nathaniel Stillman, January 28, 2001, notes in possession of the author; Irby, *Backdoor at Bagdad*, 8; Pat Kelley, *River of Lost Dreams: Navigation on the Rio Grande* (Lincoln: University of Nebraska Press, 1986), 77; Oath of Citizenship, John McAllen to Edward Downey, Cameron County, Texas, February 3, 1866 (MRA).

# 4

# *Race and Ethnicity along the Antebellum Rio Grande*

## Emancipated Slaves and Mixed Race Colonies

ROSEANN BACHA-GARZA

During the years between the outbreak of the Mexican-American War and the onset of the American Civil War, the complex character of the Rio Grande Valley borderland population was reshuffled. In the century between the Spanish colonial settlements led by José de Escandón and the Mexican-American War, the population had already homogenized into an undifferentiated Hispanic colonial type. These Spaniards had brought their cultural traditions to a string of small villages along the Rio Grande, known during the Spanish colonial era as the Rio Bravo del Norte. Eventually the Spaniards folded these new customs into the local culture shaped by Native American peoples whose ancestors had inhabited the region for thousands of years. These settlers captured members of local Indian tribes and forced them to adjust to a new way of living, either absorbing the culture and religion of Spain and assimilating themselves or leaving. Many of them made the cultural transformation, to the point where they married Spaniards and procreated with them, producing mixed offspring that have long been referred to as *Mestizo*. With the ousting of Spanish rule in 1821, this region became the northern portion of the Mexican state of Tamaulipas, which was later annexed by the United States in 1848. Families with surnames such as the Hinojosa, Ballí, Falcón, Cavazos, and Benavides—whose descendants still occupy the region—engaged with each other, forming a rich interconnected society.

A century after the establishment of the Spanish *villas* along the Rio Grande, war came to the area as the governments of Mexico and the United States disagreed on the location of the border between the two countries. The Nueces Strip—a 150 mile expanse—lay between the Rio Grande and the Nueces River. American soldiers were sent to the Rio Grande in order to secure the US claim to this largely unsettled area. In 1846, the Mexican-American War ensued, and after a two-year struggle, the United States emerged triumphant. Many soldiers who fought hard to defend the land on the left bank of the Rio Grande saw benefits in remaining in the region to resume their civilian lives, thus turning a bicultural environment into a multicultural one, blending Spanish-speaking Mexican nationals referred to as "Tejanos" on US soil with new arrivals of white settlers referred to as "Anglos." As news traveled to Europe and to the American Atlantic Coast, curious and brave entrepreneurs descended upon the sister cities of Brownsville and Matamoros, as those were the established metropolises on the natural frontier and convenient to the Gulf port at Point Isabel, which lies at the center point between the ports of Galveston and Veracruz.

Soon adventurous Anglo and Irish American capitalists like Richard King and Mifflin Kenedy, veterans of the Mexican-American War, joined the community. These newcomers married the daughters of leading Mexican landowners and business owners. Immigrants like Swede John Vale, Irishman John McAllen, and Scotsman John Young also became established merchants, traders, and ranch owners. In the 1850s, with the arrival of mixed race families such as the Webbers, Jacksons, Rutledges, and Singleterrys, a melting pot culture evolved, representing a mixture of the races. What makes these people special is their unique racial mix. The stereotypical image of an indigenous Mexican person is of someone typically short in stature, with straight black hair, dark brown, often almond-shaped eyes, and dark skin. In the South Texas borderland region known as the Rio Grande Valley, these racial mixes take on a whole new meaning. In our current historical atmosphere of tension and one-dimensional characterizations of the border and its people, this essay will clarify the region's actual historical complexity, opening dialogue about the nature of border communities and their continuing role in the evolution of American life and culture.

The complex interactions between races, ethnicities, and kin groups feed directly into the story of the Civil War in this region. While slavery was not a prominent institution in the South Texas borderlands—Tejanos collectively owned only sixty slaves before the Civil War—it edged into the life of the community in a peculiar way.[1] Slavery had been outlawed in Mexico since 1829, and a relatively unsettled state prevailed in that country during most of the nineteenth century. African Americans who could find their way to the border might control their own destinies and become free. There are two different dimensions that frame the story of the growth of unique settlements along the Rio Grande before and during the Civil War era, both of which are significant to the larger Civil War saga in the region. First, there is evidence that Nathaniel Jackson's ranch near what is now McAllen, Texas, was a depot on a southbound Underground Railroad and that he, his seven grown children, and an extended community of freedmen played active roles in smuggling runaway slaves across the river. At the same time, both Santos Benavides and John Salmon "Rip" Ford, who both played key roles in Confederate military action during the Civil War, earned bounty money as slave catchers in the region before the war began.

This contest between those who sheltered and helped convey slaves to freedom and those who were invested in preventing their escape forms another important dimension in the region's Civil War saga. Despite the rather weak political, economic, and cultural ties between the borderland and the American South generally, many residents along the river between Laredo and Brownsville signed up for the Confederate cause when the American Civil War broke out in 1861. But at the same time, many in that same region also sided with the Union. There was much more than geopolitics involved in these decisions, and understanding the human dimensions of how this community evolved and who came to occupy the region can help us comprehend this phenomenon, opening the way for telling the largely untold story of events that occurred along the US-Mexico border during the American Civil War. This essay will further illustrate how the unique racial mix of the people of the Rio Grande Valley has evolved through the descent of Spanish colonial settlers, Mexican Texan (Tejano) ranchers, Anglo merchants and businessmen, and mixed race families, as well as how they coexisted, intermingled, and eventually intermarried to create a melting pot culture.

The land along the banks of the Rio Grande was an appealing settlement location for many reasons. The climate was pleasant, the land was fertile, and the opportunity for trade was apparent. Sister towns sprang up along the two hundred mile stretch of river between Brownsville and

Laredo. Brownsville and Matamoros were the larger, more established sister-cities of the region. By the 1840s, trade routes were established along the Gulf Coast, and in Texas, port cities such as Galveston, Corpus Christi, and Brownsville were magnets for multinational visitors. With the strong French influence established by Emperor Maximilian south of the border in Mexico at that time, the entire Gulf Coast was multilingual. In addition to French, it was common to hear English, German, and Spanish spoken at any given time in the streets of Brownsville and Matamoros. Once steamboat travel appeared in the region in the late 1840s, trade opportunities emerged along the Rio Grande, moving north and west toward Laredo. With US military forts in Brownsville, Rio Grande City, and Laredo, those three locations were most attractive to the ambitious, international set. As one traveled along the river beyond Brownsville, several twin villages appeared. The next set of town sites upriver were Edinburgh (by 1855 known as Hidalgo) and Reynosa. Continuing upriver appeared the twin towns of Rio Grande City and Camargo, then Roma and Mier, followed by Guerrero (Revilla) and Zapata, and two hundred miles inland from the Gulf of Mexico were Laredo and Nuevo Laredo. Steamboat traffic sailed up and down the river, with Roma being the farthest point reachable upriver. There have been reports of an occasional successful vessel making it beyond Roma with the help of rising floodwaters, but secure river trade typically went no farther than that. Established ranches along the river took part in riverside trade as well. By 1852, with the official establishment of Hidalgo County, the County Commissioners Court had confirmed ferry licenses for the following five locations: Edinburgh, Saint Louis (Rancho San Luis), Capote, Grangeno (Granjeno), and "in front of Reynosa Viejo" (otherwise known as Peñitas).[2] Before the onset of the US Civil War in 1861, there were at least twelve ferry licenses at locations such as Rosario, Agua Negra, La Blanca, John Webber's Ranch, Benigo Leal's (Santa Ana) Ranch, Pacifico (Ignacio) Ochoa's Ranch, Tabasco Ranch, and Las Cuevas Ranch.[3] This ignited commerce and trade in the region, as resident families on these ranches were able to take advantage of the riverboat traffic to sell their excess produce and trade in animal skins.

Land travel along the banks of the Rio Grande was arduous. Riverside residents had to be skilled horsemen in order to traverse the landscape, which was covered with thick grasslands and forests filled with

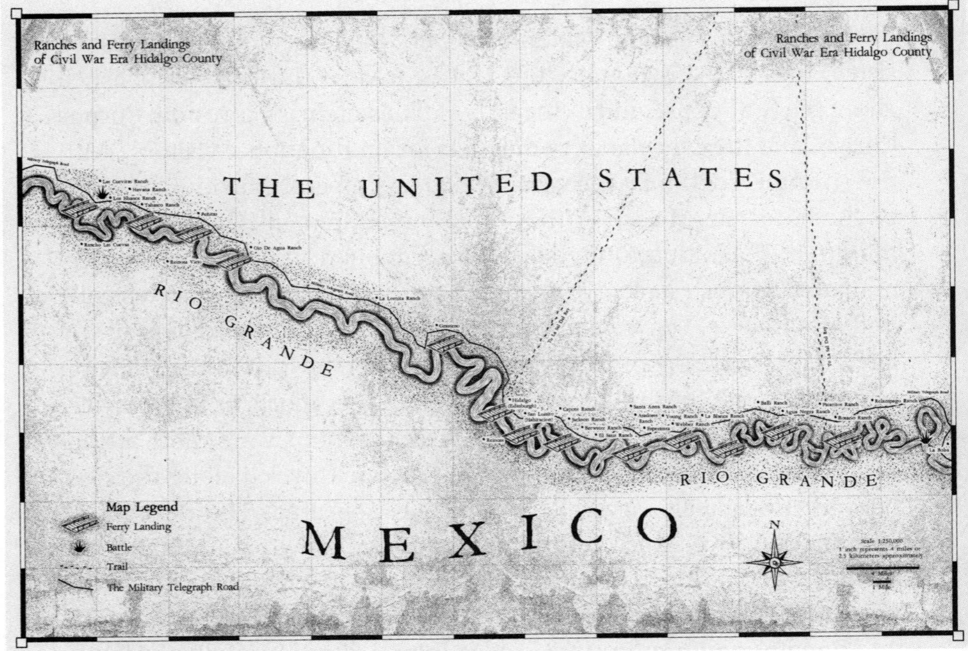


*Re-creation of riverside ranches present in Hidalgo County during the US Civil War era. Artist: Daniel Cardenas of the University of Texas Rio Grande Valley, The Studio Marketing Services.*

predatory animals.[4] A path initially carved by historic Native American peoples who inhabited the Rio Grande Valley was later developed by early Spanish settlers in order to connect with neighboring ranches during the second half of the eighteenth century and early nineteenth century. This road further progressed at the end of the 1840s as a route between Fort Brown in Brownsville and Fort Ringgold in Rio Grande City, when soldier traffic increased as a result of the Mexican-American War, when it would become known as the Military (Telegraph) Road.

Despite the multiple hairpin turns characteristic of the Rio Grande, steamboats were barreling up and down the river as trade opportunities improved. Entrepreneurs Mifflin Kenedy, Richard King, and Brownsville founder Charles Stillman were heavily invested in riverboat transportation by the 1850s, with twenty-six steamboats operating through the Civil War years.[5] Steamboats were preferred over movement by road, as land travel took twice as long than by water.[6] In addition to the increased traffic of goods that moved up and down the river, other business opportunities arose adjacent to the landings, such as cut wood stations used to fuel the steam engines necessary to propel the river vessels.[7]

With the close of the Mexican-American War in 1848, the center point of the Rio Grande's channel became the international border (also known as the Emory-Salazar Channel). The pathways traveled along the river were referred to as *Los Caminos del Rio* with continued use of Spanish as the prominent language. Traversed by foot, on horseback, or via riverboat, these thoroughfares became the lifeblood of the region. Population grew slowly as merchants and professionals from all over the world took a chance at a new adventure of life along the newly established border. On January 24, 1852, Hidalgo County was founded across from the Mexican town of Reynosa, with a total of 2,356 square miles carved out of portions of eastern Starr County and western Cameron County.[8] The county seat was settled in the original eighteenth century village known to local inhabitants as *La Habitacion*. This location later became known as *Rancho San Luis*.[9] It was then dubbed "Edinburgh" in honor of the homeland of local, successful Scottish merchant John Young, who had arrived in Matamoros in 1836 and made his way westward to expand his land and cattle holdings and to increase his merchant business.[10]

Edinburgh was a bustling place. Trade and commerce grew in conjunction with the increase in steamboat traffic. With ferries to accommodate travelers across the river and a customs house to monitor trade, various other businesses emerged with the arrival of bold entrepreneurs. White men such as Eliju Dwight (E. D.) Smith, a lawyer and merchant from Connecticut, arrived in Matamoros in 1840 and moved upriver to Reynosa, where he continued to operate a store and built the first cotton gin in the Rio Grande Valley.[11] In 1842, he bought all the acreage in Spanish land grant *porción* No. 71 originally granted to Narciso Cavazos on the northern bank of the Rio Grande opposite Reynosa and a few miles to the east.[12] After being forced out of Mexico as an American expatriate merchant at the close of the Mexican-American War, he crossed the river to reestablish himself on the US side of the border and settled in Edinburgh.[13] He returned to Brownsville in 1854 and shortly afterward sold his property, consisting of 5,565 acres of land, to Nathaniel Jackson on July 13, 1857.[14] Jackson paid $2,000 total, or 36 cents per acre.[15] The Jackson family and their ranch compound on the Rio Grande at the site of El Capote Ranch, equipped with a ferry landing, will be discussed in detail in the following pages.

As Mexico had abolished slavery in 1829, via Afro-Mestizo president Vicente Guerrero, the path to freedom for many African Americans was through Texas. Families of mixed races felt the crescendo of animosity and hate throughout the Southern states. While they were still free to do so, several of these families packed up their belongings and made their way to a place where they could settle in peace and escape quickly across the border if necessary. During the 1850s, the population of Texas increased threefold.[16] Even with the influx of new Texans, the percentage of slave owners was low and concentrated in east Texas, which was far from the temptation of escape over the border.[17]

Dreams of escape to a free land were prevalent among slaves throughout the American South. Texas slave communities grew in number, and many knew that the path to freedom was to cross the Rio Grande and then establish a new life in Mexico. Matamoros had "a reputation as a haven for runaways," and the "fluidity along the [newly established] international border" made the region appear as a "gateway to freedom and opportunity."[18] The number of escaped slaves had increased, so much so that US Army officials at border forts were ordered to "arrest any runaway slave attempting to cross the river."[19] The Fugitive Slave Act of 1850 put all slaves on notice. This law allowed for the capture and return of runaway slaves to their owners, but also after the US Supreme Court decision in *Prigg v. Pennsylvania* (1842), freedmen/women had cause to worry that they would be apprehended, regardless of their proof of freedom, and returned to servitude.[20] The population along the Rio Grande was so scattered and scant between Brownsville and points as far west as El Paso that liberation was easily attainable for runaway slaves upon arrival at the river. John Salmon "Rip" Ford, a Mexican War veteran who had become a Texas Ranger, was part of the military presence along the border in the years leading up to the American Civil War. Once Texas seceded from the Union on February 1, 1861, Ford earned the rank of colonel in the Confederate Army and was assigned to lead a cavalry patrol to protect the region between the Nueces and Rio Grande.[21] As his troops confiscated all military possessions from the opposition, they were well equipped to protect the area from hostile invaders.[22] Ford was very familiar with the region, having already traversed the terrain throughout the vast and desolate Nueces Strip. The community of Edinburgh was appealing to Ford because of its convenient location between the two military posts of Fort Brown and Ringgold Barracks. With a high-traffic ferry landing and customs brokerage station monitoring trade between Edinburgh and Reynosa, the local population grew as this location appealed to more settlers. Ford became an integral part of the community near Edinburgh when he married local merchant E. D. Smith's daughter Addie on March 31, 1861.[23]

Escape routes to Mexico were known among the slave communities in Texas. Although there were more routes on the Underground Railroad that led north into Canada, proximity to the southern US border seemed more appealing, with fewer pockets of population to encounter. US Army posts at Fort Brown, Fort Ringgold, Fort McIntosh, Fort Duncan, and Fort Davis were spread too far apart to effectively seal the border. With thousands of ads offering rewards for the capture and return of runaway slaves, numerous bounty hunters volunteered to facilitate the effort. Ford himself had often engaged in slave-catching expeditions on both sides of the Rio Grande and was a supporter of a movement called the Sierra Madre Republic, which was an effort to expand slavery through Texas and into Mexico.[24] In the mid-1850s it was feared that more than two hundred thousand slaves had escaped into Mexico. However, Ford offered a much smaller statistic: by his assertion, there were approximately four thousand runaway slaves south of the border, and at six hundred dollars per captured slave, he was determined to earn a substantial reward.[25] Santos Benavides of Laredo did not recoil from this opportunity either. As skilled horsemen with extensive knowledge of the region, these two soldiers were able to scout the terrain and intercept runaway slaves. Their connections were deep and solid in the Mexican interior, and neither of them would hesitate to traverse the border to retrieve runaways.

Felix Haywood, an ex-slave interviewed by the Works Progress Administration (WPA) as part of the Depression era's Federal Writer's Project, reported that "there wasn't no reason to run up North. All we had to do was walk, but walk south, and we'd be free as soon as we crossed the Rio Grande."[26] Clearly news spread throughout plantation communities that the porous nature of the landscape along the Rio

Grande facilitated the best chance for acquiring their freedom. Haywood further reported that "hundreds of slaves did go to Mexico and got on all right."[27]

The Texas Slave Narrative of Sallie Wroe revealed an account of her father's venture that portrayed a vivid and ironic story of crossing the Rio Grande during the Civil War. Her father and her three uncles were transporting bales of cotton to Brownsville via ox cart from their owner's plantation on Burdette's Prairie near Austin. Instead of waiting for their owner to meet them in Brownsville, they decided to roll one of the bales of cotton into the river and use it as a makeshift raft to cross the river.[28] Although modern cotton farmers confirm that it is not likely that a bale of cotton could actually float on water as this report claims, from a literary perspective it is fascinating that slaves chose to say that they rowed their way to freedom on top of the very commodity that had kept them subjugated for so long. Sallie recalled that her father "done git 'long fine with Mexico and he larnt to talk jas' like dem."[29] These former slaves made new lives for themselves in Mexico, learned to speak Spanish, and then returned for their families with some savings once slaves were officially emancipated in Texas on June 19, 1865, a date that would forever be known and celebrated annually as "Juneteenth."

When it came to runaway slave apprehension, the climate in Texas was discussed in newspaper articles and advertisements in many cities across the state. In a city such as San Antonio, located above the periphery of the region known as the Nueces Strip, slavery did exist, sparingly, and was a less prominent institution than in east Texas or other parts of the country. Runaway slaves were even less of a problem in this city not too far from the international border. Even though slaves were not happy with the circumstances of their existence, those slaves in the San Antonio region were not interested in running away. "The paid notices found in the city's newspapers of owners seeking runaways revealed that runaway slaves were not a problem in San Antonio."[30] However, there were some slaves and their offspring who were already emancipated by their owners, living within established and growing communities across the nation's Southern states. Slowly and steadily, the attitude of white people toward blacks, whether freedmen or slaves, was growing to be one of hate and marginalization. To complicate social status even more, mixed race families were increasing in numbers, and acceptance was moving from distant tolerance to animosity. With *Prigg v. Pennsylvania* (1842) and the Fugitive Slave Act of 1850 inspiring dishonest slave brokers to capture freed black men, women, and children and illegally sell them back into slavery, a run for the border looked more and more appealing. Word of established trade routes through the Mexican port towns of Matamoros and Camargo made the sister settlements of Brownsville and Rio Grande City quite attractive, but the slightly populated region that eventually became Hidalgo County was even more appealing for those who really wanted to make a fresh start. There were already forty-five ranches in existence in Hidalgo County once it was founded in 1852, and as commercial venues emerged, up sprang the perfect place to capitalize on opportunities that began on the ground floor of a new frontier.[31]

In order to paint a picture of the physical US-Mexico border landscape during the 1850s and 1860s, one must consider the route by which one would travel to get there. Arriving by land meant traversing the largely unpopulated Nueces Strip. Such an overland adventure entailed riding on horseback and pulling wagons that contained all of the family's belongings. The journey from the north meant passing through Austin and San Antonio (Bexar), or through Houston, Victoria, and Goliad. During this period of time, when the concept of Manifest Destiny lured land buyers and speculators toward westward expansion, many of them traveled via boat to Point (Port) Isabel near the mouth of the Rio Grande and commenced their journey by first moving south toward Monterrey, Mexico.[32] News of the California gold rush in 1849 also drew travelers to the region. Gold seekers, known at the time as forty-niners, arrived in Point Isabel via steamship in order to embark on the riverine trail up the Rio Grande in order to connect with the Gila Trail and make their way toward the West Coast. Travel by water up the Rio Grande was more appealing to some pioneers who could afford it in order to avoid the arduous overland trek.[33] In several cases, adventurers were convinced to stay; planting roots, they found sufficient means to survive comfortably. Clans such as the Champion family arrived in the region from Italy with the idea of pushing farther west. However, this family of brothers instead planted roots in the Rio Grande Valley by marrying local women and building ranching lives for themselves and their growing families.[34] Others who might venture upon life along the Rio Grande would have followed early trails that led to and from the salt lakes in northern Hidalgo County and eventually lead to Brownsville, Rosario, and Camargo. Why, then, would well-traveled persons choose to settle in a quiet and unassuming riverside ranch setting instead of a more cosmopolitan place at the time, such as Brownsville or Rio Grande City?

One such person who chose to plant roots in a riverside ranch was John Ferdinand Webber, the patriarch of a mixed race family that settled along the banks of the Rio Grande in the early 1850s. Webber, whose parents immigrated to America from England, was born in Vermont in 1794. He served in the War of 1812 as a private and a medic in Capt. S. Dickinson's Company, 31st US Infantry, and fought in the battle of Shadage Woods.[35] He arrived in Texas in 1826, where he was a member of Stephen F. Austin's original settlement called Austin's Colony—the first legal settlement of North American families in Mexican-owned Texas.[36] By 1832, Webber was a landowner; by 1839, his portion of land was known as Webber's Prairie.[37]

After Webber's arrival in Texas, he had an affair with Silvia Hector, who was his neighbor's slave. This tryst resulted in a pregnancy. Webber was a man of high moral and ethical standards and respected this relationship by marrying her and subsequently purchasing her freedom. Silvia's owner, John Cryor, "drove a sharp bargain" in the sale of his property, knowing how important it was to Webber to honor his actions and assure that his children be born to a legitimate union.[38] Together, John and Silvia had their first child, who they named Elsie, in 1829. Two more children, Henry and John, were born before Webber finally secured Silvia's freedom in 1834. John and Silvia had a total of eleven children; all but the two youngest were born while living in Webber's Prairie.[39] The Webbers' social status was constricted within the colony because of their mixed race marriage and their mulatto children. They acknowledged their position and kept to themselves. Interaction with local African Americans resulted in strong prejudices toward them as well. They were respected by some of their fellow citizens; white women of the settlement did not outwardly treat Silvia poorly, and she was fondly called "Puss" by her neighbors. Whenever the Webbers had visitors in their home, Silvia cooked meals and served their guests as if she were still a slave. Her neighbors were known to view her with respect and quoted as stating "if you are good enough to be Mr. Webber's wife, then surely you're good enough to sit down to the repast you have spread."[40] Despite the awkward circumstances of their family life, they remained in Webber's Prairie for more than twenty years. Even though some white settlers in Webber's Prairie were polite to Silvia, there was a contingent of new settlers who wanted to "rid the settlement of its founder and his family of mullato [*sic*] offspring."[41] It became difficult for John Webber to educate his children. He hired a gentleman from North Carolina named Robert G. McAdoo, who lived with the family as the children's private tutor.[42] No longer able to accept the cruel prejudice and discriminatory treatment toward his family, he decided to relocate to Mexico.[43]

Previously, Webber had often traveled south and further into Mexico, crossing the Rio Grande peddling tobacco. Entering into business ventures with fellow colonists Noah Smithwick, Clay Coppedge, and Silvia's owner John Cryor, they had often embarked on trips south across the Rio Grande at Laredo, past the Presidio del Rio Grande, and onward toward a Mexican settlement called San Fernando.[44] One could surmise that the multiple experiences Webber had crossing the desolate plain between Webber's Prairie and the Rio Grande were instrumental to his confident departure for the newly formed international border in the early 1850s. Although his intention was to relocate his family south of the river in Mexico, his familiarity with the region, knowledge of parallel settlements, and acquaintance with merchants and business persons along the Rio Grande provided him a logical choice for relocation. Moreover, once the Mexican War had ended in 1848, the "no man's land" of the Nueces Strip became appealing to several ambitious settlers.[45] The presence of the Texas Rangers along with US troops at the close of Mexican-American War gave American settlers a faint sense of security as they traversed the region toward the new border, thus hoping to take advantage of trade opportunities in a sparsely populated area.[46]

Having arrived in 1851, the Webbers strategically planted roots close to the terminus of the growing town of Edinburgh. This site was also conveniently located across the river from active trading partners in the Mexican town Reynosa. Traveling with them were three of John Webber's cousins John, Peter, and Andrew, who then continued their journey farther east along the river to settle in the more established and sophisticated Mexican city of Matamoros, where they married local women and built lives for themselves.[47] Two years later, after the establishment of the new county of Hidalgo, John Webber purchased two leagues of land (8,852 acres) within the Agostero del Gato land grant a few miles east of Edinburgh and built their homestead along the riverbanks south of what is today known as Donna, Texas. Shortly afterward he bought additional acreage on the nearby La Blanca tract. In order to assimilate to the region, John Ferdinand Webber became known as Juan Fernando Webber. He licensed a ferry stop at his Webber Ranch on the Rio Grande in an effort to increase his opportunities for trade.[48]

This ferry may have played a key role in the Underground Railroad into Mexico. Sylvia Webber's prior status as a slave, as well as that of her first three (mulatto) children born before John Webber married her and purchased their freedom, would have given her a natural affinity toward those seeking freedom. It would have been natural, then, for them to offer assistance to those seeking asylum across the river, and this service would have been greatly facilitated by having a ferry landing on their private property.

The Webbers were Union sympathizers during the Civil War. The ease of travel back and forth across the international border afforded Unionists a quick escape out of the country as long as they had ample warning that Col. John Salmon "Rip" Ford and other Confederate soldiers were nearby. Ford himself noted that the Webber family had "closed the doors [on his soldiers] and refused admission until [Colonel] Ford came."[49] Confederate soldiers took two of Webber's sons as prisoners. One escaped and went to Fort Brown to inform the Union troops that "Ford had only sixty odd men."[50] Despite the warning, the federal forces were underprepared for the encounter and had to retreat across the river.[51] As Confederate patrols passed near their family's property, the Webber boys often put up resistance and created difficulty for them.

Once the American Civil War was over, Juan Fernando Webber reestablished his family ranch on the US side of the border and continued to participate in economic trade along the river. He collected his pension from the US government for his military service to his country and managed his acreage until a few years before his death. He passed away in 1882, and his wife Silvia passed away almost a decade later in 1891. There is a family cemetery on the property that is maintained today by family descendants.

While the Webbers were settling in to a new life along the Rio Grande, other mixed-race families were making their way there, too. In 1857, a caravan of frontier settlers made their way from Alabama to the southern tip of Texas. Living in the Southern states prior to the American Civil War, Georgia native Nathaniel Jackson and the families that joined him had been experiencing rising ill will toward African Americans as events moved forward toward the impending secession of the Southern states. As illicit apprehensions of freed slaves increased as a result of the Fugitive Slave Act, other events going on south of the border were enticing settlers to start fresh.[52] There were seven families in the group that emigrated to the US frontier. At the time of the move, Jackson was living in Wilcox County, Alabama, with his family and the slaves that he had emancipated. One of those slaves was his wife, Matilda Hicks. Matilda had three adult children from her previous marriage: Myria, Nancy, and Emily. Together, Nathaniel and Matilda had two daughters named Matilda and Lucinda, and five sons named Columbus, Elli, Bryant, Martin, and John. The Jacksons, together with the Campbell, Champion, Hicks, McHaney, Miller, Rutledge, and Singleterry families, packed up their belongings and left their homes in Alabama behind. They were accompanied by seventeen freed slaves. After two months of maneuvering their covered wagons through unchartered territory, the adventurous party found a resting place at the southernmost boundary of the United States a few miles east of the newly established Hidalgo County seat, along the banks of the Rio Grande, a few miles west of John Webber's ranch. Soon after their arrival to the region, Jackson bought property and established a farming community where his family flourished. The accompanying families settled nearby, and all members assimilated into the local community, marrying either a fellow member of their band or within the established Tejano ranching families.

Nathaniel Jackson's family continued to expand after the establishment of the Jackson Ranch near El Capote Ranch on the Rio Grande. Equipped with a ferry landing that was one of the first licensed in Hidalgo County in 1852, the Jackson Ranch was also a stop on the Underground Railroad, according to family folklore.[53] Nathaniel and Matilda's children became integral parts of the Jackson Ranch and surrounding community. Sons Eli Jackson and Martin Jackson assumed leadership roles within the community upon Nathaniel's death in 1865. US Census records of 1860 and 1870 in Hidalgo County illustrate how newly formed families emerged via marriages of the Jackson children. Nancy (Smith) Jackson was married to Abraham Rutledge. Emily (Smith) Jackson was married to Samuel Singleterry, and after Samuel's death, she married John Dorsey, formerly of the 117th USCI.[54] Martin Jackson, after his first wife's death, married into local established Tejano ranching families: he first married Albina Cano, who died in childbirth, and then married Espiridiona Carillo.[55] There were also marital connections forged with mixed race families already living in the region. Elsie Webber, for example, married John Jackson. Rachel Amanda Webber was married to James Singleterry, son of Samuel Singleterry (white) and Emily Jackson (black). These like-minded families mixed well together, married, and procreated, deepening the mixed race lineages amongst themselves.

Standing firm on their nonprejudicial outlook on life as a mixed race family, the Jacksons boldly created a new multiracial, multicultural, and multiheritage community in a special and unique corner of the world. This community was bound together through Nathaniel's strong religious beliefs, with the fundamentals of the Methodist religion at its core. Perhaps the reason that the Jackson family and their followers did not venture farther across the border into Mexico was because Catholicism was the dominant religion there, and Nathaniel Jackson's firm devotion to the Methodist doctrine caused him to go no farther. Also, with the Webber family living nearby, the choice to stay and plant roots made sense. Their dedication to the moral grounds of family unity, no matter what skin color, was readily acceptable during a time when this region of the US was still shaping its identity. Once the Civil War broke out in 1861, the Jackson family denounced the Confederacy even though their homeland was embedded in the Southern states. Nathaniel had strong feelings of opposition to the idea of secession.[56] Due to their African American lineage, their sympathies were with the Union side of the battle. Still, the Jacksons were tolerant of all people, no matter their beliefs or status.

Despite this apparently affable atmosphere of racial comity, relationships and loyalties were complicated. For example, according to the 1860 US Census records for Hidalgo County, Texas, Abraham Rutledge was a thirty-eight-year-old farmer who owned one thousand dollars of real estate with a personal estate valued at six hundred dollars.[57] Listed below Abraham's name on the 1860 census is Nancy Jackson, a twenty-nine-year-old mixed race female born in Alabama. The Rutledge children are listed as mulatto or mixed race persons and recorded as follows—Harriet, 19; Manuel, 17; Sarah, 12; Nancy Ann, 14; Esau, 8; Martha Jane, 6—all born in Alabama. Louis, 3; Robert, 1½; and James Gilbert, 1 month, were born in Texas. On December 18, 1863, in contrast to the pro-Union views of the riverside enclave of interracial families, Rutledge mustered into the Confederate militia as a private in Capt. William D. Thomas's company of Partisan Rangers.[58] Along with several other farmers and property owners from ranches along the Military Road, Rutledge spent four months in Confederate service. His ownership of property could have been the reason that he took up arms with a legitimate armed unit—perhaps oblivious to which side of the conflict was represented—that recruited other nearby landowners who wished to protect their property.

Just as the community along the lower Rio Grande became more complicated by the settling in of Mexican-American War veterans after 1848, veterans who served in the region during the Civil War added a new presence when that conflict ran down in 1865. Again, the mixed racial and multiethnic nature of communities, as well as the potential for economic success along what remained a relatively open frontier, served as a magnet for new settlement.

Dr. William J. G. T. Brewster was originally from New Haven, Connecticut, and was a surgeon during the Civil War for the Union army. He settled near the mixed race enclave of the Jackson Ranch after having been stationed at a Union camp near Edinburgh in 1860. According to his great granddaughter, Stella Brewster de Alba, Dr. Brewster was "a wanderer and enjoyed steamboat travel and had many friends."[59] In 1866, he married Minerva Smith Singleterry, step-granddaughter of Nathaniel Jackson, and together they raised a family on the adjacent property known as El Sauz Ranch.[60] He was a schoolmaster in Hidalgo, as well.[61] Dr. Brewster had a medical practice in Matamoros across from John McAllen's general merchandise shop.[62] In 1881, during an outbreak of influenza, he contracted the disease, died, and was buried in Matamoros.

Thomas J. Handy was a Union soldier, born in Ohio, who mustered into Company F, 4th Wisconsin Cavalry, and was later promoted to sergeant.[63] "During the Civil War, courier stations were established at intervals of twenty miles, from Brownsville to Laredo, through which semi-weekly mail runs were transmitted."[64] Handy was a part of this service and was responsible for the Cuevitas Ranch station near Sullivan City. In addition to carrying mail for the Union army along the Military Highway, Handy's other responsibilities included "enforcement of revenue laws with frequent scouting expeditions to protect the many residents and their property from Indians and other marauders."[65] Apparently, at some point, Handy's duties took him to a place located in between the Jackson Ranch and Webber Ranch properties, a tract now known as the Santa Ana Wildlife Refuge. This property, originally granted to Benigo Leal by the Mexican government in 1834, was an active ranch prior to the arrival of the mixed race clans that settled nearby. Adjacent to the Santa Ana Ranch was the Asaderos Ranch, which was owned by Salvador Cavazos, a descendant of original Spanish land grantee José Narciso Cavazos. Handy married Salvador's daughter Angelita on April 25, 1866, and settled near her family's property as "a rancher, farmer and a mounted US Customs agent."[66] He was discharged from military service in June 1866 and bought a tract of land in 1878, referred to by the US Department of Agriculture as the Handy Tract. This tract of land contains two hundred acres beginning at the river's edge and crossing just north of the military road. It was here that Thomas and Angelita established the Esperanza Ranch, and they are buried in a cemetery on this property.

Another neighbor of veteran status residing among the mixed race families along the Rio Grande was Lina H. Box. Born in Blount County, Alabama, Box moved to Texas with his family in 1834. His father, John Andrew Box, was a military veteran who fought at the Battle of San Jacinto.[67] "On June 23, 1861, at the age of twenty-nine, Lina enlisted in Captain John Woodward's Company G, 1st Regiment Texas Infantry, in which he served as a private and later as a fifth sergeant."[68] He fought in four Civil War battles in Texas and later was discharged due to kidney illness. Although it is unclear exactly when Box arrived in South Texas, it is believed that he moved to Hidalgo County just after the Civil War was over; he was elected as the Hidalgo County Clerk in 1866. He purchased land in between the Jackson and Webber compounds on Rancho El Sauz, near the Brewsters. A political leader within the community, Box, a lawyer by profession, represented land and ferry investors.[69] He also served as the US Customs Deputy Collector and Inspector.[70] In 1869, Box married Martha Jane Rutledge, the mulatto daughter of

*Left: Studio portrait of Thomas J. Handy, Company F, 4th Wisconsin Cavalry, standing with sword and pistol in belt. Courtesy of the Wisconsin Historical Society. Right: Angelita Cavazos de Handy and Thomas J. Handy, with son Chancey, in 1866. Courtesy of the University of Texas Rio Grande Valley Special Collection Archives.*

Abraham Rutledge and Nancy Smith Jackson. After Martha passed away, he then married Louisa Singleterry in 1874.[71] These were interesting unions, inasmuch as Box was loyal to the Confederate cause and both Martha and Louisa were mixed race persons. Box, however, was drawn to this particular settlement near Hidalgo because of his devotion to the Methodist Church. Although the Methodist Church on the Jackson Ranch was not officially built until 1874, the Jackson family's devotion to Methodist teachings was a draw to those who wished to follow the same. Box died on August 7, 1881, in the home of Alexander J. Sutherland, the founding Methodist preacher of the Jackson Ranch Church.[72] It appeared that on the Jackson Ranch and surrounding properties along this sliver of land at the southernmost edge of the United States, folks were not viewed or judged by the color of their skin nor by their loyalty to the Union or the Confederacy. Rather, the value of successful subsistence farming, the protection of property, and simple dedication to living a clean, wholesome life was what set this community apart.

For one hundred years prior to the emergence of the mixed race enclave that blossomed at this location on the US frontier, the majority population along the river's edge was composed of a group of Spanish colonists who were a mixture of (European) white, mestizo, mulatto, and indigenous peoples. As recently as only fifty years ago, a person of Mexican American heritage was listed as white on his/her birth certificate even though there was clearly a blending of races. This legal declaration was in striking contrast to how they were labeled in society and, more importantly, how they viewed themselves. If you look at photographs of the descendants of mulatto persons who resided in this region during the Civil War era, it is difficult to immediately recognize their mixed race background. Regardless of race or ethnicity, these folks were Americans, and the image of what defines a person as an American has a very special meaning in this border society.

*Christina Webber (right), granddaughter of John Ferdinand Webber, circa 1915. Courtesy of the University of Texas Rio Grande Valley Special Collections Archives.*

When meeting with descendants of the Webbers and Jacksons, many visually present themselves as Mexican American. Most are not dark skinned and do not have hair the texture of one who is African American. Some, however, have natural skin color that is darker than most in this region. William Baize, a Jackson family descendant, has noted that there are significant differences between some relatives who particularly have the texture of hair generally associated with African Americans. He noted that as generations move along, there are less distinct markers present.[73] Sylvia Webber Ortiz reported in an interview that her father, Santiago Webber, had told her to not be surprised if someday one of the babies born into the family had hair the texture of a black person.[74] Lupe A. Flores, a descendant of intermarriage among the Jackson, Brewster, and Webber families, expressed that while the formation of a complex identity defines his family and their roots, most have not forgotten their black ancestry but rather choose to identify themselves as Mexican, even though they have been US citizens dating back five generations. He has learned a lot from observing his grandmother and conversing with her. He found that she and other relatives simply identify with their Mexican roots and speak Spanish as their native language in the home.[75] These descendants know that there is African American blood in their lineage. Even though they accept it, they choose not to define themselves by it. William Baize further confirms that his family members still present in the Rio Grande Valley continue to identify as Mexican. He indicates, "For the longest time, we were thinking Jackson was a Mexican name. I grew up thinking, 'Hey, it's a Mexican name,' and then I got into college and someone says, 'No, that's not a Mexican name.'"[76]

Today, Webber family members, for example, have been able to trace their relatives as members of sixty extended families with more than one thousand members. Descendants of the Webber clan still live in the region in towns such as Donna, Weslaco, and Brownsville. On Saturday, March 10, 2012, the National Society of the United States Daughters of 1812 Capt. Virgil McCracken, Chapter #376, conducted a dedication ceremony of a military headstone for Pvt. John Ferdinand Webber at the Webber Ranch Cemetery. Located below the Mil Acres Tract at Krenmueller Farms south of Military Highway, Hidalgo County Historical Commission officers Frances Isbell and Glenn Housley were present with many Webber family members to offer the historical remembrance and unveil the military headstone marker.

The evolution of the borderland person has blossomed into unique personae. Different blends of DNA profiles progress into truly unique human beings. One can traverse today's border landscape and find multidimensional persons living in an environment where cultures continue to converge and produce distinct features of a racially fluid society. In this region, where the majority of the population is characterized as Hispanic, one can easily encounter a blonde-haired, green-eyed, light-skinned person whose first language is Spanish. The dynamic of race and culture along the Rio Grande has acculturated over time. As escaped slaves reached for the international border in the mid-nineteenth century, their progress toward freedom often came by way of assistance from members of the Jackson Ranch and surrounding communities. Emancipated slaves found the Rio Grande to be a permanent dwelling place, a refuge in which to embark upon a new beginning. Their contribution to the racial chemistry of long-time Rio Grande Valley riverside residents, in combination with white colonial Spaniard settlers and Native American prehistoric and historic roots, has not only produced a unique caveat in the definition of what is American, but also how we perceive race in America.

## *Notes*

1. Armando C. Alonzo, *Tejano Legacy: Rancheros and Settlers in South Texas, 1734–1900* (Albuquerque: University of New Mexico Press, 1998).

2. Hidalgo County District Clerk, *Commissioners Court Meeting Minutes* (Edinburgh, September 2, 1852), 3.

Also note that the village of San Luis, also known as La Habitacíon, was founded in 1774 across from the final resting place of Reynosa, Mexico, and on the site that became Edinburgh and is now Hidalgo, Texas. It appears that the county commissioners granted ferry licenses to the similar properties of Edinburgh and Saint Louis (San Luis). Reynosa Viejo, or the original location where Reynosa was founded, is located across from Penitas, Texas. Due to heavy flooding of the Rio Grande during early settlement years, Reynosa was moved downriver to a location of higher elevation to avoid certain future floods.

3. Hidalgo County District Clerk, *Commissioners Court Meeting Minutes* (Edinburgh, November 1857 and August 1859), 50, 58.

4. M. J. Morgan, *Border Sanctuary: The Conservation Legacy of the Santa Ana Land Grant* (College Station: Texas A&M University Press, 2015), 128.

5. Ibid., 87.

6. Ibid., 84.

7. Ibid., 85.

8. Frank Cushman Pierce, *A Brief History of the Lower Rio Grande Valley* (Menasha, WI: George Banta Publishing Co., 1917).

9. Ana Cristina Downing de Juana, "Intermarriage in Hidalgo County 1860–1900" (master's thesis, University of Texas–Pan American, July 1988), 29.

10. Mary Margaret McAllen Amberson, James A. McAllen, and Margaret H. McAllen, *I'd Rather Sleep in Texas: A History of the Lower Rio Grande Valley and the People of the Santa Anita Land Grant* (Austin: Texas State Historical Association, 2003), 4.

11. "Major Elihu Dwight Smith: 1796–1868," SFAA Genealogy, http://strongfamilyofamerica.org/genealogy/getperson.php?personID=I06665&tree=dwight_2012_01_01 (accessed July 25, 2015).

12. Francis W. Isbell, "Jackson Ranch Church" (typescript, December 1982), Hidalgo County Historical Commission, Edinburg, TX, 8.

13. Congressional Series of United States Public Documents, Index to the Miscellaneous Documents of the House of Representatives for the Second Session of the Fifty-Third Congress 1893–94 (Washington: Government Printing Office, Vol. 3267, Issue 4, 1895), 3339–40.

14. Hidalgo County Courthouse, Deed Records Book A, 315–17.

15. Isbell, "The Jackson Ranch Church," 8.

16. Charles David Grear, *Why Texans Fought in the Civil War* (College Station: Texas A&M University Press, 2010).

17. Randolph B. Campbell, "Slavery," *Handbook of Texas Online*, https://tshaonline.org/handbook/online/articles/yps01 (accessed June 28, 2016).

18. James David Nichols, "The Line of Liberty: Runaway Slaves and Fugitive Peons in the Texas-Mexico Borderlands, *Western Historical Quarterly* 44, no. 4 (2013): 414, 416.

19. Joseph W. Cote, "Pathways of Freedom: Rethinking the Underground Railroad 1810–1865," Dr. Martin Luther King Task Force Inc., http://freedomexhibit.org/virtual/ (accessed June 20, 2015).

20. For further details about the *Prigg* decision, see Paul Finkelman, "Story Telling on the Supreme Court: *Prigg v. Pennsylvania* and Justice Joseph Story's Nationalism," 1994 *Supreme Court Review* 247 (1995): 247–94.

21. McAllen Amberson et al., *I'd Rather Sleep in Texas*, 179.

22. Ibid.

23. John Salmon Ford, *Rip Ford's Texas*, ed. Stephen B. Oates (Austin: University of Texas Press, 1963), 332.

24. Nichols, "The Line of Liberty," 421.

25. Cote, "Pathways of Freedom," 2.

26. "Texas Slave Narrative: Sally Wroe," Roots Web, http://freepages.genealogy.rootsweb.ancestry.com/~ewyatt/_borders/Texas%20Slave%20Narratives/Texas%20W/Wroe,%20Sallie.html (accessed June 20, 2015).

27. Cote, "Pathways of Freedom," 2.

28. "Texas Slave Narrative: Sally Wroe," Roots Web, http://freepages.genealogy.rootsweb.ancestry.com/~ewyatt/_borders/Texas%20Slave%20Narratives/Texas%20W/Wroe,%20Sallie.html (accessed June 20, 2015).

29. Ibid.

30. Bruce A. Glasrud, *African Americans in South Texas History* (College Station: Texas A&M University Press, 2011), 38–39.

31. Frances Isbell, *Hidalgo County Ranch Histories* (Edinburg, TX: Hidalgo County Historical Commission and Hidalgo County Historical Society, 1994), 3.

32. Museum of South Texas History, Margaret H. McAllen Memorial Archives, Closner Ramsey Collection, Champion file, Champion Familia C folder.

33. Ibid.

34. Ibid.

35. Andrew Forest Muir, "Webber, John Ferdinand," *Handbook of Texas Online*, http://www.tshaonline.org/handbook/online/articles/fwe59 (accessed June 20, 2015); and Isbell, *Hidalgo Ranch Histories*, 128.

36. Christopher Long, "Old Three Hundred," *Handbook of Texas Online*, http://www.tshaonline.org/handbook/online/articles/um001 (accessed July 04, 2016).

37. In 1853, a few years after Webber relocated his family to the Rio Grande Valley, the village's name changed to Webberville.

38. Noah Smithwick, *The Evolution of a State* (Austin: University of Texas Press, 1983), 166.

39. US Bureau of the Census, Travis County, Texas, 1850 United States Federal Census, August 29, 1850, 6.

40. Museum of South Texas History, Margaret McAllen Memorial Archives, Closner Ramsey Collection, 88.66.2/5A, Webber folder.

41. Ibid.

42. 1850 United States Federal Census, Travis County Texas, 6.

43. Smithwick, *Evolution of a State*, 166.

44. Ibid., xx.

45. Fred Rippy, "Border Troubles along the Rio Grande, 1848–1860," *The Southwestern Historical Quarterly* 23, no. 2 (1919): 92.

46. Ibid.

47. Museum of South Texas History, Margaret McAllen Memorial Archives, Closner Ramsey Collection, 88.66.2/5A, Box 9, Webber folder, Micaela Webber and Florencio Bravo papers.

48. Isbell, *Hidalgo Ranch Histories*, 128.

49. Ford, *Rip Ford's Texas*, 362.

50. Ibid.

51. William J. Hughes, *Rebellious Ranger; Rip Ford and the Old Southwest* (Norman: University of Oklahoma Press, 1964), 309.

52. By 1851, more than three thousand fugitive slaves lived in Mexico, many of whom lived between the Sierra Madre Orientale mountain range and the Rio Grande. The Mexican government was enticing the African American population to settle there with the promise of free land without slavery. See Rosalie Schwartz,

*Across the Rio to Freedom: US Negroes in Mexico* (El Paso: Texas Western Press, 1975), 33. In 1853, Benito Juárez was completing his exile in New Orleans and planning his return to rule in Mexico. Sympathetic to the indigenous peoples and against slavery, Juárez made it clear that African Americans would be welcome in Mexico upon his return. In 1857, Luis N. Fouché, a free negro from Florida, was granted land in Veracruz in exchange for filling this agricultural colony with one hundred negro families. This settlement was referred to as the Fouché Migration and was developed on the trade route along the coast on the Gulf of Mexico between New Orleans, Veracruz, and the Caribbean Islands. See Schwartz, *Across the Rio*, 49–50. Perhaps these events were what led the Jackson family and friends to make the journey toward the US-Mexico borderlands.

53. Isbell, "Jackson Ranch Church," 4.

54. Museum of South Texas History, Margaret McAllen Memorial Archives, Closner Ramsey Collection, 88.66.2/5A, Jackson Folder.

55. Isbell, "Jackson Ranch Church," 5.

56. Ibid., 4.

57. US Bureau of the Census, Hidalgo County, *1860 US Federal Census*.

58. Palo Alto Chapter no. 2382, United Daughters of the Confederacy, Dedication of Military Headstone for Private Abraham Rutledge, CSA, November 2012.

59. Stella Brewster de Alba, letter to the author, February 12, 2016.

60. Note: The Brewster-Bravo Cemetery is located at the southern most point of Steward Road, as the road becomes caliche, on the border of San Juan and Alamo, over the levee and to the east.

61. Frances Isbell, "Brewster Ranch Cemetery," Hidalgo County Historical Society, Cemeteries of Texas, January 1980, Cemeteries of Texas, accessed October 27, 2017, http://www.cemeteries-of-tx.com/Etx/Hidalgo/Cemetery/brewster.htm.

62. Brewster de Alba, letter to the author, February 12, 2016.

63. Samuel Handy Ybarra and Delia Handy Ybarra, *Handy Anthology: Handy Family Genealogy; History, Documents, and Photos* (Hidalgo County, TX: Blurb Incorporated, 2008), 3.

64. Ibid., 40

65. Ybarra and Ybarra, *Handy Anthology*, 40.

66. Ibid., 3.

67. Museum of South Texas History, Margaret McAllen Memorial Archives, Bexar County Historical Commission, Descendants to Honor Confederate Veteran press release, Closner Ramsey Collection, 88.66.2/5, Genealogy/Biographies Files, Box 2, C, Box Family Vol. II Folder.

68. "Descendants to Put Marker on Box's Grave," *Valley Morning Star*, October 13, 1981, A2.

69. Hidalgo County District Clerk, *Commissioner's Court Meeting Minutes* (Edinburgh, January 7, 1867), 97.

70. Museum of South Texas History, Margaret McAllen Memorial Archives, Ramsey Collection 88.66.2/5, Genealogy/Biographies Files, Box 2, C, Box Family

Vol. II Folder, Bexar County Historical Commission, press release "Descendants to Honor Confederate Veteran."

71. Louisa Singleterry was the daughter of Samuel Singleterry I and Emily Smith. Emily Smith was the daughter of Nathaniel Jackson's wife Matilda Hicks from her first marriage. Louisa was considered mulatto or mixed race in the 1860 census because her mother was black and her father was white.

72. Museum of South Texas History, Margaret McAllen Memorial Archives, Closner Ramsey Collection, 88.66.2/5, Genealogy/Biographies Files, Box 2, C, Box Family Vol. II Folder, Hidalgo County Historical Commission, letter from Frances Isbell to Mr. J. Gilberto Quezada, September 13, 1891.

73. Santos Jackson Baize and William Baize, interview by Roseann Bacha-Garza, Baize home, Edinburg, TX, Border Studies Archive: University of Texas Rio Grande Valley, January 13, 2016, 3.

74. Sylvia Webber Ortiz, interview by Roseann Bacha-Garza, Ortiz Home, Weslaco, TX, Border Studies Archive: University of Texas Rio Grande Valley, January 2016, Weslaco, TX.

75. Conversation between Lupe A. Flores and Roseann Bacha-Garza, University of Texas Rio Grande Valley, Border Studies Archive, June 15, 2016.

76. Baize interview, 4.

# 5

# *Separate Wars and Shared Destiny*

## Mexico and the United States, 1861–1878

IRVING W. LEVINSON

On a map, borders usually appear as bold and clear lines separating nations, linguistic groups, ethnicities, and economies. While those lines enable us to divide the world into distinct units, the reality we live with is not always so neat. Those borders also identify meeting places in which encounters, both planned and unanticipated, take place, and in which destinies once largely separate become intertwined. The Rio Grande Valley of the United States and Mexico is one such region.

During the first decades of the nineteenth century, the two nations pursued different paths of national development with critical decisions about those paths made in places far from the Valley. But during the 1860s and 1870s, the internal conflicts that wracked both Mexico and the United States resulted in first temporarily and then, I think, permanently intertwining two national destinies. We may best study these developments by considering them in three distinct segments. The first consists of events dating from the colonization of each nation up to the outbreak of the US Civil War. Since most English-speaking readers are familiar with the history of the United States, I will concentrate on the less well-known Mexican national narrative.

From the start of that nation's independence in 1821 until 1917, Mexico's history in large part consisted of interminable struggles of democracy versus plutocracy, of church versus state, of centralism versus federalism, of the Eurocentric versus the indigenous, and of the rule of law versus the rule of the *caudillos*.[1] The catalyst for all these struggles was the successful effort of Spain to create a highly structured (and fractured) colonial establishment along socioeconomic, cultural, and racial lines.

The Spaniards, who totaled less than 1 percent of the population, regarded themselves as physically and culturally superior to the remainder of the colony.[2] Accordingly, they reserved for themselves almost all of the senior positions in the administrative, judicial, and religious hierarchy of the colony. Below them stood the native-born whites, or *criollos*, who comprised some 17 percent of the population. During the final half century of the colonial era, the Spanish restricted criollo participation in politics to the municipal level and imposed additional layers of taxation and political surveillance.

The Indians, who composed about 60 percent of the population, suffered greater exclusion. Those who resided in the self-governing *Repúblicas de los Indios* (Indian Republics) exercised limited local autonomy under the leadership of communal elders whom the Spanish nonetheless subjected to ongoing repression and monitoring. Those residing outside of these republics rarely exercised any such authority. Since the days of the Spanish conquest, they found themselves largely consigned to the most difficult of labors and the lowest of wages.

Those of mixed ancestry, known as *mestizos*, made up most of the remaining 22 percent of the colonial population. Although individual mestizos could gain a measure of status by acquiring property or other forms of wealth, they rarely if ever found themselves accepted by the other major groups. The process of uniting the non-Spanish against the ruling minority would have proved a challenging task for the most talented of rebels. Mexico's independence movement did not enjoy the benefit of such leadership.

In 1810, a violent rebellion erupted under the leadership of Father Miguel Hidalgo y Costilla. Enshrined in Mexican memory as the father of the nation's independence, Hidalgo sought to empower the nation's disenfranchised majority and to redistribute much of the estate (hacienda) land upon which the colony's economy and social structure rested.[3] However, he lost control of his ill-trained forces almost as soon as they had gathered. As Hidalgo's followers marched from the central Mexican community of Dolores toward Mexico City, they burned estates en route. When they reached the great fortress of the *Alhondiga de Granaditas* at Guanajuato City, they found many of the region's

Spaniards, criollos, and other citizens with property sheltered within its walls. When Hidalgo's force broke through the main gate, they massacred everyone inside, regardless of age or gender.[4] In an instant, the war against Spain morphed into a conflict of white against brown, of Eurocentric against indigenous, and of rich against poor. As Hidalgo's ragtag army proceeded southward toward an unsuccessful effort to take Mexico City, his forces destroyed haciendas and forced their owners to flee for their lives. Such conflicts always became quite savage, and by the end of the struggle in 1820, an estimated six hundred thousand Mexicans lay dead.[5]

The war ended without a clear rebel victory. Indeed, the turning point came with the 1820 promulgation of a Spanish constitution that included a provision granting suffrage to all men other than those of African ancestry. The implementation of such a provision in Mexico would have transferred power to those who had joined Hidalgo. Rather than accept that fate, the leading officers of the royal army's forces in Mexico mutinied and signed a truce with the now-despondent rebels. Under the terms of the resulting Plan of Iguala, Mexico would become an independent monarchy with an official religion.[6] This plan did not specify the rights of citizens, an omission that served as further confirmation of the undemocratic intent of its authors. Therefore the Mexican war for independence resulted not in a revolutionary regime, but in a reactionary one. Two political parties emerged.

The more powerful of the two, *los Conservadores* (the Conservatives), held that the events of 1810–21 served as a grim confirmation of three essential truths: First, the majority of men did not possess the capacity to rule themselves and should not be allowed to do so. Second, humans remained fallen creatures who require a state religion with powers buttressed by the civil government to ensure their eternal salvation. Third, a strong and central authority must rule that Mexican society in order to achieve the two preceding objectives.

Their opponents, *los Liberals* (the Liberals), deemed all men fit to participate in government with the *puro* (pure) faction of this party, contending that such voting rights should be granted immediately with the *moderado* (moderate) faction arguing for universal education as a prerequisite to that status. Purists and moderates also differed in the depth of their hostility to the one permitted religion. The former sought to abolish the monopoly status enjoyed by the Roman Catholic Church and to confiscate much of that institution's wealth, while the latter viewed the Church with considerably less hostility. However, both purists and moderates regarded the state or regional governments rather than the national government as most fit to exercise the preponderance of political power. These struggles of autocracy versus democracy, church versus state, and central government (centralism) versus strong state government (federalism) would dominate Mexican life for decades.

The first effort at compromise, the Constitution of 1824, proved inadequate.[7] To satisfy the Conservatives and Moderates, the writers of that document declared the Catholic faith the only religion permitted in Mexico and gave the central government considerable power. To satisfy the Liberals, state governments received a substantial degree of autonomy. The new constitution left the critical task of determining who could vote to the states and failed to address the widespread illiteracy or the stark and extreme polarization of wealth that characterized Mexico. Subsequent events illustrated another critical problem: the central government did not have the power to subdue the caudillos.

Emerging from the chaos and economic ruin of the war of independence, the caudillos possessed the political, economic, and physical force necessary to dominate a community—be that a village, a municipality, a state, or the nation. They possessed the power to overthrow elected governments and frequently did so. The first such *coup d'etat* took place in 1829, as rebellious Liberal caudillos overthrew recently elected president Manuel Gomez Pedraza. From then until 1836, the presidency changed hands on nine occasions, often violently. By 1835, the Conservatives decided that conditions required the gutting of the 1824 Constitution. Their amendments, known as the Seven Laws (*Siete Leyes*) abolished the state and municipal governments and so transferred all administrative authority to Mexico City. This legislation also curtailed civil liberties and subsequent laws restricted suffrage to barely one percent of the population.[8]

Widespread rebellion broke out, and in the ensuing chaos, successful secession movements erupted at both geographic extremities of the nation. To the north, part of the state of Coahuila y Tejas waged a successful war of independence and emerged as the Republic of Texas (1836–45). In the south, the Republic of Central America declared independence and after a brief time, divided into the present-day nations of Guatemala, Honduras, El Salvador, Nicaragua, and Costa Rica.

From 1836 onward, Liberals and Conservatives continued their struggle. The next major eruption came in 1844 in the form of armed conflict between the powerful Liberal caudillo of Oaxaca, Juan Alvarez, and his Conservative counterpart, Nicholas Bravo. The latter, acting at the behest of President Antonio López de Santa Anna, sought to seize part of Alvarez's territory. That struggle came to an abrupt end as Alvarez called upon the peasants of his region to aid him. As they did in the time of Father Hidalgo, the peasants soon began burning estates and putting their owners to flight. Alvarez and Bravo consequently put aside their differences to crush this uprising.[9] Once again, those ruling Mexico received a reminder of the shaky ground upon which the socioeconomic structure stood.

As war with the United States approached, desperate Conservatives sought to build a sense of national unity by reinstituting the 1824 Constitution. The effort failed. When war came in 1846, many Mexicans failed to answer the call to arms unless their particular state suffered invasion. At the critical battle for Mexico City, the Liberal Alvarez disobeyed Santa Anna's order to launch a flank attack on the advancing Americans and instead took his three thousand man force back to Acapulco, thereby conserving them for the next round of civil conflict. In the countryside, multiple rebellions led by Indians and other peasants broke out. These rebellions intensified as the ability of the Mexican Army to crush such uprisings diminished with each defeat at the hands of the US Army.[10]

In 1853, a mere four years after the end of the war with the United States, Alvarez initiated a Liberal revolt that finally evicted the Conservatives from power in 1855. Two years later, the victorious Liberals wrote a constitution as uncompromisingly purist as the Seven Laws had been uncompromisingly conservative.[11] Their Constitution of 1857 abolished the Catholic Church's religious monopoly, seized all Church assets other than the churches themselves, established universal male suffrage, provided for a broad set of civil liberties, abolished remaining legal privileges of the Church and armed forces, and otherwise tore down the legal foundations of the Conservative state.

Unsurprisingly, the Conservatives' response in 1857 was the same as the Liberal response in 1836: armed rebellion. From 1857 until Christmas Day of 1860, the two sides fought the War of the Reforma. This ended in a Liberal victory. Yet the greatest loser in this process proved to be the Mexican nation.

Almost four decades of civil conflict had devastated the country. The fields that lay fallow and the mines that had flooded by 1821 often remained that way. Continuing violence meant that by 1848, one in four Mexican women was a widow. In the absence of a unified state, the infrastructure necessary to develop a nation remained unbuilt, the financial stability required for growth failed to emerge, the technological resources needed to join the industrializing world never developed, and the educational and political maturation required for modernity remained unrealized. Indeed, not until 1856 did the gross national product reach the colonial-era peak. Many of Mexico's leaders, and in particular the caudillos, were enemies of their own nation's welfare. Above all, Mexico required peace. Yet there would be no peace, and here the second segment of this essay begins with a review of events that took place during the US Civil War of 1861–65 and Mexico's War of the French Intervention (1861–67).

Mexico's war began on December 17, 1861, as Spanish troops

*Benito Juárez, president of México from 1858 to 1872 and victor in the War of the Reforma and the War of the French Intervention. Library of Congress Prints and Photographs Division, LOT 3112, no. 81.*

occupied both Veracruz and that city's harbor fortress of San Juan de Ulúa. On January 3, 1862, British and French warships arrived in support of this invasion. Ostensibly, attackers sought to force the Liberal government of Benito Juárez to reverse his July 17, 1861, default on an 82.2 million peso foreign debt. However, the objectives of French emperor Napoleon III went far beyond the collection of debt. Indeed, barely 3.5 percent of the Mexican debt was owed to France.[12]

Napoleon sought nothing less than the reestablishment of a French presence on the North American mainland and the creation of a political and cultural counterweight to the dominant British and Anglo-American ascendancy of the era. Domestic Mexican political considerations also influenced his decision to invade.[13] Monarchist sentiment within Mexico had survived both the demise of Spanish rule and the decades of internecine civil war following independence. In 1856, a monarchist faction sent two agents to Europe to solicit candidates for the throne of Mexico.[14] The outcome of the War of the Reforma only strengthened their convictions that European participation would be vital. In Paris, a small but vocal community of self-exiled Mexican Conservatives amplified the call for foreign intervention, and Napoleon received multiple assurances that Mexicans would welcome his efforts. He intended to create this new sphere of influence by combining French military power with that of the defeated but still defiant Mexican Conservatives. The latter assured both the French emperor and the prospective ruler of Mexico, Ferdinand Maximilian Joseph von Habsburg, that a substantial body of public opinion in Mexico would support the imposition of an imperial form of government.[15]

Given such assurances, the French began marching westwards from Veracruz. On April 19, 1862, the British and Spanish ships at Veracruz set sail for home, thus separating themselves from the would-be conquerors. Although Mexican forces under the command of Gen. Ignacio Zaragoza repelled the invaders at the famous May 5, 1862, Battle of Puebla, the French returned in 1863 with a far larger force, and on May 17 of that year took Puebla and soon thereafter entered Mexico City. On April 10, 1864, Maximilian received the crown offered by a carefully selected assembly of Mexican Conservatives.

The Liberal government and many Conservatives rejected the new regime and continued fighting in a conflict known as the War of the

French Intervention (1862–67). The Liberals often referred to themselves as "Juaristas," in deference to their leader Benito Juárez, or as "Republicans." Their opponents referred to themselves as the "Imperialists."

Under normal circumstances, the United States would have vigorously and, if necessary, violently opposed the reestablishment of European sovereignty on its southern border. However, the US Civil War that began with the Confederate bombardment of Fort Sumter on April 12, 1861, fully occupied Washington's attention. Indeed, during 1861 and 1862, considerable doubt existed as to whether or not the Confederacy could be subdued. The chain of events that would bring Mexico's latest civil war and the United States' first civil war together began barely two weeks after the fall of Fort Sumter, when President Abraham Lincoln declared a blockade of all Confederate ports.

As the Union Navy grew from a mere 90 warships at the start of the war to 650 vessels, the blockade became more effective.[16] The fall of the Confederacy's major port at New Orleans on May 1, 1862, rendered the South's dual task of importing war materiel and exporting the agricultural products necessary to pay for such supplies even more difficult.[17] Inevitably, the Confederate leadership sought an alternative, and they found one in the Rio Grande Valley.

Officials in Richmond realized that if much of the vital transoceanic trade flow could be diverted to a point on Mexico's Gulf coast close to the Texas border, then the material would flow northward and the agricultural exports could move in the opposite direction unimpeded by the Northern blockade.[18] By definition, a Union blockade of a Mexican port would constitute an act of war, and the Union had no need of an additional enemy, be that enemy France or Mexico.

The Confederates soon found an ideal choice: Matamoros. Located across the river from Brownsville, this city lay less than twenty miles from the Gulf of Mexico. Very quickly, Confederate partisans gave a strip of Gulf beach east of the city the grand name of Bagdad, and trade soon prospered. In the bitter words of the US consul in Matamoros, the route from that ersatz town to Matamoros became "the great thoroughfare to the Southern States."[19]

This opportunity for the Confederacy posed a dilemma for President Juárez. A *Puro Liberal* since his earliest days, he had played a prominent role in the opposition to the reactionary Siete Leyes, championed the cause of Alvarez and other Liberals who successfully forced Santa Anna from power in 1855, drafted many of the provisions of the Constitution of 1857, led the Liberals to victory in the War of the Reforma, and sternly opposed the inherently oppressive and hierarchical hacienda system throughout his adult life. To him, the Confederate plantations and the slave labor upon which they depended resembled the hierarchical and polarized society of conservative Mexico he so despised. Few if any Mexicans felt more sympathetic to the cause of the Union than he. Yet by late 1861, other considerations impinged upon those natural sympathies.

First, import and export taxes could add a significant amount of revenue to the inadequately filled coffers of his treasury. More grimly, the north of Mexico and in particular in the coastal state of Tamaulipas, as well as the adjacent state of Nuevo Leon, remained places in which the caudillos exercised a considerable amount of power.[20] For almost a century, many Tamaulipans and Nuevo Leoneses of commerce and industry eagerly generated cross-border trading profits, regardless of royal or Republican trade regulations promulgated in Mexico City. During the US Civil War, their behavior would not change.

The caudillo of Nuevo Leon and Chihuahua, Santiago Vidaurri, entrusted many of his interests in this matter to his son-in-law Patricio Milmo, who operated the most influential business in the area. Patricio soon established powerful economic ties with the leading Confederate entrepreneurs across the river. Two of the most prominent members of that group, Richard King and Mifflin Kenedy, reflagged their steamboats as Mexican vessels so they could ply the coast as well as the river with impunity. By the end of the war, Confederate shippers had transported 320,000 bales of cotton to Bagdad.[21] The cash value of that cotton was some $128,000,000, and the sale of this raw material enabled the Confederacy to buy goods of vital importance: the impedimenta of war.[22] One steamer alone, the *Love Bird*, carried 14,200 Enfield Rifles, 5 million rifle caps, 2 million rifle cartridges, and 156 revolvers.[23] In an important gesture of support for the Confederate cause, the French posted 400 of their naval infantry in Bagdad.[24]

Vidaurri initially maintained a position of neutrality in the contest between the forces of Maximilian and those of the Mexican Republic. In the conflict between the Union and the Confederacy, his sympathies lay with the Confederates, but only to the extent that he rarely allowed such

*Capt. Richard King, rancher and caudillo of South Texas. Courtesy of the King Ranch Archives.*

sentiment to stand in the way of profit. In later years, he recognized the authority of Maximilian. That decision subsequently cost Vidaurri his life; when Juarista forces under the command of Gen. Porfirio Diaz entered Monterey, they arrested him and, on July 8, 1867, executed him.[25]

The activities of lesser caudillos further compromised the Mexican government's authority. In Matamoros, Juan Cortina, who bore a fierce hatred toward Anglo-American Texans and who had led the Cortina Revolt in South Texas, held sway.[26] Although that earlier revolt ended with his flight to Mexico, his family's substantial holdings and influence, as well as Cortina's status as a folk hero who resisted Anglo-Americans, gave him a powerful base of support. Those assets, and the friendships he subsequently established with Mexico's Liberals, enabled him to function with considerable impunity during and after the War of the French Intervention. Some of the taxes collected in his jurisdiction never reached the Juaristas, and Cortina was not above staging cross-border raids.

A third caudillo, José Maria de Jesús Carbajal, also operated in Tamaulipas. When his 1840 effort to establish a Republic of the Rio Grande consisting of the states of Tamaulipas, Nuevo Leon, and Chihuahua failed, he converted from federalist to centralist and served as an officer in the national army.[27] During the conflict against France, he commanded a Juarista division. Although far more honorable than Vidaurri, his conduct nonetheless illustrated the extent to which the loyalties of powerful men shifted during this era.[28]

*Gen. Nathaniel Prentice Banks, commander of the Union forces that invaded at Brazos de Santiago. Library of Congress.*

So from the Franco-Mexican conquest of Mexico City on April 10, 1864, to the surrender of the last imperial forces on May 15, 1867, the struggle between the European invaders and the Juaristas dominated political considerations in northern Mexico while caudillos simultaneously jockeyed for power among themselves and with the Republican government of Mexico, now based in El Paso del Norte, Chihuahua. On the US side of the Rio Grande Valley, the dominant struggle remained the Confederate effort to keep the trade route to Bagdad and Matamoros open in the face of Union efforts to close them.

On November 2, 1863, the United States invaded the Rio Grande Valley by landing six brigades under the command of Gen. Nathaniel Prentice Banks on Brazos de Santiago Island. Although the invaders seized Brownsville, they did not advance far enough upriver to take either Laredo or Eagle Pass. Consequently the cotton trade shifted westward, albeit with costs increased by 50 percent.[29] A Confederate effort to drive the Union forces out of the Valley began on April 17, 1864, and ended with the fall of Brownville on July 30 of that year, as isolated Union infantry garrisons fell one by one to a far smaller Confederate cavalry force led by Col. John Salmon "Rip" Ford.

On the Mexican side of the Valley, the forces of the Imperialists and the Republicans also entered the Valley. Since their triumphant 1864 march into Mexico City, the French gradually learned to their dismay that a nation of 758,499 square miles divided by three major mountain ranges, further divided by deserts and tropical jungles and populated by largely hostile inhabitants, could not be controlled by the expeditionary force of 35,000 French soldiers and their 20,000 Mexican auxiliaries.[30]

However, the events of greatest concern to the French took place far to the north of the Rio Grande Valley. By late 1864, the Confederacy no longer stood as a barrier between Mexico and a US government hostile to French ambitions. The Southern triumphs at First Bull Run, Fort Royal, Winchester, Fredericksburg, and Chancellorsville failed to break the Union's will, and after the final Confederate invasion of the north ended in defeat at Gettysburg, US forces pushed southward, seizing Atlanta in early 1864. The French realized that they soon would confront a hostile and very powerful presence on Mexico's northern border.

In addition, Maximilian alienated many Mexican reactionaries by engaging in conduct acceptable in Europe, but wholly unacceptable to them. For example, he refused to comply with a conservative desire to return all of the Church assets seized by the Juaristas. Instead, he expressed a willingness to "sanction legitimate operations provided they are implemented honestly and in strict observance of the law which decreed the proceeding against Church property."[31]

Similarly, he refused to ban the practice of religious creeds other than Roman Catholicism. He ordered the cabinet minister responsible for such matters to "finally act in accordance with the principles of the broadest and freest tolerance and continually hold before your eyes the fact that the state religion is Apostolic Roman Catholicism."[32] Mexican Conservatives did not wish to act in accordance with principles of tolerance. Instead, they wanted a return to the provision of the Seven Laws and the 1824 constitution, which stated: "The Nation will protect it [Apostolic Roman Catholicism] by wise and just laws, and prohibit the exercise of any other whatever."[33]

Further, Maximilian issued a decree annulling all private debt of less than ten pesos. While the emperor was no doubt correct in assuming that Europeans would consider this an act of *noblesse oblige*, he did not realize that Mexican hacienda owners used such small debts as a means to keep peasants in debt peonage.

The situation on the battlefield mirrored the waning political support for the Imperialist cause. After initial triumphs seizing major cities such as Acapulco, Guadalajara, Oaxaca, Mazatlan, and Monterrey, and chasing Juárez's internally exiled government as far north as El Paso del Norte, Chihuahua, the French and their Mexican allies found themselves facing highly mobile and well-led Mexican army columns and guerrillas.[34] In desperation, Maximilian signed the Black Decree, an October 3, 1865, order directing the execution of all Republican soldiers and guerrillas upon capture. This did not reverse the tide of war.

To the Imperialists' dismay, critical US aid for the Juaristas began arriving in very substantial amounts following the April 9, 1865, surrender of Gen. Robert E. Lee's army. With the Civil War now concluded, Washington could apply undivided attention and resources to the French presence in Mexico. The United States, and in particular Ulysses S. Grant and Philip Sheridan, had long viewed the French invasion of Mexico as a blatant violation of the Monroe Doctrine, undertaken by a government in clear sympathy with the Confederate cause.[35] Both of those Union commanders believed that their own nation's civil war would not be over until the last of France's soldiers

*General Philip Henry Sheridan. Sent to Texas with fifty thousand troops, he succeeded in convincing the French of the likelihood of US intervention in Mexico. Library of Congress Prints and Photographs Division, LC-BH82-4012 B.*

and the emperor they supported, Maximilian, left Mexico. They now acted accordingly.

Grant sent Sheridan and 25,000 troops to Texas not simply to "restore Texas, and that part of Louisiana held by the enemy to the Union in the shortest practicable time" but to render assistance to the Juaristas and convince the French that war with the United States was imminent if they did not withdraw.[36] Sheridan later wrote, "During the winter [of 1865] and spring of 1866, we continued covertly supplying arms and ammunition to the Liberals—sending as many as 30,000 muskets from the Baton Rouge Arsenal alone."[37] Additional actions included sending uniformed and mounted scouts into Mexico to gather information about the terrain and the Imperial forces and the ex-Confederates who had crossed the Rio Grande. Sheridan decided to go "to Brownsville myself to impress the Imperialists, as much as possible, with the idea that we intended hostilities."[38] Sheridan very publicly opened communications with Juárez and "prepared them [his forces at San Antonio] with some ostentation for a campaign."[39] As a final touch, he assembled a pontoon bridge at Brownsville for potential use of his forces. Grant aided in the effort by sending an additional 25,000 men to Texas. US forces in Texas also engaged in several violent actions.[40]

Simultaneously, Napoleon III found himself facing increasing domestic opposition to his Mexican project. Increased Juarista resistance and the Union's conquest of the Confederacy convinced French politicians of all political parties that their troops should return home.[41] On April 11, 1866, Napoleon III ordered all French troops in the interior to retreat to Mexico City. Later that year, he advised Maximilian to give up the throne and return to Europe.[42] He decided to remain, arguing that a Habsburg never abandoned his throne.

Less than two months after that French withdrawal southward, on June 2, 1866, Republican general Mariano Escobedo inflicted a crippling defeat on the remaining imperial forces in northeastern Mexico. At the battle of Santa Gertrudis/Cervalo, his combined force of 1,500 infantry and 500 dragoons destroyed the substantial forces escorting two supply convoys vital to a continued imperial presence in Nuevo Leon and Tamaulipas. His troops killed 396 of the enemy, wounded 165, took hundreds of prisoners, and seized eight pieces of artillery and more than 1,000 muskets while suffering only 155 fatalities.[43] The Rio Grande periphery of the empire soon crumbled, with the last imperial troops departing Matamoros three weeks later on June 23, 1866, and sailing from Bagdad two days later.[44]

This victory might have ended formal hostilities in the Valley. But the caudillos proved unwilling to holster their weapons. For example, in August 1866, Juárez ordered the arrest of Gen. Servando Canales for having abandoned Matamoros in the face of an imperial assault and sent Gen. Santiago Tapia to replace him. In response, Cortina declared himself governor of Tamaulipas.[45] The two rebels joined forces.

Following Tapia's death due to cholera, Juárez sent Escobedo to Matamoros in early November with orders to reestablish federal authority. Given the uncertain situation, the US consul in Matamoros requested a US force to protect American citizens and property. In response, Gen. Thomas Sedgwick sent nine companies of troops into the city, where they remained until December 1, 1866. On that day, they evacuated at the request of Escobedo, who promptly began a bombardment and soon took control of the city.[46]

Even when not defying the central government, caudillos often sought to accumulate as much power as possible. Before his untimely demise, Vidaurri had remained so territorial that at one point he had accumulated 10,000 rifles and a dozen cannons for use in resisting any encroachment upon his power.[47]

The Republicans continued their attacks throughout Mexico. By early 1867, their ranks grew to some 60,000 men, with their Imperialist foes now reduced to half that number.[48] In April, 28,000 Juarista troops under the command of Gen. Porfirio Diaz liberated Mexico City after a lengthy siege.[49] Maximilian then gathered his remaining forces in Querétaro, where he and 7,000 soldiers soon came under siege. On May 15, Juárez announced the fall of Querétaro, and scarcely more than one month later, on June 19, 1867, the former emperor, Gen. Tomás Mejia, and Gen. Miguel Miramón fell before a firing squad.

Sadly, the end of hostilities between national armies did not bring peace to either side of the Valley. Consideration of this 1867–77 period constitutes the third section of this essay.

On the northern side of the Rio Grande, the economic collapse catalyzed by the 1865 downfall of the Confederacy continued. Undoubtedly, the end of the wartime cotton trade represented the greatest single economic loss, and this loss affected northeastern Mexico as well.

On both sides of the river, substantial numbers of military deserters

*Porfirio Diaz, caudillo of Mexico and president from 1876 to 1880 and from 1884 to 1911. Library of Congress, Prints and Photographs Division, LC-USZ62-10027.*

from the Confederate, Union, Imperialist, and Juarista armies, as well as unconquered indigenous bands, inflicted a considerable level of violence on the civilian population. The federal governments of both nations failed to control their territory. Given the debilitated state of the national government and economy, Mexico City's control over much of Mexico remained partial in 1867.[50] Many urgent priorities required government attention, and the task of destroying the power of the numerous and habitually uncooperative caudillos did not rank as the highest priority. Indeed, a caustic observer might well have noted that much of the Liberal party's strength traditionally flowed from such regional power bosses.[51] In addition, the Mexican Army faced high desertion rates because of irregular pay, a politicized officer corps, and supplies so irregular that the soldiers used fourteen different patterns of small arms.[52]

Across the river, Union forces occupied Texas. However, a sweeping demobilization soon reduced the US Army to a shadow of the powerful Civil War juggernaut. As late as 1877, only 2,522 soldiers guarded both the western and southern frontiers of Texas. Of those, 678 were infantry soldiers, who were of little if any use in pursuing mounted raiders. By contrast, the minimum deemed necessary for controlling the southern frontier of Texas were 4,000 troops.[53] The lack of cross-border cooperation between the national or state authorities did not improve matters.[54] Local law enforcement proved similarly weak.

While many in the United States preferred to think that cross-border violence was of Mexican origin, a significant body of evidence points to substantive raids launched from US territory by Anglo-American and Mexican American gangs. That material, gathered by a select committee of Mexican legislators, documented a variety of Texan practices identical to those of which the US accused Mexicans.[55] Upon reviewing that report, John Watson Foster, the US Ambassador to Mexico and future US Secretary of State, cited the Mexican authors for their "fairness and impartiality."[56]

In that report, the Mexican commissioners cited ongoing refusals by Texas judges to punish Americans for engaging in cross-border raiding and the refusal of US courts to honor warrants of arrest issued by their Mexican counterparts. Further, they alleged that leading US *hacendadoes* (hacienda/estate owners) and men of commerce, such as Adolphus Glaevecke and Richard King, bore responsibility for organizing cross-border looting expeditions. Other documented complaints included repeat purchases by US citizens of cattle stolen by Indians from Mexican ranches and haciendas, and a general failure of Texas authorities to control the border area.[57] Lastly, repeated excesses committed by Texas Rangers left many in as much fear of those enforcing the laws as of those violating them.[58]

The results of this were summarized by Jonathan Evans, a representative of the Great Northern Railway Company: "At that time it was not considered safe for any man to travel alone, and every one carried arms for his own defense. As provost-marshal, it was my duty to aid the civil authorities in the execution of the laws. I found the civil authorities wholly powerless to sustain themselves against the flood of thieves and desperadoes who swarmed across the river on their mission of pillage and murder."[59]

Local law enforcement in Mexico proved equally inept. As the US consul in Matamoros pointed out, the problems in large part flowed from the absence of competent local authority to perform a range of activities.[60] However, the two sides of the Valley still shared a common and largely Mexican heritage. As one US cavalry officer assigned to the area wrote: "This country on the Rio Grande is a queer place. . . . I should judge that at least nine-tenths of the population . . . are Mexicans. . . . All of the interests of the people are with Mexico. All of the trade . . . is with the interior of Mexico. . . . We receive from Mexico all the commerce of these posts here."[61]

Like a three-legged stool, the economy rested on bases consisting of haciendas, ranchos, and the small community of merchants. Those *comerciantes* made their livelihood by doing more than transporting finished goods to and raw materials from the countryside. Utilizing the advantages of the free trade zone previously created by the Mexican government, they also made considerable profit from the import and export trade of Monterrey and much of the north of Mexico.

On both sides of the Rio Grande, the haciendas remained the dominant economic and political institution, with the ranchos playing a secondary role. Those Anglo-Americans who migrated to South Texas in the wake of the 1836 Texas War of Independence and the 1846–48 war between Mexico and the United States did not seek to destroy that structure. Rather, they sought a place for themselves as Anglo-American hacendados and *rancheros*. Indeed, the traditions of *patronismo* familiar to Spaniards and Mexicans would become features of life on the ranches of men such as Richard King and Mifflin Kenedy.[62] For both Anglo-Americans and Mexican Americans, as well as Mexicans, patronismo, predicated on an agrarian economy, would remain a dominant feature of life until the end of the nineteenth century and, in many instances, well into the twentieth century.

Both hacienda owners and merchants had demonstrated a high level of adaptability to changing situations. For example, after the conclusion of the 1846–48 war, the mercantile houses of both northeastern Mexico, be they in Monterrey or Matamoros, accelerated their participation in land development and sought to earn profits from the changed circumstances.[63] In Nuevo Leon, prominent comerciante Patricio Milmo joined with Evaristo Madero and the mercantile house of José San Ramon to forge profitable cross-border linkages.[64]

During the 1857–60 War of the Reforma, the US Civil War, and the 1861–67 War of the French Intervention, the intertwined rural and urban leaders of the Valley suffered no long-term threat to their dominance. Some of them managed to profit from the situation, with perhaps the best-known example being the profits earned by both Santiago Vidaurri and Richard King from the cross-border cotton trade during the US Civil War.

In Mexico, the weakening of national administrative structures usually resulted in regional elites strengthening their power.[65] The vacuum created by the collapse of intra-Mexican trade during the War of the French Intervention enabled astute caudillos who could provide a semblance of order with opportunities to expand their authority.

So in 1867, the transnational Rio Grande Valley was a hierarchical, agrarian, socially polarized community of predominantly Mexican origins and culture with an Anglo-American minority reflecting a similar level of economic and social polarization. On both sides of the river, prominent hacendadoes enjoyed considerable autonomy. Through a complex chain of events, the caudillos on both sides of the border united to end the violence.

That process began soon after Mexico's 1875 presidential contest between two great heroes of the War of the French Intervention, Sebastian Lerdo de Tejada and Gen. Porfirio Diaz.[66] Unwilling to accept his electoral defeat and convinced that his loss in part resulted from electoral fraud, Diaz began accumulating resources for the traditional remedy of dissatisfied caudillos: a violent overthrow of the government. In New York City, he met with American investors who would welcome a new regime in Mexico City. The group included James Stillman, who was president of the National City Bank and a son of Charles Stillman, founder of Brownsville.[67] Diaz gained their support and, accompanied by one of Stillman's lawyers, proceeded to South Texas. There, in February 1876, he met with local financiers and regional hacendadoes led by Richard King at Kingsbury, Texas. They agreed to provide Diaz with weapons, munitions, capital, and the space necessary to equip and train an armed force. In return, Diaz promised to pacify the border, to grant the Americans substantial concessions for Mexican rail and agricultural development, and to honor previous commitments placed in abeyance by the Lerdo de Tejada government.

During the preparation for that invasion, Diaz lived quite openly in Brownsville, residing in the house built by the town's founder, Charles

*The Stillman House in Brownsville, Texas. Built by the founder of Brownsville, this residence later served as Porfirio Diaz's home while he planned the overthrow of the Mexican government. Photo by the author.*

Stillman. Only after repeated Mexican protests did President Rutherford B. Hayes issue a March 9, 1876 order, calling for the detention of Diaz.[68] Even then, a period of three weeks passed before the US government was prepared to implement the order. At that point, Diaz launched his attack on Matamoros and began his successful campaign to overthrow Mexico's elected government on April 1, 1876. On that day, he crossed the river and took Matamoros with little opposition. Although he subsequently suffered a series of tactical defeats in April and May of that year, Diaz rallied his forces and, having obtained additional supplies in both Matamoros and Brownsville, subsequently overthrew the elected government of Mexico.[69] He would keep all of his commitments to the Americans, particularly those concerning border security. Both nations soon intensified their commitment to pacify the region.

In mid-1877, Diaz gave two of Mexico's most powerful caudillos, Gerónimo Treviño and Servando Canales, the authority and the troops necessary to end the disorders caused by smugglers, bandits, filibusterers, and of course, Indians.[70] In doing so, Diaz began a successful policy of co-opting rather than crushing caudillos. The success of this particular tactic stands as perhaps the principal cause of his retaining power for more than thirty-four years.[71] The most powerful of northern Mexico's dynasties, the Terrazas, subsequently accepted similar terms.[72]

On the US side of the frontier, disgruntled supporters of ousted Mexican Pres. Sebastian Lerdo de Tejada received shipments totaling 1,000 rifles and $12,000 in gold. An American Valley caudillo and former colonel of the Confederate army, Santos Benavides, sent some of these across the border to his Mexican cousin, Gen. Garza Ayala, and to the senior Lerdista general, Mariano Escobedo. Soon an American force of 1,500 men led by Col. Ranald Mackenzie set out to subdue the Lerdistas on both sides of the Rio Grande. When he tried to carry this mission into Mexico, he advanced no further than the Rio Grande. There he encountered a force of one hundred Mexicans under Col. Jesús Nuncio, who informed the US commander of his order to repel any incursion onto Mexican soil.[73] Mexico now stood committed to securing her own territory from both external invasion and internal disorder. The situation remained volatile as the two national armies sought to restore order or, perhaps for the first time, to establish order in their nations' respective border territories. The challenge involved not only Mexican and United States raiders, but also indigenous tribes.[74]

In all this, a potential for a larger conflict lay in unforeseen incidents, as well as in a deliberate clash between armed forces. One particularly tense incident that took place during September 1878 involved the successful escape of two convicted Mexicans from the Rio Grande City jail, the ensuing murder of the jailer and his wife, and the murderers' subsequent crossing into Mexico. This prompted a sharp response from the US commander at Fort Ringgold, Maj. William R. Price. He took his entire force plus two Gatling guns and a detachment of Texas Rangers to the north bank of the river. There, Col. Francisco Estrada told him that if Americans crossed the border, war would begin.[75] Price did not cross, and the Mexican government soon extradited the two escaped criminals.

In spite of such events, both national armies achieved considerable success in controlling conditions within their territory, and this lessened the level of fear between the two states. Perhaps more importantly, President Diaz clearly understood that to have access to the flow of American technology and capital that he sought to start Mexico's modernization he would need to address American dissatisfactions. Indeed, pacification of the border region had been a prerequisite for the funding Diaz received from King and his group to overthrow Lerdo's government.[76] Lastly, Diaz and his lobbyist, Manuel Murphy Zamacona, joined with similarly minded Americans to convince President Rutherford B. Hayes of the benefits that would flow from converting Mexico from a suspect state into a market for American products and a source of raw materials.[77]

As tensions lessened, Diaz summoned the last Valley caudillo of that age, Juan Cortina, to Mexico City. There, Cortina accepted a pension and permanent surveillance instead of arrest. Treviño's forces subdued a number of Indian bands and border bandits, while the US Army brought the last of their nation's Indian Wars to their desired conclusion. In an ending appropriate for an opera, Governor Gerónimo Treviño of Nuevo Leon, the caudillo who had served as a member of the federal cabinet and who as commander of his nation's forces in northeastern Mexico had been preparing for a US invasion, stood in full dress uniform at the wedding of his forty-three-year-old son to the daughter of Gen. Edward Otho Cresap Ord, the commander of US forces in Texas.

A traditional sort of conclusion to this narrative would identify two roles that Mexico played in US Civil War. Most importantly, Mexico provided a blockade-free outlet for the trans-oceanic shipment of weapons and munitions from Europe to the Confederacy, and of cotton from the South to overseas markets. The dual consequences of this included both a prolongation of Confederate resistance and the Union decision to invade the Rio Grande Valley. The second role played by Mexico was that of a refuge for a mélange of people, including deserters from both armies, Union sympathizers, marauding Indians, and bandits of Mexican, Anglo American, and Mexican American ancestry.

Yet to end an assessment of the 1860s and 1870s with only those conclusions ignores a more important outcome: the linking of the US and Mexican economies because of the agreements made in New York and Kingsbury. Those pacts tied together one of the most powerful financial syndicates in the United States, the long-reigning dictator of Mexico, and the most powerful Anglo American caudillos in the Rio Grande Valley. The consequence proved nothing short of stunning.

By 1902, "a remarkable consortium of capitalists held 80 percent of Mexico's railroad stock."[78] American investors also held 80 percent of the capital of Mexico's mining industry.[79] Most significantly, the combined effect of the encouragement Diaz gave to foreign investors, as well as the technological and financial strength of US investors, enabled them to purchase 27 percent of the land in Mexico.[80] The roots of that expansion rested upon actions taken in Texas. Important Porfirians such as Yreno Longoria of Nuevo Laredo and Antoni [de] Balli of Tamaulipas joined American industrialists such as Ennis Cargill, James A. Baker, and B. F. Yoakum to form the Rio Grande Valley Land and Irrigation Company, an entity that acquired control of much valuable land on both sides of the river.

Although temporarily broken by the Mexican Revolution of 1910–17, these linkages would be reestablished starting in 1940. As of 2015, the United States again played a dominant role in Mexico's economic life, buying 77.6 percent of Mexican exports and selling Mexico more than half of all the goods and services that nation imports.[81] The binational linkages formed because of Diaz's seizure of power and the consequent US-led industrialization of Mexico survive to this day. The hundreds of billions of traded items and millions of people crossing that border each year are a continuation of the ties forged in this Valley in the year 1876. That relationship, rather than the battles of US Civil War, is the greatest inheritance of those years.

If there is one final lesson in this story, it is: do not obstruct caudillos (on either side of the Rio Grande)—for you are soft and moist and you taste very good with barbecue sauce, salsa, or mole.

## Notes

1. A *caudillo* is an individual who possesses the political, economic, and physical force necessary to dominate a village, municipality, state, or nation. A caudillo's power flows from both that base of power and from agreements made between similarly minded individuals and groups. The most famous caudillo in Mexican history is Antonio Lopez de Santa Anna, who held the presidency for eleven terms of varying length during the early and middle parts of the nineteenth century. The longest-serving caudillo was Porfirio Diaz, who held the Mexican presidency for more than three decades.

Another term requiring clarification is *federalism*. In the context of United States history, the word refers to the belief that the national government rather than the state governments ought to exercise preponderant power. In the Mexican context, federalism refers to the opposite: the conviction that the preponderance of political power should be at the regional or state level rather than at the national one. A Mexican who favored a strong central government would have labeled his philosophy as centralist.

2. The demographic figures in this paragraph and the two following paragraphs

are based on Fernando Navaro y Noriega's 1814 *Memoria sobre la población del reino de Nueva España*, as cited by Timothy Anna, *The Fall of the Royal Government in México City* (Lincoln: University of Nebraska Press, 1978), 6.

3. A hacienda is a largely self-sustaining agricultural estate of one thousand or more acres owned by a family or extended family and staffed by a mixture of tradesmen, resident peons, and day laborers. A variant, the *plantacion*, produced only a few crops, and those were largely for export. These estates often comprised several hundred square miles of territory. By contrast, a *rancho* (ranch) is an agricultural property of less than one thousand acres. Thus large US ranches such as the King Ranch or the XIT Ranch would be called *haciendas* in Mexico.

4. As remembered by the leading conservative intellectual of the era, Lucas Aleman, "This pillage was more merciless than might have been expected of a foreign army. . . . All that could be heard was the pounding by which the doors were opened and the ferocious howls of the rabble when the doors gave way. . . . The women fled terrorized to the houses of neighbors, climbing along rooftops without knowing if that afternoon they had lost a father or a husband at the granary." Lucas Aleman, *Historia de México* (Ciudad de México: Editorial Jus, 1942), 1: 403–4.

5. Catalina Sierra, *El Nacimiento de México* (Mexico City: D.F., 1960), 119, discussing the estimate of Jose Luis Maria Mora and cited by Hugh M. Hamill in "Was the Mexican Independence Movement a Revolution?," a paper delivered in Mexico City, January 29, 1976, and edited by Josefina Vasquez in *Dos Revoluciones*: *México y los Estados Unidos* (Mexico City, 1976), 47.

6. A copy of Plan of Iguala can be found in the compilation by Thomas Brabson Davis and Amado Ricon Virulegio, *The Political Plans of México* (Lanham, MD: University Press of America, 1987), 151.

7. The Constitution of 1824 can be reviewed at http://tarletonlaw.utexsa.edu/constitutions/text/AT1S.html. One of the first United States ambassadors dispatched to Mexico, Waddy Thompson, took note of the economic and ethnic disparities: "The lands of the country belong to a few large proprietors, some of whom own tracts of eighty and one hundred leagues square, with herds of sixty and eighty thousand head of cattle grazing upon then, whilst the Indian laborers upon those farms rarely have enough meat to eat. . . . It is a very great mistake to suppose they enjoy anything like a social equality, even with the Indian population; and although there are no political distinctions; the aristocracy of color is quite as great in México as it is in this country: and the pure Castillian [*sic*] is quite as proud that he is a man without 'a Cross' as was Leather-stocking, even if that cross should have been with the Indian race, however remote." Waddy Thompson, *Recollections of México* (New York: Wiley and Putnam, 1846), 12, 150.

8. The very severe restrictions on political participation were set forth by the Ministro de Relaciones Exteriores, Gobernacion y Policia in the Bases Generales (Mexico City, D.F), Archivo General de la Nacion, Ramo Gobernacion. Sin Seccio, 1846, caja 319, expediente 3, foja 1.

9. A complete review and analysis of the Alvarez rebellion is provided by John

Mason Hart, *The 1840s Southwestern México Peasant's War: Conflict in a Transitional Society*, included in *Riot, Rebellion, and Revolution*, edited by Friedrich Katz (Princeton: Princeton University Press), 1988.

10. Irving Levinson, *Wars within Wars: Mexican Guerrillas, Domestic Elites, and the United States of America 1846–1848* (Fort Worth: Texas Christian University Press, 2005).

11. A complete copy of the 1857 Constitution is in the compendium edited by Walter Fairleigh Dodd, *Modern Constitutions: A Collection of the Fundamental Laws of Twenty-Two of the Most Important Countries of the World, with Historical and Biographical Notes* (Chicago: University of Chicago Press, 1909), II: 39–78.

12. To be specific, Mexico owed 70,000,000 pesos to British financial institutions, 9,400,000 pesos to Spanish financial institutions, and 800,000 to French ones. David Marley, ed., *Wars of the Americas: A Chronology of Armed Conflict in the Western Hemisphere, 1492 to the Present* (Santa Barbara, CA: ABC-CLIO, 2008), II: 824.

13. Additional considerations included Napoleon's desire to recoup prestige lost as a result of his duplicitous conduct towards his Sardinian ally following the conclusion of the Franco-Austrian War in 1859. To his dismay, his Liberal French critics, now empowered by an 1859 amnesty, used the Mexican Intervention as an opportunity to criticize him. Jean Mayer, *Las Oposiciones Francescas a Expédition du Mexique*, in *El Poder y la Sangre: Guerra, Estado y Nación en la Decada de 1860*, ed. Guillermo Palacios and Erika Pani (Ciudad de México: El Colegio de México, 2014), 451–52.

14. Brig. Gen. Jésus de Leon Toral, *Historia Militar: La Intervención Francesa en México* (Ciudad de México: Sociedad Mexicana de Geografia y Estadistica, 1962), 9.

15. The British foreign secretary (and later prime minister) Lord William Russell remarked that the Mexican exiles in Paris were notable for "the extravagance of their hopes in respect to external intervention." Napoleon III would satisfy them, if only briefly. Ibid., 457. By contrast, French opposition to the project erupted from the start of the venture. Ibid., 454.

16. James Kirby Martin, Randy J. Roberts, Steven Mintz, Linda O. McMurry, James H. Jones, *America and Its Peoples* (New York: Pearson Longman, 2007), 396.

17. Although the port of Mobile did not fall to Union forces until August 23, 1864, the steadily tightening sea blockade prevented the constant flow of seaborne trade that would have been necessary to provide the South with the required sustenance.

18. In the Rio Grande Valley, plans for re-routing considerable overseas commerce through Mexico were being formulated even earlier. In August 1861, Charles Stillman, one of the founders of Brownsville, expected to ship all of Texas' cotton through Matamoros. Daddysman, *The Matamoros Trade*, 30.

19. Leonard Pierce Jr. to Secretary of State William Seward, March 1, 1862, OR, I, 9, 674, cited by Jerry D. Thompson and Lawrence T. Jones III, *Civil War and Revolution on the Rio Grande Frontier: A Narrative and Photographic History* (Austin: Texas State Historical Association, 2004), 40, 144.

20. "Weakened by years of civil war and foreign invasion, the Mexican central government had acquired a healthy respect for the power of the individual states . . . and consequently regional *caudillos* enjoyed considerable latitude." Richard H. Zeitlin, "Brass Buttons and Iron Rails: The United States Army and American Involvement in Mexico, 1868–1881" (PhD diss., University of Michigan, 1985), 25.

21. This equates to 153,600,000 pounds using a weight of 480 pounds per bale. The cited measurement is found at http://www.unc.edu/~rowlett/units/scales/cotton.html.

22. Daddysman, *The Matamoros Trade*, 143.

23. Ibid., 167. To ensure that trade revenue would be used to support the war effort, Confederate president Jefferson Davis in spring 1864 stated that "half of all export exchanges [be reserved] for incoming orders of strategic goods." Daddysman, *The Matamoros Trade*, 141.

24. Toral, *Historia Militar*, 133.

25. *Diccionario Porrúa de la Historia, Biografía, y Geografía de México* (Ciudad de México City: Editorial Porrúa, S.A., 1995), 3729. Many supporters of Maximilian paid a high price even if they kept their lives. For example, prior to the outbreak of the War of the French Intervention, the ranches of the Sanchez-Navarro families encompassed an area larger than the combined size of fabled King Ranch and the XIT Ranch of Texas. In retaliation, the victorious Júaristas dissolved this holding. For further information, see Charles Harris III, *A Mexican Family Empire: The Latifundio of the Sanchez Navarros, 1765–1867* (Austin: University of Texas Press, 1975).

26. A brief summary of Cortina's life can be found in *Handbook of Texas Online*, https://tshaonline.org/handbook/online/articles/fc073. For a most complete and well-written biography of Cortina, I recommend the work by Jerry D. Thompson: *Cortina: Defending the Mexican Name in Texas* (College Station: Texas A&M University Press, 2007).

27. While no English-language study examining the short-lived Republic of the Rio Grande exists, readers of Spanish can refer to the brief book by Josefina Zoraida Vasquez, *La supeusta republica del Rio Grande* (Ciudad Victoria, Tamaulipas: Instituto de Investigaciones Historia de la Universidad de Tamaulipas, 1995), A very brief online summary can be found in *Handbook of Texas Online*, https://tshaonline.org/handbook/online/articles/ngr01.

28. At one point, Juárez was establishing a base of operations in Monterrey while Canales, Carbajal, and Cortina simultaneously claimed the governorship of the adjacent state of Tamaulipas. Pedro Pruneda, *Historia de la Guerra de Méjico desde 1861 a 1867, con Todos los Documentos Diplomáticos Justificativos* (Madrid: Editores Elizade y Compañia, 1867), 370.

29. Thompson and Jones, *Civil War and Revolution*, 75.

30. Figures of the size of the imperial force were provided by Toral, *Historia Militar*, 71–72.

31. Ferdinand Joseph Maximilian von Hapsburg, *Alocuciones cartas ofciales é instruciones del Emperador Maximiliano durante los años de 1864, 1865 y 1866*, cited by Samuel Siegfried Karl Ritter von Basch and translated by Hugh McAden Oechler,

*Memories of México: A History of the Last Ten Months of Empire* (Leipzig: Verlag von Ducker und Humblot, 1868), and republished (San Antonio, TX: Trinity University Press, 1973), 18.

32. Ibid., 17–18.

33. Article I, Section 3, of the 1824 Constitution of the United Mexican States, to be found at http://tarletonlaw.utexsa.edu/constitutions/text/AT1S.html.

34. Proud of having been the home of the national government during this conflict, the residents of El Paso del Norte subsequently changed the name of their community to the one it bears today: Ciudad Juárez.

35. Grant "looked upon the invasion of México by Maximilian as part of the [Confederate] rebellion itself, because of the encouragement that invasion received from the Confederacy, and that our success in putting down [Southern] secession would never be complete till the French and Austrian invaders were compelled to quit the territory of our sister republic." Philip H. Sheridan, *Personal Memoirs of P. H. Sheridan, General, United States Army in Two Volumes* (New York: Charles L. Webster & Company, 1888), 210.

36. Ibid., 208.

37. Ibid., 226.

38. Ibid., 213, 214.

39. Ibid., 215.

40. In one particularly sharp incident, a force of American soldiers crossed the Rio Grande on January 5, 1866, and sacked Bagdad. In doing so, they overwhelmed the small Imperial Guard force and took three hundred prisoners. Mary Margaret McAllen, *Maximilian and Carlotta: Europe's Last Empire in México* (San Antonio: Trinity University Press, 2014), 229. Various explanations as to the cause of this raid exist. McAllen suggests that former Union general Richard Clay Crawford, who had joined the Juaristas, led this raid of African American troops as part of the war against the French. By contrast, Richard Zeitlin suggests that racially inflammatory articles published by Confederate exiles served as the catalyst for the raid.

41. Jean Mayer, *Las Oposiciones Francescas a Expédition du Mexique*, in *El Poder y la Sangre: Guerra, Estado y Nación en la Decada de 1860*, ed. Guillermo Palacios and Erika Pani (Ciudad de México: El Colegio de México, 2014), 466, 468.

42. Quoted in Basch, *Memories of Mexico*, 12.

43. Thompson and Jones, *Civil War and Revolution*, 120–23.

44. Ibid., 105.

45. More detailed information about Cortina's role can be in Thompson, *Cortina*.

46. Milo Kearney and Anthony Knopp, *Boom and Bust: The Historical Cycles of Matamoros and Brownsville* (Austin: Eakin Press, 1991), 147–48.

47. Ibid., 50.

48. Pedro Pruneda, Historia de la Guerra de Méjico desde 1861 a 1867, con Todos los Documentos Diplomáticos Justificativos (Madrid: Editores Elizade y Compañia, 1867), 411.

49. McAllen, *Maximilian and Carlotta*, 346–47.

50. "Weakened by years of civil war and foreign invasion, the Mexican central

government had acquired a healthy respect for the power of the individual states" and consequently regional *caudillos* enjoyed considerable latitude. Zeitlin, "Brass Buttons and Iron Rails," 25.

51. For a more complete consideration of this point, see Laurens Ballard Perry, *Juárez and Diaz: Machine Politics in México* (DeKalb, IL: Northern Illinois University Press, 1978).

52. *Report of the Committee of Investigation sent in 1873 by the Mexican Government to the Frontier of Texas*, translated from the official edition made in Mexico (New York: Baker and Godwin, 1875), 69–70.

53. The precise number of US troops available to meet challenges on both the southern and western frontiers of Texas at any one time remains in dispute. While several authors cite the figure of 3,100, Gen. William Tecumseh Sherman stated that the 1877 total only came to 2,522 men divided into a cavalry force of 1,844 troopers and 678 infantry. Gen. William Tecumseh Sherman, cited in Testimony Taken by the Committee on Military Affairs in Relation to the Texas Border Trouble, 45th Congress, 2nd Session, US House of Representatives, Miscellaneous Document no. 64 (Washington, DC: Government Printing Office, 1878), 18. Sherman stated that the task of patrolling only the southern front in Texas would have required four thousand men. Ibid., 19.

54. "The Mexican authorities, as a rule, civil and military, have been cognizant of these outrages and have (with one or two honorable exceptions), protected the offenders, defeated with technical objections attempts at recovery of the stolen property, assisted in maintaining bands of thieves, or directly and openly dealt in plunder." US Commission on Inquiry (Washington, DC: Government Printing Office, May 7, 1872), 28. This was one a series of reports issued by federal officials of the United States during this decade. Other such documents includes Testimony Taken by the Committee on Military Affairs in Relation to the Texas Border Troubles, 42nd Congress, 2nd Session, House of Representatives, Miscellaneous Document Number 64 (Washington, DC: Government Printing Office, 1878), Volumes 1 and 2. Message of the President of the United States in Answer to a Resolution of the House of Representatives, Transmitting Reports from the Secretaries of State and of War in Reference to the Mexican Border Troubles, 46th Congress, 1st Session, Executive Document Number 13 (Washington, DC: Government Printing Office, 1877). Texas Frontier Troubles, 44th Congress, 1st Session, House of Representatives, Report 343 (Washington, DC: Government Printing Office, 1876).

55. *Report of the Committee of Investigation sent in 1873 by the Mexican Government to the Frontier of Texas.*

56. Zeitlin, "Brass Buttons and Iron Rails," 29. Typically an American group of investigators would allege that Texas had suffered far more at the hands of Mexican marauders than Mexicans had suffered at the hands of American marauders. Mexican commissions argued precisely the opposite. Juan Fidel Zorilla, Maribel Mió Flaquier, and Octavio Herrera Pérez, *Tamaulipas: Una Historia Compartida I, 1810–1921* (San Juan Mixcoac, Mexico: Universidad Autónoma de Tamaulipas, Instituto Investigaciones Históricas, 1993), I.

57. *Report of the Committee of Investigation sent in 1873 by the Mexican Government to the Frontier of Texas*, 34, 91, 105, 107, 277, 376, 396–97, 401.

58. On just the Texas side of the border, the Texas Rangers reliably were reported to have killed, often by lynching, some one hundred Mexican Americans for no valid reason. Governor Edmund Jackson Davis to US Secretary of War William Belknap, letter of June 26, 1875 (Microfilm 666, National Archives and Records Administration, Washington, DC), 0073–0075

59. Jonathan Evans cited in Testimony Taken by the Committee on Military Affairs in Relation to the Texas Border Trouble, 45th Congress, 2nd Session, US House of Representatives, Miscellaneous Document no. 64 (Washington, DC: Government Printing Office, 1878), 16.

60. Thomas F. Wilson, United States Consul in Matamoros, as cited from *US House of Representatives Report 701* (Washington, DC: Government Printing Office, 1875), 143.

61. Report of Col. William R. Shafter, Fort Clark, Texas, April 4, 1868, in Records of the Adjutant General's Office, Department of War, Record Group no. 94, personnel file (cited as ACP hereafter), Box 570.

62. Patronismo is a paternal relationship between estate owner and employee in which the owner controls not only the employee's livelihood, but the house in which he lives, the community in which he votes, and the employee's future prospects. In nineteenth century Mexico, ranch hands often served in the caudillos' private armies.

63. Mario Cerruti and Miguel A González Quiroga, *El Norte de México y Texas (1848–1880): Comerico, capitales y trabajadores en una economía de frontera* (Ciudad de México: Instituto de Investigaciones Dr. José Maria Luis Mora, 1999), 76. Other prominent Mexican comerciantes cited by Cerruti and González include Guadalupe Garza, Antonio de la Garza y Chapa, Juan José la Garza, and Guadalupe Garcia. Ibid., 43–45.

64. Evaristo Madero, one of the most affluent and powerful of Northern Mexico's landowners, was the father of Francisco Madero, who led the first phase of the Mexican Revolution and subsequently became president.

65. Juan Fidel Zorilla, Maribel Mió Flaquier, and Octavio Herrera Pérez, *Tamaulipas: Una Historia Compartida I, 1810–1921* (San Juan Mixcoac, Mexico: Universidad Autónoma de Tamaulipas, Instituto Investigaciones Históricas, 1993), I: 57.

66. Sebastian Lerdo de Tejada had been a member of the triumvirate that led Mexico's republicans during the War of the French Intervention. Along with Benito Juárez and Jose Maria Iglesias, he symbolized independent Mexico. At the time he decided to stand for president, Lerdo de Tejada was serving as Chief Justice of the Supreme Court. By contrast, Diaz was the proverbial man on horseback. He led the Mexican Army in its victorious charge against the French at the Battle of Puebla, subsequently escaped from a French prison camp following a later defeat, and returned to the field in time to lead the army that liberated Mexico City.

67. In addition to founding Brownsville, Charles Stillman developed a "network of mercantile and industrial enterprises, including cotton brokerage and real estate

firms, silver mines in Nuevo León and Tamaulipas [the two Mexican states bordering the Rio Grande Valley], merchandise outlets, a shipping company that carried passengers and goods from the Gulf Coast up the river as far as Rio Grande City, and an off-loading, warehousing, and transportation company that carried goods to the Mexican interior as far as Guadalajara. Stillman and his partner, José Morell, established retailing outlets and founded one of the first textile factories at Monterrey. Stillman's Vallecillo mines, between Laredo and Monterrey, produced more than $4 million in silver and lead during the 1850s, and he sold their stock on the New York Stock Exchange" (*Handbook of Texas Online*, https://tshaonline.org/handbook/online/articles/fst57). Charles's son James subsequently became one of the most powerful of American capitalists, with assets including 20 percent of the stock of First National City Bank (today known as Citibank). He played a critical role on the development of irrigated agriculture throughout the Rio Grande Valley. For a brief summary of his commercial activities and of relationship with Porfirio Diaz, see *Handbook of Texas Online*, https://tshaonline.org/handbook/online/articles/fstbp.

68. Zorilla et al., *Tamaulipas*, 79–83.

69. Those present at the meeting included Thomas Wentworth Peirce (president of the Galveston, Harrisburg, and San Antonio Railroad), Andrew Wentworth Peirce (president of the Texas International Railroad), Thomas T. Buckley (a vice-president of the Bank of the Republic of New York, treasurer of the Cleveland, Youngstown, and Pittsburgh Railroad, and a board member of the Atlantic and Pacific Railroad). Also present was John Salmon Ford, captain of the Texas Rangers and former colonel of the Confederate Cavalry of the West. For decades, King hosted the Rangers at his ranch, offering them considerable support. John Mason Hart, *Empire and Revolution: The Americans in México since the Civil War* (Berkeley: University of California Press, 2002), 62–66.

70. Juan Fidel Zorilla, Maribel Mió Flaquier, and Octavio Herrera Pérez, *Tamaulipas—Una Historia* Compartida, I, 94.

71. This Porfirian policy was known as *pan o palo* (bread or stick). Caudillos received incentives in return for their loyalty. Typical concessions would have been a railroad diverted through a caudillo's land or the right to condemn and purchase land they had long wanted or nomination to a high political office. By contrast, defiance brought a variety of repressive responses. Perhaps the most singular was a federal Secretary of Education who, after committing a policy offence, received appointment to a diplomatic post in Russia.

72. Reliable legend holds that once in office, Diaz gave caudillos who were both powerful and hesitant a theatrical performance. The caudillo would be invited to the grand presidential office in the National Palace. There, Diaz would open a desk drawer and pick up a pistol in one hand and a fistful of high-denomination pesos bills in the other. At that point, he would ask the caudillo if he wanted "*la pistola o los pesos.*" Wise visitors who desired a long and healthy life invariably took the latter choice.

73. Zeitlin, "Brass Buttons and Iron Rails," 178.

74. In testimony before a committee of the US House of Representatives, the

commanding general, Edward O. Cresap Ord, went farther. He argued that the border area had never been tranquil. Citing a 1744 document written by Father Joseph Sadelmayer in which that cleric characterized the indigenous tribes as people given to plunder and dishonesty, Ord concluded: "These observations of Father Sadelmayer show that these savages—except that they now have rifles—were the same two hundred years ago as today." Gen. Edward O. Cresap Ord cited in *Testimony Taken by the Committee on Military Affairs in Relation to the Texas Border Trouble*, 45th Congress, 2nd Session, US House of Representatives, Miscellaneous Document no. 64 (Washington, DC: Government Printing Office, 1878), 14.

75. Zeitlin, "Brass Buttons and Iron Rails," 109.

76. The first such American insistence is described in detail by one of the participant, John Salmon "Rip" Ford, in John Salmon Ford, *Rip Ford's Texas*, ed. Stephen B. Oates (Austin: University of Texas Press, 1963), 412–14.

77. Zeitlin, "Brass Buttons and Iron Rails," 211.

78. The consortium's leaders were James Stillman, Edward Henry Harriman, John D. Rockefeller, Jay Gould, and, after Gould left the consortium, Jacob Schiff. Edward Henry Harriman controlled three major railroads (the Illinois Central, the Southern Pacific, and the Union Pacific) as well as the Pacific Mail Steamship Company and the Wells Fargo Express Company. Jay Gould relinquished control of the Erie Railroad following assorted financial irregularities, and his place in the consortium was taken by Jacob Schiff, who headed the banking house of Kuhn, Loeb, and Schiff, who also served on the boards of Harriman's Union Pacific and Stillman's National City Bank. John Mason Hart, *Revolutionary México: The Coming and Process of the Mexican Revolution* (Stanford: Stanford University Press. 1997), 134–35.

79. Ibid., 142. One of the largest holdings was the 4,700,000 acres (approximately 7,300 square miles purchased by the Texas Oil Company (subsequently Texaco). Ibid., 158, 160.

80. Ibid., 158, 160.

81. Andrea Burgess et al., *The Economist Pocket World in Figures 2015* (London: Profile Books, 2015), 181.

# 6

# *Col. José de los Santos Benavides and Gen. Juan Nepomuceno Cortina*

## Two Astounding Civil War Tejanos

JERRY THOMPSON

No ethnic group has been as neglected by Civil War scholars as the Tejanos of South Texas. More than four thousand Spanish-surnamed soldiers from the region are known to have fought in the Confederate army, while 950 Tejanos and Mexicanos enlisted in the Union army in the Lower Rio Grande Valley in 1863–64. Several hundred Union-inspired guerillas, operating in the Nueces Strip and from camps south of the border, were also active in the war. Two of the most important individuals in South Texas during the war were José de los Santos Benavides, a lifetime native of Laredo, and Juan Nepomuceno Cortina, who was raised in Camargo, Brownsville, and Matamoros. Benavides rose to the rank of colonel during the war, the highest ranking Tejano in the Confederate army, while Cortina became a general in the army of Benito Juárez and governor of Tamaulipas.[1] The semi-literate Cortina also became a supporter of the Union cause. The lives of these two individuals paralleled some of the most violent and tumultuous years of the nineteenth century. What is so amazing is that Benavides and Cortina came from very similar socioeconomic backgrounds, yet went in such opposite directions: One was a supporter of secession, the status quo, and the Confederacy, while the other started a revolution in the lower valley in 1859–60 and tried to start another revolution south of the border. One was admired and beloved by Anglos in Texas, while the other was hated with great passion.

*Santos Benavides (courtesy of Webb County Heritage Foundation) and Juan Nepomuceno Cortina (courtesy of Jerry Thompson).*

The two began their paths to such varied destinies when the US Army under Gen. Zachary Taylor came to the Rio Grande and raised their flag on a tall willow pole on the morning of March 8, 1846. Santos, his well-known uncle Basilio, and their large and extended family at Laredo cooperated with the US Army during the Mexican-American War and became a significant part of the political establishment in the decade that followed. In the lower valley, Cortina enlisted in the Mexican *Defensores de la Patria*, a company of the *Guardia Naciónal de Tamaulipas* that was organized in Matamoros, but included men from both sides of the Rio Grande. Gen. Pedro Ampudia, commanding the Mexican Army in Matamoros, enlisted the services of the Defensores de la Patria and Cortina as scouts. While Santos Benavides and his uncle tolerated and even cooperated with Capt. Mirabeau B. Lamar and the American army at Laredo, Cortina fought for the Mexican Army at Palo Alto and Resaca de la Palma, and it is likely that he was with Mexican guerillas who were active in the American rear when the Americans moved against Monterrey.[2]

Benavides's and Cortina's loyalties during the Civil War are best explained by examining the economic and political conditions in Laredo and Brownsville in the decade that preceded the war. In the years after the Mexican-American War, socioeconomic inequality and deep-rooted racism engulfed Brownsville and Cameron County. A customs official remembered how in Brownsville "lawless and unprincipled Americans were much in the habit of grossly maltreating the Mexicans."[3]

To maintain themselves politically in Cameron County and in the Lower Rio Grande Valley, the European and Anglo minority were largely reliant on the Tejano majority to keep them in office, yet only on rare occasions were Tejanos elected to public office. "An hour before the election they are 'fast friends,'" the *Brownsville American Flag* recorded, but "an hour after the election they are a 'crowd of greasers.'"[4] Only in 1853, when two Mexican Texans became county commissioners, did the majority come close to comprising a meaningful political minority in Brownsville and Cameron County. Petit and grand juries, often used as a political tool and as an instrument of intimidation, rarely included Mexican Americans.[5]

In the lower valley, there was great insecurity over the ability of the Tejanos to hold on to their ancestral lands. In February 1850, there was even talk in Brownsville that the Americans, either in Austin or Washington, DC, would annul all the land titles in the Nueces Strip. One prominent American in the lower valley advertised in the *Brownsville American Flag* as early as June 2, 1847, that "Mexican law and authority are forever at an end" in the Nueces Strip and that "by the laws of Texas no alien can hold real estate within its limits."[6] In a number of instances, to defend their property the grantees were forced into expensive litigation and ruinous lawsuits. Several individuals in the lower valley went as far as to propose a territorial government that would adjudicate land titles. The Anglo-dominated separatist movement gained neither momentum or legitimacy; however, Sen. Thomas J. Rusk denounced the Separatists on the floor of the US Senate and Gov. Peter H. Bell and the Texas legislature moved to establish a commission to investigate and recommend for confirmation to the state legislature all land claims.

William H. Bourland and James B. Miller, experienced public officials, were appointed to what came to be known as the Bourland

Commission. Claimants were asked to submit evidence of title and a description of the land they claimed. An affidavit was to also be submitted stating that their documents were not forged or antedated.[7] After several delays, the Bourland Commission arrived in Laredo in the heat of July 15, 1850, and commenced hearings. At first, Laredoans such as Santos and Basilio Benavides were suspicious of the commissioners and their attorney, Robert Jones Rivers, but County Clerk Hamilton P. Bee assured the landowners of the commission's honest intentions. Fifteen claims, including all the lands the Benavides family had inherited through decades of Spanish and Mexican rule, were eventually submitted. Sensing the urgency of the situation, Bourland hurried back to Austin and submitted the list to Governor Bell. On September 4, 1850, the legislature confirmed the rancheros' fifteen claims, and a sigh of relief was felt all the way to the border.[8]

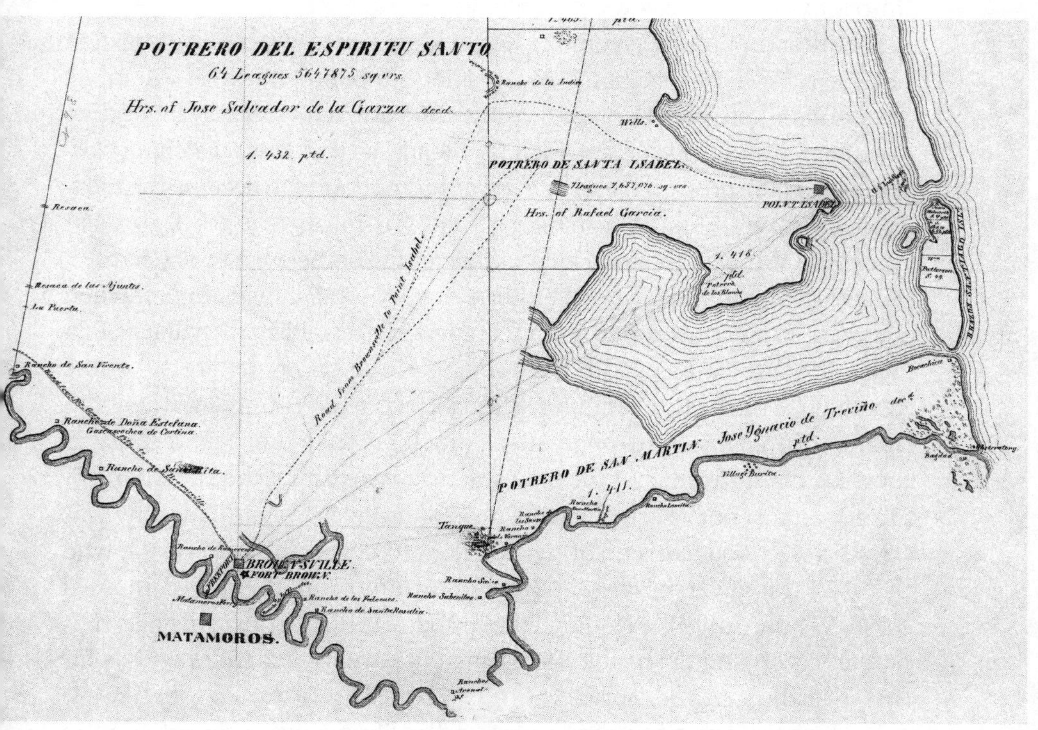


*Map of the Portrero del Espiritu Santo land grant with Dona María Estéfana Goseascochea de Cortina's Ranch. Courtesy of the Texas General Land Office. Map of Cameron County compiled and drawn by E. Schutze, 1873.*

Although Cortina's mother inherited a large part of the Potrero del Espiritu Santo Grant in the lower valley and the grant was also declared valid by the Texas Legislature, María Estéfana Goseascochea de Cortina was forced to sacrifice thousands of acres of land to her attorneys to defend her claims. Cortina blamed a "multitude" of Brownsville lawyers for conspiring against the owners of the land. To Cortina, these were "vile men" in a "secret conclave" whose "sole purpose" was "despoiling the Mexicans of their land."[9] The simmering discontent in the lower valley exploded into the Cortina War in the summer and fall of 1859. Twice Cortina and his *Cortinistas*, a guerilla army numbering as many as six hundred, defeated the Brownsville militia and the Texas Rangers, one of the few times the Rangers were ever defeated in battle. It was not until December 1859 that a combined force of Rangers and US Army regulars decisively defeated Cortina at Rio Grande City and drove him into Mexico.[10]

Although he would come of age in Matamoros, Cortina was born in a large rock and adobe house in the small sunbaked village of Camargo, Tamaulipas, on May 16, 1824. At the time of his birth, Cortina's father, Trinidad, was alcalde of the town. Trinidad married María Estéfana Goseascochea the previous year, and it was his mother who became the moving and inspirational force in his early life. Cortina's great-great-grandfather, Blas María de la Garza Falcón, was captain of the presidio of Cerralvo, Nuevo León, on the far northeastern edge of the Spanish empire, when he was given permission by José de Escandón to establish the village of La Villa de Santa Ana de Camargo, the first of the "villas del norte," at the confluence of the Rio San Juan with the larger Rio Grande. With a high mass, the singing of hymns, and as much pomp and pageantry as was possible on the frontier at the time, Camargo was established on March 5, 1749, as part of the province of Nuevo Santander. Cortina's destiny was more closely tied to his great-grandfather, José Saldivar de la Garza, who in 1772 was given the large Espiritu Santo land grant that was composed of 408 square miles, including what is today the city of Brownsville, that stretched up and down the Rio Grande for twenty-five miles and as far north as the Arroyo Colorado.

More than one hundred miles up the life-giving waters of the Rio Grande, half again by ox cart, Santos Benavides's great-great-grandfather, Tomás Sánchez de La Barrera y Garza, founded the small and often troubled community of La Villa de San Agustín de Laredo on the north bank of the Rio Grande in 1755. Named after a Cantabrian village on the Bay of Biscay in northern Spain, Laredo was the last of Escandón's Villas del Norte and his only successful settlement on the north bank of the river. Both of Santos's parents were born in this small river community. Not long after Mexico made its break from the Spanish empire, on November 1, 1823, Santos was born to Margarita and José de Jesús Benavides a little more than six months before Cortina was born in Camargo. The infant was christened eight days later in a small rock and adobe church on the east side of the barren San Agustín Plaza.[11] At the time of her death, Margarita owned a sizeable herd of 635 sheep, along with a few other animals. Her personal possessions included household items valued at 675 pesos. After Santos's father took his half of the estate, the boy was given thirty-eight pesos.[12] It was not much, but with time and hard work, Santos would turn his meager inheritance into one of the largest and most profitable mercantile firms in the community.

Although the adjustment to American rule was difficult for Santos, in 1856 and again in 1857 he was elected mayor of Laredo. One of his primary responsibilities as mayor was to preside over the municipal court that tried both civil and criminal cases, even those for capital murder. Another responsibility was leading the city council, which passed ordinances to regulate Laredo's traditionally rowdy and frequently violent fandangos. Licenses were required of all dance halls, and the presence of a town marshal to keep the "public peace" was mandatory.[13] The council also passed an ordinance prohibiting the firing of weapons within the city limits after seven at night, unless in self-defense. Pistols could be discharged on private property during the day, but not on the two public plazas or in the streets.[14] As mayor, Santos had the opportunity to employ friends, relatives, and other political allies. Nepotism laws were a thing of the future, and political patronage grew unchecked. Two years after serving as mayor, just as Basilio was becoming state representative, Santos was elected county judge.[15]

At the same time the Benavides family was coming to dominate Laredo and Webb County politics, Santos was able to enlarge his mercantile business and maintain his extensive ranching interests. Largely due to his growing political influence, he was awarded the lucrative ferry franchise that connected Laredo to Nuevo Laredo. Santos and his brothers profited from a growing commerce with the interior of Mexico and with Laredo's sister community of Nuevo Laredo.[16]

When Basilio was elected state representative, the Benavides family gained additional political clout and influence in both Texas and Mexico. During the tumultuous decade of the 1850s, Santos and Basilio began corresponding with José Santiago Vidaurri y Valdez, the powerful governor of Nuevo León and Coahuila. In one of his first letters to the governor, Basilio congratulated Vidaurri for his endorsement of the Plan de Ayutla and his opposition to the dictatorial administration of Antonio Lopez de Santa Anna.[17] Although Vidaurri despised the extent of Mexican centralism, the government he created in Nuevo León and Coahuila was not so different.

On February 1, 1861, before a packed and boisterous gallery of citizens in Austin, the Secession Convention voted 166 to 8 to present a secession ordinance to the people of Texas. Three weeks later, Texans voted 46,129 to 14,796 in favor of disunion. Surprisingly, the secession ordinance was even more popular on the Rio Grande frontier where there were few, if any, slaves than it was in other areas of the state, including the slave-holding and agricultural counties in East Texas. In the counties along the river from Laredo to the Gulf—Webb, Zapata, Starr, Hidalgo, and Cameron—the ordinance was approved by a vote of 1,124 to 41.[18] In Webb and Zapata Counties, not a single vote was cast against secession. Most of those who led the fight for secession on the border tended to be of the ranching and mercantile elite, with close ties to the political establishment in Austin. Many others who voted for secession were the economically disadvantaged within the feudal patronage system of which Santos, along with the rest of the Benavides family, were an integral part.

With the departure of the federal troops from Laredo, Santos received authorization from the State of Texas to raise a company of as many as one hundred men for defense of the frontier. Interestingly, the fighting that began the Civil War on the Rio Grande, which took place at Carrizo in May 1861, was rooted not in the issues of slavery and secession, but in the Cortina War that swept over the lower Rio Grande Valley in 1859 and 1860.

Since its creation in 1856, Zapata County was administered by a clique of merchants and large landowners headed by Henry Redmond, a crafty Englishman who arrived on the border in 1839, shortly after Texas independence. Redmond acquired land, married into an influential local family, and wisely made friends with the Benavides family in Laredo. By 1861, he had developed a lucrative trading business in San Bartolo, or what some called Redmond's Ranch, a short distance upriver from the small rock and adobe county seat of Carrizo. The rotund Redmond was instrumental in organizing the county that was named after his revolutionary friend from across the river in Guerrero, the mulatto hero of the Republic of the Rio Grande, Col. Antonio Zapata. Redmond became postmaster at Carrizo, justice of the peace, the first county judge, and for a few years, collector of customs at San Bartolo.[19]

The political machine that ran the county included many of Santos's friends. John D. Mussett, an articulate Arkansas lawyer, was the acting deputy collector of customs at Carrizo; Pedro Díaz was the county sheriff; Trinidad Zampano was county clerk; Fernando Uribe was tax assessor and collector; while Agustín Díaz was district clerk. Another player in county politics and a friend and political ally of Santos was Blas María Uribe, a wealthy merchant and rancher who controlled the votes at the small mud village of San Ygnacio, thirteen miles upriver from Carrizo.

The degree to which the *patrón* system controlled Zapata County was indicated by the role played by then county judge, Isidro Vela, who was part of Redmond's cabal, in the secession vote in the county.[20] Realizing that there was a strong contingent of local pro-Unionists, on the eve of the vote, Vela made it known that anyone who failed to vote in favor of secession would be fined fifty cents, a considerable amount of money for the poor who eked out a living in the small villages along the river.[21] The ploy seemed to work: officials announced that the vote for secession was unanimous, 212 to 0. However, when Vela learned that several individuals had not voted and others publicly protested the legitimacy of the vote, Vela ordered them arrested. What resulted was a full-fledged revolt that played right into the hands of Cortina.

On April 12, 1861, the day before the surrender of Fort Sumter in the harbor of Charleston, South Carolina, forty armed Tejanos and Mexicanos under the leadership of a thirty-nine-year-old ranchero named Antonio Ochoa seized control of the southern part of the county. Proclaiming a pro-Unionist stance, Ochoa and his followers also took great pride in calling themselves Cortinistas, and threatened to kill all the "gringos" in the county and hang Sheriff Díaz.[22] Certain that Cortina was coming to their aid, Ochoa and his men were reported to be "marching about the county in armed bodies threatening the lives of Tom, Dick, and John Doe."[23] They "were not only attempting to prevent the county officers from taking the [Confederate] oath of office," but were "also threatening to forcibly take all public money."[24] Some feared that Ochoa had enough men to seize the county seat of Carrizo. Eventually the men were confronted by Judge Vela, owner of the large Rancho Clareño, who persuaded them to return to their homes. Although the dissidents backed down, they issued a *pronunciamiento* against the Confederacy and presented it to Judge Vela.

From his fortified ranch near San Bartolo, Redmond was in a state of panic. The insurrectionists demanded that their *pronunciamiento* be "forwarded to the US," which Ochoa thought was "a few miles on the other side of Bexar," as noted by Redmond. "[It is] hard to say how far their ignorance will lead them," he went on to say.[25] From Fort Brown, Col. John Salmon "Rip" Ford, commanding Confederate forces on the Rio Grande, assured Redmond that the troops at Laredo under Capt. Santos Benavides were more than capable of protecting him and the other Zapata County officials. Ochoa and his men were public enemies, and their actions were treasonous, Confederate authorities asserted.[26]

The secessionist press in Texas reported that the insurrection in Zapata County was inspired by ignorant Unionists. Ochoa and his men, it was reported, were in favor of "Old Abe, the rail splitter," and were demanding to communicate with federal authorities. With its ethnic and socioeconomic undercurrents, the threatened violence was, in reality, a reaction to Zapata County boss rule. Although Ochoa owned a small ranch near Clareño, most of his followers were poor vaqueros and *labradores*, many from Guerrero, across the river from Carrizo.[27] Some had ridden with Cortina during the Cortina War and were tired of the abuse and discrimination that had for some time been a part of the Texas political and social landscape.

To ensure peace in the county, Capt. Matthew Nolan, commanding a hastily organized Confederate company of twenty-two men, rode downriver from Santos's headquarters at Fort McIntosh. After a fifty-five-mile ride, Nolan bivouacked near Redmond's Ranch on the afternoon of April 14, 1861.[28] Although fatigued, the captain was determined to crush any resistance to state authority in the county. Judge Vela quickly issued warrants for the arrest of Ochoa and eighty of his men. With little hesitation, Captain Nolan, Judge Vela, and Sheriff Díaz, whom the insurgents were still threatening to hang, marched for Rancho Clareño, where Ochoa was said to have his headquarters. Reaching the small river village before daylight on April 15, Nolan deployed his men around the ranch, and Sheriff Díaz ordered Ochoa's men, many of whom were still half asleep, to surrender. Most were in the process of doing so when one insurgent, according to Nolan, fired at Nolan's men, although one of the Confederate volunteers later confessed that not a single shot was fired by Ochoa or his men.[29] Nolan ordered an all-out attack on the ranch.

Outnumbered and caught off guard, Ochoa's men tried to surrender, but they never had a chance. Many were gunned down where they stood, while others were killed as they fled toward the river. Although Nolan later bragged that "nine Black Republicans" were killed in the skirmish, several of those were reported to have been noncombatants and were probably unarmed. Ochoa, the leader of the movement, was across the river in Guerrero at the time, but two of his lieutenants, Nepomuceno and Santiago Vela, were killed in the attack.[30] Looking into the incident twelve years later, a committee sent by the Mexican government to investigate problems on the border concluded that "inoffensive inhabitants were assassinated."[31]

In the days following the massacre at Rancho Clareño, unsubstantiated rumors rapidly spread along the Rio Grande: Cortina had formed an alliance with federal authorities in the North, as well as Unionists in Texas, and he prepared yet another attack on Texas.[32] Furnished with arms and horses paid for by the Unionists and hoping to reassert himself on the north bank, Cortina was again recruiting men.[33] Along with Teodoro Zamora, a leading lieutenant and the former county judge of Hidalgo County, as well as Antonio Ochoa, Cortina was reported to be marching on Carrizo to avenge the victims of the Clareño massacre.

Fearing for his life, Judge Vela fled with his family to Redmond's Ranch. Although he received assurances from Mexican authorities across the river in Guerrero that they would do everything possible to apprehend Cortina and Ochoa, Vela took no chances. Cortina was so popular on the Rio Grande that even members of the Mexican Army were deserting to join the wily revolutionary.[34] When Colonel Ford received a plea for help from Redmond, he sent Santos downriver to assist the Zapata County officials. Santos hastily assembled his men on the plaza in Laredo, and they galloped off across Zacate Creek, bound for Redmond's Ranch. Pausing briefly at San Ygnacio, Santos was told by several villagers who were thought to sympathize with Cortina that the revolutionary was already in possession of Carrizo and that if the captain cared for his life, he should immediately return to Laredo. Still, Santos pushed his men downriver, past Ramireño, and then to Redmond's Ranch, where the men were deployed around the small village.

Near Guerrero, Cortina was joyfully greeted by Ochoa and a number of Zapata County insurgents as a conquering hero. However, Cortina had no idea that the seemingly sympathetic alcalde of Guerrero, Juan G. Garza, was keeping Santos informed of his every move.[35] Garza went as far as to dispatch twenty-five men under José María Hinojosa to watch the main ford on the Rio Grande, just below Guerrero, in an attempt to impede Cortina's crossing. But, after finding another crossing, Cortina splashed across the Rio Grande into Texas, and the next day, his advance guard skirmished with three of Santos's pickets below Carrizo. Reinforced by twenty men from Guerrero and a few men from

*Confederate colonel John Salmon "Rip" Ford. Courtesy of the DeGolyer Library, Southern Methodist University, Lawrence T. Jones III Texas Photography Collection.*

Zapata County, including relatives of those killed at Rancho Clareño, Cortina's force was said to be growing hourly.[36]

By the morning of May 21, 1861, Cortina and seventy of his men had Santos completely surrounded at Redmond's Ranch. Cortina sent waves of fear across Texas during the Cortina War in 1859, but he now sent two of his men under a flag of truce to the ranch in an attempt to persuade Santos to leave and let Redmond, Vela, Mussett, and their friends defend themselves. Influential citizens and friends from Guerrero crossed the river to tell Santos that Cortina's intention was to seek revenge only on Redmond and those responsible for the bloodshed at Rancho Clareño. Cortina was determined, they said, "to have Redmond's head before sundown."[37] But Santos stood firm and refused to forsake his friend. The two men knew and respected one another for over a decade, since the time Santos was serving as Webb County judge and Redmond as judge in Zapata County.

In the meantime, all sorts of rumors reached the besieged Confederates. Cortina was reported to have between 1,500 and 2,000 men under his command, and he was in control of both Roma and Rio Grande City. Two residents of Carrizo, Anselmo Flores and Pedro Reyna, attempted to persuade Santos to leave and let Redmond and his gringo friends defend themselves, but Santos had no doubt that Redmond's Ranch could easily be defended, especially the largest of the buildings, which was constructed solidly of stone and had been used before the war by the army. Moreover, enough water and food were available to last for several weeks. The men's morale was heightened by their possession of a six-pounder cannon, along with an abundant supply of ammunition.

Several of Cortina's men were able to get within a few hundred yards of the ranch complex and fire a volley of shots at the defenders. Other Cortinistas were seen on the small cactus-studded hills east of the ranch and across the river in Mexico. They did little more than ride around on their horses, however—a tactic Santos felt was being used to confuse his besieged Confederates. Santos, Mussett, Vela, and Redmond took turns gazing through a spyglass at the Cortinistas from Redmond's front porch.

Just as he had done when he seized Brownsville in 1859, Cortina cut all communications between Redmond's Ranch and the outside world, and through the night his men continued to fire indiscriminately into the ranch. One of Santos's couriers was captured on the river road from Carrizo to Roma, and another rider, Ángel Jiménez, was seized on the road leading upriver to Laredo. A third rider, mounted on Santos's horse, set off at a gallop and was able to get past Cortina's pickets and reach Laredo safely, however.[38] Within hours, thirty-six men under Capt. Refugio Benavides and Basilio Benavides, along with Lt. Charles Callahan, were on their way to Carrizo, riding through the night to reach the besieged Confederates.

On the morning of May 22, 1861, after riding sixty-five miles in thirteen hours, the Laredo reinforcements ran into a party of Cortinistas near San Bartolo, and a skirmish ensued. Hearing the sounds of gunfire, Santos and his men saddled their horses and galloped out of Redmond's Ranch to join the fray. Cortina, too, heard the sounds of battle and pushed his men forward. In a running fight that began at 1:00 p.m. and lasted forty minutes, Santos and thirty-six of his men completely routed Cortina's raiders. A number of the Cortinistas appear to have been preoccupied with sacking the small two-story Zapata County courthouse and Mussett's store, and were caught by surprise.[39] Seven of Cortina's men were killed in the initial charge, while several others were severely wounded. At the head of his men, Santos pursued the partisans to the river, where several more Cortinistas drowned while attempting to swim the Rio Grande to Mexico. With ten of his men, Cortina "gained the opposite side of the river in safety, and in ascending its banks, faced about, took an apparent disdainful view of his recent antagonist and master, uncovered, and with characteristic dignity, waved his hat, bidding them in the blandest tone . . . a courteous temporary adieu, informing them that he would give them another call in a few days."[40]

"Before attacking Cortina," Santos wrote in his official report, "I particularly ordered my men not to arrest any of the bandits, but to kill all that fell into their hands. Consequently I have no prisoners."[41] Eleven prisoners, some of whom were badly wounded, were shot by Santos.[42] Such had long been the fate of captured "bandits" on the Rio Grande frontier. Santos later admitted that he intended to exterminate the "whole band" and that his "prisoners were mostly dead men."[43] None of Santos's men were wounded or killed in the brief battle, although Lt. Juan García Soto and Pvt. Dario Areola lost their horses in the fight. Pvt. Ángel Jimenez, who had been captured by the Cortinistas the previous day, was liberated.

Only days after the battle at Carrizo, Santos gleefully carried the news of his defeat of Cortina north to San Antonio. When word reached Austin, accolades for the Laredo captain reverberated across the state. Ford promised to send enough Colt pistols to equip Santos's company as soon as possible, and although he did requisition the revolvers, Santos only received fifty old muskets that came by boat from Brownsville, along with some subsistence rations. In fact, many of the recruits in Texas were so desperate for weapons that the state legislature contemplated raising a regiment of Mexican Texans and arming them with lances.[44]

On May 29, 1861, Ford trumpeted Santos's defeat of Cortina in a proclamation entitled "Rout of Cortina," which repeated what Santos said in his letter to Confederate headquarters in Houston on May 23.[45] Any defeat of the elusive Cortina was good news in Texas. "Thanks are due to Captain [Santos] Benavides and his men for their gallantry in expelling a foe from our territory," Ford wrote. "Thanks are also due to the Hon. Basilio Benavides, Refugio Benavides and the citizens of Webb County for their promptitude in going to the rescue of their fellow citizens of Zapata County, when threatened by imminent danger. They have shown themselves to be loyal to the government of the Confederate States under trying circumstances and deserve the commendation of every true friend of the South." Ford also sent a congratulatory letter to Santos: "Your judgement [*sic*], ability, and gallantry in the affair receive encouragement from every quarter. I sincerely congratulate you upon your success. You and the people of Webb County have furnished indisputable evidence to the world of your devotion to the cause of Constitutional liberty."[46]

In Austin, Gov. Edward Clark was equally felicitous. Prior to the battle at Carrizo, the governor appears to have had serious doubts as to the loyalty of the Benavides family, and he was overjoyed at the defeat of Cortina. "Whenever our enemies have appeared on our soil," the governor told the captain, "you and your brave men have been present and driven them back, with great honor to yourselves and the gratification of your state."[47] Clark even sent Santos an elegantly engraved pistol along with a congratulatory letter: "I am happy to believe in your hands it will always be used in the defense of your country and prove an instrument of terror and destruction to her enemies."[48] Governor Santiago Vidaurri also wrote from Monterrey to offer his congratulations.[49]

Despite the resounding defeat at Carrizo, Santos Benavides and the Confederacy had not heard the last of Juan Cortina. Able to maintain a guerrilla army of several hundred men on the Mexican bank of the Rio Grande, Cortina continued to plot and scheme against his old political enemies in Texas, many of them now in the Confederate army or in positions of power. Communicating with Union officials in New Orleans, Cortina was certain that with his assistance, the Confederates could be forced out of Brownsville, if not the entire Lower Rio Grande Valley.[50] Cortina had the small Confederate force in Brownsville so unnerved that reports of his crossing the river became a common rumor on the north bank. Once jittery Confederates rushed to the riverbank and opened fire on several Mexican soldiers and civilians who were peacefully bathing in the river.[51]

Knowing that Cortina was bitterly opposed to the Confederates, John L. Haynes, one of the leading Texas Unionists who had gone to Washington, DC, to help persuade Lincoln to "reinaugurate the National Authority on the Rio Grande," who also had been one of the few Anglo-Texans to provide a meaningful explanation for the origins of the Cortina War, and who had now become a colonel in the 1st Texas Union Cavalry, was in correspondence with Cortina from New Orleans. As a result, Cortina welcomed a Union presence on the frontier.[52]

In November 1863, Cortina watched from Matamoros as Union forces waded ashore on Brazos Island and began marching on Brownsville. Commanded by Gen. Nathaniel P. Banks, 6,998 men in 26 ships from New Orleans came out of the gray, cold dawn. "The flag of the Union floats over Texas today, General Banks proudly wired President Abraham Lincoln.[53] The Bluecoats were hoping to cut the flow of cotton into Mexico and strangle Texas economically. Believing the French Imperialists in Mexico to be in violation of the basic tenets of the Monroe Doctrine, Lincoln hoped to wave the stars and stripes at the Imperialists and their Mexican allies and coerce them into leaving Mexico. The presence of a federal army on the border could also serve to provide a safe haven for hundreds of persecuted German Texan Unionists who were being driven out of the Texas hill country.[54]

The expected arrival of the Union army on the Rio Grande helped spark a violent mutiny by the unpredictable eighteen-year-old Capt. Adrian J. Vidal, Mifflin Kenedy's impetuous stepson, who was in command of a Confederate cavalry company at the mouth of the river. There remains little doubt that Vidal fell under Cortina's influence and was, perhaps, thinking that he could somehow duplicate Cortina's 1859 raid on Brownsville. On October 28, 1863, Vidal seized control of the small community of Clarksville at the mouth of the river.[55] Fearful that Vidal would be assisted by Cortina and the two would sack Brownsville, Confederate authorities were in a panic. Crying "*¡Muerte a los Americanos!*," Vidal and his men passed within a mile of Brownsville at night, plundering several ranches and killing at least ten unoffending citizens. As Vidal and his men crossed the river about nine miles above Brownsville, near Cortina's mother's ranch, a large body of Texas Unionists gathered on the south bank of the river to greet him and his men. Less than three weeks after the arrival of the federals in Brownsville, Vidal crossed the ferry and enlisted in the Union army.[56]

After setting fire to Fort Brown, at midnight on November 3, 1863, Gen. Hamilton P. Bee and his small force of Confederates bid a fatigued and drunken adieu to Brownsville. On the south bank, Cortina and the Unionists cheered. With looting, violence, and disorder engulfing Brownsville, community leaders sent an urgent plea to Cortina in Matamoros for assistance in restoring order, but Cortina refused. Before daybreak on November 6, just hours before the Union army entered Brownsville, Cortina seized power in Matamoros.[57]

In the months following the arrival of the federals in the lower valley, Cortina cooperated with the Bluecoats, even allowing the federals to take control of three of King and Kenedy's steamboats that had been under Mexican registry. "I will do everything that tends to the good and prosperity of the American Union," Cortina wrote.[58] Perhaps his greatest contribution was facilitating the recruitment of hundreds of Tejanos and Mexicanos into the Union army. A number of men who enlisted in blue had been with Cortina in 1859 and were now joining the army they had fought against at the time. With Cortina's assistance, Union recruiters enlisted an entire regiment, the 2nd Texas Cavalry, composed almost entirely of Tejanos and Mexicanos.[59]

With the Imperialists closing in on Matamoros, Cortina went over to the French, an act that Benito Juárez and the Liberals would never forgive. Although he returned to the Liberal fold, he was deeply mistrusted. Despite this, he did rise to the rank of general and was with the Republican army at Querétaro on May 15, 1867, when Emperor Maximilian surrendered what remained of the once grand Mexican Imperial army. On a sunny morning of June 19 on El Cerro de las Campanas, Maximilian and two of his leading generals were lined up against a wall and shot. The Empire "died in a lake of blood," Cortina wrote.[60] On the border after the war, he began orchestrating cattle raids into Texas. So lucrative and so extensive were the raids that Cortina was able to purchase several large ranches in Tamaulipas and accumulate a fortune of $800,000.[61]

With the Union army in control of the Lower Rio Grande Valley, Santos Benavides and his small command at Laredo and Eagle Pass were the only Confederates on the Rio Grande. In March 1864, Benavides fought off a small Union force that was attempting to seize the 5,000 bales of cotton stacked in San Agustín Plaza.

In 1864, Confederate authorities offered to commission Benavides as a brigadier general, if he could raise a regiment. Although Benavides's regiment did become reality on paper, by 1864 Texas manpower was seriously depleted, and Benavides was never able to complete his regiment or gain the promotion he wanted so badly.[62]

After the war, Benavides fought bandits and Native Americans, and beginning in 1879, he was elected three consecutive times to the Texas House of Representatives, an accomplishment unequaled by any other Tejano in the nineteenth century. In fact, at the time he was the only Tejano in the legislature. In the last decade of his life, Benavides became somewhat of an international diplomat. He befriended President Porforio Díaz and traveled to Mexico City several times to visit with the Mexican caudillo.[63]

In Laredo in November 1890, Benavides's health made a turn for the worst, and many in the city feared for his life. "His legion of friends in Laredo hope for his speedy recovery," the *Laredo Times* reported.[64] But Santos did not recover. Bedridden and deathly ill for almost a year, he slowly slipped into unconsciousness, and the end finally came early on the morning of Sunday, November 9, 1891, eight days after his sixty-eighth birthday.[65] The saddening news of Santos's death spread quietly over the city. At nine the next morning, a large somber crowd gathered on Market Plaza in front of his residence to escort his remains to San Agustín Church, four blocks away, where a lengthy high mass was conducted before a large congregation, rich and poor, that filled the cathedral to capacity and spilled over into the plaza. At the conclusion of the mass, a long line of carriages carrying relatives and the elite of the city, along with hundreds of mourners on foot, including men who had ridden and fought with him in the Civil War, followed a black-draped hearse with Santos's casket to the Catholic Cemetery.[66]

Cortina outlived Benavides by almost three years. In the twilight of his life, Cortina was said to have remarked that at last he had made peace with the "Texas people," and that he wanted to leave the world without enemies. On the evening of October 30, 1894, the old general died painlessly at his residence in Azcapotzalco on the outskirts of Mexico City of pneumonia and heart failure. It was said his mind was clear to the end. The high-riding border caudillo, or *el jefé de fronterizo* as the Mexico press labeled him, was seventy years old.

Cortina and Benavides lived through a period of great tumult and drama on the South Texas borderlands. Through all the sound and fury that was the history of the Civil War on the border, these two remarkable men seemed to always be at the forefront of events, always ready to lead.

### Notes

1. Jerry D. Thompson, *Cortina: Defending the Mexican Name in Texas* (College Station: Texas A&M University Press, 2007); Jerry D. Thompson, *Tejano Tiger: José de los Santos Benavides and the History of the Texas-Mexico Borderlands, 1823–1891* (Fort Worth: Texas Christian University Press, 2017).

2. Thompson, *Cortina*, 14–16.

3. W. P. Reyburn to F. A. Hatch, November 21, 1859, US Congress, House, "Difficulties on Southwestern Frontier," 36th Cong., 1st Sess., no. 1050, 65.

4. Ibid.

5. Thompson, *Cortina*, 28–30.

6. *Brownsville American Flag*, June 2, 1847.

7. Armando C. Alonzo, "Mexican-American Land Grant Adjudication," *Handbook of Texas Online*, http://www.thshaonline.org/handbook/online/articles/pqmck (accessed April 15, 2016).

8. Ibid.

9. Cortina Proclamation, September 30, 1859, Letters Received, Adjutant General's Office, Record Group 94, National Archives.

10. Thompson, *Cortina*, 73–80.

11. Certificate of Baptism, José de Santos Benavides, July 28, 1986. This particular document by Rev. Thomas A. Davis mistakenly lists his birth as October 31, 1823.

12. Margarita Ramón, Probated Will by José de Jesús Benavides, May 5, 1835, Document F 114, Laredo Archives, St. Mary's University, San Antonio, Texas. For the English translation, see Robert D. Wood, trans., *Death and Taxes* (San Antonio, TX: San Mary's University Duplication Services, 2001), 47–48.

13. Ordinances approved by the City Council of Laredo, January 15, 1856, Ordinance no. 1, Laredo Archives, Microfilm Roll 15.

14. Ordinances approved by the City Council of Laredo, January 18, 1856, Ordinance no. 2, Laredo Archives, Microfilm Roll 15.

15. Minutebook no. 1, April 1, 1856, to April 1, 1857, Special Collections, City Library, Laredo, TX; and Election Returns, 1856 and 1857, Laredo Archives, Microfilm Roll 15.

16. Santos Benavides to the Mayor and Council of the Corporation of Laredo, October 14, 1859, Laredo Archives, Microfilm Roll 15.

17. Basilio Benavides to Santiago Vidaurri, n.d., Correspondencia de Vidaurri, Archivo General del Estado de Nuevo Leon, Monterrey, Nuevo Len.

18. Maverick County voted 80–3 against secession, but the returns from Eagle Pass arrived in Austin too late to be tabulated. Glen Sample Ely, *Where the West Begins* (Lubbock: Texas Tech University Press, 2011), 28, 139; and Jesse Sumter, *Paso del Aguila: A Chronicle of Frontier Days on the Texas Border*, ed. Ben E. Pingenot (Austin: Encino Press, 1969), 83; and Glen Sample Ely, *The Texas Frontier and the Butterfield Overland Mail, 1858–1861* (Norman: University of Oklahoma Press, 2016), 342–43.

19. Virgil N. Lott and Mercurio Martinez, *The Kingdom of Zapata* (Austin: Eakin Press, 1983), 42–43.

20. Juan O. Sanchez, "Vela, Isidro," *Handbook of Texas Online*, http://www.tshaonline.org/handbook/online/articles/fvepu (accessed August 15, 2016).

21. Gardner W. Pierce to John Z. Leyendecker, June 1, 1861, Leyendecker Papers, Center for the Study of American History, University of Texas at Austin; Dale Baum, *The Shattering of Texas Unionism: Politics in the Lone Star State During the Civil War Era* (Baton Rouge: Louisiana State University Press, 1999), 75–76.

22. *Corpus Christi Ranchero*, April 20, 1861.

23. Pierce to [Leyendecker], June 1, 1861, Leyendecker Papers, CAH.

24. *Corpus Christi Ranchero*, April 20, 1861.

25. Henry Redmond to John S. Ford, April 12, 1861, Edward Clark Papers, Texas State Archives, Austin. Also, John D. Mussett to Captain Brown, October 18, 1861, LR, Confederate District of Texas, New Mexico, and Arizona, RG 109, NA.

26. Ford to Redmond, April 15, 1861, Ford Papers, Nita Stewart Haley Library and J. Evetts Haley Center, Midland, TX.

27. Eighth Census (1860), Zapata County, TX, NA.

28. *Corpus Christi Ranchero*, April 27, 1861. As a result of his service during the Mexican War, Nolan was known in South Texas as the "Boy Bugler of the Battle of Cerro Gordo." In the years after the Mexican-American War, Nolan had served with Ford's company of rangers in the Nueces Strip as a bugler. Later he was elected sheriff of Nueces County but was murdered in Corpus Christi on December 22, 1864. Bill Walraven, *Corpus Christi: The History of a Texas Seaport* (Woodland Hills, CA: Windsor, 1982), 53.

29. Gardner Pierce to Leyendecker, June 1, 1861, Leyendecker Papers, CAH.

30. *Corpus Christi Ranchero*, April 27, 1861. Santiago Vela, fifty-seven, a victim of

"una armada de aquel estado," was buried in Guerrero at 10:00 a.m. on the same day, April 15, 1861. Registro Civil de Guerrero, Libro de Defunciones, 1860–1861, 26–27, Guerrero Archives, Nuevo Guerrero, Tamaulipas. Copy courtesy of Stanley Green.

31. Reports of the Committee of Investigation Sent in 1873 by the Mexican Government to the Frontier of Texas (New York: Baker and Godwin, 1875), 66. For a more detailed study of the turmoil in Zapata County, see Jerry Thompson, *Vaqueros in Blue and Gray* (Austin: State House Press, 2000), 15–23; and Jerry Thompson, *Mexican Texans in the Union Army* (El Paso: Texas Western Press, 1986), 1–7.

32. Henry Redmond to John S. Ford, May 14, 1861, Ford Papers, Haley Library. Besides the originals of the Ford Papers at the Haley Library, copies are available at the Texas State Archives in Austin.

33. *Austin Texas State Gazette*, June 8, 1861, TSA.

34. Isidro Vela to Ford, May 14, 1861, Ford Papers, Haley Library.

35. Juan G. Garza to Gefe Politico del Distrito del Norte, May 19, 1861, Correspondencia del Alcalde de Guerrero, Guerrero Archives, Nuevo Guerrero, Tamaulipas.

36. Juan G. Garza to Santos Benavides, May 18, 1861, Correspondencia del Alcalde de Guerrero.

37. Pierce to Leyendecker, June 1, 1861, Leyendecker Papers, CAH.

38. Redmond to Ford, May 23, 1861, Broadside File, TSA.

39. *Galveston Weekly News*, June 18, 1861.

40. Benavides to Ford, May 14, 1861, Ford Papers, Haley Library; Corpus Christi Ranchero, June 1, 8, 1861. "I have no prisoners," Santos said in his official report. Santos told José María Hinojosa that ten of Cortina's "men were left dead on the field and that the others were dispersed in all directions." [Juan G. Garza] to Gefe Politico del Distrito del Norte, May 22, 1861, Correspondencia del Alcalde de Guerrero. Yet in a letter to his friend Vidaurri, Santos said seven Cortinistas were killed. Benavides to Vidaurri, June 10, 1861, Correspondencia de Vidaurri, AGNL. Also, *Galveston Weekly News*, June 15, 18, 1861.

41. Benavides to Ford, May 14, 1861, Ford Papers, Haley Library.

42. Lewis E. Daniell, *Types of Successful Men of Texas* (Austin: E. Von Boeckmann, 1890), 327.

43. Ibid.

44. Francis Richard Lubbock, *Six Decades in Texas or the Memoirs of Francis Richard Lubbock*, ed. C. W. Raines (Austin: Pemberton Press, 1968), 380.

45. "Rout of Cortina," May 29, 1861, contained with Benavides to Ford, May 23, 1861, Ford Papers, Haley Library.

46. Ford, Order no. 21, May 27, 1861, Ford Papers, Haley Library.

47. Daniell, *Types of Successful Men of Texas*, 327.

48. Ibid. Wallace E. Oakes, a friend of the governor, gave the pistol to Benavides personally in November 1861. Wallace E. Oakes to Clark, August 27, 1861; and Benavides to Clark, October 24, 1861, Clark Papers, TSA.

49. Vidaurri to Benavides, June 22, 1864, Correspondencia de Vidaurri, AGNL.

50. Cortina to John L. Haynes, September 12, 1863, letter in private collection.

51. Hamilton P. Bee to Manuel Ruiz, September 12, 1863, *War of the Rebellion:*

*A Compilation of the Official Records of the Union and Confederate Armies* (Washington, DC: Government Printing Office, 1889), I, 26, pt. 1, 396 (hereafter referred to as OR, by series, volume, and part). Also, Banks to H. W. Halleck, November 4, 1863, OR, 1, 25, pt. 1, 397–98; and Banks to Halleck, November 6, 1863, OR, 1, 26, pt. 1, 399–400.

52. A. Lincoln to Edwin M. Stanton, August 4, 1862, *The Collected Works of Abraham Lincoln* (New Brunswick, NJ: Rutgers University Press, 1953), 5: 357.

53. Nathaniel P. Banks to Abraham Lincoln, November 3, 1863, OR, I, 26, pt. 1, 396.

54. Jerry Thompson and Lawrence T. Jones III, *Civil War and Revolution on the Rio Grande Frontier: A Narrative and Photographic History* (Austin: Texas State Historical Association, 2004), 51–52.

55. James Duff to E. R. Tarver, November 11, 1863, OR, I, 26, pt. 1, 439–43; Bee to Edmund P. Turner, October 28, 1863, OR, I, 26, pt. 1, 448–49; Adrian J. Vidal, Compiled Service Record (Union), RG 54, NA; *Houston Tri-Weekly Telegraph*, November 12, 1863; and Thompson, *Vaqueros in Blue and Gray*, 71–74.

56. Duff to Tarver, November 11, 1863, OR, I, 26, pt. 1, 439–43.

57. Thompson, *Cortina*, 115–17.

58. Cortina to John A. McClernand, April 7, 1864, OR, I, 34, pt. 3, 73–74.

59. Thompson, *Mexican Texans in the Union Army*, 15–21.

60. *Brownsville Daily Ranchero*, September 24, 1870.

61. Thompson, *Cortina*, 202–3.

62. Thompson, *Tejano Tiger*.

63. Ibid.

64. *Laredo Times*, November 12, 1890.

65. *Laredo Times*, November 10, 1891.

66. *Laredo Times*, November 11, 1891. During the Great Depression his remains were moved to the new Catholic Cemetery.

# 7

# *Los Algodones*

## The Cotton Times on the Rio Grande

KAREN G. FORT AND TOM A. FORT

*[A]ll the cotton that is shipped from this port comes from Texas, and it is probable that most of the merchandise brought here finds its way into the interior of the Southern states.*
—LEONARD PIERCE JR., UNITED STATES CONSUL IN MATAMOROS, APRIL 24, 1862[1]

Throughout the Civil War years, wagons loaded with cotton bales creaked and rumbled across southern Texas en route to the Rio Grande. Their destination was Bagdad, a ramshackle port on the Gulf of Mexico east of Matamoros, Tamaulipas. Anchored offshore were ships from European countries whose textile mills demanded Southern cotton, and whose usual sources were mostly sealed off by the Union blockade. But cotton *was* available at Bagdad, the Confederacy's only port immune to the federal blockade. In addition, it was an unblockaded entry point for military and civilian cargoes for the Confederacy, along with shipments for another war—Mexico's fight against the French invaders. In time, both sides in that contest would be supplied in part through Bagdad.

Cotton—"white gold"—became the primary means of financing the Confederate war effort and in time was subject to layers of bureaucratic regulations at the national, military, and state levels to control its sale and export. Because cotton was regarded as a medium of exchange, the Confederate government in Richmond, Virginia, sought to buy bales for use in purchasing military and other supplies from foreign sources. Government and army agents tried to buy cotton from planters with paper notes, bonds, and currency. Increasingly, the Rio Grande trade severely impacted government purchases because foreign agents involved in it dealt only in gold. In the western or Trans-Mississippi Confederacy, this effectively cut out the government, military, and state buyers with their paper bonds and currency, and opened the door to speculators. For some it was *very* profitable: "Manipulators, sharpers and scoundrels contested with the shrewd agents of the great mercantile firms in London, Paris, and Bremen for the Rio Grande cotton trade which was so vast in its possibilities for profit that control of even a part of it could mean millions."[2]

This chapter looks at the cotton trade and, in particular, the logistics and challenges of moving thousands of bales, mainly from central and southeast Texas to the Rio Grande, and from the river to Bagdad and the fleet of foreign merchant ships offshore. It will describe the impact of the federal blockade as well as the importance of steamboat traffic on the Rio Grande. Steamboats carried cotton bales from river landings to Matamoros and Bagdad, while also taking deck loads of inbound cargoes—such as military weapons and supplies for Confederate troops—to those same upriver points for shipment into Texas. And then there was salt, the other "white gold," mined from salt lakes in South Texas and transported north to San Antonio and beyond, as well as south to the Rio Grande.

Before it ended in 1865, the cotton trade drew international commerce to the Lower Rio Grande and transformed the tiny fishing village of Bagdad into a major port. The trade also became so notorious for greed and corruption that, later, many involved in it were reluctant to admit it. "[T]he tone of public feeling is such that every man, jealous of his reputation, hesitates to have his name associated with any government transaction in cotton."[3] Decades after the war, residents along the Lower Rio Grande remembered that frenzied, prosperous era as *los algodones*, "the cotton times."

### *Cotton, Trails, and the "Bagdad Trade"*

*[W]e entered a chaparral, or thick covert of mosquite-trees and high prickly-pears. These border the track, and are covered with bits of cotton torn from the endless trains of cotton wagons.*

—Lt. Col. Arthur J. L. Fremantle, South Texas, 1863[4]

## Introduction

Charleston harbor, April 12, 1861. In the predawn darkness a cannon shell arced over the Union's Fort Sumter and exploded. The Confederate bombardment literally blasted all remaining hope for a peaceful solution to the divisive issues of slavery and states' rights. The beleaguered federal garrison, outnumbered and short of supplies, lowered the stars and stripes on the following day, and the troops evacuated to US Navy ships a day later. Neither the South nor the North was truly prepared for war, but ready or not, the conflict had begun.

Southern cotton planters normally sent their annual crop to Northerner and European markets by sea. In Texas, rivers such as the Trinity and Brazos flowed toward the Gulf Coast, providing cheap water transportation to ports such as Galveston, Velasco, and Matagorda. Toward the end of each year, streams of bale-laden carts and wagons rolled to river landings, where they were loaded aboard steamboats and flatboats bound for the Gulf. Then came Sumter, and almost overnight the situation changed.

## Blockade and Evasion

On April 18, US President Abraham Lincoln ordered a naval blockade of Confederate ports. This came in response to the Confederates' decision to issue letters of marque, permitting privateers to prey upon Union merchant ships. Later the blockade was extended to the Confederacy's entire Atlantic and Gulf of Mexico coastlines. With the blockade, the Union sought not only to prevent the Confederates from privateering but also to shut down Confederate international commerce and to undercut the Southern war effort by restricting or stopping vital imports of weapons and materiel, along with clothing, foods, salt, medicines, and other essentials. The export of cotton was not yet a major factor; the Confederate government in Richmond ordered it withheld in the belief that the resulting shortage would prompt England or France to intervene in the war on behalf of the Confederates. In 1862, after such "cotton diplomacy" failed, cotton became the means of financing the Confederate war effort, and large-scale exports resumed to England, France, and other consumers—including the northeastern United States, where Southern cotton traditionally was the lifeblood of the textile industries. The chief obstacle to exporting cotton was the Union blockade.

For the US Navy, the blockade challenge was daunting. In 1861 the Union had fewer than a hundred vessels; less than fifty were in serviceable condition, and most of those were deployed overseas.[5] There were about a dozen warships available to interdict all seaborne commerce into and out of the Confederacy with its 3,500 miles of coastline, indented by numerous bays, sounds, inlets, and river mouths.[6] Not surprisingly, for months the blockade remained more an idea than a reality.

However, the federal navy's strength grew during that year through the addition of more ships to the blockade squadrons and the capture of merchant ships trying to slip past the cordon. Expansion of the federal navy, along with the likelihood of seizure and loss of vessels and cargoes, reduced the number of ship owners willing to risk losing their investments. By late fall, when cotton shipments usually began, little of the crop was moving. "In country sheds, in city warehouses and out in the pale November sunlight at the gin yards, the South's baled cotton crop of the war year 1861 waited, with the world waiting for it, and with no accustomed way to go."[7]

Blockading ships had reached Texas on July 2, 1861, when the USS *South Carolina* took up station off Galveston. Within days she captured nearly a dozen sailing merchant vessels.[8] Although an encouraging start for the federals, the Texas blockade was hardly watertight: well into 1862 there were no more than five Union warships available for duty along the coastline, with most of those off Galveston, the state's only deepwater port and the center of blockade-running activity.[9] But the threat to merchant shipping was real enough, and so was the economic impact. The tightening squeeze on Texas' maritime trade adversely affected not only port communities such as Galveston and Houston but also towns, plantations, and farms inland, where livelihoods, based on cotton, depended on sea transport for access to distant markets. Within this cotton-based infrastructure were the planters, merchants, factors (or agents), speculators, buyers for international firms, and shippers, identified collectively as the "cotton interests." For decades, most of the state's cotton had been exported by sea, but with that option now too risky, men involved in the cotton business in Texas as well as Louisiana and Arkansas began looking for a way through or around the blockade.

They found it on the Lower Rio Grande, in what became known variously as the "Rio Grande trade," the "Matamoros trade," or simply the "cotton trade." It was fostered by the proximity of Mexico, a neutral nation off limits to the Union blockade; foreign vessels in business with Mexico could enter Mexican ports unmolested by the US Navy. Another factor was the international boundary. The portion along the Rio Grande was defined in the Treaty of Guadalupe-Hidalgo (1848): "The boundary line between the two Republics shall commence in the Gulf of Mexico, three leagues from land, opposite the mouth of the Rio Grande, otherwise called Rio Bravo del Norte, or opposite the mouth of its deepest branch, if it should have more than one branch emptying directly into the sea; from thence up the middle of that river, following the deepest channel, where it has more than one, to the point where it strikes the southern boundary of New Mexico."[10] The treaty also stipulated that the Rio Grande (Rio Bravo del Norte) was "free and common to the vessels and citizens of both countries."[11]

The boundary was placed at the center of the Rio Grande's deepest (or main) channel; however, its exact location could and did change as the then undammed river flooded periodically, shifting the main channel elsewhere. Where the river discharged into the Gulf, the boundary extended three leagues or eighteen nautical miles offshore. It was this protective, invisible line in the ocean that permitted the cotton trade to survive. South of the boundary merchant ships, including English, French, German, Spanish, and others, could anchor, unload cargoes for the Confederacy, and take on Confederate cotton, all safely in Mexican waters where Union blockade ships could not legally interfere.

Aboard Union vessels on blockade duty just north of the invisible line, captains and crews watched in frustration as the foreign ships arrived, discharged cargo and loaded bales, and then weighed anchor and departed. In international waters, Union warships could and did stop and search foreign-flag vessels suspected of trading with the Confederates through Mexico. The majority had their manifests and documents in order, maintaining that their inbound cargoes were consigned to Mexican merchants, and their outbound cotton was Mexican in origin. Unless a US Navy skipper was prepared to question the authenticity of the documents and perhaps spark an international incident, there was little more he could do except permit the merchant vessel to sail on.

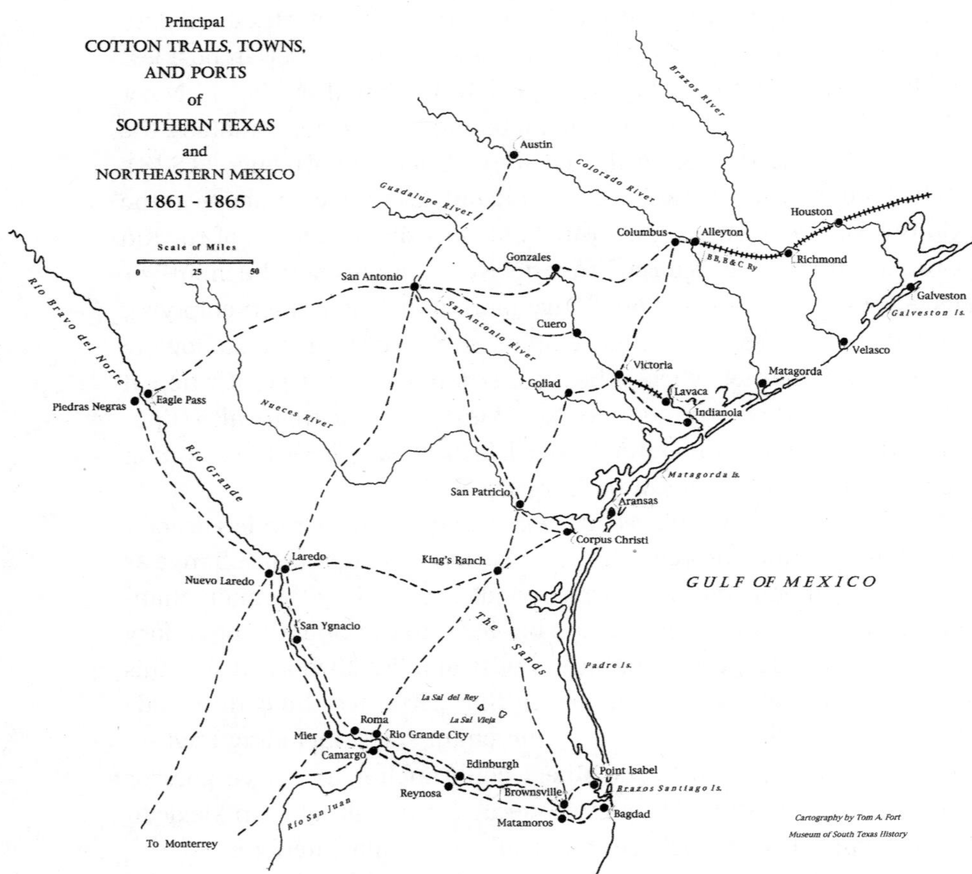


*Map of South Texas cotton trails, showing main wagon roads (or routes) used in transporting cotton from Northeast Texas through Alleyton and San Antonio to Mexico, 1861–65. Courtesy of the Museum of South Texas History.*

## Cotton Trains and Trails

By 1862, Bagdad was the only port open to the Confederacy that could not be blockaded by the Union. Thus it was a powerful magnet for cotton interests in the Trans-Mississippi region. But moving bales to Bagdad was no simple matter. With no rail line to the border, cotton mostly followed long, rough wagon roads that led across arid southern and southwestern Texas to the Rio Grande. Until the end of the war these overland "cotton trails" from Texas, Arkansas, Louisiana, and Indian

Territory (Oklahoma) were the economic lifelines for planters, buyers, and shippers, who also had bureaucratic hurdles to deal with. The Confederate government in Richmond imposed restrictions on the sale and export of cotton, which it regarded as the key to financing the war. In the cotton-growing regions of Texas and along the Rio Grande, agents of the Texas State Cotton Bureau, the Confederate military, and officials of the Trans-Mississippi Quartermaster Department's Cotton Bureau competed with one another to buy cotton, for which they offered government bonds in payment. To their dismay, however, the various agents found out quickly that the Rio Grande cotton trade dealt only in gold specie, against which their paper bonds, notes, and currency were considered worthless. Cotton was being purchased with specie by Matamoros business interests not only at the Rio Grande but also in the cotton growing areas of central and eastern Texas. Small wonder that cotton continued rolling to the Rio Grande!

In response, the Confederate and Texas governments enacted regulations and laws intended to encourage the sale of cotton to the Confederacy before it could be shipped to the border. That strategy, mixing patriotic appeals with strong-arm tactics, had mixed results as thousands of Trans-Mississippi bales kept rolling southward. A postwar newspaper article reported that some 320,000 bales had been exported through Bagdad.[12]

Before being transported to the Rio Grande, cotton had to be ginned and baled. Cotton cultivation at that time required a great deal of manual labor, and most cotton planters—particularly those with large plantations—relied on African American slave labor. Typically slaves handpicked a cotton crop in the late summer and early fall, and carried it to the planter's or a neighbor's cotton gin, where the seeds were removed from the fibers.[13] After the cotton was ginned, slaves carried it in basket loads to a large, outdoor bale press, where a vertical wooden screw was turned by horses or mules harnessed to two long wooden beams, called "buzzard wings" because they angled down from the top of the press. A heavy wooden plunger, mounted on the bottom of the screw, was fitted into a wooden enclosure termed a "bale box." The basket loads of cotton were dumped into the bale box. As the animals walked in a circle around the press, the wooden screw descended, forcing the plunger down into the bale box and squeezing the cotton into a rectangular bale. To raise the screw, the animals walked in the opposite direction. When the plunger was lifted, the bale was wrapped in old clothes, flour sacking, or burlap, and tied with ropes. A finished bale weighed between 450 and 500 pounds, ready to travel.[14]

This "white gold" destined for the Rio Grande came from farms and plantations in southeast and central Texas, as well as Louisiana, Arkansas, and Indian Territory. On the Trinity River in eastern Texas, merchant and planter James Madison Hall wrote in his journal on June 8, 1863, "We met 26 wagons in one train all loaded with cotton, they were from Louisiana and bound for Brownsville for army supplies."[15] Like small tributaries feeding into a stream, numerous back-country roads led from the cotton-growing areas to converge at points where the trails to the Rio Grande started. The principal "trail head" was the town of Alleyton, near Columbus in Colorado County, and at that time the western terminus of the Buffalo Bayou, Brazos and Colorado Railway. This line tapped the southeastern Texas cotton-growing country from Buffalo Bayou (near Houston) to Stafford Point, Richmond, Eagle Lake, and Alleyton. Lt. Col. Arthur Fremantle, a British army officer traveling through Texas in 1863, visited Alleyton: "This little wooden village has sprung into existence during the last three years, owing to its being the present terminus to the railroad. It was crammed full of travelers and cotton speculators."[16]

For cotton growers west of the Brazos River, the main "jumping off point" was San Antonio. There, wagon trains departed from the Main Plaza, bound for the Rio Grande. Others, meanwhile, arrived from the south bringing goods imported through Bagdad and Matamoros. Eliza Ripley, an eyewitness, described the scene in 1864:

> San Antonio was now the business point to which all the wagon-trains from Mexico converged. Hundreds of huge Chihuahua wagons were to be seen 'parked' with military precision outside the city, waiting their turn to enter the grand plaza, deliver their packages of goods, and load with cotton for their outward trip. Everything was hurry, bustle, and confusion. The major-domo, urging his train of wagons through the streets, was loud and vociferous in his language, and each driver and outrider added copiously to the babble of tongues. Merchants

> of every clime were here, anxious to sell or exchange for cotton, or to procure transportation for their goods far into the interior of Louisiana and Arkansas.[17]

Meanwhile, newspapers advertised various goods, including "bagging, bailing rope and twine, blankets, leather, lead, various foodstuffs, and 'segars.'"[18]

Oxcarts and wagons were the primary vehicles. Early in the trade, two-wheeled Mexican-style carts, or *carretas*, were common on the trails through South Texas. August Santleben, then a seventeen-year-old teamster, described these big Chihuahua carts has having beds fifteen feet long by six-and-a-half feet wide; they could carry loads of two to three tons, pulled by five to six pairs (or yokes) of oxen.[19] The carts often were constructed entirely of wood, which caused problems with prolonged wear. "The wheels and axles . . . after long use, wore away until the former wobbled considerably, and the screeching noise they made was awful."[20] Teamsters lubricated the wheels by shoving prickly pear pads into the wheel hubs.

In time many of the *carretas* were replaced by large, four-wheeled American-style freight wagons. Resembling the familiar sway-backed, canvas-topped "prairie schooners," these were heavy, stoutly built vehicles. Santleben recalled wagons with beds (bodies) twenty-four feet long and four-and-a-half feet wide, with axles made of solid iron. Protecting the bed and its contents were curved wooden bows with heavy canvas covers. "An average load for such wagons was about seven thousand pounds, but generally, with ten small mules attached, sixteen bales of cotton was a load."[21]

Wagons normally traveled in caravans or "trains." "Each train consisted of ten or fifteen wagons, a few saddle horses, and twenty or thirty spare draft animals. The train generally had one wagon master, two section captains, twelve teamsters, a couple of armed outriders, and a 'corporal' to ride herd on the extra animals."[22] The wagon master was in charge of the train, keeping up the pace, finding watering places, and selecting a campsite each night.

Anglo-Texans in almost any occupation could be conscripted into Confederate army service. For that reason, planters might use their own African-Texans as wagon drivers to take their cotton to the jumping-off points: "The planters' negro teamsters could place the cotton at Alleyton or Goliad, their owners being paid a better price for the cotton so delivered."[23] For the longer hauls through South Texas, Mexican-Texans (Tejanos) or native Mexicans frequently were hired, since they also were exempt from conscription. Not all drivers were men. Fremantle described one unusual teamster: "I had a long talk with a big mulatto slave woman, who was driving one of Ward's wagons. She told me she had been raised in Tennessee, and that three years ago she had been taken from her mistress for a bad debt, to their mutual sorrow."[24] Ward was the wagon master for a train close to Fremantle's. In 1864, on a wagon train to Mexico, Eliza Ripley also saw other women going along. "Near the Frio [River] we met the only American train I saw, accompanied with a woman (it was not unusual to see women in Mexican trains, making chocolate and *tortillas* for their teamster lords). A Texas teamster, with a wife and two children, returning from the Rio Grande, was camping by the road-side in a drenching rain, dismally trying with wet [cow] chips and twigs to make a fire, as they had no cooked provisions."[25]

Armed outriders protected the trains. Vigilance was essential: cotton was nicknamed "white gold" because of its high commercial value, and renegade bands roamed South Texas looking for opportunities to attack trains, kill teamsters, and make off with loaded wagons. "The trains were under constant danger from Indian raids, bandits, jayhawkers, and bushwhackers. This was especially true on the homeward journey, when they were loaded with necessities, luxuries, and specie. At night the wagons were drawn into a defensive circle to protect men and animals."[26] It was a risky trade, but a rich one, and the potential for profit turned it into a "white-gold rush." From the inland plantations to the Rio Grande, people were eager to cash in: "nearly everybody [became] wild with the cotton mania [and] about 5,000 wagons [were] employed in hauling cotton from Louisiana, Texas and the Indian territory to Matamoros."[27] Everyone, it seemed, saw gold in cotton: "various merchants in Texas and Mexico advertised for cotton. From Eagle Pass, Adolfo Duclos, a French immigrant, offered to accept cotton delivered there, then sell it in Mexico on commission, or for goods. Later, Guilbeau and Herman of Monterrey advertised a similar arrangement."[28]

During the course of the war, cotton trains followed several routes to the Rio Grande. The original trail led from Alleyton southwest to Goliad, and then south to King's ranch near present-day Kingsville, and continued to Brownsville. Late in 1861 the first trains headed south along this trail, the most direct route. It was heavily traveled through 1862 and 1863, but the traffic south of King's ranch stopped when Union forces occupied the Lower Rio Grande Valley late in 1863. During the next eight months, wagon traffic diverted west to Laredo, where another cotton trail crossed the river. When the federals withdrew to Brazos Santiago Island in July 1864, the Brownsville-Matamoros crossing reopened. But the Alleyton-Brownsville trail remained less used during the rest of the war, due to fear of federal attacks from the coast and the debilitating effects of a two-year drought that dried up water holes and grasslands across South Texas.[29] However, once the Valley returned to Confederate hands, "it was possible for cotton trains freely to cross as low down as Rio Grande City, or even Edinburg."[30]

Richard King, a Rio Grande steamboat captain and rancher, established his Santa Gertrudis Ranch near the Gulf Coast during the 1850s. King was a dyed-in-the-wool Confederate, and his ranch became the main stopping place for cotton trains, as described by author Tom Lea: "[King] could stand on the watchtower at ranch headquarters and see the cotton wagons moving south on the road across his pastures toward Brownsville. He could talk to the train bosses and the teamsters and the brokers' agents who stopped to camp under the trees by the Santa Gertrudis water, who came into the ranch commissary to buy camp supplies, who bought horses and mules and beef for the last leg of the long haul to the border."[31] In addition, King's long experience with border trade enabled him to advise government agents and cotton shippers—and also to become a buyer.

> Strangers bringing cotton from afar, to trade for the hard money offered at Matamoros, had their difficulties delivering the travel-stained bales into the hands of dependable brokers. Moreover, the passage of cotton into Mexico was soon restricted by taxes and attempted controls; official agents and buyers and collectors sent out by the Confederate government and the Military Board of Texas appeared with confusing orders and inconsistent demands and competitive instructions. From his point of vantage on the cotton road, Captain King quickly

> found himself an adviser of cotton-owning strangers, a counselor and assistant of government agents, a contractor for the cartage of cotton to the river, and a speculative cotton buyer himself. By March, 1862, the ranch headquarters at the Santa Gertrudis was an official receiving, storage and shipping point for the bales arriving from East Texas, Louisiana, Arkansas and finally as far as Missouri.[32]

South of King's ranch lay "the sands," the worst part of the route: "With few watering places, it was a dreary waste of mesquite, prickly pear, salt licks and sand, infested with rattlesnakes, tarantulas, scorpions, ticks, and fleas. To cross this treacherous strip of more than 120 miles, the teamsters took extra oxen along to assist in pulling through the more difficult places and to replace animals that became too weak to continue."[33]

In spite of these difficult conditions, the sands "became a broad thoroughfare along which continuously moved two vast, unending trains of wagons; the one outward bound with cotton, the other homeward bound with merchandise and army supplies."[34]

To avoid the sands, especially in the summertime, some wagon trains headed west from Goliad or King's ranch, and then continued either to Laredo or cut southwest to the river towns of Roma and Rio Grande City in what is now Starr County. These routes avoided most of the South Texas interior, ravaged by drought and plagued by outlaws. Another western route led to Eagle Pass. Laredo and Eagle Pass had attracted cart and wagon trains since before the war; the old Spanish Royal Road, or *camino real*, crossed the Rio Grande at Eagle Pass. These two crossing points received heavier use after Union troops occupied the Rio Grande Valley late in 1863. For all practical purposes, they were beyond the reach of the federals, and cotton trains continued to use them until the war ended. "One Little Rock, Arkansas, merchant brought 100 wagons of cotton through Eagle Pass, and the customs inspector . . . noted that 'there was scarcely a day that hundreds of bales were not unloaded . . . and crossed [over] . . . as fast as possible.'"[35] Trails from San Antonio also led to King's ranch, as well as to Roma, Laredo, and Eagle Pass.

## At the River

After weeks on trails that were dusty in dry weather or quagmires when it rained, the trains arrived at the Rio Grande. Cotton buyers, representing mercantile interests in Matamoros, often were waiting there with money in their hands. A wagon master could sell the cotton at the river crossing and thereby pay his teamsters with part of the proceeds.[36] "Because of their scarcity and the dangers of the trail, private teamsters received substantial wages. Those working for private merchants were the better paid, reportedly getting $9.00 per day and ox feed."[37]

It was not unusual to sell the cotton while it was still on Texas soil. With the Union blockade in place, "Matamoros cotton speculators by the summer of 1862 were taking technical precautions: they bought their cotton and transferred its title to the names of bona fide Mexican citizens and branded the bales accordingly, *in Texas*, before the cotton ever crossed the river. Blockaders were then unable to say, much less prove, that cotton moving through Matamoros and Bagdad was not the property of neutrals. The ancient skills of Matamoros merchants had not been acquired for nothing."[38]

By wagons and carts, thousands of cotton bales crossed the Rio Grande onto Mexican soil. Their destination was Matamoros. Wagons crossing at Brownsville could head directly into the city. Upriver, wagons crossing at Rio Grande City or Roma could follow the river road to Matamoros, or they could be unloaded and the bales put aboard a steamboat for the downriver trip. Before starting north again, the

*Cotton bales on the Rio Grande south bank; Brownsville, under Union occupation, is across the river.* Frank Leslie's Illustrated Newspaper, *December 5, 1863.*

wagons would be loaded with merchandise destined for the Confederate military forces and the home front. If they crossed at Laredo or Eagle Pass, wagon and cart trains headed southeast along trails that followed the Rio Grande's south bank. Accompanying a train on this route, Eliza Ripley wrote that "we found the four or five days from Laredo to Matamoras [*sic*] the most forlorn and depressing, partly perhaps from the accumulated fatigue and exposure incident to repeated trips of a similar nature. There were not even the usual number of *jeccals* [*sic*] (huts) by the road-side to enliven the mournful scene. At long intervals two or three small collections of adobe huts, surrounding the inevitable dusty plaza, marked as many towns."[39]

As an alternative, at Mier or Camargo (both on tributaries of the Rio Grande), bales could be loaded aboard one of M. Kenedy & Co.'s steamboats and thus avoid both the river road and the higher cost of additional overland transport. The carts and wagons, reloaded with inbound goods, then headed back the way they came.

### Bales by Sea

Besides the overland routes, cotton also reached Matamoros by means of the Texas coast. Its long, shallow bays, or *lagunas*, provided relatively calm waters protected from the open Gulf by low barrier islands, of which Padre Island is perhaps the best known today. The lagunas made convenient waterways for moving bales toward the Rio Grande. "Safely out of reach of the large Union blockaders, shallow-draft schooners sailed these lagoons and bays running cotton and contraband between the Gulf ports of Texas and the neutral waters of Mexico. Drawing about three feet of water and manned by crews of three to six men, these small, swift ships usually carried forty to eighty bales. Frequently, smaller sloops carrying from fifteen to forty bales and two- to three-man crews were used."[40] The volume of such commerce was limited somewhat by fear of drawing federal attacks to interrupt it.[41]

Through 1861, the maritime trade of Brownsville went by way of Point Isabel and Brazos Santiago Pass.[42] "In October 1861, there were as many as nine vessels recently arrived in Brazos harbor."[43] Side-wheel steamboats moved cargoes between Point Isabel and Brownsville, while lighter-draft stern-wheelers handled the upriver trade. Late in that year, with more Texas ports blockaded, the first cotton wagons started coming to Brownsville; with no blockaders offshore, the bales were loaded

VERY NEARLY CAPTURED IN A CALM.

*Schooner* Rob Roy, *commanded by William Watson, running the blockade off the Rio Grande, 1864.* The Adventures of a Blockade Runner, or Trade in Time of War, *by William Watson, 1892.*

THE UNITED STATES SLOOP OF WAR "BROOKLYN."

*US Navy sloop-of-war USS* Brooklyn *capturing a cotton-laden blockade runner off Point Isabel in May 1863.* Harper's Weekly, *January 19, 1861.*

onto ships at Point Isabel. Late in February 1862, the sloop-of-war USS *Portsmouth* arrived off the Brazos Santiago pass. "The blockade of the harbor of Brazos de Santiago . . . resulted in the diversion of trade from the Texas to the Mexican side of the river below Matamoros."[44] Yet throughout the war the sometimes-tenuous nature of the blockade along the Texas coast encouraged "runners," mainly using small, shallow-draft sailing vessels to continue slipping into and out of Point Isabel and other ports. "This type of blockade running was impossible for the Union to stop."[45]

But US Navy vessels still posed a threat, if not directly off Bagdad, then farther out in international waters. American-owned vessels using Confederate ports (such as Point Isabel) could be stopped, inspected, and possibly seized along with their cargoes. Foreign-owned ships also could be stopped and their cargo manifests examined. Shippers resorted to creative subterfuges in listing their cargoes: "Various goods arrived [in Mexico] . . . such as Enfield guns labeled with some nicety 'Hollow Ware,' barrels of gunpowder branded 'Bean Flour,' boxes of percussion caps bearing the legend 'Canned Goods,' cargoes of lead marked 'Bat [*sic*] Metal.'"[46]

### Matamoros, Bagdad, and Lightering the Bales

Early in 1865, a Union army officer wrote, "Matamoros is to the rebellion west of the Mississippi what New York is to the United States—its

Loading wagons on the Calle de Cesar, Matamoras, for Piedras Negras. *Frank Leslie's Illustrated Newspaper*, February 20, 1864

*Freight wagons being loaded on the Calle de Cesar, Matamoros, bound for Piedras Negras.* Frank Leslie's Illustrated Newspaper, *February 20, 1864.*

great commercial and financial center."[47] After the blockade of Brazos Santiago, "the trade" shifted largely from Brownsville to the city of Matamoros, on the river opposite Brownsville. In 1862, Matamoros became the nexus of the Rio Grande trade, with an army of merchants, brokers, and buyers representing countries around the world, as well as Monterrey, Saltillo, and other cities in Mexico. "Business was booming in Matamoras [*sic*]," recalled Eliza Ripley, "large warehouses were opened and filled, vessels of every size and nationality unloaded at the *Boca*—several miles below the city at the mouth of the Rio Grande—and goods were hauled to Matamoras in an endless stream of wagons. A regular fast stage-line was in full operation also for business-men to travel to the *Boca* and back again."[48] Blockade runner William Watson also visited Matamoros: "The whole town was enveloped in a cloud of dust. By the long drought the soil on the roads and streets had by the enormous traffic been ground into a fine powder, which covered them to the depth of several inches; this was whirled about by the wind in every direction."[49]

As bales arrived in Matamoros, cotton merchants processed paperwork and stored them in their warehouses until the "white gold" was transported to Bagdad. By road, wagons and carts carried bales, unloading them at one of the scarce warehouses or directly onto the dunes. Bales also arrived from Matamoros on steamboats, with deck hands rolling bales down the stages and onto the riverbank. Bagdad fronted directly onto the Gulf and had no harbor—just dunes and a beach. Offshore lay a sandbar that could prohibit taking cargoes to or from the waiting ships for days at a time. Evidently there were few warehouses. Eyewitnesses reported hundreds, if not thousands, of cotton bales and cargo crates piled in the open on the riverbank and the sand dunes, awaiting transport. Some cargoes never left. Years after the war, William Watson recalled that "immense piles of goods which had been landed from the ships lay wasting, and on most of them the enormous charges for lighterage, which had been laid on heavily, when added to the freight, port dues, and import duties far exceeded the value of the goods, and in many cases the owners had disowned and abandoned them altogether."[50]

By "lighterage" Watson referred to the moving of cargoes from and to the ships anchored offshore. A "lighter" was a vessel used to ferry crates, sacks, barrels, and any other incoming shipments from the merchant ships to the beach, and to ferry cotton bales and other goods back out. "Every small vessel that would do for a lighter," remembered Watson, "had been brought to the place [Bagdad], put under the Mexican flag and converted into a lighter."[51] Popular for use as lighters were "scows"—small, blunt-ended sailing craft with wide decks that carried substantial loads. Schooner-rigged, they were easily handled by only two or three crewmen, and having shallow hulls they could nose directly onto the beach at Bagdad to load and unload. In Southern and Gulf waters there was precedent in using them to carry cotton bales: "The scow had been used in Southern rivers since the early nineteenth century; . . . both scow sloops and schooners were used to haul cotton and tobacco to market. . . . The area of greatest popularity seems to have been west of New Orleans and extended as far as the Mexican border."[52]

Steamboats were used as lighters also. Fremantle observed "two small steamers" taking bales out to waiting ships."[53] A British warship captain wrote that it "frequently required two to three months to load a vessel . . . because the small steamboats used to transport the cotton could not cross the bar . . . when the water was low."[54]

Over time the "fleet" off Bagdad grew as more international customers came for cotton. In the spring of 1863, Fremantle told of seeing seventy ships or more anchored off Bagdad.[55] At about the same time, "Rear Admiral Theodorous Bailey, acting commander of the Eastern Gulf Blockading Squadron, received reports that off Bagdad there were from 180 to 200 vessels of all nations waiting to discharge their cargoes and load cotton."[56]

## The French Intrusion

Complicating the Rio Grande trade was Mexico's concurrent struggle against the French invasion. During the three-year War of Reform, the Liberal government of Benito Juárez had finally defeated the Conservatives opposed to it. France, Spain, and England had assisted Juárez by making financial loans for his war effort; now those countries' bondholders wanted to be repaid. Juárez, however, had to suspend interest payments while his government recovered. In response, Spanish, English, and French troops were sent to occupy Mexico's chief port of Veracruz late in 1861; by seizing the custom house, the three governments would repay their bondholders from tariff revenues. Collecting on debts with fixed bayonets was not unheard of at the time. However, it soon became clear that France had imperial designs on Mexico, prompting England and Spain to begin withdrawing their forces.

Driving the French action was the boundless ambition of Louis Napoleon of France. Napoleon III, as he was also known, sought to reestablish a French empire in the New World. French military leaders held the Mexican Army in low regard and considered the country an easy conquest after its long internal War of Reform. With Mexico in hand, Louis probably believed he could influence the outcome of the American war and regain former French territory such as Louisiana (lost in 1803 when Louis's uncle, Napoleon Bonaparte, sold the immense region to the United States). Louis may also have wanted Texas to become an independent republic again, and to ally with France in curbing US westward expansion.[57] With such goals, the French began their "Mexican Adventure." An initial thrust toward Mexico City ended with the Mexicans' resounding victory at Puebla on May 5, 1862. Stunned, the French withdrew to Veracruz and prepared to strike again. Reinforced and reequipped, they marched inland again in 1863, taking Mexico City and forcing the Juárez government into Northern Mexico.

The next year Louis made the Austrian archduke Maximilian the emperor of Mexico. One of Maximilian's objectives was to put Imperial troops on the Rio Grande; in September 1864, Austrian, Belgian, and French soldiers landed by sea at Bagdad, took Matamoros, and soon occupied the south bank. Also present were Imperial Mexican troops, loyal to the Conservatives, who preferred French rule to that of Juárez and the Liberals.

Years later, Eliza Ripley recalled her wagon train's entering Matamoros that fall.

> Arriving at Matamoras [*sic*] early in the afternoon, we drove like tired, travel-stained emigrants straight to the plaza. . . . We were surprised to find the city in the hands of the French, garrisoned and picketed by an invading army! . . . A few miles away, on the south bank of the Rio Grande, the Mexican Government [of Juárez] held possession; the opposite [Texas] bank was under Confederate control. Here the French were exulting over the

> capture of the city; and across the river the Federal army occupied Brownsville—the flags of four nationalities floating almost in sight of each other, amid the Pride, pomp, and circumstance of glorious war.[58]

The presence of French Imperial troops on the border could have disrupted the cotton trade, since the business relationships that encouraged it had been made between Confederate and Mexican interests. Among the latter was Santiago Vidaurri, the powerful, autocratic governor of Nuevo Leon, Coahuila, and later Tamaulipas. Vidaurri was an opportunist who favored the cotton trade; in 1861, mercantile firms in the states under his control were selling supplies to the Confederates in return for cotton.[59] Vidaurri had only lukewarm support for Juárez; when offered an alliance with the French but told by Juárez to fight, he went to Texas instead, leaving others to decide matters. In the end, the Confederates proved as adept at cultivating the French as they had Vidaurri, with the result that the trade went on.

French warships, meanwhile, blockaded Mexico's Gulf coast to try to prevent shipments of foreign weapons and supplies for Juárez from coming in through Tampico and other ports. Nevertheless, rifles of English, French, and Austrian origin were used by the Juaristas. So were guns of American manufacture; the Juárez government found ways to purchase arms from US makers despite the federal ban on arms exports while the Civil War was going on.[60] Shipments of weapons for Juárez could enter Mexico through Bagdad, because the French were not blockading the port: the textile mills in France also needed cotton.

That US president Lincoln viewed the French actions as a violation of the Monroe Doctrine was unquestioned, but he refused to be drawn into a war with France over the issue, deciding to fight "one war at a time." Still, Lincoln and his advisors regarded the presence of French troops in Mexico as a threat to US interests, and the thought of a French/Confederate alliance must have been worrisome. Rumors were spreading that Louis Napoleon would side with the Confederates to conquer the Union, in return for the reacquisition of part of the original Louisiana Territory.[61] By mid-1863, as more of Mexico fell under French control, plans were being made for a Union invasion at Brownsville, not only as a way to sever the cotton trade but also to put a federal military presence along the Rio Grande.

## The Federals Invade

*I am satisfied that it is impossible to prevent illicit trade on the Rio Grande unless we can take possession of Brownsville and the American side of the Rio Grande from there to its mouth.*
—Commander Sam. L. Swarthout, USS *Portsmouth* on blockade duty off the Rio Grande, letter to Admiral Farragut, 1862[62]

The Union strategists knew they could not destroy Bagdad itself: the ramshackle port was on Mexican soil, and an attack likely would have started still another war. Instead, the US could do the next best thing—seize the river's north bank and block the crossing points for Confederate cotton shipments. On a blustery November 1, 1863, a Union fleet entered Brazos Santiago Pass. Federal troops under Gen. Nathaniel P. Banks came

*Confederates evacuating Brownsville after hearing of Union forces landing at Point Isabel.* Harper's Weekly, *February 13, 1864.*

ashore, seizing Point Isabel and nearby Brazos Santiago Island. While a detachment began constructing a fortified supply depot on the island, most of the Union force marched toward Brownsville. Word of the invasion set off a panic in the city. Civilians frantically crossed the river to Matamoros, as outnumbered Confederate troops, under Gen. Hamilton Bee's orders, set fire to Fort Brown and withdrew northward. The fires quickly spread into adjoining Brownsville. Stores began to burn, and four tons of gunpowder exploded, hurling flaming debris across the town (and the river), destroying half of the business district.

When the Bluecoats arrived, they found charred ruins where the fort and much of Brownsville had been. What was left came under US control, and Old Glory waved again. While army engineers began to rebuild Fort Brown, Union cavalry units made long-range sweeps deep into South Texas, intercepting cotton trains and harassing any inhabitants with Confederate sympathies. (King's ranch was the target of one such foray.) Meanwhile, other federal units marched upriver to seize crossings at Edinburgh and Rio Grande City. Earlier, a gradual withdrawal of Confederate forces from the Rio Grande had begun, their numbers being too few to resist a Union invasion if it came: "Only a few hundred [Confederate] cavalry were left below Rio Grande City by December, 1862."[63]

By that point, it looked as if the Union would achieve its goal of closing the Rio Grande and shutting off the cotton trade. But the numbers of federal troops were too few to hold the region. By late July 1864, Cols. John Salmon "Rip" Ford and Santos Benavides led Confederate cavalry in turning back a Yankee thrust at Laredo, sending the Bluecoats retreating to Fort Brown. Subsequently they abandoned that post and withdrew to their depot on Brazos Santiago Island. The north bank of the Rio Grande returned to Confederate hands.

## End of the Trade

With the federal forces back at the coast, the Brownsville/Matamoros trade resumed. But by March 1865, the cotton frenzy was winding down. Cotton trains were few, as more planters in Texas' cotton regions hoarded their bales for the postwar market. Overseas the price of cotton fell; ships still anchored off Bagdad, but they found it harder to get a paying load. An economic depression settled over Brownsville, where idle steamboats tied up at the levee.

Then, in May, a federal infantry column set out from Brazos Santiago for Brownsville, intent (perhaps) on securing cotton bales to use as currency after local Confederates surrendered. A last chance for battlefield glory may have been a motive also; officers with combat achievements would have better opportunities for promotion in the peacetime army. Whatever the reasons, the intrusion ended with Confederate cavalry and artillery hitting the column and forcing its withdrawal to Brazos. The last land fight of the Civil War was over, and with it the rich and prosperous cotton-trade era, long remembered on both sides of the Rio Grande as *los algodones*, "the cotton times."

### *The Steamboat Era on the Rio Grande*

Camargo, Tamaulipas, June 1863. Workmen stack the last of four hundred bales of cotton on the battered main deck of a steamboat. Fully laden, the stern-wheel vessel has barely a foot of hull above the swirling brown water. From her tall jack-staff at the bow ripples the eagle-and-serpent flag of the Republic of Mexico. Ready to go, deckhands haul in the landing stage, or gangplank, and coil the dripping mooring lines around cleats. At the blistering boiler fronts, sweating firemen heave four-foot lengths of mesquite into the roaring furnaces, keeping up steam pressure.

Overhead on the hurricane deck, the bell begins to clang loudly,

*Brownsville riverfront and Levee Street businesses, circa 1864, with steamboats tied up. Photographer: Louis de Planque, Matamoros. Courtesy of the DeGolyer Library, Southern Methodist University.*

announcing that the boat is about to move. In his wheelhouse the pilot pulls on a stout brass ring with a line fastened to it, signaling the engineer down below for "backwater." Levers are pulled, steam hisses, clanking engine valves lift and drop, and the massive wooden pitmans slide backward and then forward, slowly turning the paddle wheel. With wood smoke rolling from her rusty sheet-iron chimneys, the boat backs away from the landing into the river current. Then, with the engines set for "ahead," the pilot gives a long blast on the whistle and guides the vessel downstream toward the juncture with the Rio Bravo del Norte, better known as the Rio Grande. Ahead lies a voyage of some 190 miles down the winding river that could take four to five days. At the journey's end are Brownsville and Matamoros, twin focal points of the Rio Grande cotton trade.

## Steam on the River

Throughout the Civil War years, steamboats carried cotton bales down the Rio Grande and cargoes of military and civilian goods upriver. While the wartime cotton trade was a new phenomenon, the river traffic itself was well established. As early as 1829 there was an attempt at commercial steam navigation on the Rio Grande: Henry Austin, cousin to Texas empresario Stephen F. Austin, brought a side-wheeled boat named *Ariel*. For several months he ran her up and down the river, but the venture proved unprofitable, and Austin soon took his boat north.[64]

The true "steamboat age" on the Rio Grande began during the Mexican War. In the summer of 1846, US troops occupied both sides of the river from its mouth at the Gulf of Mexico west to what is now Starr County. Gen. Zachary Taylor, commanding the US forces, was preparing his army for a march overland to assault the fortified city of Monterrey in Nuevo León. As the jumping-off point for his campaign, Taylor chose the town of Camargo, Tamaulipas, on the Rio San Juan a few miles south of today's Rio Grande City, Texas. One of the challenges facing Taylor and his staff was transporting from Matamoros to Camargo the mountain of material needed for the impending march. The army on the Rio Grande did not have sufficient wagons to carry out the task. Since the Rio Grande and Rio San Juan both were navigable, Taylor sent quartermaster officers to the Ohio River to obtain steamboats. The army bought some vessels and contracted the use of others;

all had civilian crews. Descending the Ohio and Mississippi Rivers, the boats followed the coasts of Louisiana and Texas to Brazos Santiago and the Rio Grande.[65] In addition to the army's vessels, a few privately owned boats came to the Rio Grande, carrying nonmilitary passengers and freight, both barred from the "government boats."

Besides carrying army supplies, the puffing steamboats also hauled troops, some bound for Taylor's base camp, and others—their enlistments having expired—headed back to Matamoros and a return home. The potential for postwar river commerce was not lost on the steamboat captains and owners. Northern Mexico, remote from mercantile centers far to the south, was a ready market for manufactured goods, a situation perceived by European and American entrepreneurs before and during the Mexican War. In the Rio Grande they saw a water highway for commerce once the war ended. When that occurred in 1848, the Rio Grande officially became part of the international boundary between the two republics, a circumstance that would define the region's later Civil War role.

With the war with Mexico over, the US Army prepared to depart the Rio Grande, leaving several posts to keep watch over the border country: Fort Brown at Brownsville, Ringgold Barracks (later Fort Ringgold) near Rio Grande City, and Fort McIntosh at Laredo. Wanting to get out of the steamboat business, late in 1848 the army announced that it would auction off the remaining boats—those that had not succumbed to hard service and irregular maintenance.[66] Private owners bought some of the vessels, and the Rio Grande's commercial riverboat era was underway.

### M. Kenedy & Co.

The 1850s became a decade of thriving commerce along the Lower Rio Grande, establishing patterns that continued into the Civil War. Arriving by sea, manufactured goods from Europe and the US poured into Matamoros. English, French, German, and other nations' mercantile houses processed the documents and sent the shipments along various routes into the interior of northeastern Mexico. Across the river (and the international boundary), the new city of Brownsville, adjacent to Fort Brown, quickly became the principal trade center for the Texas side. Among its merchants, bankers, and steamboat operators were three men who came to dominate the river trade before and during the Civil War.

Charles Stillman of Connecticut was a long-time resident of Matamoros and a wealthy businessman and investor who was at home on both sides of the river, with connections from Matamoros to Monterrey and New York. Mifflin Kenedy of Pennsylvania was a Quaker steamboat captain who had assisted the Army Quartermaster Corps in selecting steamboats for Mexican War service. Richard King, orphaned son of Irish immigrants to New York City, brought his steamboat piloting experience from Florida to the Rio Grande during the Mexican War. Later, King became a boat captain and a cattleman; his ranch south of Corpus Christi served as the principal way-stop for Confederate wagon trains to and from Brownsville. In time, King himself became a cotton buyer and shipper. Both Kenedy and Stillman also owned South Texas ranches.

While there were others cashing in on the border trade bonanza, the partnership of Stillman, Kenedy, and King—known officially as M. Kenedy & Co.—eventually ruled the river. The trio started with surplus army boats from the Mexican War. As those vessels wore out, Kenedy and King ordered new steamboats from builders near Pittsburgh. Stoutly constructed side-wheelers were called "outside boats" because they carried seaborne cargo from the anchorage at Point Isabel along the coast (outside of the barrier islands) to the Rio Grande and then upriver to Brownsville. Beyond Brownsville the Rio Grande became shallow in places; to handle those stretches, the partners ordered "inside boats," stern-wheelers that almost sat on the water's surface and could, as steamboat men liked to boast, "navigate on a heavy dew." The paddle wheel, mounted at the stern behind the hull, was at less risk of damage from floating logs and other debris than the side-mounted wheels of the outside boats.

M. Kenedy & Co. flourished, adding more boats and buying out competitors. (In the partners' view, there was room for only *one* steamboat company on the Rio Grande). By 1861, they had amassed the fleet that would carry the Rio Grande trade during the Civil War. In addition, they effectively controlled all commerce on the Rio Grande and would have a firm grip on the cotton trade through their extensive connections with the merchants and financial interests in Matamoros and Monterrey. The existence of such organizations as M. Kenedy & Co. helped make the Lower Rio Grande the nexus of the Civil War trade. "The large commercial firms in Brownsville and Matamoros had obvious advantages in exploiting the Rio Grande cotton trade. They already had the ships, organization, Mexican contacts, markets, and credit and capital resources needed by the newly formed Confederate and Texas governments. That they withal also aggrandized their own fortunes is a matter of record."[67]

## Wartime Trade on the Rio Grande

During the war years, steamboats carried Rio Grande cargoes in both directions. Loads destined for Confederate Texas included rifles, pistols, and other weapons plus blankets, hats, shoes, accoutrements, uniforms, medicines, and other military essentials. Foodstuffs, condiments, table wares, cigars, wines, ladies' fashions, and other items arrived also, bound for Texas consumers deprived of such luxury goods by the blockade. Crated rifles and ammunition for Benito Juárez's guerrillas also made the trip. Downriver, the primary cargo was cotton. Three hundred or more bales could be loaded aboard a steamboat, the equivalent of about thirty wagons. Before federal troops occupied the Lower Rio Grande during 1863 and 1864, cotton could be loaded at Roma or Rio Grande City, where trail branches met the river. Later, with wagon trains crossing at Laredo and Eagle Pass and coming down the south bank, steamboats could load cotton at Mier on the Rio Alamo or Camargo on the Rio San Juan, while unloading their incoming cargoes at those same points. (Both the Rio Alamo and Rio San Juan flowed into the Rio Grande.) Roma, a few miles upriver from Rio Grande City, was the practical head of navigation; any boats making it that far usually turned around to begin their downriver trip. During periods of high water it was possible for a steamboat to navigate as far as Laredo, although with the risk of becoming stranded if the river level dropped before the boat returned.

At the other end of the river there were hazards of a different kind. "Outside" boats taking cargoes from Point Isabel to the Rio Grande ventured into the Gulf of Mexico via the narrow Brazos Santiago Pass, and then steamed about ten miles south along Brazos Santiago Island and past Boca Chica inlet before entering the river mouth with its notorious sandbar. Many seagoing vessels, and a few steamboats, ended their days on the island or the bar.

From the river mouth to far beyond Brownsville, the Rio Grande posed still other headaches for steamboat men. It twisted, looped, and curled back on itself so much that a steamboat bound upriver could spend as much time going the *opposite* direction as it did heading for its destination. Floods brought high water that spread the river across miles of landscape and caused it to change course. Both sides of its channel were marked by "ox bows," or cutoff bends, along with abandoned stretches of channel known locally as *resacas*; some of these were dry, others water-filled. Another problem was the international boundary, which was supposed to be in the center of the deepest channel. Recording the changes no doubt kept government surveyors and officials busy on both sides. Yet during the war that same boundary line would prove heaven-sent for M. Kenedy & Co. and the Confederates.

Early in 1862 came the added threat of seizure by Union ships. In his memoirs, Col. John Salmon "Rip" Ford recalled: "King & Kenedy felt cramped in their transporting operations. They could not visit Brazos Santiago without being captured by the blockader. They consulted Ford in regard to placing their boats under the Mexican flag . . . to render them free from capture by the Federals."[68] Ford, then commanding Confederate forces in the Rio Grande Valley, was well known and respected on both sides of the river. The partners followed his advice. Soon Mexican flags flew from their steamboats, but the crews—and management—remained the same, and the cargoes they carried were marked as Mexican-owned. While Union troops occupied the Valley in 1863 and 1864, the steamboats of King and Kenedy churned merrily along, their pilots keeping scrupulously south of the midchannel boundary line and safely in Mexican waters. No doubt their crews waved (and possibly gestured) to Yankee troops on the Texas side.

While the Union forces held the Valley, they also used steamboats. Several boats belonging to M. Kenedy & Co. fell into federal hands and were put to use carrying supplies and troops from Brazos Santiago to Fort Brown, as well as to Union outposts farther upriver. To avoid the river mouth altogether, the federals built a supply depot at White's Ranch, downriver from Brownsville. Transport ships unloaded cargoes at Union-held Point Isabel, and wagons brought the supplies overland to White's landing. There they were loaded onto steamboats for the run to Fort Brown.

In April 1864, Lt. Benjamin F. McIntyre, of the 19th Iowa Infantry, noted steamboat activity in his diary: "Camp near Brownsville Texas Apr 11th 1864, Monday, The Steamer James Hale arrived today from the Point having on board six heavy cannon which are intended to be placed on Fort Brown."[69] In July, steamboats were being used to evacuate the Union troops: "Fort Brown Texas July 19th 1864 Tuesday The James Hale and Mustang has arrived & will be loaded tonight. A large number of Refugees and citizens left on the packets Sunday evening & will go to NO—many more will leave tomorrow."[70] The *Mustang* was a former M. Kenedy & Co. boat used by the US Quartermaster Department. Along with the *James Hale*, the *Alamo*, and the *Matamoros* (all mentioned by McIntyre), the *Mustang* made numerous runs on federal army business, as noted in the time book or log kept by Theodore M. Warner, the boat's purser (or clerk), on July 9, 1864:

> *Saturday 9th*
> *Str Mustang left B[rownsville] at 4.50 a. m.*
> *Gen. Herron is aboard*
> *Arrived at wood yard at 8.40 a.m.*
> *Left same at 9.20 a.m.*
> *Stopped at White Ranch at 5 min to 12[?]*
> *Landed Gen Herron and left at 1.25[?] p.m.*
> *Arrived at Clarksville at 4.20[?] p.m.*[71]

## End of the Era

Steamboats continued to ply the Rio Grande after the Civil War. But conditions along the river were changing, and the old boom days would not be back. In 1866, Charles Stillman suffered a stroke and left for New York City; he never returned. His partners reorganized the firm as King, Kenedy & Co. They sold several boats, such as the *Antonia*, to the French for use as gunboats. But time was running out for Imperial forces on the Rio Grande. With the end of the Civil War in 1865, US troops under Gen. Philip Sheridan arrived on the Lower Rio Grande, bringing crates of weapons. "Sheridan supplied Juarez's troops with tens of thousands of surplus rifles and pistols. These weapons, Sheridan later wrote, 'we left at convenient places on our side of the river to fall into their hands.'"[72] The Juaristas gained the upper hand, and Imperial forces left the Rio Bravo del Norte; in June, 1866, the *Antonia* carried the last Austrian and Belgian troops from Matamoros to Bagdad for embarkation to Veracruz. Napoleon III began pulling his troops out of Mexico, leaving the puppet emperor Maximilian I to his fate. In 1867 Juárez defeated the last Imperial forces and rode triumphantly into Mexico City. Subsequently, King, Kenedy & Co. reacquired the *Antonia*.

That same year also brought a disastrous hurricane that destroyed Bagdad and devastated Matamoros and Brownsville. A number of steamboats were sunk at their moorings; others were wrecked beyond practical repair. As river trade declined, fewer boats operated on the Rio Grande. Kenedy and King eventually sold out to another partner and became full-time ranchers. By the 1870s, only a few boats still ran on the river, and by 1890 there remained only one, the *Bessie*, which made her last voyage around 1900. With her ended the Rio Grande's steamboat trade and a last commercial link with the Civil War "cotton times," *los algodones*.

### *The Other White Gold: Salt*

An ex-Confederate officer was giving a lecture in Syracuse, New York, a few years after the close of the Civil War. In the course of the day he had been driven about the city by his host and had, naturally, been given a view of the extensive salt wells and salt works for which that city was noted. In opening his lecture that evening, he startled his audience with the somewhat remarkable query, "Do you know why you northerners whipped us southerners?" On the surprised ears of his audience fell the terse answer, "Because you had salt."[73]

It may be said that while cotton financed the Confederate war effort, it was salt—the other "white gold"—that actually sustained it. Salt was used in the diets of millions of soldiers and civilians; in feeding livestock and draft animals, including many thousands of army mules and horses; in preserving beef, pork, bacon, fish, butter, eggs, and other foods; in tanning leather for military accoutrements and harness; in making gunpowder; and for scores of other uses. Before the war, the Southern states usually imported the quantities of salt they needed—and they needed a lot of it. As many as fifty pounds of salt were consumed per person per year, or some 225,000 tons annually for a population of some nine million. Most of it arrived by ship from England and the West Indies; "only a very small part of that amount had been produced in the Southern states before the Civil War."[74] In 1861, with the blockade in place, salt imports began falling off, salt prices began rising, and domestic sources took on a new—and valuable—importance.

From Saltville, Virginia, to Avery Island, Louisiana, and Grand Saline, Texas, enterprising Southerners exploited known salt mines and began looking for additional sources.

One long-practiced means of recovery was boiling down salt water from coastal lagoons. The method was most used in Florida, surrounded by salt water and with ample forests for wood fuel.[75] Texans, like Richard King of the Santa Gertrudis Ranch, knew the method also: "Alert to enlarge ranching income, early in the war Captain King essayed a new venture. A salt shortage in the Confederacy made the extracting of salt from saline lakes on the boggy coastal prairies near the Santa Gertrudis a modestly profitable enterprise. He gathered and sold salt."[76] Likewise, King's business partner Charles Stillman produced and sold salt from his Los Laureles Ranch on the Laguna Madre.[77]

Salt lakes were another important source. In South Texas, some thirty miles north of the Rio Grande, are two historic salt lakes: La Sal Vieja and La Sal del Rey. Both provided salt during the Civil War. La Sal Vieja, "the old salt," lies in gently rolling terrain in what is now western Willacy County. In Civil War days, the site was probably dry during much of the year, but since 1940 water has filled La Sal Vieja, channeled into it as a flood-control measure. Today it is actually two lakes, a large one and a much smaller one, separated by a narrow natural isthmus.

La Sal del Rey, in north-central Hidalgo County, is the better known of the two lakes. (Its name in older sources often appears as El Sal del Rey.) Lying in a natural depression, the lake is a geological phenomenon, a seemingly inexhaustible source of salt. During the late 1700s, the Spanish crown recognized the value of the lake by declaring it royal property and issuing leases for mining. A percentage of the profits was paid to the Crown, and for that reason it was named La Sal del Rey, "the King's salt." Unlike La Sal Vieja, La Sal del Rey remains dry or nearly so throughout much of the year. No floodwater is diverted into it, and today the lake and its surrounding lands are within the Lower Rio Grande Valley National Wildlife Refuge.

In centuries past, both lakes were known widely for their salt production, and both were mined. Archaeological traces indicate that Native Americans dug salt for thousands of years. One local tradition suggests that traders from Aztec Mexico obtained salt from La Sal del Rey and possibly La Sal Vieja. Spanish colonial ranchers were granted the surrounding lands and mined salt under royal leases. A Spanish chronicler noted that La Sal Vieja supplied "all of northern Mexico with salt."[78] After Spanish rule ended in 1821, there came Mexican *salineros* or salt miners, followed by Anglo-Americans during the Republic of Texas days. La Sal del Rey was so rich that in the 1840s the Republic of Texas recognized its value and, following Spanish legal precedent, declared it a government resource.

To collect the salt, the crystals were hand-dug from shallows around the lake perimeter by miners wading into water that was often only a few inches deep. The salt was then piled onto wooden piers or onto the lakeshore and allowed to dry in the sun. Afterward it was shoveled into baskets or bags for transport by muleback and oxcart to the Rio Grande and on into Mexico. Mining at La Sal Vieja ceased before 1920, but at La Sal del Rey the age-old process continued well into the 1930s. Photographs from that time suggest that the mining procedures had changed little in more than two hundred years.

When the Civil War began in 1861, these salines took on new importance for the war effort in Texas. Due to the blockade, salt imports began to shrink, and salt deposits such as those in South Texas became an increasingly valuable source of supply. In 1862 the Texas governor, Francis Lubbock, declared La Sal del Rey to be under state control. However, although the two lakes were rich producers, their remote location

*Wagons and carts at Matamoros in the 1860s. Photographer: Attributed to Louis de Planque, Matamoros; copied by Robert Runyon, Brownsville. Courtesy of the Robert Runyon Photographic Collection, di_11071, The Dolph Briscoe Center for American History, University of Texas at Austin.*

was a problem. The salt had to be hauled by carts and wagons over distances of several hundred miles, through arid country where water holes were scarce. Much of the salt went north and east, to San Antonio, Houston, and other population centers, where the mineral was most needed for food processing, manufacturing, and military distribution. Other loads rolled toward the Rio Grande as they had for many years.

Soon after Union forces occupied Brownsville late in 1863, the federals sent cavalry to seize both lakes and drive away the state officials and miners. It should be noted that popular histories of South Texas during the war usually mention Union forces "destroying the salt works" at La Sal del Rey and La Sal Vieja. Exactly what this entailed is not clear, and one wishes that the military reports were more descriptive. Salt at these sites evidently was produced mainly by digging it from the lake bed and drying it in the sun. The main "works" may have consisted of shovels and possibly a wharf or two on which to pile the crystals. Boilers, kettles, and pans, such as were used often in recovering salt from brine, may not have been needed here.

To prevent Confederates from reopening the works, Union troops returned on occasion and not always on horseback. On January 7, 1864, Union major general N. J. T. Dana on the Rio Grande wrote to Brig. Gen. C. P. Stone at Point Isabel: "I sent the Ninety-first Illinois Infantry about a week ago to visit Salt Lake. It will return now in a couple of days. There was no special object more important than giving them proper occupation."[79] One can only surmise what the foot soldiers said about being sent on such a march for "proper occupation"! Dana's dispatch did not specify which salt lake they were sent to.

La Sal del Rey and La Sal Vieja were among a number of salt sources in Texas. Others included the Aransas Salt Works and Lamar Salt Work (both in Aransas County); Double Mountain Salt Works (Stonewall County); Grand Saline Salt Work (Van Zandt County); and the Palestine Salt Works (Anderson County).[80] Texans apparently fared somewhat better than residents in other Confederate states, where shortages of salt became acute. Union army troops and Union navy landing parties often targeted Confederate salt works, knowing that an absence of salt could undercut the Confederate war effort at many levels. In time salt became so scarce that people recovered and reused it until its preservative value was lost. "Every grain was carefully shaken from the cured meat before the latter was used and religiously saved."[81] As Confederate currency lost its value, salt became a primary article of barter.

With increased scarcity, the price of salt surged upward. Before the war, salt imported from Liverpool sold in New Orleans for 50 cents a sack, or about a quarter of a cent per pound. By late 1861 the price in Georgia and Virginia was six dollars a sack and rising. To try and hold the line, during the fall of 1864 the State of Texas fixed the price of salt for army use at $2.50 per bushel.[82] As with the cotton trade, the wartime salt trade attracted its share of speculators and extortionists—those intent on cornering the market and raking in huge profits. "It is currently reported," wrote an editor, "that all the salt in New Orleans and elsewhere is now in the hands of speculators."[83] A planter wrote, "Blessed are they that have no hogs. These extortioners are worse than the Hessians & doing our cause more damage."[84]

Meanwhile, by early in 1864, Union troops had advanced from Brownsville up the Rio Grande, seizing river crossing points as they moved toward Laredo. Driven back by the cavalry of Cols. Santos Benavides and John Salmon "Rip" Ford, the federals retreated to Brownsville and finally to Brazos Santiago Island. Once enemy troops had left the mainland, salt mining resumed at La Sal del Rey and La Sal Vieja. By this time wagons and carts were in short supply; those not being used in the cotton trade were commandeered as army transports.

The early spring of 1865 brought a reluctant awareness to the Confederacy that the Civil War had reached an end. After the last Confederate armies surrendered east of the Mississippi, troops in the Trans-Mississippi states (Louisiana, Arkansas, and Texas) held out for a brief time before they also surrendered. The war's final land engagement took place near the Rio Grande, east of Brownsville, in May 1865. Afterward, Union occupation forces came to South Texas, and the long period of Reconstruction began.

Salt mining continued at the two lakes as it had since Spanish colonial times. Yet La Sal del Rey was destined to play one more role in history. Legal disputes about the ownership of the salt—whether it belonged to the property owner or to the state—led to a landmark court case in which the state ruled that those who owned Texas lands also owned the rights to the minerals beneath them. The significance of this ruling for the subsequent rise of Texas' petroleum industry may well be imagined. But that is another story.

## *Conclusion*

Looking back in later years, Eliza Ripley summed up the Rio Grande trade:

> The Confederate Government made stupendous efforts to procure army supplies through Mexico; but the great distance, scarcity of transportation, lack of harmony between the several branches of the service, and the unscrupulousness of speculators, interfered with well-laid plans, diminished anticipated results, and subjected the officers of the department to severe criticism for their failure to furnish the army with everything needed, and vituperation from every contractor who did not get the pound of flesh demanded. Traders shipped hither merchandise of every description, with the expectation of selling to the Confederate authorities at such fabulous profit as would warrant taking proportionate hazard in regard to securing payment, all tending to wild speculation, reckless business methods, and amazing complications.[85]

In the end, the Rio Grande cotton trade benefitted the merchant, the speculator, and the sharp operator far more than it did most of those who labored in it, or the Confederate soldiers and civilians in need of what it brought. As often happens, the lure of gold and immense profits, coupled with greed, finally ruled the day.

## *Notes*

1. James A. Irby, *Backdoor at Bagdad: The Civil War on the Rio Grande* (El Paso: Texas Western Press, 1977), 23.

2. Ibid., 7.

3. Ibid., 17.

4. Lt. Col. Arthur J. L. Fremantle, *Three Months in the Southern States: April–June 1863* (Lincoln: University of Nebraska Press, 1864, reprinted 1991), 30.

5. Rodman L. Underwood, *Waters of Discord: The Union Blockade of Texas in the Civil War* (Jefferson, NC: McFarland & Company Inc., 2003), 27.

6. Ibid., 23.

7. Tom Lea, *The King Ranch* (Boston: Little, Brown and Company, 1957), I: 182.

8. Richard V. Francaviglia, *From Sail to Steam: Four Centuries of Texas Maritime History 1500–1900* (Austin: University of Texas Press, 1998), 194.

9. Ibid., 194.

10. The Avalon Project, Documents in Law, History, and Diplomacy, "Treaty of Guadalupe-Hidalgo: Article V, February 2, 1848," Lillian Goldman Law Library, Yale Law School, http://avalon.law.yale.edu/19th_century/guadhida.asp (accessed January 16, 2016).

11. Ibid., Article VII.

12. James W. Daddysman, *The Matamoros Trade: Confederate Commerce, Diplomacy, and Intrigue* (Newark: University of Delaware Press, 1984), 143; n. 175; *Weekly Texas State Gazette* (Austin), March 22, 1865; *New York Times*, September 6, 1865, 150.

13. The term "cotton gin" derives from "cotton engine," referring to the machine devised originally in 1793 by Eli Whitney and improved in subsequent years by other inventors.

14. Karen G. B. Fort, *Bale o' Cotton: The Mechanical Art of Cotton Ginning* (College Station: Texas A&M University Press, 1992, reprinted 2015), 24–27.

15. Karen Gerhardt Fort, *A Feast of Reason: The Civil War Journal of James Madison Hall* (Abilene, TX: State House Press, 2017). The handwritten journal is located at the Briscoe Center for American History, University of Texas at Austin.

16. Fremantle, *Three Months in the Southern States*, 63.

17. Eliza M. Ripley, *From Flag to Flag: A Woman's Adventures and Experiences in the South during the War, in Mexico, and in Cuba* (New York: D. Appleton and Company, 1889), 95–96. Documenting the American South, University Library, University of North Carolina at Chapel Hill, 2004, http://docsouth.unc.edu/fpn/ripleyflag/menu/html.

18. Daddysman, *The Matamoros Trade*, 108.

19. August Santleben, *A Texas Pioneer: Early Staging and Overland Freighting Days on the Frontiers of Texas and Mexico*, ed. I. D. Affleck (New York: Neale Publishing, 1910; complete facsimile edition by W. M. Morrison, Waco, Texas, 1967), 107–8.

20. Ibid., 108.

21. Ibid., 108–9.

22. Ibid.

23. LeRoy P. Graf, "The Economic History of the Lower Rio Grande Valley, 1820–1875" (PhD diss., Harvard University, 1942), II: 496.

24. Fremantle, *Three Months in the Southern States*, 41.

25. Ripley, *From Flag to Flag*, 104.

26. Daddysman, *The Matamoros Trade*, 110.

27. Ibid., 108–9, n. 9; *Cincinnati Gazette*, April 16, 1865, 143.

28. Ronnie C. Tyler, "Cotton on the Border, 1861–1865," in *Lone Star Blue and Gray: Essays on Texas in the Civil War*, ed. Ralph A. Wooster (Austin: Texas State Historical Association, 1995), 217.

29. Graf, "The Economic History of the Lower Rio Grande Valley," II: 529.

30. Ibid. Edinburgh, to use its correct spelling, was the river town known today as Hidalgo, Texas. Scottish merchant John Young named it for Edinburgh, Scotland, when he settled there in 1852.

31. Lea, *The King Ranch*, I: 184.

32. Ibid., 184.

33. Tyler, "Cotton on the Border," 109.

34. Ibid., 216.

35. Ibid., 219.

36. Graf, "The Economic History of the Lower Rio Grande Valley," II: 496.

37. Daddysman, *The Matamoros Trade*, 111.

38. Lea, *The King Ranch*, I: 186–87.

39. Ripley, *From Flag to Flag*, 111–112.

40. Daddysman, *The Matamoros Trade*, 112.

41. Graf, "The Economic History of the Lower Rio Grande Valley," II: 523–24.

42. Ibid., II: 494.

43. Ibid., II: 532, n. 1.

44. Ibid., II: 494–95.

45. Underwood, *Waters of Discord*, 60.

46. Lea, *The King Ranch*, I: 193.

47. Official Records of the Union and Confederate Armies, Series 1, Vol. 48, Part 1, 512–13, "Making of America," Cornell University Library, http://ebooks.library.cornell.edu/m/moawar/waro.html (accessed January 18, 2016).

48. Ripley, *From Flag to Flag*, 121–22.

49. William Watson, *The Civil War Adventures of a Blockade Runner* (College Station: Texas A&M University Press, 2001), 24.

50. Ibid., 26.

51. Ibid.

52. Howard I. Chapelle, *American Small Sailing Craft: Their Design, Development, and Construction* (New York: W. W. Norton & Company, 1951), 332–33.

53. Fremantle, *Three Months in the Southern States*, 8.

54. Tyler, "Cotton on the Border," 218.

55. Fremantle, *Three Months in the Southern States*, 8.

56. Underwood, *Waters of Discord*, 70–71.

57. Ibid., 106–7.

58. Ripley, *From Flag to Flag*, 113–14.

59. Underwood, *Waters of Discord*, 109.

60. René Chartrand, *The Mexican Adventure 1861–67*, Men-At-Arms Series, no. 272 (London: Osprey Publishing, 1994, 1998), 12–13.

61. Underwood, *Waters of Discord*, 106–7.

62. Ibid., 65.

63. Graf, "The Economic History of the Lower Rio Grande Valley," II: 526.

64. Harbert Davenport, "Notes on Early Steamboating on the Rio Grande," *Southwestern Historical Quarterly* XLIC (1945): 286.

65. For an account of one boat's voyage from the Mississippi to Texas in 1847, see "The Del Norte Goes to Texas," the diary of Chief Engineer Andrew Jackson Printz, in the *S&D Reflector: Sons and Daughters of Pioneer Rivermen* (December 2006), 35–38.

66. Irby, *Backdoor at Bagdad*, 8.

67. John Salmon Ford, *Rip Ford's Texas*, ed. Stephen B. Oates (Austin: University of Texas Press, 1963, reprinted 1987), 329.

68. Nannie M. Tilley, ed., *Federals on the Frontier: The Diary of Benjamin F. McIntyre 1862–1864* (Austin: University of Texas Press, 1963), 327.

69. Ibid., 375.

70. Theodore M. Warner, *Time Book of the Steamer* Mustang, *1864*, Theodore M. Warner Collection, Margaret H. McAllen Memorial Archives, Museum of South Texas History, Edinburg, Texas. Maj. Gen. Francis J. Herron was appointed commander of the Union's XIII Corps and served at Fort Brown after General N. P. Banks left the Rio Grande in mid-November to prepare for the Red River Expedition.

71. Ibid.

72. Patrick J. Kelly, "Lincoln Looks South of the Border," *The New York Times*, November 22, 2013, http://opinionator.blogs.nytimes.com/2013/11/22/lincoln-looks-south-of-the-border/?_r=0 (accessed January 18, 2016).

73. Ella Lonn, *Salt as a Factor in the Confederacy* (Tuscaloosa: University of Alabama Press, 1965), 13.

74. Ibid., 14. One estimate put the Confederacy's total wartime salt consumption, for all uses, at three hundred million pounds per year.

75. Ibid., 30.

76. Lea, *The King Ranch*, I: 181.

77. Graf, "The Economic History of the Lower Rio Grande Valley," II: 433–34.

78. Ruth Musgrave Coole, "La Sal Vieja," *Handbook of Texas Online*, https://www.tshaonline.org/handbook/online/articles/r0101. For information about La Sal del Rey, see Eloise Campbell, "La Sal del Rey," *Handbook of Texas Online*, https://www.tshaonline.org/handbook/online/articles/gplpe (accessed January 22, 2016).

79. Official Records, Ser. 1, Vol. 34, Part 2, Chapter 66, 39.

80. Bill Winsor, *Texas in the Confederacy: Military Installations, Economy and People* (Hillsboro, TX: Hill Junior College Press, 1978), 53–54.

81. Lonn, *Salt as a Factor in the Confederacy*, 51.

82. Ibid., 45.

83. Ibid., 36.

84. Ibid.

85. Ripley, *From Flag to Flag*, 121–22.

# 8

# *From the Bluegrass to the Rio Grande*

## Kentucky's US Colored Troops on the Border, 1865–1867

W. STEPHEN McBRIDE

In May 1865, the US government sent a large military force to South Texas to establish and maintain order; to guard the Rio Grande border against smuggling, Indian and bandit raids from Mexico, and escaping ex-Confederates from Texas; and generally to intimidate the Imperialist forces under Emperor Maximilian, who were attempting to conquer Mexico.[1] Among the forces sent to South Texas were roughly 16,000 to 20,000 men of the 25th Corps US Army, under Maj. Gen. Godfrey Weitzel, who traveled by ship from City Point, Virginia. The 25th was the army's only corps made up entirely of African American regiments, designated United States Colored Troops (USCT), although they did have white commissioned officers. Among the USCT were seven infantry regiments and one heavy artillery regiment from Kentucky. All of these regiments had been sent to eastern Virginia during the Civil War and were stationed around Richmond and Petersburg. Between late May and June 1865, four of these regiments (the 109th, 115th, and 122nd Infantry and 8th Heavy Artillery) were sent to the ports of Indianola and Corpus Christi, while the other four (the 114th, 116th, 117th, and 118th Infantry regiments) were sent to the Rio Grande.[2] The latter regiments, which will be the subject of this chapter, landed at Brazos de Santiago in late June 1865, and then spent the next year or two performing a variety of duties between the river's mouth and Laredo. For newly emancipated and enlisted men from Kentucky, this assignment was truly extraordinary.

### *Kentucky's US Colored Troops*

Although Kentucky was the last state to enlist African American soldiers, it provided the second most of any state (after Louisiana), with nearly 24,000. Because of Kentucky's status as a loyal Union state and a slave state, the federal government did not press African American enlistment into US Colored Troops in Kentucky in 1863, when such enlistment was authorized elsewhere. It was feared that Kentucky might secede over the enlistment and emancipation of her enslaved men. Also as a loyal state, Kentucky was not affected by the January 1, 1863, Emancipation Proclamation.

In 1864 the US Army needed more soldiers and Kentucky was not meeting its quota, so by April 1864 the enlistment of US Colored Troops began. Initially enlistment was very slow due to limiting this enlistment to free blacks and enslaved men with their owners' permission, but it sped up dramatically in late May 1864 when these restrictions were lifted. Two of the early Kentucky USCT regiments created were the 114th and 116th US Colored Infantry regiments, which began enlisting men at Camp Nelson, Kentucky, in late May 1864 and were officially organized in early July 1864. These two regiments were filled with men from the central Bluegrass section of Kentucky, and nearly all had been enslaved. The other two Kentucky USCT regiments to serve along the Rio Grande, the 117th and 118th Infantry, were organized in July and August 1864 in Covington and Owensboro, Kentucky, respectively. Formerly enslaved men from western Kentucky filled most companies of these two regiments, although one company of the 118th was organized in Louisville, Kentucky.[3]

While most Kentucky USCT performed duty within Kentucky or nearby Tennessee and southwestern Virginia, one regiment (107th) was sent to Washington, DC, and eight regiments were sent to eastern Virginia. These eight regiments eventually became part of the 25th Corps, US Army of the James, and performed mostly siege and fatigue duties around and near Richmond and Petersburg, while also participating in a number of engagements. For instance, the 117th was involved in a battle with Confederates at Deep Bottom, Virginia, on October 27, 1864, and the 116th participated in the early April 1865 attack of the Petersburg defenses and was one of the first US regiments to enter that city. It also participated in the pursuit of Gen. Robert E.

Lee's Confederate Army of Northern Virginia to Appomattox Court House, and was present at their surrender.[4]

### *Off to Texas*

Following the surrender of Lee's army, the 25th Corps was placed under Maj. Gen. Henry Halleck's Military Department of Northern Virginia and expanded to include all US Colored Troops that had been in the former Armies of the James and of the Potomac. As General Halleck did not relish the idea of having thousands of African Americans under his command, and troops were needed in Texas, he designated the entire 25th Corps to be sent to South Texas and be placed within Maj. Gen. Philip Sheridan's Military Division of the Southwest (soon to be changed to Military Division of the Gulf).[5]

But why the Rio Grande? There were a number of reasons why the federal government decided to send troops to this region. For one, when the movement to South Texas was first planned, Confederates west of the Mississippi had yet to formerly surrender, and although Confederate general Edmund Kirby Smith did surrender his forces on May 25, 1865, many officers and soldiers did not individually surrender and sign loyalty oaths. They simply dispersed, often with their arms and equipment, much of which now belonged to the US government. The US government was particularly concerned about former Confederates crossing into Mexico and continuing the Civil War from there.

Another factor was that with the surrender of Confederate forces, the state and local governments in Texas also disbanded and the state was in a rather chaotic condition in terms of government and general law and order. Much banditry was occurring along the Rio Grande and elsewhere, and one of the army's goals was to restore order and reestablish loyal state and local governments.[6]

Another major factor in sending US troops to South Texas, particularly along the Rio Grande Valley, was the civil war occurring in Mexico between the Imperialist forces of Emperor Maximilian and the Republican forces (known as Liberals) of Benito Juárez, the elected president of Mexico. The US government was sternly opposed to Maximilian's attempt to create a monarchy in the Western Hemisphere and his use of French and Austrian troops in this endeavor. This was seen as a direct assault on the Monroe Doctrine and on the viability of the Republican/

Democratic form of government. Both Generals Grant and Sheridan and Secretary of War Stanton believed that the Europeans saw the Civil War in the United States as an opportunity to invade Mexico because the US would not be able to respond. US officials saw this attack on Mexico as an assault not only on a neighboring country, but also on democracy as a form of legitimate government. Thus in their view, confronting the attack on Mexico was perceived as an extension of the Union's war mission. Sheridan stated in November 1866, "I have always believed that the occupation of Mexico was a part of the [Confederate] rebellion; and believing that the contest in our own country for the vindication of republicanism, I did not think that the vindication would be complete until Maximilian was compelled to leave."[7]

Grant earlier stated in June 1865, "I regard the act of attempting to establish a monarchical government on this continent in Mexico by foreign bayonets as an act of hostility against the Government of the United States."[8]

US troops were stationed between Brazos de Santiago and Laredo, and later Fort Duncan at Eagle Pass to intimidate the Imperial forces, provide moral support for the Liberals, and prevent illicit cross-river trade and any aid to the Imperialists from ex-Confederates—particularly immigration. Although US forces were ordered to maintain "strict neutrality," they occasionally stretched this neutrality and sometimes materially aided the Liberals and undermined the Imperialists.[9]

Between May 1 and June 2, 1865, the USCT regiments of the 25th Corps, including those from Kentucky, boarded ocean going steamboats at City Point, Virginia, and began their long trip to South Texas. This trip involved stops at Mobile, Alabama, and New Orleans, and finally Brazos de Santiago for most regiments, although one brigade each landed at Indianola (including the 8th US Heavy Artillery, 109th US Infantry, and 115th US Infantry) and Corpus Christi, Texas (including the 122nd US Colored Infantry), for duty in or around those parts.[10]

For most of the Kentucky USCT and other men in the 25th Corps, this was by far the longest trip of their lives. According to Lt. Ludlum Drake of the 114th US Colored Infantry, "Part of our regiment was transported on the C.C. Leary, an old screw propeller so worn out that the captain was afraid to use the sails to increase the speed and we were 23 days reaching Brazos."[11]

An officer of the 114th USCI reported that "[t]he command stood the voyage well and had general good health," but a captain of the 117th noted that "[o]ne man died in the company [Company C] and was buried at sea."[12] Chaplain A. E. Everest of the 118th USCI stated: "Only two deaths occurred. One of these was from Pneumonia and the other from drowning. The man was washing his clothes and fell into the river at New Orleans."[13]

This voyage was an extraordinary event for many of these soldiers, as Pvt. Edward Francis of the 114th US Colored Infantry noted, "I traveled on the Atlantic Ocean. I was very sick but I soon got well. . . . I can't get any further from home than I am."[14]

The Kentucky USCT arrived at Brazos de Santiago from June 20 to 23, 1865, and set up temporary camp there with much of the rest of the 25th Corps. At Brazos there was a lack of both wood and water, and conditions were quite primitive and overcrowded. Water condensing machinery was brought in but could not keep up, and men were still only rationed three pints of boiling hot water per day.[15] The sandy unvegetated nature of the Brazos landscape was quite striking to the soldiers, as was the wildlife. Lt. Warren Goodale of the 114th stated that "[a]ll vegetable life seems thorny, and insect and reptile life venomous," and Lt. Ludlum Drake, also of the 114th, noted that "[a]t Brazos . . . there was no chill to the air, no shade, nothing green, just clean white sand. Here we had condensed water that had not yet lost its steam heat."[16]

Fortunately, most USCT soldiers did not stay at Brazos for long, and by late June/early July received orders to march toward Brownsville. River flooding due to mountain snow melt made this march very difficult with "the command having to wade through water and mud to a depth of two feet or more."[17] According to Lt. Ludlum Drake of the 114th: "No one will ever forget the three days march up the river to Brownsville. . . . The mud and water was all the way from ankle deep to waist deep pouched up by the tread of six thousand men and their wagons. . . . One of my men stumbled and went clean under, gun, knapsack, haversack, and all. As he scrambled up out of that ooze, his hair, ears, nose, and mouth full of it."[18]

Three of the four Kentucky USCT (114th, 117th, and 118th) soon went into camp in or near Brownsville, where they remained for at least a few months. The remaining Kentucky regiment, the 116th, briefly encamped at White's Ranch, downstream from Brownsville on the Rio Grande until July 12, when it broke camp and marched upriver to Roma, arriving there on July 25 after marching through Brownsville, Edinburgh, and Rio Grande City.[19] Most companies of the 116th would remain at Roma until February 1866, when they returned to White's Ranch. While the regiment was at Roma, Companies A, D, H, and K performed detached garrison duty at Edinburgh. After the move back to White's Ranch, Company I was detached to Clarksville, and Companies D and K were detached to Arenal Ranch (located ten miles below Brownsville). The 116th would stay at White's Ranch and other points along the Rio Grande until mid-September 1866, when it was transferred to New Orleans and Greenville, Louisiana.[20]

The regimental headquarters of the 114th remained the longest in Brownsville—for a full nine months before transferring to Ringgold Barracks in April 1866. The regiment remained at Ringgold until mid-March 1867, when they marched to Brazos de Santiago to be mustered out on April 2, 1867.[21] While the regiment was stationed at Brownsville, Company F did detached duty at Arenal Ranch, while Company H performed garrison duty at Fort Brown itself, and remained there until mustering out. While the regiment was at Ringgold Barracks, two companies (A and F) were detached to Redmond's Ranch, located sixty miles upriver; two companies (A and I) were detached to Laredo; and one each was detached to Rancho Santa Maria (Co. E), Edinburgh (Co. G), and Roma (Co. K).[22]

Unlike the relatively geographically stable 114th and 116th, the 117th moved their regimental headquarters many times, usually back and forth between Brownsville and Ringgold Barracks every few months, but also to Brazos de Santiago. The regiment's longest assignments were between October 1865 and March 1866 at Ringgold Barracks and between March and October 1866 at Brownsville.[23] Detached companies of the 117th also performed duty at White's Ranch and Clarksville (Co. A), Edinburgh (Cos. D, H, and K), Roma (Co. E), Laredo (Cos. F and G), Brazos de Santiago (Cos. I and K), and even Galveston (Co. E). The 117th was finally mustered out at Brazos de Santiago in August 1867, making it the longest serving Civil War regiment in the Rio Grande Valley.[24]

The final Kentucky USCT stationed along the Rio Grande, the 118th US Colored Infantry, spent its entire relatively short tour in the lower valley at Brownsville (June–August 1865), Clarksville (September 1865–January 1866), and finally White's Ranch, where it was mustered out on February 6, 1866.[25] Separate companies of the 118th generally did not perform duty detached from the regiment. The early mustering out of this regiment may have been related to its participation in the January 1866 invasion of Bagdad, Mexico (as discussed in more detail later), but the four Kentucky USCT stationed north of the Rio Grande were mustered out at this same time.[26]

While stationed at the various large and small posts, the Kentucky USCT performed a lot of what was described as "guard and fatigue duty." In fact, some officers complained about the intensity of this duty to the exclusion of other activities. An officer from the 114th USCI complained that "[d]oing heavy fatigue and guard duty during the month [December 1865], one half of the command being on duty each day, and the white separate Brigade doing no fatigue, consequently there was no battalion exercises and very few company drills."[27]

The fatigue duty included cutting wood for fuel or construction, policing camp, digging ditches, constructing buildings, constructing or repairing roads and railroads, and even constructing pontoon bridges. The construction of a winter camp near Brownsville was described as follows: "Huts were made of a frame of poles covered with shelter tents. The huts were 7' x 9' or 10' and are 5' high on the sides and 8 & 1/2' at the ridge with two bunks at one end . . . with mud or sod chimney on one side. The end of the hut to company street. Very good poles were found in a swamp about four (4) miles up river from Brownsville."[28]

While at Ringgold Barracks in October 1865, soldiers of the 117th USCT, besides the normal guard and fatigue duty, were "employed to make brick to build adobe quarters." In February 1866 Company F of the 114th was stationed at Arenal Ranch near Brownsville, where it was "chopping and drawing wood for government steamboats." Company G of the same regiment was "assigned duty, care and instruction of the Pontoon train and in laying Pontoon Bridge" at Brownville in February 1866, while Co. H was "on special duty caring for the artillery in Ft. Brown and drilling in artillery manual."[29] Company H, 114th US Colored Infantry, spent most of their Rio Grande duty at Fort Brown and participated in the November 1866 movement into Matamoros, Mexico (discussed later in more detail).

As the Company H quote provided suggests, these soldiers did have some time for drill, particularly after their camps were established. "Guard and fatigue" in reports often became "Guard, fatigue, and drill." While in Brownsville, in spring 1866 an officer of the 117th noted, "The drill of the Bayonet Exercise had been introduced and now forms part of our military accomplishments."[30]

Relations between the local population and the US Colored Troops seemed to be mostly positive during the 1865–67 period, although some newspaper articles written by whites disparaged the African American soldiers.[31] Sgt. Maj. Thomas Boswell of the 116th communicated a positive view of the area when he wrote, "Roma is a nice little village, situated on a high bluff, and is kept very clean. There are but two or three Americans in the place. If our regiment stays any length of time we will all speak Spanish, as we are learning very fast."[32]

Pvt. Edward Francis of the 114th also seemed to experience positive relations with the local population (although with a language barrier) when he wrote, "The people is very friendly, but I can't understand nothing they say to me."[33] Lt. Col. Charles Kireker of the 116th stated that the local people "show no malice toward the northern freedmen."[34] The generally positive experiences of the Civil War USCT with locals along the Rio Grande sharply contrast with the experiences of USCT stationed farther north in Texas (who encountered more open hostility and violence from whites) or the later experiences of regular US Army African American troops.[35]

One of the major challenges faced by the Kentucky and other USCT in the Rio Grande Valley was disease. Soon after their arrival in the Valley there was a major outbreak of scurvy that affected upward of 60 percent of the USCT soldiers.[36] This disease, which results from a lack of fresh fruits and vegetables, likely began on the voyage to Texas and reached epidemic proportions by July and August 1865. The 114th regimental return for July–August 1865 stated that "the general appearance of the command was not good. During the past two months scurvy has prevailed . . . in the Reg't epidemically."[37] On September 11, 1865, the chaplain of the 114th, Thomas Stevenson, reported that "much suffering has been experienced and many deaths have occurred among the men of this Regiment" due to scurvy.[38] The 118th USCI lost forty-three men to the disease during the summer and fall of 1865.[39]

The US Army moved to remedy the scurvy epidemic by purchasing and providing more fruit and vegetables but also by utilizing a local product, American agave. According to Stevenson, "By use of appropriate remedies especially the Agave Americana the health of the Regiment has for some weeks exceedingly improved."[40] The agave plant was processed into a drink known as "pulque." The effectiveness of this remedy was also reported in the 114th field and staff returns of July–August 1865. "The disease is now fast disappearing by improved rations and the use of 'Pulque' from the Agave Americana."[41] Interestingly, the production of pulque was seen as so vital that instructions on how to produce it were sent out by 25th Corps commander Maj. Gen. Godfrey Weitzel to his division commanders on July 26, 1865.

> The Aloe tree is cut down, brought in, or pressed in a rough press, which can easily be put up at any post. The juice collected and then issued to the patient at the rate of an ounce or two per day. The juice in a few days commences to ferment. During the fermentation it has a very disagreeable smell and taste. In the open air the fermentation lasts only a few days, and after this it again has a more pleasant but very acid taste. It can then again be used. But it is always better and more pleasant before fermentation. In order to cure your scurvy patients, and to prevent it . . . until fresh vegetables can be issued . . . you will send out detachments from each post or brigade, with two or three wagons, to collect this tree and make this drink which is called by common people "pulque."[42]

One Kentucky company, Company K of the 114th, "was sent about 50 miles into the country [from Brownsville] and made pulque from the Agave Americana for the use of the Division until the 24th [of September 1865]."[43]

Another major disease outbreak occurred a year later, when cholera struck. This disease spread to a number of regiments in a number of locales including the 114th at Ringgold Barracks and Edinburgh, the 116th at White's Ranch, and the 117th at Brownsville, causing the death of many men. According to Lt. Col. Charles Kireker of the 116th, "August 12th, 1866, cholera made its appearance in the regiment as an epidemic and continued as such until August 28th, when it entirely disappeared, having destroyed the lives of forty-five men. The members of the regiment behaved nobly during the prevalence of the epidemic, each on trying to help the other."[44]

Interestingly, four months before the cholera outbreak, Kireker had issued General Order No. 6 to try to prevent this disease, which he described as "the scourge of the human race." He ordered on April 28, 1866, "The utmost cleanliness of their premises is therefore recommended to the inhabitants of White's Ranch. All animal and organic matter, slops and etc. calculated to emit offensive odors or poison the atmosphere must be burned or removed a safe distance. It is also recommended that lime be Liberally applied to all kinds of wood work, sinks and such other places of deposit as may require disinfecting."[45] Obviously, his order did not prevent the August outbreak.

Other more general or poorly diagnosed ailments occurred throughout the Rio Grande occupation of the USCT. In late fall 1866, "nearly all of the enlisted men of the company [Co. G, 114th] have been sick at different times with fever and ague and fever of a malaria type." An officer of the 114th also reported "much diarrhea and dysentery from bad and hasty meals for early parties, fatigues and guards being ordered too early at sunrise generally."[46] In a letter home from Brownsville dated July 10, 1865, Pvt. Edward Francis of the 114th reported to his wife Liza, "Tommy [Francis] is not very well. He is complaining today and answer this as soon as you can. . . . Arch Elmore is very sick. He has dropsy. He is at the hospital in Brownsville. I have not seen him for a week. We don't think he will ever get well."[47]

Another major challenge and concern of the Kentucky African American soldiers was the well-being of their families back in Kentucky. The wives and children of most Kentucky USCT were not emancipated until a March 3, 1865, congressional act, and this often was not enforced until the passage of the Thirteenth Amendment in December 1865. While many families escaped into refugee camps at US Army bases, such as Camp Nelson and Louisville, others remained on the farms where they had been previously enslaved, and still others were turned out by their former owners. The soldiers were concerned about their fate; wrote letters or had others, such as company sergeants or chaplains, write for them; and attempted to send money home. Pvt. Edmund Delaney of the 117th USCI even resorted to writing from Brownsville to

*Pvt. Edmund Delaney, 117th US Colored Infantry. Edmund Delaney Civil War Pension Application, National Archives Records Administration, Washington, DC.*

his former owner, Henry Graves, to inquire about his wife and why she had not written him back, saying, "I wish you would write to my wife and see if you can find out why she don't write to me."[48]

Sending money home was sometimes logistically difficult, as soldiers of 116th USCI expressed to President Johnson and Secretary of War Stanton from White's Ranch on May 30, 1866: "[W]e has not any way to send our Money home . . . and thire is no Person that we could trust for we has sent large amounts of Money to our famuleys and they has not got it. And I larns that thire is a number of our famuleys has been turned out of Doors, and they has no Place to lay thire heads and we has no way to help them."[49]

In a series of letters home to his wife, Liza, Pvt. Edward Francis of Company B, 114th USCI at Brownsville, writes that he has sent her money and requests, "The next time you write, I wish you would let me know whether you got it or know I have been uneasy about it. I have heard of the rest of the boys money getting home and I have not heard of mine."[50] Of perhaps greater concern was when soldiers heard that their family members were ill. This sometimes, as in the case of

Pvt. William Sayles of the 117th USCI, led them to request a leave or early discharge so that they could care for their sick family members. Interestingly, Private Sayles, who wrote directly to President Andrew Johnson, was given an early discharge in November 1866, four months after his letter.[51]

The letters soldiers wrote home and to government officials touch on another issue: literacy. The vast majority of Kentucky USCT was illiterate when they enlisted. Those that were literate, like Sgt. Maj. Thomas Boswell, were often promoted to noncommissioned officers to aid in paper work. By their mustering out, however, many of those soldiers had learned to read and write. The army was transformed into a school for these soldiers, often taught by the regimental chaplains. In fact, teaching literacy to the soldiers was an official responsibility of the USCT chaplains.[52] As Chaplain Thomas Stevenson of the 114th USCI reported from Brownsville: "There is an ardent and universal desire among these men for books. . . . Many of these Colored men possess minds of the very highest order, and were they placed in circumstances favorable to mental Culture and intellectual development they would exhibit such talents such aptness to acquire useful knowledge make such proficiency in the arts and sciences as would forever confound their implacable enemies, and gladden the hearts of their genuine friends."[53]

Stevenson went on to note that "[n]early all the men in my Regiment can spell and read with more or less accuracy, many can write with considerable mechanical excellence." Similar progress likely occurred with the other Kentucky USCT along the Rio Grande. As historian Keith Wilson stated, "School attendance became an experience of liberty and an act of defiance against slavery."[54]

The more mundane "guard and fatigue" duty of the Kentucky USCT was occasionally disrupted by more dramatic duty related to the US Army's purpose along the Rio Grande to stop cross-border smuggling and raiding and to intimidate the Imperialist forces in Mexico. The USCT were often placed at known fords and ports along the river, or sent in pursuit of raiders or smugglers spotted by scouts or citizens. For instance, on August 11, 1865, a combined detachment of the 116th (Cos. D and H) and the 31st USCI (Cos. A and G), numbering nearly 175 men, left Roma in pursuit of "a party of hostile Indians, supposed to be in the vicinity of Redmond's Ranch."[55] According to the expedition commander, Maj. L. Wright:

> Arrived at Redmond's Ranche on the morning of the 14th . . . in the Afternoon a Mexican came and informed me that the Indians had possession of his Ranche, which is situated about forty miles NorthEast of Rancho Solominino. I marched immediately for Solominino which I reached next morning. I then concluded not to move East but to push in the direction of Laredo. . . . I arrived at Rancho Perueno within twenty five miles of Laredo on the morning of the 17th. . . . I therefore concluded to allow [the men] one days rest, and proceed alone to Laredo to communicate with Lt. Jones who . . . informed me that . . . four of those [Indian] parties had returned from this Expedition driving off large herds of Cattle and Horses—The fifth party was still thought to be below Laredo—These Indians are part of the Kickapoo tribe. . . . I left Laredo, returned to my Command on the eve of the 18th marched enroute for Roma on the 19th where I arrived this a.m.[56]

Although this expedition was unsuccessful in intercepting the Indians, Major Wright did gather much useful information on local geography and the patterns of raiders and smugglers. According to Major Wright,

> [T]he inhabitants of Texas lose more by thieving parties in Mexico than by the Indians. . . . [T]housands of head of Cattle, Horses and sheep, are crossed every week between Laredo and Roma—There are many Fords on the River well adapted for this purpose, Redmond's Ranche appears to be a more central point than any other, and I think used more than any other. . . . In my opinion it is essential for the welfare of the inhabitants of the frontier to place at least a Regiment from Laredo down to Roma, and allowing what little cavalry there is at Laredo to scout around the Country.[57]

A November 5, 1865, report by Lt. W. Myers of the 117th USCI also noted that "I was informed at Roma that cattle were frequently crossed into Mexico, above there, at a place known as Redman's Ranch."[58] The army soon took Major Wright's and Lieutenant Myers's reports and recommendations seriously and stationed a detachment of soldiers, including Kentucky USCT, at Redmond's Ranch.

At about the same time as Lieutenant Myers's report, an expedition of 117th men successfully intercepted a cattle smuggling operation below Ringgold Barracks. As Lt. Henry Miller reported:

> I started from this Post [Ringgold Barracks] on the morning of the 1st [of November] in Command [of] (25) Twenty five En-Men with 5 days Rations. . . . I marched down the River Patrolling its Banks. . . . About 12 O clock on the 2nd inst. I discovered men engaged in crossing Cattle from Texas into Mexico. I detached 1 Serg. & 5 men with orders to proceed down the River as fast as possible for them to march to the point where these men were at work and arrest them and seize the boats. Whilst I proceeded down the road to prevent them from getting into the Chaparral and also to prevent the cattle from being turned loose if they should have any ready to cross. . . . I then took them in charge and proceeded on to Edinburg Patrolling the River as previously.[59]

Lieutenant Miller did not catch any additional smugglers on this expedition, although he did learn of smugglers "engaged in crossing goods from Mexico to Texas," and ended his report by stating, "There is a great Deal of Smuggling done along the River, evidence presents itself every few miles."[60] Miller's report indicates that boats were also utilized to cross livestock, so the crossing was not limited to the river fords.

The use of riverboats to smuggle goods from Mexico into Texas was also reported by Lt. Col. Charles Kireker of the 116th USCI in March 1866. Kireker stated, "I have the honor to inform you that I hold . . . the following articles smuggled from Mexico and confiscated at White's Ranche Texas . . . while the parties were in the act of crossing the articles from the Sloop to their Shop; Viz—1 Box of French Wine, 2 Baskets containing 5 Bottles of Absinthe, 1 ½ Doz. of Sardines."[61] He goes on to report, "I have reason to believe that smuggling is carried on to some extent at this Station there being a Sloop plying continually between the Mexican and this side of the river: the goods are carted from Bagdad to a point nearly opposite White's Ranche and run across at night."[62] The smuggling of goods and animals across the river was a constant and insurmountable problem that required considerable time and effort from the USCT stationed on the Rio Grande.

Although the US forces along the Rio Grande were ordered to maintain "strict neutrality," there were a number of incidences where they were clearly supporting the Liberal forces of Benito Juárez. For instance, Liberal leader Juan Cortina and his men were allowed to cross into Texas near Brownsville and resupply, and then reenter Mexico.[63] On a few occasions US forces crossed into Mexico to aid Liberal forces or "protect" American interests, particularly American merchants based in Mexico. Two of these troop movements involved Kentucky USCT, one into Bagdad, Mexico, in January 1866, and one into Matamoros, Mexico, in November 1866.

The Bagdad incident or occupation began on January 5, 1866, when the Imperialist army in town was captured by a party of American filibusters from Clarksville, Texas, under the leadership of cashiered former lieutenant colonel Arthur F. Reed and former army captain R. Clay Crawford.[64] This party consisted of about 60 to 120 men, including "a number of colored soldiers—perhaps (30) thirty in all from the 118th Regt. USCI."[65] After their capture of Bagdad, "this organized gang of thieves" began looting and plaguing the town. Most of the surviving men of the 118th (at least two were killed) returned to Clarksville in the early morning hours of January 6.[66] Meanwhile, Liberal forces under Gen. Mariano Escobedo entered the town and requested that the US Army send two hundred soldiers into Bagdad to stop the plundering and restore order. On January 6, Col. John S. Moon of the 118th US Colored Infantry at White's Ranch was ordered by Major General Weitzel "to send two hundred men to Bagdad to protect private property and preserve order."[67] Moon then ordered his subordinate Lt. Col. Issac D. Davis at Clarksville to comply with this order. Apparently the plundering did not stop immediately, and General Escobedo requested a hundred more men, which Colonel Moon soon sent. Apparently order was soon restored after these additional hundred men were sent in. Later the 118th men were replaced by troops of the 46th USCI who were later replaced by the 2nd US Colored Cavalry. On January 22, 1866, the US soldiers were withdrawn across the river to Texas, and on January 25, 1866, the Liberals abandoned Bagdad, and it was soon reoccupied by the Imperialists.[68]

The Imperialists complained that this action was a breach of neutrality, but the Americans stated that it was a humanitarian effort and that Davis was ordered "under no circumstances to interfere between the contending parties [Liberals versus Imperialists] and not even guard prisoners."[69] The American commanders also denied any knowledge or complicity in the original filibuster attack by Reed and Crawford. In summarizing the Bagdad affair, Weitzel stated, "During the whole time that the Liberals had possession there was continual quarrelling amongst the leaders. . . . The whole affair was disagreeable in the extreme from the beginning to the end."[70]

Even so, the Company D, 118th USCI January–February return stated, "For its conduct [at Bagdad] the Company was highly complimented by Comdg. Genls. of both the US and Liberal armies."[71] Soon after the Bagdad affair, the 118th was mustered out of service. Whether this was related to their conduct in Bagdad is unclear.

The second invasion of Mexico involving the Kentucky USCT occurred at Matamoros in November 1866. Like the Bagdad affair, the movement into Matamoros was motivated, or at least justified, as "protecting private property"—particularly American merchants' private property—and was perhaps even more confusing and convoluted than the Bagdad affair.

The difficulty in Matamoros began in August 1866 when the legitimate Liberal government of Tamaulipas, under Gov. Juan Maria Caravajal (also Carabajal), was overthrown and a new government under Gen. Servando Canales was installed. A major force behind this coup was the wealthier merchants of Matamoros, many of whom were US citizens and who were unhappy with Governor Caravajal's policies, which forced loans on them.[72] Major General Sheridan did not have a high opinion of these merchants and stated, "the merchants of Matamoros—most of them foreign born and some claiming American citizenship, but ultra Maximilian adherents, and blockade runners during the Rebellion—induced Canales (a noted character) to pronounce against the Liberal Government."[73]

The uprising was quick and, in the case of Matamoros, bloodless. As US Bvt. Maj. Gen. George W. Getty reported on August 12, 1866, "A revolution in the city of Matamoros yesterday resulted in the overthrow of the Government of Caravajal . . . General Pedro Hinojosa (Juarist) is in Command of the military forces in the city and it is said Canales has been proclaimed Governor of the state."[74]

This new government under Canales was seen as illegitimate by

Liberal president Benito Juárez, and he ordered General Escobedo to recapture Matamoros and install Santiago Tapia as the new governor. As Escobedo and his 3,500 troops neared the city in November 1866, the merchants "proposed that Canales should surrender the city to Escobedo, if Escobedo would agree to pay them the money [they gave] to Canales."[75] This supposedly amounted to $600,000. When Escobedo refused this offer, the merchants turned to Bvt. Brig. Gen. Thomas Sedgwick, commander at Brownsville and colonel of the 114th US Colored Infantry. They convinced Sedgwick that US troops were necessary to protect American citizens and their property from the pending battle between Escobedo and Canales/Hinojosa.[76]

On the evening of November 24, 1866, Sedgwick sent one company of the 19th USCI and one company (Co. H) of the 114th USCI from Brownsville across the Rio Grande in boats to secure the Mexican side. The next day a pontoon bridge was constructed across the river, and a company of the 4th US Cavalry was sent across and into Matamoros.[77] Initially Company H of the 114th guarded the southern or Mexican end of the bridge, but later they also entered Matamoros. Company H, 114th USCI, "crossed the Rio Grande River into Mexico on the 25th of November, 1866 and remained there in possession of the Plaza of the City of Matamoros until the 1st day of Dec. 1866 when it recrossed the River at Brownsville, Tex."[78]

*Sedgwick's Pontoon Bridge. Courtesy of the University of Texas Rio Grande Valley Special Collection Archives, Norman Rozeff Collection.*

On November 27, the Matamoros army of General Hinojosa and Governor Canales was able to repel the initial attack by General Escobedo. Soon after Escobedo and Canales entered into negotiations, and Sheridan ordered Sedgwick to withdraw US troops from the city, which Sedgwick complied with on December 1. Later that same day, the Liberal army took possession of Matamoros.[79]

Soon after the Matamoros withdrawal, Sheridan traveled to the Rio Grande and placed Sedgwick briefly under arrest. Sedgwick also received some bad press for the Matamoros affair. For instance, the *Rio Grande Courier* (December 7, 1866) reported, "In the late fiasco, for such as it was, Col. Sedgwick has been simply outwitted by a combination of military and civilian influence, the latter mostly of American nationality."[80]

Sheridan, however, did not take the event too seriously, and felt that the merchants had made Sedgwick "their 'cats paw' to protect their interests. This was the point of the whole affair."[81] Sheridan summarized his opinion of the whole affair as follows:

> The occupation of the city was a mere matter of form and had the consent of General Escobedo, who made no objection and since the city passed into his hands has called on General Sedgwick in the most friendly manner, and asked me to forgive his action.
>
> There is little doubt but that this unauthorized and harmless intervention does much to reconcile and bring about the very good condition of affairs they existed in Matamoros when I left Brownsville.[82]

By the fall and winter of 1866, there were only eight USCT regiments left along the Rio Grande, but three of them were Kentucky regiments—the 114th, 116th, and 117th. The earlier discharge of Northern USCT, which began in late summer and fall 1865, did not pass unnoticed by the Kentucky soldiers, and they felt it was grossly unfair. As Sgt. Maj. Thomas Boswell of the 116th complained: "We were in high hopes of being mustered out soon, but it seems that they have slighted us. Our Corps is pretty much all gone home; but it is said that we are to be retained because we are 'slave state troops.' Is this a good reason for our retention? No. We earnestly hope that the Government will not be guilty of this great wrong toward us, as we have tried to do our duty."[83]

As noted previously, Boswell's 116th finally left the Rio Grande for Louisiana in late September 1866 and mustered out in January 1867. Interestingly, at least 113 men of the 116th reenlisted into two of the new regular African American regiments, the 9th US Cavalry and the 39th US Infantry, which were recruiting in New Orleans at the time.[84] Some of the men in the 9th US Cavalry returned to the Rio Grande in April 1867.

The 114th and 117th US Colored Infantry regiments were the last two Civil War volunteer units to leave the Rio Grande Valley. The 114th was mustered out at Brazos de Santiago in April 1867, while the 117th did not depart until August 1867. As these units left bases such as Ringgold Barracks, Brownsville, and Fort McIntosh, they were replaced by US regulars, including the recently organized 9th US Cavalry and 41st US Infantry, both African American units soon to be known as "Buffalo Soldiers."[85]

By the late winter of 1867, following negotiations between the United States and Napoleon III, and just before the 114th and 117th were mustered out, the French troops were withdrawn from Mexico. Although it was hoped that Maximilian would return to Europe as well, he stayed and fought on until May 1867, when he was at last defeated and captured at Querétaro, Mexico. One month later, he and his leading generals were executed.[86]

### *Conclusion*

Much can be said about the legacy of the USCT stationed along the Rio Grande. They certainly helped maintain order in the region after the collapse of the Confederate state government and many local agencies. They likely also reduced cross-border smuggling and raiding, although it is difficult to measure how significantly. Sheridan's use of these troops to guard Texas ports certainly reduced the movement of former Confederates into Mexico. He felt that the USCT played a vital role in the ultimate Liberal victory in Mexico. Early in the border occupation, Sheridan wrote, "The necessity of troops along the Rio Grande has been very demoralizing to the Imperial cause, and has withdrawn all Mexican support for it."[87] Later, in a November 1866 summary of the Rio Grande occupation, he reported, "The effect of this large movement of troops on the destiny of Imperialism in Mexico has not been fully appreciated by our people. . . . But the appearance of our troops and the knowledge that friends were on the border went like electricity to the houses and hearts of the Mexican people."[88]

While Sheridan may have overstated the impact of the USCT on the border, they certainly helped with the morale of the Liberals and undermined the Imperialists' abilities to acquire supplies and likely recruits from Texas—particularly ex-Confederates.

Following their discharge, most of the Kentucky USCT returned to Kentucky and began their new lives as freedmen. Some returned to the farms where they had previously worked as slaves—but now as paid laborers. Others moved to or created rural hamlets, such as Ariel near the former US Army depot of Camp Nelson in Central Kentucky. Still others moved to more urban areas, including Lexington, Louisville, and Covington, looking for work. While most remained in Kentucky, some such as the Reverend Gabriel Burdett and William Wright, both formerly of the 114th, became discouraged with racism in Kentucky and migrated to the Midwest in the 1870s—Burdett to Kansas and Wright to Iowa. It was reported that William Wright left Kentucky because "he had fought so hard for his freedom in the Civil War."[89] Burdett bitterly stated that staying in Kentucky would be "remaining where they will be oppressed all of their life and where it will be impossible for them to rise any higher than a mere mud sill."[90]

There were of course exceptions to the move back to Kentucky. As noted previously, some men decided they liked military life and enlisted into one of the six regular army African American regiments. One who did was William W. Green, formerly of the 116th, who served in the 9th Cavalry from 1867 to 1872 and then again from 1883 to 1888.[91] Another exception was former Sgt. Maj. Thomas Boswell of the 116th, quoted previously, who after his 1867 muster out in New Orleans stayed in that city, became a clerk, married twice, and died in 1896.[92]

It is probably safe to conclude that these men from Kentucky were proud of their service in the USCT, including their service along the Rio Grande. Unlike African American soldiers from most other states, those from Kentucky earned their freedom from slavery by joining the army. As Sgt. Maj. Thomas Boswell stated, "We are Kentucky boys and there is no regiment in the field that ever fought better."[93]

*Pvt. William Wright, 114th US Colored Infantry. Courtesy of Ron Coddington.*

## Notes

1. William A. Dobak, *Freedom by the Sword: The US Colored Troops, 1862–1867* (Washington, DC: Center for Military History, United States Army, 2011); Jerry Thompson, *Cortina: Defending the Mexican Name in Texas* (College Station: Texas A&M University Press, 2007); William L. Richter, *The Army in Texas During Reconstruction, 1865–1870* (College Station: Texas A&M University Press, 1987); Larry Knight, "United States Colored Troops in Texas during Reconstruction," *Southwestern Historical Quarterly* 109, no. 3 (2006): 337–57.

2. National Archives and Records Administration (NARA), Record Group 94, Records of the Adjutant Generals Office, Compiled Records Showing Service of Military Units in Volunteer Union Organizations, Microfilm Publication M594, Roll 205 (8th US Colored Heavy Artillery), Roll 216 (109th, 114th, 115th, 116th, 117th, and 118th US Colored Infantry), Roll 217 (122nd US Colored Infantry), Washington, DC.

3. Ibid.

4. Ibid.

5. Dobak, *Freedom by the Sword,* 434; Work, "United States Colored Troops in Texas," 340.

6. Dobak, *Freedom by the Sword,* 438–39; Work, "United States Colored Troops in Texas," 338.

7. Maj. Gen. Philip H. Sheridan to Bvt. Maj. Gen. John A. Rawlings, November

14, 1866, *The War of the Rebellion: A Compilation of Official Records of the Union and Confederate Armies*, Series I, Volume 48, Part 1 (Washington, DC: 1896), 300 (hereafter cited as OR).

8. Lt. Gen. Ulysses S. Grant to President Andrew Johnson, July 19, 1865 (OR), Series I, Volume 48, Part 2 (Washington, DC), 923.

9. Sheridan to Rawlings, November 14, 1866, 297–303; Dobak, *Freedom by the Sword*, 438; Richter, *The Army in Texas* 23–24; Work, "United States Colored Troops in Texas," 338–39.

10. National Archives and Records Administration (NARA), Record Group 94, Records of the Adjutant Generals Office, Compiled Records Showing Service of Military Units in Volunteer Union Organizations, Microfilm Publication M594, Roll 205 (8th US Colored Heavy Artillery), Roll 216 (109th, 114th, 115th, 116th, 117th, and 118th US Colored Infantry), Roll 217 (122nd US Colored Infantry), Washington, DC.

11. Ludlum C. Drake, "Recollections of the Civil War," Papers of the Military Order of the Loyal Legion of the United States, Michigan Commandery (Detroit, Bentley Historical Society, University of Michigan, Ann Arbor, 1891), 15.

12. NARA, M594, Roll 216, 114th and 117th USCI Reg. Returns, May–June 1865.

13. Chaplain C. Everest to Adj. Gen. L. Thomas, July 1, 1865. NARA, Record Groups (RG) 94, Records of the Adjutant Generals Office, Entry 363, Letters Received by Adj. Gen. L. Thomas, E: 398, Washington, DC.

14. Edward Francis to Liza Francis, July 10, 1865, in Marshall Myers and Chris Propes, eds., "'I Don't Fear Nothing in the Shape of Man': The Civil War and Texas Border Letters of Edward Francis, United States Colored Troops," *The Register of the Kentucky Historical Society* 101, no. 4 (2003): 469.

15. Work, "United States Colored Troops in Texas," 342

16. Warren Goodale to Dear Children, June 8, 1865, Warren Goodale Papers, Massachusetts Historical Society, Boston; Drake, "Recollections of the Civil War," 16.

17. NARA, M594, Roll 216, 114th USCI Reg. Returns, July–August 1865.

18. Drake, "Recollections of the Civil War," 16–17.

19. NARA, M594, Roll 216, 116th USCI Reg. Returns, July–August 1865.

20. Ibid., July–August 1865 to September–October 1866.

21. NARA, M594, Roll 216, 114th USCI Reg. Returns, July–August 1865 to March–April 1867.

22. Ibid.

23. NARA, M594, Roll 216, 117th USCI Reg. and Co. Returns, July–August 1865 to July–August 1867.

24. Ibid.; Dobak, *Freedom by the Sword*, 453.

25. NARA, M594, Roll 216, 118th USCI Reg. Returns, May–June 1865 to January–February 1866.

26. Dobak, *Freedom by the Sword*, 474.

27. NARA, M594, Roll 216, 124th USCI Reg. Returns, November–December 1865.

28. Ibid.

29. NARA, M594, Roll 216, 117th USCI, Co. K Reg. Returns, September–October 1865, 114th, Co. F USCI Reg. Returns, January–February 1866, Co. G Returns, January–February 1866, Co. H Returns, January–February 1866.

30. NARA, M594, Roll 216, 117th USCI, Co. D Returns, May–June 1866.

31. Work, "United States Colored Troops in Texas," 337–38.

32. Edwin S. Redkey, ed., *A Grand Army of Black Men: Letters from African-American Soldiers in the Union Army, 1861–1865* (New York: Cambridge University Press, 1992), 203.

33. Myers and Propes, "'I Don't Fear Nothing in the Shape of Man,'" 471.

34. Col. C. Kireker to Lt. Col. D. D. Wheeler, April 5, 1866, NARA RG 94, Records of the Adjutant Generals Office, Entry 57C, US Colored Troops Regimental Papers, 116th US Colored Infantry, Washington, DC.

35. Dobak, *Freedom by the Sword*, 438–39; Work, "United States Colored Troops in Texas," 337–38, 347–52; Antonio N. Zavaleta, "Colored Death: The Tragedy of Black Troops in the Lower Rio Grande, 1864–1906," *Studies in Rio Grande Valley History* 6 (2005): 351.

36. Josepth T. Glatthaar, *Forged in Battle: The Civil War Alliance of Black Soldiers and White Officers* (New York: Free Press, 1990), 200; Work, "United States Colored Troops in Texas," 344.

37. NARA, M594, Roll 216, 114th USCI Reg. Returns, July–August 1865.

38. Chaplain T. Stevenson to Adj. Gen. L. Thomas, September 11, 1865, NARA RG 94, Entry 363, S-2247.

39. Zavaleta, "Colored Death," 351.

40. Chaplain T. Stevenson to Adj. Gen. L. Thomas, September 11, 1865, NARA RG 94, Entry 363, S-2247.

41. NARA, M594, Roll 216, 114th USCI Field and Staff Returns, July–August 1865.

42. Lt. Col. D. D. Wheeler to Brig. Gen. G. A Smith, July 26, 1865, NARA RG 393, Records of the US Army Continental Commands, 1821–1920, Entry 512, 25th Corps Letters Sent, Washington, DC.

43. NARA, M594, Roll 216, 114th USCI Reg. Return, September–October 1865.

44. Charles Kireker, *History of the 116th Regiment USC. Infantry* (Philadelphia: King and Baird, 1866), 10.

45. Lt. Col. Charles Kireker, General Order 6, April 28, 1866, NARA, RG 94, Entry 576, 116th USCI.

46. NARA, M594, Roll 216, 114th USCI, Co. G Returns, November–December 1865, Reg. Returns, November–December 1866.

47. Myers and Propes, "'I Don't Fear Nothing in the Shape of Man,'" 469.

48. NARA, RG 94, Compiled Service Records of Volunteer Union Soldiers Who Served in the US Colored Troops, 117th USCI, Edmund Delanley, Washington, DC.

49. G. E. Stanford et al. to President and Secretary of War, May 30, 1866, in Ira Berlin, Joseph Riedy, and Leslie S. Rowland, eds., *Freedom, A Documentary History of Emancipation, 1861–1867, Series II: The Black Military Experience* (New York: Cambridge University Press, 1982), 780.

50. Myers and Propes, "'I Don't Fear Nothing in the Shape of Man,'" 475.

51. Work, "United States Colored Troops in Texas," 355.

52. Keith P. Wilson, *Campfires of Freedom: The Camp Life of Black Soldiers during the Civil War* (Kent, OH: Kent State University Press, 2002), 83–87.

53. Chaplain T. Stevenson to Adj. Gen. L. Thomas, September 11, 1865.

54. Wilson, *Campfires of Freedom*, 83.

55. Maj. L. Wright to Capt. M. H. Baillache, August 24, 1865, NARA RG 393, Part 2, Entry 533, Washington, DC.

56. Ibid.

57. Ibid.

58. Lt. W. Myers to Capt. J. W. Looby, November 18, 1865, NARA, RG 393, Part 2, Entry 533, Washington, DC.

59. Lt. Henry H. Miller to Capt. J H. Looby, November 18, 1865, NARA RG 393, Part 2, Entry 533, Washington, DC.

60. Ibid.

61. Lt. Col. Charles Kireker to Lt. Col. D. D. Wheeler, March 13, 1866, NARA. RG 94, Entry 57C, 116th USCI.

62. Ibid.

63. Dobak, *Freedom by the Sword*, 449–50; Richter, *The Army in Texas* 23–24; Thompson, *Cortina*, 162–69.

64. Dobak, *Freedom by the Sword*, 449.

65. Maj. Gen. H. G. Wright to Col. G. L. Hartsuff, January 30, 1866, NARA, M619, Letters Received by the Office of the Adjutant General, 1861–70, Roll 452, Washington, DC.

66. Dobak, *Freedom by the Sword*, 449–50.

67. Lt. Col. D. D. Wheeler to Col. J. S. Moon, January 6, 1866, NARA, M619, Roll 452.

68. Dobak, *Freedom by the Sword*, 449–50; Thompson, *Cortina*, 162–69.

69. Maj. Gen. Godfrey Weitzel to Col. C. H. Whittlesey, January 27, 1866, NARA, M619, Roll 452.

70. Ibid.

71. NARA, M594, Roll 216, 118th USCI, Co. D Returns, January–February 1866.

72. Dobak, *Freedom by the Sword*, 451.

73. Maj. Gen. Philip H. Sheridan to Gen. John A. Rawlings, December 11, 1866, NARA, M1635, Headquarters of the Army, Letters Received, Roll 943, Washington, DC.

74. Brig. Gen. G. W. Getty to Maj. Gen. H. G. Wright, August 12, 1866, NARA, M1635, Roll 94.

75. Sheridan to Rawlings, December 11, 1866.

76. Ibid.; Dobak, *Freedom by the Sword*, 451.

77. Ibid.

78. NARA, M594, Roll 216, 114th USCI, Co H. Returns, November–December 1866.

79. Dobak, *Freedom by the Sword*, 451.

80. *Rio Grande Courier*, December 7, 1966, NARA, M1635, Roll 94.

81. Sheridan to Rawlings December 11, 1866.

82. Ibid.

83. Redkey, *A Grand Army of Black Men*, 203.

84. Dobak, *Freedom by the Sword*, 453; Kireker, *History of the 116th USCI*, 52.

85. Dobak, *Freedom by the Sword*, 453.

86. Richter, *The Army in Texas* 24; Dobak, *Freedom by the Sword*, 452–53; Work, "United States Colored Troops in Texas," 356–57.

87. Maj. Gen. Philip H. Sheridan to Lt. Gen. U. S. Grant, August 1, 1865 (OR), Series I, Vol. 48, Part 2, 1148.

88. Sheridan to Rawlins, November 14, 1866.

89. Ronald S. Coddington, *African American Faces of the Civil War* (Baltimore: Johns Hopkins University Press, 2012), 210; Richard D. Sears, *Camp Nelson, Kentucky: A Civil War History* (Lexington: University Press of Kentucky, 2002), lxii.

90. Ibid.

91. William W. Green, NARA, Civil War Pension, Washington, DC.

92. Thomas Boswell, NARA, Civil War Pension, Washington, DC.

93. Redkey, *A Grand Army of Black Men*, 203.

# 9

# *Archeological Insights into the Last Battle of the Civil War*

## Palmito Ranch, May 12–13, 1865

ROLANDO GARZA

The Battle of Palmito Ranch is embroiled in myth and legend. The historical record provides conflicting accounts of why and how the battle occurred, and is laden with personal and cultural biases. It provides diverging accounts about the battle, such as why the federal troops were marching on the mainland, the number of battle participants and casualties, as well as the intensity of the battle. It is up to the researcher to wade through these inconsistencies and deduce what they perceive to be an accurate portrayal of the battle. Conversely, the material cultural objects deposited during the battle, the archeological record, have the potential to provide a more accurate and objective representation of the battle when systematically examined in conjunction with the historical record. To date, however, the dearth of professional archeological investigations at the site of the Battle of Palmito Ranch provides limited insights into the nature of the engagement on the afternoon of May 13, 1865. Accordingly, in order to gain a more precise understanding of the Battle of Palmito Ranch based upon the physical evidence, more archeological investigations need to be conducted and the collection of battle-related artifacts by hobbyists needs to stop in order to preserve what is left of the archeological record. This chapter will outline the confusion inherent in the historical documents relating to Palmito Ranch and make some suggestions about how the archaeological record can help straighten out our understanding of the events that took place there.

### *The Historical Record*

The historical record consists of primary and secondary sources. At the heart of the primary sources for a mid-nineteenth century battle are the accounts from battle participants. These are composed of official military reports and documents, personal journals, letters, and memoirs written at a later date. Other items, such as contemporary factual newspaper articles, photographs, or drawings are also useful primary sources. Military documents such as muster rolls, quartermaster reports, or orders to the field can provide a somewhat accurate glimpse into the situation of the troops in the field; however, these provide little light on actions during the battle. Official military reports can provide an in-depth description of the events during the battle, but are usually highly biased and are generally driven by specific agendas. Each account comes from a perspective that is influenced by which army the soldier was with and the reason why the soldier was putting the account in writing. For example, the commander from the defeated army might be inclined to bend the truth, whether consciously or subconsciously, in the official report to his superiors to make it appear that he made all the right decisions and gave all the proper commands but circumstances beyond his control caused the defeat. Such circumstances could include unanticipated enemy reinforcements or special weapons, subordinate officers failing to obey battle commands, or even sudden changes in the weather. Likewise, the commander from the victorious army might be inclined to bend the truth, again consciously or subconsciously, in the official report to his superiors in order to make it appear that the odds against his force were much greater than they actually were and that only through his quick and ingenious decisions and heroism was victory achieved.

The same holds true for personal accounts from battle participants, such as letters, journals, and memoirs. It is human nature to perceive yourself and your actions differently than others do. Generally people tend to view themselves in a more positive light, but that is not always the case. Regardless of whether it is positive or negative, this self-perception is transcribed within every diary or journal entry. This biased self-perception comes through in letters as well, although letters are also greatly influenced by the intended audience. For example, a soldier may write home after a battle and play up the skill and strength of the enemy, as well as his brave deeds, to make his family proud. While another soldier, who fought beside the previous one, may write home after a battle and downplay the danger and the gore of the battle to ease his family's distress. As for memoirs, these are usually written well after the time of the battle and the individual is usually concerned with their legacy. Consequently, memoirs usually provide the least accurate depiction of the battle.[1]

Secondary sources for a mid-nineteenth century battle consist of historical and biographical publications derived from the examination of primary resources. Researchers generally analyze a wide scope of primary sources to produce what they perceive to be an accurate description of the battle or an individual's role in the engagement. The accuracy of these descriptions, however, can be skewed by personal and cultural bias. This can be illustrated by how the depiction of the battle changes in these publications through time and through the influence of the cultural origins of the researcher.

The remainder of this section will compare a selection of primary and secondary sources for the Battle of Palmito Ranch. We begin with the Union commander Col. Theodore Barrett's official reports on the battle to his superiors.[2] On May 16, 1865, Barrett sent his first report to Lt. Col. J. Schuyler Crosby, Assistant Adjutant General, Department of the Gulf. In this report, Barrett states that he had sent two hundred and fifty troops from the 62nd United States Colored Infantry (USCI) and fifty troops from the 2nd Texas Cavalry (not yet mounted) under the command of Lt. Col. David Branson for the purpose of procuring beef and capturing a herd of two hundred horses that was reported to be in the vicinity of Port Isabel.[3]

He reports that he ordered Branson to cross Boca Chica at 7:00 p.m. and attack a Confederate post about ten miles from that point at or before daylight to secure their horses and cattle. Branson's forces were delayed while crossing Boca Chica due to a severe storm. The delay prevented Branson from arriving under the cover of darkness and securing all the men and horses, but he was able to take three prisoners and a few horses and cows. Branson drove off the enemy and then fell back three miles to White's Ranch, where he and his men bivouacked for the night.[4]

Barrett then reports that at daylight on the morning of May 13th, he, along with two hundred and fifty troops from the 34th Indiana Volunteer Infantry under the command of Lt. Col. Robert G. Morrison, joined Branson at White's Ranch. The Union force now under his command proceeded, with slight resistance from enemy cavalry, to the Confederate camp that Branson had captured the day before. Barrett states that in order to get to the reported herd of horses, he needed to travel approximately five miles farther up the road to Brownsville to a road that split off to the north.[5]

He says he advanced cautiously about two or three miles up the road before encountering a considerable enemy force. Barrett deemed it prudent to go no farther and retired to a suitable area to camp, with the intention of going to Port Isabel the next morning. He states that at 4:00 p.m. the Confederate cavalry appeared in front in full force, and three pieces of artillery opened fire on them, while a large contingent of cavalry was attempting to gain their rear by flanking their right under the cover of heavy brush.[6]

Barrett states that if it had not been for needless panic on the part of a portion of the 34th Indiana, they would have sustained no losses. He goes on to report that the 34th Indiana had one enlisted man wounded, and that two officers and seventy-eight enlisted men were missing. The 62nd USCI had five enlisted men wounded and two missing. Finally, the 2nd Texas Cavalry had one enlisted man wounded, with two officers and twenty-three enlisted men missing.[7]

He goes on to say that the point at which the enemy opened artillery fire was about twelve miles from Boca Chica. He estimated the Confederate forces at not more than nine hundred troops with three pieces of artillery. A captured federal soldier, who eventually escaped, reported to Barrett that Confederate forces suffered seventeen dead and wounded. Barrett also reports that his men took fire from parties on the other side of the Rio Grande. He concludes this first report with the statement that "Every officer and man in the 62nd USCI did his duty."[8]

Barrett's next report to Crosby was dated May 21st. In this report, Barrett makes very slight adjustments to the casualties his forces suffered. The major difference in this report is that he goes into detail about what happened to the 34th Indiana. Barrett states that Capt. A. M. Templer of Company B and forty-eight enlisted men, mostly of Companies B and E, were taken prisoner while bravely fighting on the skirmish line that was put out to cover their regiment. He says that when the order to retreat was given to the 34th Indiana's commanding officer, he failed to pass on that order to his troops on the skirmish line, leaving them unprotected from the enemy. Barrett reports that the 34th Indiana lost their regimental and national colors and threw away their arms, ammunitions, and accoutrements; all the while there was a well-organized and unbroken regiment (62nd USCI) in between them and the enemy.[9]

Barrett also includes a brief account of the actions of the 2nd Texas Cavalry during the battle. He commends this small force for fighting bravely, but said they became disorganized and sought shelter from enemy fire under the bluff at Palmito Ranch, where they were soon surrounded and overtaken. He appears to excuse their actions on the grounds that they had been on picket duty the previous night and on skirmish lines during the day, and were therefore very fatigued. Barrett also mentions that they were inexperienced troops and lacked discipline.[10]

He then goes on to reinforce that the reason for the expedition was to secure horses and cattle, since they could no longer get cows on South Padre Island. He states that if it had not been for the enemy mistaking their foraging raid as an attack on Brownsville, his forces would have been able to accomplish their mission successfully. Barrett explains that his quick decision to retreat from his position was because the enemy attacked in numbers larger than their own, supported by six pieces of artillery. At this point he requests that this report serve as charges and specifications against the commanding officer of the 34th Indiana, concluding with additional praise for members of the 62nd USCI.[11]

Barrett's third report was to Bvt. Maj. Gen. L. Thomas, Adjutant-General, US Army, and is dated August 10, 1865.[12] This report has a much different tone than the previous two reports. Barrett starts off by stating that on the evening of May 11th he sent an expedition of two hundred and fifty men of the 62nd USCI, properly officered, and fifty men and two officers of the 2nd Texas Cavalry (not yet mounted) under the command of Lt. Col. David Branson of the 62nd USCI. Barrett makes no mention of a foraging run. He describes the force's crossing of Boca Chica as "effected with difficulty" due to a severe storm.[13] He writes that "the force marched nearly all night, and after a short rest, early next morning attacked a strong outpost of the Confederates at Palmetto Ranch."[14] He states that the enemy force was driven in confusion from its position, and that Branson's forces took their camp, camp equipage, and stores. Barrett reports that some horses and cattle were captured, as well as a number of prisoners, and that Branson fell back to the vicinity of White's Ranch after destroying the stores that could not be transported.[15]

He goes on to report that on the morning of the 13th, about two hundred men of the 34th Indiana, under the command of Lt. Col. Robert G. Morrison, joined Branson forces. Barrett then writes, "Assuming command in person of the forces thus united, I at once ordered an advance to be again made in the direction of Palmetto Ranch," which was once again occupied by Confederate forces.[16] Barrett states that enemy cavalry were quickly encountered and that his forces drove the enemy in front of them back to Palmito Ranch by 7:00 or 8:00 a.m., where they compelled the rest of the Confederate forces to abandon the outpost once again. Barrett then destroyed all stores that had escaped destruction on the previous day and burned all structures. He reports that a detachment was sent back to Brazos Island with their wounded and the prisoners captured, and ordered the remainder of his troops to advance. Barrett states that nearly the entire forenoon was spent in skirmishing and that "[t]he enemy, though taking advantage of every favorable position, was everywhere easily driven back."[17] He says that a sharp engagement occurred early in the afternoon in which his forces charged the enemy, forcing them from their cover and driving them across the open prairie beyond the rising ground and out of sight. He states that at this point he decided to relinquish pursuit and fall back to a hill about a mile from Palmito Ranch because his troops needed a rest after driving the enemy back several miles.[18]

Barrett goes on to report that at 4:00 p.m. the Confederates, now greatly reinforced, reappeared in the front and opened fired on his troops with both small arms and artillery. Meanwhile a large body of Confederate cavalry with a section of an artillery battery had already succeeded in flanking his right under the cover of the dense chaparral. Barrett describes his situation at this time as extremely critical, with the Rio Grande on his left, a superior force of enemy to his front, and a flanking force on his right. He says he decided to fall back fighting because his position had become untenable, as he had no artillery to oppose the enemy's six twelve-pounder field pieces. Barrett states that his troops were receiving heavy fire from both their front and their flank as they fell back.[19]

Barrett mentions the forty-eight men of the 34th Indiana under

Captain Templer, who had been put out as skirmishers to cover their regiment, stubbornly resisted the enemy until they were cut off and captured by the enemy's cavalry. He does not mention anything about Colonel Morrison and the rest of the 34th Indiana abandoning their skirmishers.

The report goes on to say that Barrett ordered the 62nd USCI to cover the federal forces as they fell back. More than half of the regiment were deployed as skirmishers, while the remaining troops acted as their support. It states that the skirmish line was nearly three quarters of a mile in length. It goes on to report that every attempt of the Confederate cavalry to break the Union skirmish line was repulsed with enemy losses, and that the entire US 62nd USCI regiment fell back with precision and in perfect order. He states that these troops seized upon every advantageous position and returned the enemy's fire deliberately and with effect. Barrett says that the fighting lasted for about three hours and that the last volley of the war, it is believed, was fired by the 62nd USCI at sunset between Boca Chica and White's Ranch. He reports that their entire loss in killed, wounded, and captured was 4 officers and 111 enlisted men.[20]

Barrett concludes the report by saying that he learned a few days after the federal occupation of Brownsville that a detail of the engagement was forwarded to the department headquarters at New Orleans shortly after the battle. Because these reports may never have reached the Adjutant General's Office, he is respectfully submitting this report on "the last conflict of the great Rebellion."[21]

It is interesting to see how three official military reports written by the same person within a three-month time span immediately following the battle can provide varying views of what actually happened. It appears that in the first two reports, those addressed to Crosby, Barrett is seemingly trying to shrug off responsibility for the battle and the defeat. Here he reports that the purpose of the expedition was a foraging run, even though he does state that the expedition had orders to attack a Confederate outpost. In his second report he becomes more insistent that the expedition was to obtain horses and cattle, and then goes on to blame Confederate forces for the engagement by mistaking his foraging run as a raid on Brownsville. The third report, however, presents a different tone. This is most likely because of who he is reporting to.

Regardless, in the third report, Barrett presents himself more as if he was in charge and responsible for the actions. He does not mention anything about an expedition to secure cattle and horses. Although he does not say it directly, the report can be interpreted as if he purposely sent out his forces to engage the enemy. He presents his actions and the actions of his troops as correct and valiant; it was just that the enemy greatly outnumbered and outgunned him that resulted in his being defeated. It is also interesting that the reported intensity of the fighting increased with each telling.

The transcript of Lt. Col. R. G. Morrison's court martial provides several accounts of the Battle of Palmito Ranch by Union battle participants in the form of testimony under oath within three months of the engagement.[22] Although these accounts are largely focused on the actions of Morrison and the 34th Indiana during the battle, they do provide additional detailed descriptions of the battle.

On July 29th Lt. Col. David Branson, commander of the 62nd, was asked to give a full account of the expedition from the time it left White's Ranch on the morning of May 13th to its return to Boca Chica, including the part played by Morrison and the 34th Indiana Volunteers.[23] Branson begins his testimony by stating that at daylight on the morning of the 13th he and his troops were at White's Ranch, with half of his men on skirmish duty and engaging Confederate cavalry, which fled when Colonel Barrett and the 34th Indiana troops arrived. Branson states that Barrett ordered the skirmish line forward toward Palmito Ranch, along with the remainder of the 62nd USCI in support. The 34th Indiana would follow shortly afterward. In his testimony, Branson makes no mention of any enemy resistance during their march from White's Ranch to Palmito Ranch, or of any Confederate troops being compelled to abandon Palmito Ranch. Instead, Branson just says that the entire command under Colonel Barrett stacked arms, rested, and ate breakfast when they arrived at Palmito Ranch.

Branson states that after about two hours of rest, Barrett resumed the advance to a hill or ridge partially covered with chaparral about one mile farther on, with skirmishing going on all the way. The 62nd was left in reserve. Shortly after noon, Branson says he was ordered to move his regiment around the rear of the 34th to the bank of the river and to proceed upriver about a mile, concealing his movements in the reeds and chaparral, with the purpose of driving the enemy out of the brush. Branson executed this order effectively, having one man seriously wounded. He says that at about 2:00 p.m. the main skirmish line was called in and was allowed to rest. He notes that the 34th had halted on the side of the hill furthest upriver from Palmito Ranch and stacked arms. Branson adds that at about this time Barrett ordered him to take his regiment and return to the hill where the 34th Indiana was resting and to rest his troops as well. Branson says that while they were resting, most of the men eating, the enemy's cavalry reappeared in considerable force from upriver, marching by a flank movement in a direction to intercept their retreat.

Branson goes on to say that once Barrett became aware of the enemy's movement, he ordered him to put out some skirmishers to cover his regiment and to fall in and take arms. Branson describes how he and the 34th adjusted their positions to take better ground. While they were doing this, Branson says that the enemy's artillery began firing on them from a position on Telegraph Road, about one mile away and fairly close to the river. He points out that at the first artillery shot some of the men of the 34th increased their gait, causing some confusion and disorder within that regiment.

Branson says that in a very short time Barrett ordered the retreat. He says that Barrett, after consulting with some of his officers, said in low, clear, and distinct tone of voice, "Very well then, we will retreat in good order, and good order let it be. Men keep your ranks. They can't hurt you, we'll get out of this yet."[24] Branson describes the retreat of the 62nd and 34th troops in detail, focusing on the disorder of the 34th. He testifies that the men of the 34th Indiana continually straggled from the ranks, throwing away guns, accoutrements, haversacks, canteens, and clothing all the way to Boca Chica.

Branson's extensive questioning focused primarily on the actions of Morrison and the 34th Indiana, for which the charges were brought against Morrison. Branson's testimony does provide some good detail on the actions and troop movements in the core battle area on May 13th. He reveals that when the reinforced Confederate troops caught the federal troops at rest, there were no pickets in place—only four to five men on high ground to notify the command of any enemy approach. Branson estimates that on May 13th Barrett had about 430 federal troops against about 550 Confederate cavalry supported by six pieces of artillery, only four of which were actually fired.[25]

On August 11, 1865, 2nd Lt. Charles A. Jones of Company K, 34th Indiana, testified as a witness for the defense. Jones provides the perspective of the commander of one of the skirmishing lines that advanced westward from Palmito Ranch on the morning of May 13th. Jones provides an in-depth account of his company's action, although with a somewhat boastful tone. He describes heavy exchanges of fire while advancing the skirmish line under his command. In his testimony, Jones takes responsibility for sending Branson's party up the river banks to flush out the Confederate troops from the brush. Jones says that he did not receive clear orders on the objectives of advancing the skirmish line under his command, and that Barrett sought his counsel and followed his direction. Jones's testimony makes Barrett look like a weak and indecisive commander. He directly contradicts portions of both Barrett's and Branson's testimony.[26] The August 18th testimony of Cpl. Joseph A. Keller, Company K, 34th Indiana, supported Jones's account that Barrett let Jones take charge of the left advance and that Jones gave Branson the command to advance up the river banks to flush out the enemy from the brush.[27]

The transcript of Morrison's court martial clearly illustrates how battle participants from the same army can provide strongly conflicting accounts of a battle only months after the engagement. It is possible that some of the witnesses intentionally misrepresented the truth in order to protect themselves or someone else. But the fact that these accounts were given under oath in a military court makes it even more perplexing. Regardless, Lt. Col. R. G. Morrison was acquitted on all charges, which puts into question Barrett's credibility and the credibility of his account of the battle.

Almost twenty years after the battle, Col. John Salmon "Rip" Ford, the commander of the Confederate reinforcements that joined the engagement at Palmito Ranch on the afternoon of May 13th and drove the Union forces back to Brazos Island, wrote his memoirs. Ford's stated purpose for writing his memoirs was to aid his fellow citizens in finding the true history of the making of Texas. Ford felt it was his responsibility because he had experienced much of that history firsthand. Stephen B. Oates edited Ford's memoirs and published them as *Rip Ford's*

*Texas* in 1963.[28] In Oates's forward to the book, he acknowledges that "Ford's two accounts of the Civil War in the original memoirs duplicate and often contradict one another."[29] Oates later notes that the memoir's account of Palmito Ranch was obscure and incomplete, so he integrated it with Ford's detailed article on the battle that appeared in the *San Antonio Express* on October 10, 1890.[30]

The following is the account of the Battle of Palmito Ranch that appears in Ford's edited memoirs. On May 12th a report came from Capt. William Robinson, who was in command of six companies of Giddings's battalion, which was on picket duty at Palmito Ranch. Robinson reported that the federals had advanced and that he was engaged with them just below San Martin Ranch. Ford directed Robinson to hold his ground if possible and that he would come to his aid as soon as men could be collected at Fort Brown. That night couriers were sent to different camps scattered about the region to hurry the troops back to Fort Brown. Ford also notes that he and his commanding officer, Gen. James E. Slaughter, had supper at Ford's quarters. During their meal Ford asked Slaughter what he intended to do, to which Slaughter replied, "Retreat." Ford then thundered, "You can retreat and go to hell if you wish. These are my men, and I am going to fight."[31]

On the morning of May 13th, Ford waited at Fort Brown until 11:00 a.m. for General Slaughter, who failed to appear. Placing himself at the head of the few men that were present, Ford began his march to a location just a short distance from the San Martin Ranch. When Ford saw the federal lines some half mile down from the San Martin Ranch, he thought to himself, "This may be the last fight of the war, and from the number of the union men I see before me, I am going to be whipped."[32] Then according to Ford, "He buoyed up his spirits, made a short talk to the boys, and found them in such good fighting trim that he made haste to put them to work."[33]

After having made a reconnaissance, and determined to attack, Ford directed Capt. O. G. Jones of the 3rd Texas Field Battery to place a section of his battery in the road under Lt. J. M. Smith, another section under Lt. S. Gregory to the left supported by Lt. Jesse Vineyard's detachment of Giddings's battalion, and the remaining section was to be held in reserve. Ford directed the artillery to move in advance of the line. Ford placed Captain Robinson in command of the main body of cavalry, with Anderson's battalion under Capt. D. W. Wilson on the right and Giddings's battalion on the left. Ford ordered Gregory to move under the cover of the hills and chaparral, to flank the enemy's right, and if possible get an enfilading fire.[34] Capt. G. A. Gibson's and Capt. F. B. S. Cocke's companies were ordered to the extreme left and to turn the enemy's right flank. Ford then advanced skirmishers.[35]

Ford recalls that his artillery opened fire before the enemy was aware that they had artillery pieces on the field. He says that Smith fired several well-directed shells and round shot into the enemy's lines, while Gregory's fire annoyed the enemy. Ford claims at this point the skirmishing became brisk. He waited until he heard Gibson and Cocke open on his left, and when he saw that the enemy's skirmishers were left without support, he ordered an advance. "Very soon," Ford describes, "Captain Robinson charged with impetuosity."[36] Ford states the federal skirmishers were captured as expected and the enemy troops were retreating at a run, continuing that the artillery pieces pursued at the gallop and shouting men pressed to the front, occupying the hills adjacent to the road and firing from behind the security of the crests. He notes that the enemy endeavored to hold various points, but was driven from them. Ford recollects the pursuit lasting for about seven miles until he ordered his officers to withdraw their men. He says he ordered the halt because "the artillery horses were fatigued and the cavalry horses were jaded," and he thought the federals would be reinforced at White's Ranch.[37]

Ford initially states that the enemy lost twenty-five to thirty men killed and wounded, and 113 captured. He goes on to say that some were killed while swimming the river and that many escaped to Mexico. He then approximates that the enemy lost about two hundred killed, wounded, and missing. Ford claimed that the Confederate troops suffered five wounded, "none of them supposed to be dangerous."[38]

The account of the Battle of Palmito Ranch presented in *Rip Ford's Texas* has a much different flavor than that of the firsthand accounts from the federal battle participants. In Ford's edited memoirs, the Confederate troops appear to be more skillful and able to dominate the federal troops when they engaged. Ford describes himself as leading the few troops present on the morning of the 13th, and describes his first site of the federal line as intimidating because they outnumbered his troops and were strategically positioned. In reading the edited memoirs with the various footnotes, the Confederate forces at the battle ranged from 200 to 800. Even more intriguing, somewhere in the body of Ford's original papers, he says his force of about 1,300 engaged a federal column of about the same size at the Battle of Palmito Ranch.[39]

In 1889 Hubert H. Bancroft published a brief account of the Battle of Palmito Ranch in his book, *The History of the North Mexican States and Texas: Vol II, 1801–1889*.[40] Bancroft's account is highly influenced by Colonel Barrett's third report on the engagement, to the point of using some of the same wording.[41] I believe that it was Bancroft's account of the Battle of Palmito Ranch that incited Ford to write the 1890 article that he sent to the *San Antonio Express*. Regardless, Bancroft's brief account has multiple factual errors. He spells Branson's name as Bronson. He has Confederate General Slaughter in command of the troops occupying Palmito Ranch on the morning of the 13th. Bancroft goes on to state that at "about four o'clock in the afternoon, however, the federals were assailed from in front by a strong body of infantry with six 12-pounders."[42] Bancroft concludes that a running fight was maintained for about three hours without the Confederate troops being able to break the federal line. It is unclear why Bancroft would make such errors, when he apparently had access to Barrett's official report. One explanation may be the fact that Bancroft and his army of assistants were in the process of producing numerous historical volumes on the west, and this volume itself (vol. 11) was more than five hundred pages and he uses less than a page to describe the battle. Regardless, Bancroft's treatment of the Battle of Palmito Ranch exemplifies the confusion that envelopes the historical record of the last land battle of the Civil War.

In 1899 the Confederate Publishing Company of Atlanta published *Confederate Military History*.[43] It is self-described as a library of the Confederate States' history, in twelve volumes, written by distinguished men of the South and edited by Gen. Clement A. Evans of Georgia. The account of the Battle of Palmito Ranch in this publication begins with a statement from Capt. W. H. D. Carrington of Carter's battalion. According to Carrington, "the United States forces under Colonel Barrett (brevet brigadier-general), consisting of the Thirty-second Indiana, better known as the Morton rifles, a regiment of negro troops officered by Lieutenant-Colonel Branson, a part of a New York regiment, and a company of the Second (Federal) Texas, under command of Lieutenant or Captain Hancock, numbering about 1,600 or 1,700 men advanced from Brazos island upon Brownsville. They were held in check by Captain Robinson, commanding Giddings' regiment, on the evening of the 12th of May, 1865."[44]

Col. John Salmon "Rip" Ford is given credit for furnishing the subsequent report of the battle that ensued on May 13, 1865.[45] As expected, the account of the battle is very similar to the account that appears in Ford's edited memoirs. One interesting addition to Ford's account is that it states that on the 12th, Capt. W. N. Robinson, commanding Giddings's battalion, three hundred strong, reported that the advancing enemy had driven in his pickets, captured their rations, clothing, two sick soldiers, and burnt "Palmetto rancho."[46] The account goes on to state that in the evening Captain Robinson with a force of sixty troops attacked the Union force and drove them back to White's Ranch. The remainder of the account of the battle is almost identical to the account presented in the 1890 newspaper article and in *Rip Ford's Texas*. The Confederate Publishing Company obviously published these volumes to promote the Southern version or perspective on the military history of the Civil War; as the nineteenth century was coming to a close, the former Confederate states were still reeling from Reconstruction and trying to regain their identity and pride. The perspective of the Battle of Palmito Ranch in this account accordingly places the Confederate troops and commanders in a favorable light.

During the twentieth century, the fabled "Last Battle of the Civil War" was only sporadically examined by historians. The accounts are generally brief and continue to put forth inconsistent accounts of how and why the Battle of Palmito Ranch was fought. In 1960, one researcher put forth that Colonel Barrett was ordered by his commanding officer to march on Brownsville to capture the thousands of bales of Confederate cotton that were still on the north side of the Rio Grande.[47] Regardless, the story of the Battle of Palmito Ranch continued to be glossed over in the pages of history until the turn of the twenty-first century, when two separate researchers conducted in-depth examinations of the battle.

In 2001 Philip T. Tucker published *The Final Fury: Palmito Ranch, the Last Battle of the Civil War*,[48] and in 2002 Jeffrey William Hunt published *The Last Battle of the Civil War: Palmetto Ranch*.[49] Both authors do an excellent job of examining a vast array of primary source documents and of presenting the conflicting accounts put forth in the historical record. They also make valiant attempts to draw objective conclusions in order to finally present an accurate depiction of the Battle of Palmito Ranch. However, despite their thorough and scholarly effort, the authors fail to provide a consistent account of information fundamental to the battle, such as why the federals were marching on the mainland or how many casualties each army suffered.

Both Tucker and Hunt seem to discount the explanation of a foraging run for the expedition. Tucker suggests that the motivation behind the expedition was driven by Barrett's desire to capture military glory before the close of the war in order to further his postwar political aspirations.[50] Hunt, on the other hand, acknowledges the evidence behind that opinion, but believes that idea was pushed forward due to personal animosities between Barrett and the commander and members of the 34th Indiana. Hunt concludes that probably the best statement regarding Barrett's motive for the expedition was made by Capt. Joshua Fussell, Company D, 34th Indiana, when he said the expedition was made "either without any definite purpose or for some purpose that has never been made clear."[51]

Both authors go on to acknowledge the numerous discrepancies in the historic record regarding the number of casualties suffered. Hunt concludes that despite the large number of prisoners lost on the federal side, the number of men from each side who were shot in battle was almost equal: ten Union soldiers and six Confederate soldiers.[52] Tucker, on the other hand, sees the battle as having had much heavier losses, possibly due to a Confederate policy to give no quarter. Tucker suggests the full magnitude of the federal defeat was covered up because of the intended joint Union-Confederate operations against the French in Mexico, and that the actual number of casualties from both sides was downplayed.[53] Tucker supports this theory by stating, "To this day, some historians, relic hunters, and those familiar with the remote battlefield of Palmito Ranch still uncover the remains of Union soldiers identified by US buttons and buckles."[54]

In conclusion, these two modern scholarly examinations of the Battle of Palmito Ranch reveal that even after 150 years of research, the historical record fails to provide a consistent, objective, and accurate account of the battle. Despite this, it is still critical for a society to have an accurate understanding of the past events that played a role in shaping its current state. The field of archeology can help provide that objective and accurate understanding.

### *The Archeological Record*

The archeological record of a battle is composed of the material remains that were deposited during the battle. If preserved in pristine condition, the archeological record can reveal an objective and accurate depiction of the battle. However, the archeological records associated with mid-nineteenth-century battlefields are typically disturbed. This usually begins with battle participants picking up souvenirs or trophies from the battlefield immediately after the battle and can continue for months or years. Civilians also joined in the collecting of souvenirs from battlefields during this period. In the case of the Battle of Palo Alto, the first battle of the US-Mexican War (1846–48), an inn was established shortly after the battle on the historic road near Palo Alto, enticing guests to stay by offering activities such as collecting souvenirs from the battlefield.[55] During the twentieth century, the archeological records associated with the majority of unprotected mid-nineteenth century battlefields in the US have been highly compromised and often destroyed by modern land management practices and urban development. In addition, the development and availability of modern metal detector technology has allowed new generations of individuals to effectively collect artifacts from mid-nineteenth-century battlefields. This activity, which often goes on for decades on unprotected sites, can devastate the integrity of the archeological record, sometimes to the point of rendering the record scientifically unserviceable.

To date there have been three reconnaissance-level archeological investigations conducted within the core battlefield area at Palmito Ranch. National Park Service (NPS) archeologist Charles M. Haecker conducted the initial investigation in 2001 in fulfillment of an NPS American Battlefield Protection Program (ABPP) grant. The primary research objective of this investigation was to "ascertain the presence or absence of battle-related artifacts within an area believed by historians to comprise the western portion of the battlefield."[56] The second archeological investigation was conducted by the author in an effort to supplement the data collected from the previous investigation by surveying a parcel of land directly to the east. The primary research objective of this investigation was to identify any physical evidence of the Union retreat—in particular, the contested retreat and capture of the 34th Indiana skirmishers and the 2nd Texas Cavalry.[57] The third archeological investigation was conducted by the Texas Historical Commission's chief archeologist Dr. Jim Bruseth in 2010 in fulfillment of an ABPP grant. The primary research objectives of this investigation were to verify if Union forces utilized Palmito Hill as terrain to gain observation of the surrounding prairie and as an avenue of approach during the final day of the battle, as well as to add valuable archeological data to further the geographical understanding of the battle.[58]

Combined, these three archeological investigations systematically examined less than forty of the more than three thousand acres

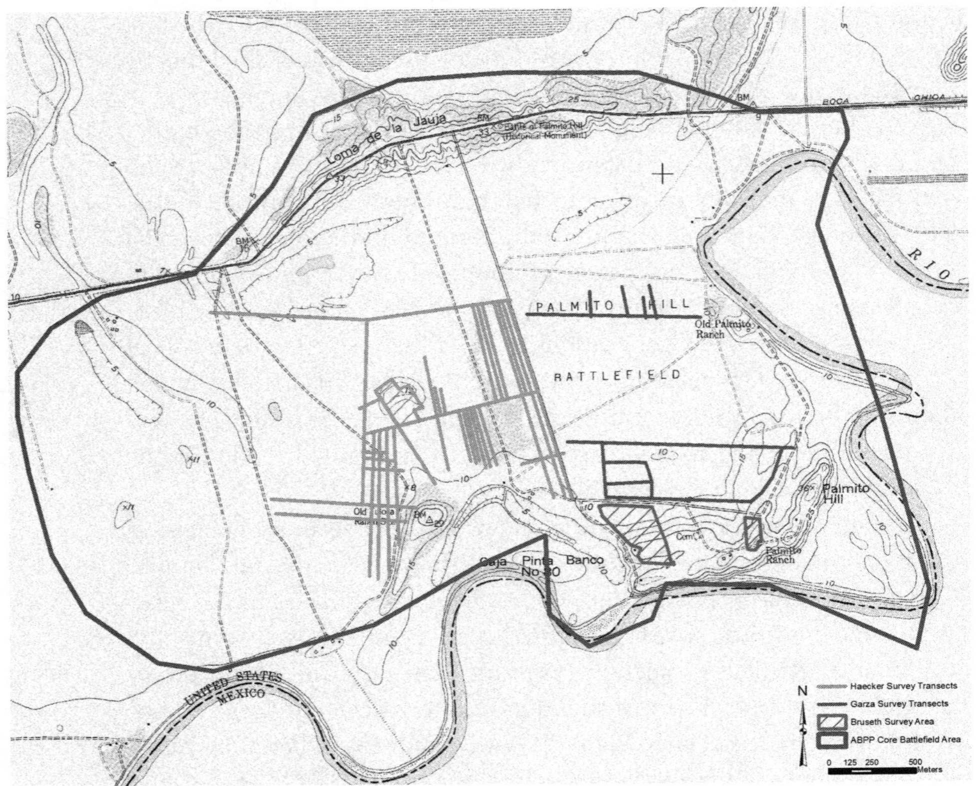


*This map shows the total survey of the core battlefield areas at the Palmito Ranch battlefield site. Three separate surveys were conducted, in order to look for battle-related artifacts. Courtesy of the author.*

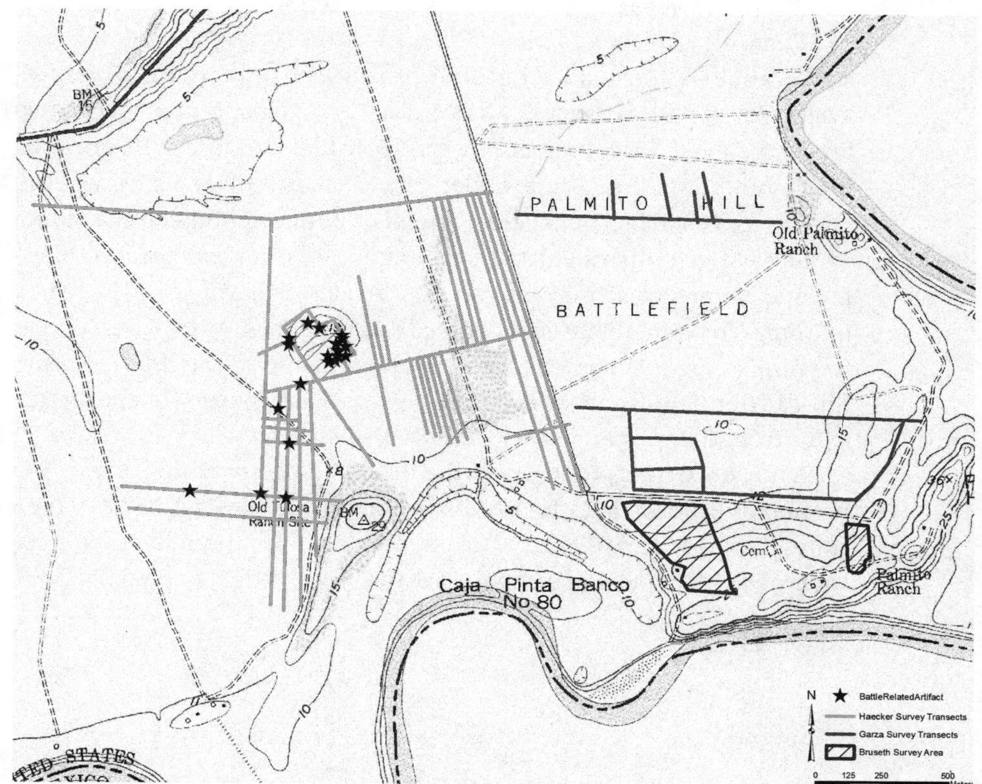


*This enlarged map of the three survey sites at Palmito Ranch battlefield shows that battlefield-related artifacts such as bullets and buttons were found only at the Hacker survey transects. Courtesy of the author.*

designated as constituting the Core Battlefield Area by the NPS American Battlefield Protection Program. Only twenty possible battle-related artifacts were recovered in the course of these investigations. Nineteen of these artifacts are Civil War period bullets and lead shot, and the other artifact was a button. All twenty of these artifacts were recovered by the investigation that examined the western arena of the core battlefield area. No other Civil War period military items were recovered during these investigations. Generally items such as uniform buttons, uniform accoutrements, remains of weapons, canteens, and other metal military objects are found in conjunction with bullets on Civil War battlefields during archeological investigations.

Regardless, eleven of these bullets were recovered in a northeast-southwest axis linear cluster in close proximity to an unnamed low rise. These eleven bullets consist of five unfired .58 caliber Minie bullets, two fired .58 caliber Minie bullets, one fired .65 caliber musket ball, one fired Sharps and Hankins carbine bullet, one fired .44 caliber pistol ball, and one fired .34 caliber buck shot. The distributional and compositional artifact pattern of this cluster is consistent with a small federal infantry line being attacked by a force of Confederate cavalry supported by infantry. The other eight bullets were recovered widely scattered across the project area. When examined in relationship to the linear cluster, the distributional pattern of these eight bullets suggests the attack came from the west and southwest along a broad front.[59]

The above interpretation of the artifact pattern could support the portion of Branson's testimony during Morrison's court martial, which states that no federal pickets were put out and only four or five men were stationed as lookouts on a small rise to the west, while the main body of

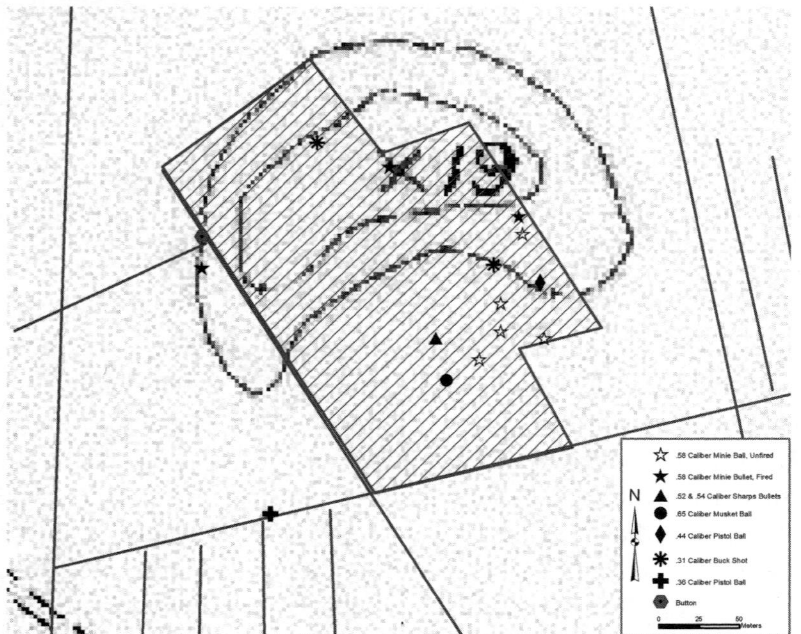


*This enlarged section of the Hacker survey transects shows the detailed location of battlefield artifacts recovered, with a key to indicate exactly what was found. Courtesy of the author.*

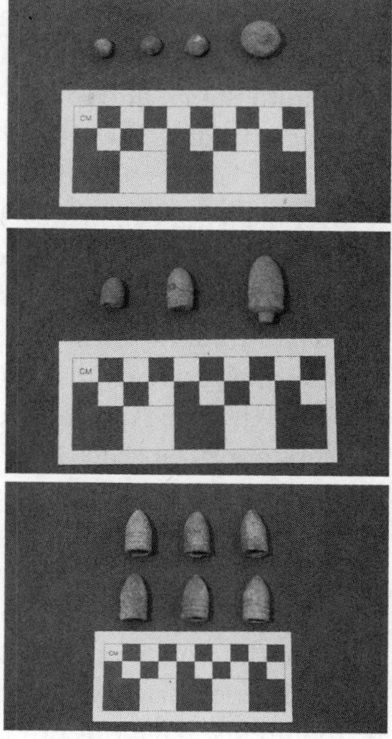

*Lead bullets collected during the 2001 archaeological project at Palmito Ranch (41CF93) and curated at the Museum of South Texas History. Top (left to right): FS #1 36 caliber, FS #10 36 caliber, FS #20 36 caliber, FS #7 69 caliber; Middle (left to right): FS #4 36 caliber, FS #5 44 caliber, FS #9 54 caliber used in Sharps and Hankins rifles; Bottom: all 58 caliber, above (left to right) FS #3, FS #6, FS #8, below FS #12, FS #13, FS #14.*

federal troops rested the afternoon of the 13th. Conversely, the lack of potential battle-related artifacts recovered in the remainder of the core battlefield area investigated does not support the balance of Branson's account, or for that matter, the majority of the other accounts. To add confusion to the interpretation of the artifact pattern exposed in these investigations, the historical record reveals that in early September 1864, Confederate and Union forces clashed in a series of attacks and counterattacks at and around Palmito Ranch.[60] However, the depictions of these actions are even more inconsistent and contradictory than the accounts of the 1865 Battle of Palmito Ranch.

Nevertheless, the archaeological record seems to be consistent with the account of only four or five federal troops being present during the early afternoon of May 13th. The artifact pattern suggests that this small body put up a very brief resistance in a formal firing line before being overtaken by a broad line of rapidly advancing Confederate troops. The very limited amount of battle-related artifacts, as well as their absence throughout most of the area investigated, suggests that neither the Union nor the Confederate forces engaged in running exchanges of fire or in close-quarters fighting in the areas to the west of Palmito Ranch and to the north and west-northwest of Palmito Hill, which contradicts the majority of the historical record.

It may be questioned whether the latter two investigations did not recover evidence of the May 13th engagement because of varying field methodologies or the competency of the field crew. The second investigation utilized virtually the same field methodologies by examining a series of long survey transects that stretched across the broad prairie at parallel and perpendicular orientations to each other. This investigation also used the same mower and mowing equipment to cut the vegetation for the survey transects. In addition, more than half of the metal detector operators had participated in the previous investigation. The 2010 investigation did not utilize long-running mowed survey transects, but examined two separate survey areas and prepared the survey areas differently. In the survey area on top of Palmito Hill, the grassy areas in between the woody vegetation were mowed to similar conditions as the previous two surveys. This provided ample area to recover a sample of the archeological record of the May 13th battle if it were present. The second survey area, which was about six hundred meters to the west, was a plowed field that had been overgrown with tall grasses and weeds but still possessed considerable areas of exposed soil. The vegetation in this area was not prepared; instead, the metal detector operators systematically searched the field in a back-and-forth survey-transect fashion, following the formerly plowed rows. Again, the core of metal detector operators had participated in the previous investigations. Consequently, the absence of battle-related artifacts recovered during the latter two investigations is probably not the result of varying archeological field methodologies or competency of the crew.

It may also be questioned whether the absence of battle-related artifacts in the latter two survey areas is due to postbattle human or natural actions. Natural actions that could remove or obscure the archeological record in these areas could include the burying of the record under alluvium due to intensive flooding or the removal of land due to the shifting of the river. The Rio Grande has definitely shifted its course in this area since the time of the battle, yet most of the landforms described in the historical record appear to be intact today. This is supported by the 1898 International Boundary and Water Commission survey map of the area and a modern topographic map with the 1853 and 1898 river channels and Telegraph Road from the previous map superimposed. The prairie in the core battlefield area certainly has flooded since the time of the battle, due to torrential rains and river overflow generated by tropical storm activity. Nonetheless, the prairie in the core battlefield area is contiguous and displays no surface variance between the areas where battle-related artifacts were present or absent. Therefore the absence of battle-related artifacts in the latter two survey areas is probably not due to natural actions.

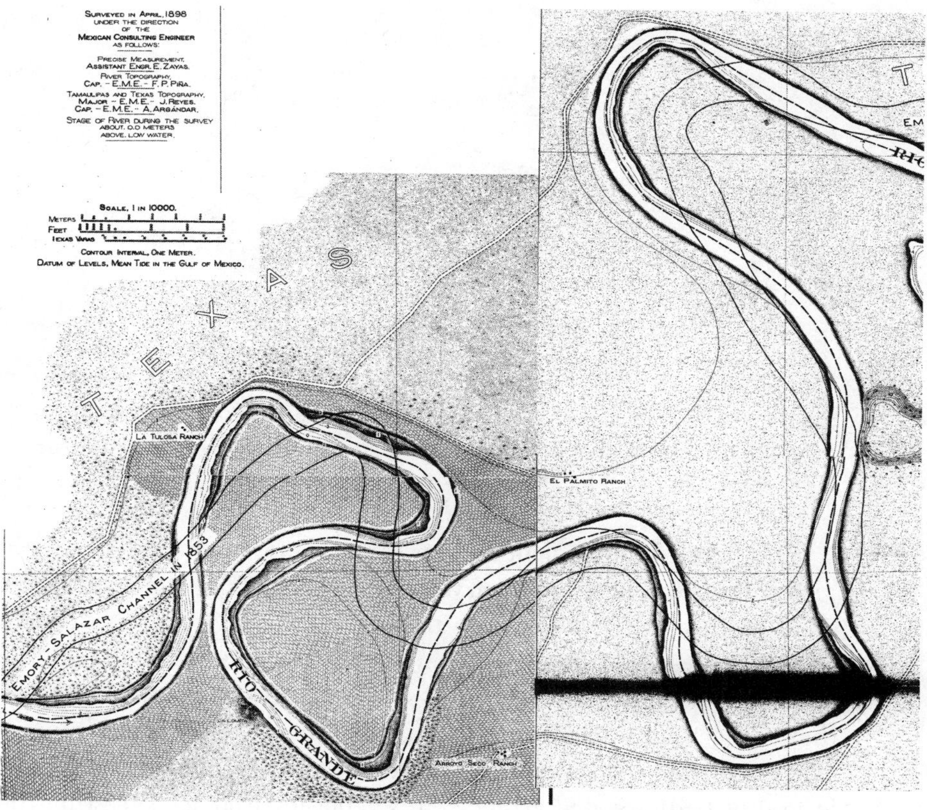


*Survey map of the Rio Grande near Palmito Ranch battlefield to show the location of Palmito Ranch and its position as it related to the actual river channel. Note the Emory-Salazar Channel maps the course of the Rio Grande in 1853 prior to the US Civil War. The outlined Rio Grande shows how the course of the river changed by the time this map was created by the International Boundary and Water Commission in 1898. Courtesy of International Boundary and Water Commission.*

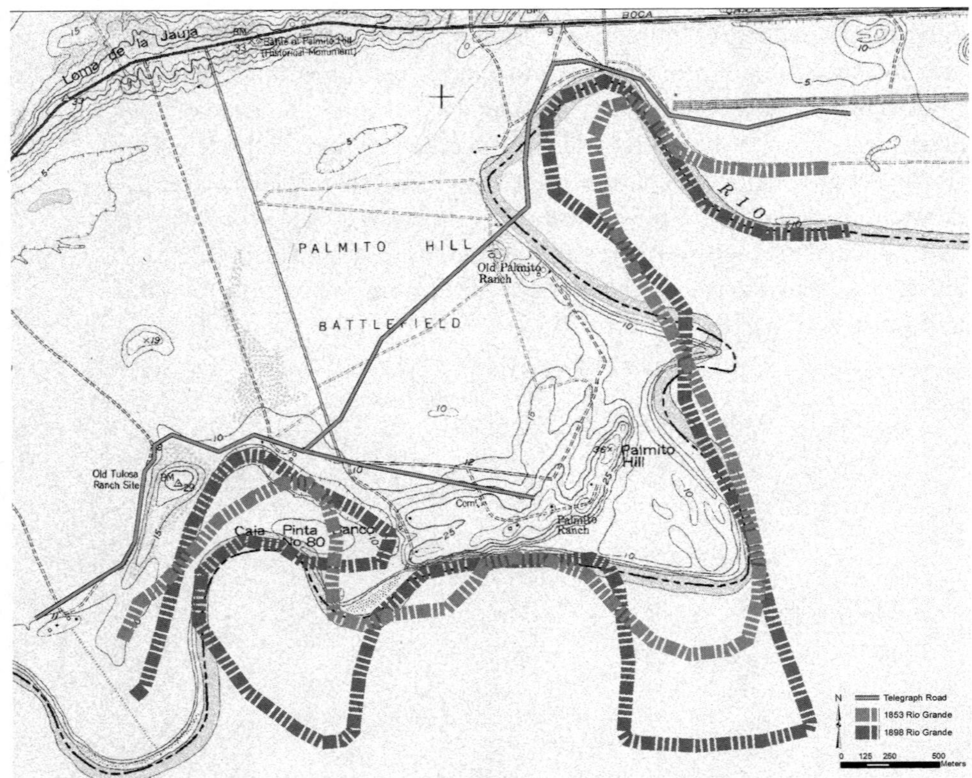


*This map shows the position of Palmito Ranch battlefield site and the surrounding topography as it related to the location of Telegraph Road and the river channels, both in 1853 and in 1898. Courtesy of the author.*

Postbattle human actions may have removed the archeological record from the latter two survey areas. These might include large-scale earth-moving projects or the undocumented intensive collection of battle-related artifacts. However, there is no evidence that this landform has undergone any large-scale human alteration. It is agreed that the terrain in and around the core battlefield area appears much as it did during the time of the battle.[61] As to the undocumented collection of battle-related artifacts, it is generally well accepted that the area between the Brownsville Ship Channel and Rio Grande to the coast has experienced varying levels of undocumented artifact collecting by numerous individuals for several decades, if not longer. However, the vegetation—particularly the dense stands of Gulf cordgrass that dominate the prairie and the dense thorn scrub on higher elevations—serves as a protective barrier for the ground surface and the underlying archeological record. In addition, previous systematic archeological investigations on battlefields that are known to have been collected generally show that this activity is not likely to remove the entire archeological record. That said, the undocumented collection of artifacts from any archeological site always results in adverse impacts to the archeological record and its ability to provide a complete and accurate view of the events that the record represents. Certainly decades of relic hunting has adversely affected the integrity of the archeological record, not only for the Battle of Palmito Ranch but also for the other historic and prehistoric resources in the area. Nonetheless, it is not likely that human activities have completely removed the May 13th battle's archeological record from the latter two survey areas.

In conclusion, the results of the archeological investigations have provided some accurate and objective insights into the actions of the Battle of Palmito Ranch. However, it is important to note that these data are the product of three relatively narrowly scoped archeological investigations and thus represent just a small sample of the archeological record. That said, the data suggest that after the reinforced Confederate troops burst upon the scene and overtook the small party of federal lookouts that were stationed on the small unnamed rise, there was very limited exchange of fire between the two armies in the core battlefield area. Additional extensive and intensive archeological investigations within the core battlefield area would provide a more accurate depiction of the battle based upon more physical evidence and a lot less conjecture. Until such investigations can be conducted—a matter dependent upon funding and focused interest—the events at Palmito Ranch in May 1865, the last land battle of the Civil War, will remain contested and confused.

## *Notes*

1. Respecting the use of such different forms of primary records as diaries, letters, and memoirs, see George Mason University, "What Kind of Historical Source Are Letters and Diaries?" History Matters: The US Survey Course on the Web, http://historymatters.gmu.edu/mse/letters/whatkind.html (accessed April 19, 2016). With respect to the reliability of eyewitness accounts more generally, see Hal Arkowitz and Scott O. Lilienfeld, "Why Science Tells Us Not to Rely on Eyewitness

Accounts," *Scientific American* (January 1, 2010), http://www.scientificamerican.com/article/do-the-eyes-have-it/.

2. Colonel Barrett authored three reports to his superiors on May 16, 1865, May 21, 1865, and August 10, 1865. The third (and official) report was published in 1893 in *The War of the Rebellion: A Compilation of the Official Records of the Union and Confederate Armies*. Official Records, US Government, Series I, Vols. 41, 48, Part 1, pp. 265–67; hereafter cited as (OR). Barrett's first two reports, along with the third, can be found transcribed in appendix C of Charles M. Haecker's "An Historical Archaeological Study of the Battlefield of Palmito Ranch, 'The Last Conflict of the Great Rebellion,'" in *From These Honored Dead: Historical Archaeology of the Civil War*, ed. Clarence R. Geier, Douglas D. Scott, and Lawrence E. Babits (Gainesville: University of Florida Press, 2014), 57–71.

3. "Not yet mounted" refers to a cavalry regiment whose enlisted men do not currently have horses. Haecker, "Historical Archaeological Study of the Battlefield of Palmito Ranch," appendix C, 6.

4. Ibid.

5. Ibid.

6. Ibid.

7. Ibid.

8. Ibid., 7.

9. Ibid., 8.

10. Ibid.

11. Ibid., 8–9.

12. Barrett's third report was published in (OR), Series I, Vols. 41, 48, Part 1, pp. 265–67.

13. Ibid., 266.

14. Ibid.

15. Ibid.

16. Ibid.

17. Ibid.

18. Ibid.

19. Ibid., 266–67.

20. Ibid., 267.

21. Ibid.

22. US Army, 1865, Proceedings, Findings, and Court Martial Convened by Order of the US Army in Special Orders no. 36, Headquarters of the Army of the Rio Grande, Brownsville, TX, July 19, 1865, in the Case of Lt. Col. R. G. Morrison, 34th Indiana Veteran Volunteer Infantry. RG 153, Records of Judge Advocate General. National Archives, Washington, DC.

23. This and the subsequent four paragraphs are a summation of Lt. Col. Branson's testimony in Morrison's Court Martial, US Army, 1865, pp. 41–62.

24. Ibid., 42.

25. Ibid., 41–62.

26. This a very brief summation of Lt. Charles A. Jones's testimony in Morrison's Court Martial, US Army, 1865, 79–87.

27. Ibid., 117–19.

28. John Salmon Ford, *Rip Ford's Texas*, ed. Stephen B. Oates (Austin: University of Texas Press, 1963).

29. Ibid., xi.

30. Ibid., 393.

31. Ibid., 389.

32. Ibid., 390.

33. Ibid.

34. "Enfilading fire" is defined as gunfire directed along the length rather than the breadth of a formation.

35. Ibid.

36. Ibid. ,391.

37. Ibid.

38. Ibid., 392.

39. Ibid., xxxix.

40. Hubert H. Bancroft, *The History of the North Mexican States and Texas: Vol II 1801–1889* (San Francisco: History Company Publishers, 1889).

41. Bancroft's only footnote for the account of the Battle of Palmito Ranch references Colonel Barrett's Report. Bancroft, *History of the North Mexican States and Texas*, 476.

42. Ibid., 475.

43. Clement A. Evans, *Confederate Military History: A Library of Confederate States History*, 12 vols. (Atlanta: Confederate Publishing, 1899).

44. Ibid., XI: 125.

45. Ibid.

46. Ibid., XI: 126.

47. Explanation described in L. J. Shuler, *The Last Battle in the War between the States May 13, 1865* (Brownsville, TX: Springman-King, 1960), 18.

48. Phillip T. Tucker, *The Final Fury: The Last Battle of the Civil War* (Mechanicsburg, PA: Stackpole Books, 2001).

49. Jeffrey William Hunt, *The Last Battle of the Civil War: Palmetto Ranch* (Austin: University of Texas Press, 2002).

50. Tucker, *The Final Fury*, 65–67.

51. Hunt, *Last Battle of the Civil War*, 57.

52. Ibid., 128.

53. Tucker, *The Final Fury*, 163.

54. Ibid., 159.

55. Advertisement published in the *Brownsville American Flag*, July 4, 1847.

56. Haecker, "Historical Archaeological Study of the Battlefield of Palmito Ranch," 38.

57. Ibid., appendix D.

58. Texas Historical Commission, "Palmito Ranch Battlefield National Historic Landmark Final Technical Report with Archeological Survey Report: Grant Number GA-2255–09–008." Report prepared for the National Park Service American Battlefield Protection Program (Washington, DC: National Park Service, 2011).

59. Ibid., 48.

60. (OR), Series I, Vol. 41, Part 1,1893, 184–85, 742; Ford, *Rip Ford's Texas*, 309–10.

61. Terri Myer, *Palmito Ranch Battlefield National Historic Landmark Nomination* (Washington, DC: National Park Service, 1994), 4.

# 10
# *The Black Military Experience in the Rio Grande Valley*

JAMES N. LEIKER

It is no exaggeration to state that Civil War historians hijacked the nineteenth century. At heart, historians segment time by establishing certain events as narrative benchmarks, and in this task Civil War specialists have triumphed gloriously. Popular and scholarly understandings of the nineteenth-century United States follow a "before and after 1861 to 1865" approach. Terms like "antebellum" imply an inevitable, teleological drift toward the bombing of Fort Sumter, just as "reconstruction" assumes the centrality of the war's aftermath as a national defining feature for the twelve years following Appomattox. The problem with this periodization—as people in border areas can appreciate—is one of geographic imbalance; it relegates the West to a sideshow. The Civil War remains for many an eastern affair, as restricted spatially as it is chronologically. Although military campaigns destroyed or disrupted lives and communities in the hinterlands, the typical "western" challenges of border control, Indian pacification, and overall frontier violence seem far removed from the issues over which the war was fought.

Unsurprisingly, western historians challenge this perception. A bevy of books and dissertations have attempted to remove the region from its usual periphery, but one in particular—with great innovation—has suggested a new periodization. Elliott West has called the period 1845 to 1877 the *Greater Reconstruction*, a thirty-two year segment beginning with the US annexation of Texas and Oregon, followed by war with Mexico and acquisition of the contemporary American Southwest, and concluding with the final campaign of the Plains Indian Wars. Within this period, what we term *the Civil War*, the failed secession of Southern polities, appears as a subcategory (with apologies to Civil War specialists). Consider the many tasks which the US Army undertook during the three-decade span, as well as the similarities that connect them: subduing white Southerners who tried to leave the Union and western Indians and Hispanics who resisted joining it in the first place; building schools and other assimilating institutions for people of color, African Americans and Native Americans both; and providing a symbol of powerful federal authority in the face of passionate loyalty to states and tribes. True, in this light, the Civil War loses uniqueness. But reconceptualized within the Greater Reconstruction, it attains broader significance on a continental scale. "Reconstruction," however, is a linear term that implies rebuilding after a war, which is inaccurate in that several overlapping wars were responsible for subduing local governments in the South and West. For this reason, we might tweak the naming of the period from 1845 to 1877 (the timeframe of this collection) and call it the *Greater Consolidation* when the country endured a series of internal conflicts sparked by westward expansion. All those conflicts ended with greater centralized control, won through a building of military muscle that transformed the US into a modern, industrial nation-state.[1]

The process of Greater Consolidation can best be seen through the dual lens of a particular people working in a particular place. Like most "border" societies, the Rio Grande Valley in 1845 remained provincial in structure and outlook: dependent on subsistence agriculture, not easily accessible, and not the sort of place where one might expect struggles over national identity to unfold. But during the three decades of war that followed—between Anglos and Hispanics, Unionists and Confederates, Conservatives and Juaristas, federals and Texans—the question of literally where one nation ended and another began was settled through military force. That African Americans served in this arena adds another layer of complexity. The Greater Consolidation entailed more than an establishment of territorial sovereignty; it also meant answering difficult social and racial questions. Who should be eligible for citizenship? Is the United States truly one nation, one people? What is an American, really? To most, such questions may seem annoyingly abstract. In border areas, they require answers based on precision and clarity, and the consolidation period required a lot of them—and quickly. The emancipation of slaves was a consequence, not a cause, of the war, and by no means did it guarantee citizenship to the four million African Americans who were freed; indeed, the term "African American" is anachronistic when describing the period, since their place in the consolidating nation was far from settled. But neither was it settled for Spanish-speaking Latinos or Confederate Texans, all of whom had resisted or had reason to resist incorporation into a national polity. Blacks were the exception, finding in national military service a path toward equality. Their participation in the various campaigns that shook the Rio Grande Valley offers a window into the shifting loyalties and conflicts that characterized national consolidation on the US-Mexico border.

Probably for most Valley residents in 1845, "border" was a purely legalistic, even meaningless, term, but not so for faraway politicians. Mexican officials had disputed Texan claims to the region south of the Nueces River since independence nine years before. When the United States annexed the Republic of Texas, arch-expansionist President James K. Polk dispatched an army to occupy the contested zone, sparking a war that culminated in the Treaty of Guadalupe Hidalgo and the fixing of an international boundary at the Rio Grande. Although the treaty promised protection for Texas-born Latinos, a gradual process of land seizure ensued as Anglos used every means available, including outright fraud, to acquire property. Aggrieved Latinos responded by fleeing to Mexican towns like Matamoros and Nuevo Laredo, or by aligning with charismatic *caudillos* (strongmen) like Juan Cortina. The number of blacks in the Valley remained miniscule: as of 1860, only 357 of the state's 182,921 black residents resided south of the Nueces River. More than one-third of these lived as free people, a sharp contrast to East Texas' Cotton Belt. Fifty-three free black men and women resided in Brownsville, along with seven slaves.[2]

Despite slavery's weak presence in the Valley, the distant institution lay at the heart of many local conflicts. Anglo Texans' enslavement of blacks—a violation of Mexico's antislavery policy—had been one of several contributing factors to the revolution of 1836 and Mexico's subsequent refusal to recognize the Republic of Texas. Until the end of the Civil War, thousands of runaways sought their freedom by attempting to cross the Rio Grande. Texas officials estimated that by 1855, more than four thousand had jumped the border through Eagle Pass and Piedras Negras alone. Latinos had no love for the peculiar institution and often aided fugitive slaves by concealing them in homes and churches before shepherding them into Tamaulipas or Coahuila; scholars would do well to remember that the Underground Railroad ran south to Mexico as well as north to Canada. Suspicious of Black-Latino friendship, Anglos in several central counties passed laws prohibiting communication between slaves and "Mexicans." Texas Rangers like John Salmon "Rip" Ford, an implacable enemy of Cortina, frequently crossed the border for ostensible purposes of tracking outlaws and Indians, but with the real goal of capturing runaway slaves.[3]

"Unconsolidated" best describes the Valley of the antebellum years, a region legally part of the United States but politically and socially a confusing melee of competing factions fighting for local control. While the 1860s war between the Union and the Confederacy did little to immediately change this reality, it did increase the federal military presence in the area, as well as introduced the new element of black men in federal uniform. Long excluded from formal military service, enslaved people often interpreted the wearing of uniforms and the carrying of firearms as indications of trust—a recognition of manhood in one willing to share the burden of defense. A common spiritual heard in slave quarters opened with the line "Do you think I'll make a soldier?" Even slave revolts could become military affairs, with rebels organizing themselves through soldier-like discipline. Although Blacks had served in previous wars, the 1863 emancipation and the Union army's recruitment of freedmen provided their first substantial use in combat roles. Seen this way, the War Department's issuance of General Order No. 143, approving the creation of the United States Colored Troops (USCT), was a revolutionary act that gave free blacks and freedmen an opportunity to prove their capacity for citizenship on the battlefield. Ultimately the USCT numbered about 180,000 men, more than 10 percent of Union forces and one of a handful of advantages that tipped the scale to the North's favor during the war's concluding stages.[4]

Enlisted men in the USCT (only whites could serve as officers) hailed mostly from slave states, especially from parts of the South then controlled by Union forces: North and South Carolina, Louisiana, Virginia, and Maryland. After Grant's victories in the summer and fall of 1863, this especially meant enlistments in cities located on the Mississippi

River between St. Louis and the Gulf of Mexico. Black regiments sent to the Rio Grande Valley included the 87th and 95th Colored Infantries, both recruited in and around New Orleans. Also known respectively as the Corps d'Afrique's 16th Infantry and 1st Engineer, the regiments were attached to a small expedition under Maj. Gen. Nathaniel Banks. In September, this expedition landed at the mouth of the Rio Grande and marched inland, occupying Brownsville by early November. Joining them in 1864 were the 91st Illinois (white) and the 62nd US Colored Infantry (USCI). Initially named the 1st Missouri Colored, the 62nd had the distinction of being the first black regiment organized in a border state. As such, it recruited not only freedmen and fugitive slaves from the Confederacy, but fugitives from areas loyal to the Union as well. Lincoln's emancipation had no legal effect on slavery in Missouri, but this did not stop dozens of enslaved men from emancipating themselves, absconding from their plantations, often taking new names and heading toward federal recruitment centers in St. Louis.[5]

Black soldiers who entered the Valley discovered a confusing muddle that transcended a simple dichotomy of "North and South." Texas, of course, joined the Confederacy by adopting an ordinance of secession in February 1861, but the area had seen secession movements before. Besides the detachment of Texas itself from Mexico a generation earlier, Latino elites in 1840 tried to establish an independent Republic of the Rio Grande, a scheme also contemplated by Anglos like John Ford in the 1850s when debates over slavery grew fierce. These kinds of loyalties to *patria chica*, local identity, remained strong during the Civil War. Complicating the situation was Mexico's own "civil war" south of the border. In order to defeat his Conservative rivals who opposed plans to secularize the government, Liberal president Benito Juárez suspended repayment of foreign loans. Juárez's victory over the Conservatives, after two years of intense bloodshed, was soured by the actions of creditor nations—Britain, France, and Spain—who sent a naval fleet to occupy the port of Veracruz in December 1861. Britain and Spain in time withdrew, but the French emperor, Napoleon III, and his Austrian puppet, Archduke Maximilian, raised an army that marched inward, captured Mexico City, and elevated Maximilian to the throne as ruler of Mexico in spring 1864. As Juárez rallied his Liberal forces to fight the invasion from strongholds on the US border, Liberals and Imperialists jockeyed for control over strategic locations. The most precious of these lay at the Rio Grande's mouth, where a steady commerce in cotton and military supplies gave the victorious faction access to markets and allies in the Caribbean and Europe. Black Union soldiers, like white ones, had the dual responsibility of upholding US sovereignty against internal secessionists north of the river and external expansionists south of it.[6]

The USCT regiments spent much of the war quartered on the island of Brazos Santiago, from which they could prevent Confederate cotton shipments through the port of Bagdad. Following a massive redistribution of Union troops in the summer of 1864, Confederate forces reoccupied Brownsville, leaving Brazos as the only federal stronghold on the South Texas coast. As soldiers of the 62nd USCI wintered there in 1864–65, their commanding officer, Lt. Col. David Branson, had the opportunity to observe morale and discipline. He was disappointed. Branson described some of these Missouri recruits as "lazy, dirty & inefficient," but attributed most of the blame for the regiment's poor state to its white officers, who issued punishments with their fists or the flat of a sword. Branson wrote his superiors that "Men [black enlisted] will not obey as promptly an officer who adopts the systems of the slave driver." Not all commanders shared Branson's view of the 62nd. In a request for regiments to join him in an expedition to Mobile in February 1865, Brig. Gen. William A. Pile specifically asked for the 62nd, "a well drilled and disciplined regiment and well fitted for field service." Black recruits typically entered the service with minimal or nonexistent literacy, yet at least in the case of the 62nd, some progress had been made in learning to read and write during its first year. Besides insisting on formal instruction while stationed at Brazos, Branson promoted education in a severe manner, ordering any soldier caught playing cards to stand at a prominent position in camp with a book in hand, reciting aloud to demonstrate his literacy. Harsh tactics like these must have worked; unlike most USCT regiments, the 62nd filled its noncommissioned officer positions—jobs that demanded heavy processing of army paperwork—with black soldiers rather than white ones.[7]

Branson personally led troops in what some call the last battle of the Civil War at Palmito Ranch on May 13, 1865, a month after Lee's surrender in Virginia. The Union commander at Brazos Santiago, Col. Theodore Barrett, ordered Branson with eleven officers and two hundred and fifty men of the 62nd to the mainland, in what may have started as a simple foraging expedition, but which Barrett's detractors believe was a last-ditch effort to win distinction. After several days of slow advancing westward toward Brownsville, they were joined by Barrett himself, leading two hundred men from the 34th Indiana and fifty white troops from the 2nd Texas (Union) Cavalry. Confronting them was Col. John Salmon "Rip" Ford and several hundred mounted Confederates—along with a half dozen French volunteers from Mexico—who fired on Barrett's command and halted its advance in the thick underbrush along the river. Barrett ordered his infantry to fall back to the coast. Though technically the skirmish at Palmito Ranch was a Union defeat, Branson nonetheless praised his men's conduct, having lost only five wounded and two captured.[8]

Union forces finally did enter Brownsville two weeks later, on May 30, 1865, as part of a massive movement of sixteen thousand black infantry, cavalry, and artillerymen of the XXV Corps who arrived from City Point, Virginia. The end of formal hostilities in Virginia allowed the army to focus more attention on the Texas coast and the increasingly tense situation in Mexico. For the next two years, black soldiers outnumbered white ones in Texas three to one. Men of the USCT dispersed far beyond Brazos Santiago: to Fort Brown in Brownsville, Ringgold Barracks in Rio Grande City, Fort McIntosh at Laredo, Fort Duncan in Eagle Pass, and many smaller posts. Soldiers who hailed from the Deep South did not find the physical climate of the Rio Grande Valley very inviting. A chaplain wrote "as far as the eye can reach nothing but sand is seen"; an assistant surgeon, complaining of the swampy roads leading into Brownsville, told his wife the town was "one of the most forsaken looking holes you ever saw"; and a USCI captain declared southern Texas "some of the hardest soldiering I have ever seen and in the meanest part of the world."[9]

These observations by whites, however, may not have represented the view of the typical black enlisted man. Certainly he endured the same heat, mosquitoes, humidity, and barren physical landscape as his officers, but his assessment of the social landscape may have differed. Consider this quote from a colonel of the 19th USCI, stationed at Edinburgh in 1866: "The Mexicans are without much prejudice against negroes on account of color, and if let alone by the whites would give no trouble." If Hispanics regarded national boundaries with ambivalence, they did the same for racial ones; within the as yet unconsolidated space of the Lower Valley, African Americans and Latinos found room for mutual sympathy and even affection. Certainly not all interactions were friendly. Residents of Roma, for instance, complained that black soldiers supplemented their meager diets by killing livestock, stealing from gardens, and generally thieving and plundering. Three companies of the 8th US Colored Artillery were even ordered to split a fine of seventy-five dollars for stealing potatoes. Yet examples of fellowship abound as well. Black enlisted men sold weapons (illegally) to Mexican soldiers fighting for Juárez, encouraged desertions from Maximilian's French Army, and in rare cases even deserted themselves by jumping the border and vanishing into Mexico's interior. While the US Army formally practiced neutrality in the Liberal-Imperialist conflict, black soldiers openly empathized with the Liberals' cause and possibly even saw it as continuous with their nation's own war to defeat the slave owning aristocracy. Contrasted against the hostile reception that the Reconstruction army suffered elsewhere in Texas, Sgt. Maj. Thomas Boswell's observation seems remarkable: "If our regiment stays here [Roma] any length of time we will all speak Spanish, as we are learning very fast."[10]

However, events did not permit a testing of Boswell's prediction of bilingualism. Napoleon III's withdrawal of troops and the subsequent collapse of Maximilian's Imperial regime in early 1866 diminished the need for a strong presence of Union volunteers. Through the remainder of the year, more than half the regiments of the XXV Corps mustered out. Those who remained dealt with a situation that remained violent and unstable, despite the Liberals' uneven victory. In November, black infantry companies from the 19th and 114th USCI, intervening in a dispute in Matamoros, crossed the Rio Grande over a hastily constructed pontoon bridge and secured order in the town while the last Imperialist sympathizers clashed with Juárez's Liberals. The companies' commander, Col. Thomas Sedgwick, was relieved of command and arrested for this action, which violated army neutrality policy. Elsewhere, the US Army diminished its forces rapidly. The last USCT regiment to depart the Valley, the 117th USCI, mustered out from Fort McIntosh and Ringgold Barracks in July 1867.[11]

The near-simultaneous defeats of the Confederate and French

armies underscore Lower Valley residents' memory of the 1860s as a period of not one civil war but two. Yet neither conflict should be classified as a complete victory in the march toward national consolidation. Mexico's centralized government struggled for years afterward to exert control over its border region. Similarly, the US period of "Reconstruction" was characterized by a reluctant use of federal power against violent secessionist urges. Indeed, the persistence of ideologies about state sovereignty and the weaknesses of both the US and Mexican governments on their mutual border explains much of the region's history into the twenty-first century. Consolidation's victory was less ambiguous for freedmen, free blacks, and runaway slaves for whom the wars brought not only emancipation but a chance to join the national polity as US soldiers and, by extension, as US citizens. The 62nd Infantry, whose service in the Valley exceeded that of any other USCT regiment, exemplifies this. Following disbandment in spring 1866, they returned to Missouri to receive their discharges and final payments. 1st Lt. Richard Baxter Foster, like Branson a staunch advocate of education while stationed in Texas, led a fund-raising campaign among USCT veterans for establishment of a black university in Jefferson City. Former enlisted men of the 62nd collectively donated $4,000 for the cause, which culminated in the founding of Lincoln Institute—later Lincoln University—in September 1866. The school took its place beside Fisk, Howard, and other historically black colleges in elevating African Americans "up from slavery" (Booker T. Washington's phrase) thanks to the efforts of men whose own education developed at Brazos Santiago.[12]

The experience of the US Colored Troops anticipated a new place for blacks in the Regular Army. Since the republic's earliest days, federal law had restricted peacetime enlistment to whites, even barring people of color from government jobs like mail delivery. But in the closing months of the rebellion, the topic of black military service grew entwined with that of black citizenship. Abraham Lincoln, impressed with the USCT's record, recommended black veterans for suffrage rights during discussion of a reconstruction government in Louisiana. Following that lead, Congress, in July 1866, approved an army reorganization bill that both expanded the Regular Army's size—it had shrunk dramatically in the year after Appomattox—and allowed for establishment of six new regiments composed exclusively of blacks. Radical Republicans may have passed the measure merely as a political and social hammer to hold above Southerners' heads, but idealistic motives were in play as well. The act mandated the appointment of a chaplain to each regiment and emphasized the teaching of literacy to new recruits—neither of which was required in white regiments. The reorganization act flowed from the same set of beliefs as the Freedmen's Bureau and pursued the same goal: helping former slaves become useful and productive citizens. Army officers seldom shared the lofty principles of eastern reformers. Gen. William T. Sherman wrote in 1877, "The experiment of converting them into soldiers has been honorably and in good faith tried . . . and has been partially successful; but the army is not and should not be construed a charitable institution."[13]

In 1869, Congress reduced and merged the number of infantry regiments, leaving two regiments of black infantry, the 24th and 25th, and two of cavalry, the 9th and 10th. Henceforth, African Americans constituted a proportion of the Regular Army roughly equivalent to their Civil War numbers, about 10 percent of aggregate strength, a proportion that stayed consistent until the turn of the century. Black and white soldiers were expected to cooperate in the field but otherwise served in segregated units, with separate barracks, dining, and training. The term "buffalo soldier" has been used to describe men of the frontier cavalry, and colloquially to describe all black men who served during the western Indian Wars. However, historians have debunked the term as anachronistic, probably not used by soldiers themselves until the twentieth century. Nor were "buffalo soldiers" victims of systematic discrimination in terms of food, supplies, and stations, as many have claimed. With scarce resources stretched thin from the Pacific Coast to the Deep South, army leaders could ill afford to consider racial prejudice in their decisions about budgets and allocations of manpower. For the remainder of the Greater Consolidation, black regulars participated in many key episodes of western conquest: guarding settlements, breaking up labor disputes, protecting mail and payroll shipments, and—ironic given their own experiences with racial oppression—removal of American Indians to government reservations.[14]

Only in Texas did military Reconstruction overlap with Sherman's frontier army. The last USCT regiments had not quite mustered out when the 9th Cavalry arrived in San Antonio in March 1867. With the arrival of the entire 24th and 25th Infantries over the next three years, nearly two thousand black soldiers were stationed along the Rio Grande between Brownsville and El Paso. In the Lower Valley, their task, as always, was to enforce national sovereignty. Local Hispanic caudillos like Cortina who had fought Maximilian now waged a new war of resistance against US authorities, plundering cattle ranches and raiding American border towns. Outlaw gangs and bands of nomadic Indians also traversed the area, enjoying the sanctuary offered by the Rio Grande because of its lax law enforcement. Black soldiers learned and performed all the duties expected of an occupying force, raiding Mexican and Indian villages, striking at noncombatants, capturing prisoners, and destroying provisions in order to impoverish enemies and encourage submission.[15]

In contrast to the favorable reception extended to the USCT, blacks in the Regular Army endured years of animosity and harassment during their stay in the Lower Valley. Some of this stemmed from Texans' general suspicion of standing armies. Like many Americans, they inherited from colonial times an assumption about local militias as the bastions of liberty, an obstacle against the tyrannical instincts of distant centralized government. Anglos repeatedly ridiculed federal soldiers as naïve and ineffective, even lobbying for their removal and the shifting of responsibilities for law enforcement to Texas Rangers. Many Hispanics also hated black troops, for similar reasons. Ringgold Barracks, where the 9th Cavalry was garrisoned, saw a recurring pattern of civilian-military antagonism. In December 1874, Col. Edward Hatch ordered the arrest and removal of a gambler from Rio Grande City who had been relieving his men of their earnings. This action led a grand jury in Starr County—overwhelmingly Latino—to indict Hatch for false imprisonment, forcing him to retain a lawyer's services. The following month, a party of Hispanic men from Solesis Ranch exchanged shots with black cavalrymen patrolling the border for illegal crossings of cattle. Two soldiers died in the ambush, prompting Hatch to order a raid on Solesis the next day, arresting twenty-seven people whom he believed to be followers of Cortina.[16]

The attack at Solesis embroiled the 9th Cavalry—and for that matter, all of South Texas—in a web of legal and military trouble. The ranch lay partly on a piece of disputed territory, land created by a capricious change of river course since the Treaty of Guadalupe-Hidalgo. US commanders regarded it as part of Texas, but from the standpoint of Cortina and his followers, the ranch lay in Tamaulipas—meaning American soldiers had invaded Mexican soil and killed Mexican citizens. In April 1875, Starr County's court indicted for murder three men, Sgt. Edward Troutman, Pvt. Charley Blackstone, and Pvt. John Fredericks, who languished for weeks in the Rio Grande City jail, unable to raise the five hundred dollars each required for bond. As federal attorneys for the soldiers applied for a change of venue, even Anglo Texans—no friends to border Hispanics—condemned Hatch and his men for intruding in local affairs. In June, the soldiers' case was moved to East Texas federal district court, which acquitted all three a few months later. Yet justice still eluded the black cavalrymen. Forced to obtain legal counsel at their own expense, they spent months unsuccessfully trying to collect compensation. While stationed at Fort Stockton in April 1876, Private Blackstone killed Fredericks in a quarrel over responsibility for legal costs.[17]

Other types of retaliation followed Hatch's raid. In March 1875, two parties of *Cortinistas* rendezvoused near Edinburgh and rode northward, robbing and burning ranches and stores as part of a 130-mile raid into US territory that reached the vicinity of Corpus Christi. Work and commerce slowed to a halt as rural people fled to towns for protection. At Roma, a company of the 9th Cavalry prevented one band from robbing the customs house. Most of the "outlaws," Hatch believed, escaped capture because sympathetic locals kept them informed of his troops' whereabouts. A wave of anti-Mexican violence initiated by white vigilantes and Texas Rangers ensued, prompting fears that more Latinos would join Cortina and precipitate a formal war. Federal authorities moved additional cavalry and infantry to Fort Brown, and even made naval vessels available at the fort commander's discretion. Despite the strengthened military presence in the Rio Grande Valley, army leaders seemed to understand that both Latinos and Anglos objected to that presence more strenuously, and resisted federal authority more often, when the occupying troops were black. In June, Mexican bandits attacked a station house and threatened the black employee, declaring that "they did not care for black soldiers" and intended to stalk and kill any detachment of the 9th Cavalry they encountered. By this time, Colonel Hatch had already received orders to transfer his regiment to Fort Clark, thereby removing all outlying companies from the Ringgold Barracks area and its hostile atmosphere.[18]

Episodes like these led to much questioning about the role of African

Americans as border protectors. Describing the 9th Cavalry's travails in Starr County, Brig. Gen. Edward O. C. Ord wrote:

> An unfortunate condition of affairs arose between the colored troops and the native population, under which native Mexicans living on the American side were indisposed to cooperate with the officers of colored regiments. They were averse to having that sort of troops among them. For that reason, I gave order . . . that no patrols or small parties should be sent out from posts, except under command of a white officer, and as there are very few white officers available, this, in a great measure, prevented such patrols being sent.

According to Ord, once the 9th had been replaced with the white 4th Cavalry, local Hispanics showed "zeal and activity" in cooperating with US troops. Other officers like Lt. Col. John Mason held the opposite view that blacks' exceptionally friendly relations with Hispanics made them ineffective soldiers: "[T]he class of Mexicans along that frontier are generally of the lowest order, part Indians, and they fraternize with the negro more readily than with the white people; . . . there are a great many lewd women, and there are dance-houses and gambling-houses which are frequented by the men."[19]

Mason's racist fears about black-Mexican affinity notwithstanding, he identified a key element in understanding black soldiers' experience in the Rio Grande Valley. "Crossing the river" carried a different meaning at night than by day. Officially, the Rio Grande represented a national border that US troops were obliged to defend; unofficially, the social life of the river's "other side" beckoned with lures of sex, drinking, gambling, and other temptations that young men came to expect as a feature of military life. An assistant surgeon at Fort McIntosh worried about soldiers visiting "fandangos" in downtown Laredo, places he described as "of a very low order." Alcoholism was an endemic problem in the frontier army; one study in the 1880s concluded that 4 percent had been hospitalized for problems related to overconsumption. Heavy drinking seemed to be less of a problem for black regiments, but they did share equally in the army's other great scourge—prostitution. Lower Valley communities like Brownsville and Rio Grande City saw the inevitable proliferation of brothels that appeared adjacent to military bases. Black soldiers at Fort Brown and Ringgold Barracks suffered high rates of syphilis and gonorrhea. Mexican men cared as little for interracial sex between blacks and native women as did whites in Mississippi, even though some had reason to tolerate and even encourage such liaisons. Cattle rustlers apparently used Hispanic women as spies to monitor troop movements: "The reason that troops do not stop this [stealing cattle across the river], or attempt to, is that the colored soldiers have more or less Mexican women about camp, who—when the soldiers are going out—give information to their friends."[20]

White fears about black men as bestial rapists motivated hundreds of lynchings in the period following Greater Consolidation—at least in the Deep South. Violence in the Lower Valley never reached that kind of scale, even though sexuality did take its place beside race as a cause of civilian-soldier tension. The transcript of a court-martial at Ringgold Barracks, which involved a fight between Privates George McKay and James Holt, reveals some context:

> The reason I [McKay] am accused of this [drunkenness and firing a weapon] is because Private James Holt has a Mexican woman that is very fond of me, and he accused me of persuading her to leave him. . . . We [the woman, McKay, and Holt] had been talking about Mexican women and I saye [*sic*] to her How is it that when a colored man marries a Mexican woman that the Mexican don't like it and tries to kill him; and she say I don't know the reason but that is the truth. And there I said "It is best for Mexican men to marry Mexican women and colored men, colored women"—and she says "Yes that is the best way." Then Holt spoke up . . . and called me a dirty liar, and he picked up an axe and threw it at me."

Apparently, sexuality caused tensions between soldiers as well. Yet by their very nature, disciplinary records reveal only the superficial or violent aspects of soldiers' sexual relationships. Some black enlisted men formed lasting and apparently loving partnerships with Hispanic women as well. Such was true for George Forniss of the 24th Infantry, who in 1871 married Cesaria Perazo in El Paso. The marriage lasted until Cesaria's death in 1886, after which George received his discharge, remained on the border by finding work as a tailor, and in 1892 began living with Severiana Tijernia. The couple moved to Brownsville and for whatever reason did not marry until 1903 when their daughter Josephine was ten years old.[21]

For all of war's horrific legacies, it also brings into intimate contact people from different backgrounds, people who defy the borders that separate them either through romantic liaisons or cultural mixing. In establishing jurisdiction over local polities, the Greater Consolidation not only eroded political boundaries, but racial and ethnic ones as well. But the extent of such mixing should not be overstated. Of the hundreds of black enlisted men stationed in the Lower Valley, only a small number chose to remain and form families with native Hispanics after their expiration of service. Compared to the overall friendliness described by USCT officers in the mid-1860s, black Regulars' relations with the local populace in the 1870s appear cold and hostile. Desertion rates for black regiments on the Rio Grande never exceeded that for the army as a whole, which is odd considering that desertion there simply meant fording the river and vanishing into Mexico. Unlike earlier decades when runaway slaves perceived Mexico as a land of freedom and Mexicans as sympathetic allies, African American soldiers by the end of consolidation regarded both as "other"—a sign perhaps of their own growing sense of national loyalty and identity.[22]

Ultimately peace in the Rio Grande Valley depended on the Mexican government's own ability to assert jurisdiction. Civil war gripped the country again in 1876 as the administration of Sebastian Lerdo de Tejada was challenged by forces under Gen. Porfirio Diaz. Facing a possible expansion of the conflict onto US territory, the Regular Army obtained permission to arrest and confine foreigners who plotted insurrection north of the border. The following year, President Rutherford Hayes—whose own rise to power resulted from a compromise between internal factions—authorized post commanders to cross the Rio Grande at will for purposes of recapturing stolen goods and arresting criminals. Mexican newspapers condemned Hayes's order, calling it an affair "of national honor." While Mexicans wasted their energies fighting each other, *Norteamericanos* again invaded their land: "In the presence of the common enemy all are brothers; the same sentiment impels all—the defense of the flag, the integrity of the country."[23] A skilled manipulator of public opinion, Diaz used these expressions of outrage to his advantage. Placing his troops at key points along the river, he could slow illegal crossings and give US officials the appearance of cooperation, but among his countrymen he kept the threat of foreign invasion very much alive, with himself as protector. After November 1876, when he evicted Lerdo from office, Diaz asserted iron-fisted control over the northern border, starting with Cortina's removal. Mexican *federales* rather than *Cortinistas* soon patrolled the Rio Grande; bandits and revolutionaries were simply impressed into federal service, temporarily eliminating their threat to US towns and ranches. Thus began the thirty-four year reign of the *Porfiriato*, as Diaz brought relative peace and industry, but also economic instability through an accommodation with American capitalists that exploded into another revolution in 1910.[24]

Though the Rio Grande Valley remained a violent place that continued to attract outlaws and rebels, the scale of such violence declined. In response, the US Army greatly reduced its strength in the area, gradually replacing black regiments with white ones and then reassigning the latter. By the mid-1880s, posts like Fort Brown and Ringgold Barracks held only small garrisons. As the twentieth century dawned, African American soldiers returned to the border after a two-decade absence to find a populace that remembered and resented their earlier service. During a smallpox epidemic in March 1899, troops from the 10th Cavalry at Fort McIntosh tried to remove infected patients into a government quarantine center. Amid cries of "nigger soldiers," an angry crowd of Laredo Hispanics confronted them over a three-day period, resulting in at least one civilian death from gunfire. Later that fall, the commander of Ringgold Barracks, Lt. Erubian Rubottom, ordered the firing of several rounds from a Gatling gun to frighten residents of Rio Grande City, whom he believed were launching an imminent assault against men of the 9th Cavalry—Hatch's old regiment. And in 1906 came the most remembered incident of border violence: the purported shooting by black infantrymen into civilian homes and businesses of Brownsville. Claiming discrimination by the town's Latino residents, 167 men of the 25th Infantry were summarily dismissed from service without honor by President Theodore Roosevelt, who charged them with "a conspiracy of silence" to protect guilty parties. The infamous "Brownsville affair" diminished the army's peacekeeping power in southern Texas, resulting in the closing of Fort Brown and Ringgold Barracks, and within the year, the relocation of remaining black regiments to Cuba and the Philippines.[25]

At first glance, this proliferation of violent incidents involving African American soldiers suggests animosity among Valley residents based on race. Yet, as Albert Rodriguez has noted, the census of 1900 shows Cameron and Hidalgo counties as having among the highest rates of interracial marriage involving at least one black spouse in the United States at that time. These marriages were mostly of black men marrying ethnic Mexican women or first-generation Tejanas.[26] Given that Latinas were legally defined as white, such marriages in fact quietly violated Texas's antimiscegenation laws. A reconciliation of two such contradictory phenomena leads to the conclusion that black soldiers endured prejudice partly as blacks but more as US soldiers. Whatever limited tolerance South Texans had for them as coworkers and even family members, African Americans in uniform represented unwelcome federal authority, an outside intrusion into provincial affairs. In this regard, Valley Hispanics differed little from unreconstructed Confederates or even western Indian tribes; all carried lingering resentment against the US Army and the men who filled its ranks. As General Ord had observed in the 1870s, civilians might grudgingly cooperate with white troops, but the sight of former slaves in military garb often provoked violent outrage.

The black military experience in the Rio Grande Valley, then, is the story of a deteriorating relationship simultaneous with a strengthened one. At the beginning of the Greater Consolidation, when principles of "manifest density" were in ascent but "borders" remained fluid and ill-defined, the Rio Grande offered to blacks a potential escape from slavery and persecution—an openness with respect to race that was enjoyed even by the US Colored Troops in the 1860s. By 1877, however, such friendliness was replaced by hostility, not coincidentally at the exact time when territorial expansion reached its limits and "the border" acquired meaning as a division of peoples and nations. As residents' political relationship with the United States solidified, their social one with black men who sought equality by enforcing US hegemony declined. The Civil War of 1861 to 1865 did not by itself accomplish this transformation; rather, a series of wars, spanning a three-decade breadth of the nineteenth century, subsumed a host of feuding polities and factions beneath centralized control by the modern nation-state. Within that new order, African Americans earned a permanent place, first as freedmen, then as legal citizens, and finally as fellow Americans expected to shoulder the burden of national defense.

## *Notes*

1. Elliot West, *The Last Indian War: The Nez Perce Story* (Oxford: Oxford University Press, 2009), xviii–xxii.

2. Armando C. Alonzo, *Tejano Legacy: Rancheros and Settlers in South Texas, 1734–1900* (Albuquerque: University of New Mexico Press, 1998); US Census Bureau, *Population of the United States in 1860* (Washington, DC: Government Printing Office, 1864), 484–87.

3. James M. Smallwood, *Time of Hope, Time of Despair: Black Texans during Reconstruction* (Port Washington, NY: Kennikat Press, 1981), 19–21; Ronnie C. Tyler, "Fugitive Slaves in Mexico," *Journal of Negro History* 57, no. 1 (1972): 1–12; "Report of the Committee of Investigation Sent in 1873 by the Mexican Government to the Frontier of Texas," 1874, Biennial Reports of the Adjutant General of the State of Texas, 1873–1904, Governors' Papers, 1875–1899 (Austin: Texas State Archives), 178–79.

4. Theophilus G. Steward, *The Colored Regulars in the United States Army* (Philadelphia: AME Book Concern, 1904), 57–59; and Elizabeth Fox-Genovese, *Within the Plantation Household: Black and White Women of the Old South* (Chapel Hill: University of North Carolina Press, 1988), 305. Two authoritative works on the USCT are Joseph T. Glathaar's *Forged in Battle: The Civil War Alliance of Black Soldiers and White Officers* (New York: Free Press, 1990), and William A. Dobak's *Freedom by the Sword: The US Colored Troops, 1862–1867* (Washington, DC: Center for Military History, US Army, 2011).

5. Dobak, *Freedom by the Sword*, 121–22, 191.

6. A useful overview of Mexico's internal unrest is found in Paul Vanderwood's "Betterment for Whom? The Reform Period: 1855–75," in Michael C. Meyer and William H. Beezley, eds., *The Oxford History of Mexico* (Oxford: Oxford University Press, 2000), 371–96.

7. Dobak, *Freedom by the Sword*, 428–30, 444–46.

8. Ibid., 431–44; and William L. Richter, *The Army in Texas during Reconstruction, 1865–1870* (College Station: Texas A&M University Press, 1987), 23–27.

9. Dobak, *Freedom by the Sword*, quotes on 434–37.

10. "The Mexicans" quote by Col. J. Jenkins to Assistant Adjutant General (AAG), District of the Rio Grande, April 7, 1866, Letter and Order Book, 19th USCI, Record Group (RG) 94, National Archives (NA); "If our regiment," quoted from Edwin S. Redkey, ed., *A Grand Army of Black Men: Letters from African-American Soldiers in the Union Army, 1861–1865* (New York: Cambridge University Press, 1992),

203; Dobak, *Freedom by the Sword*, 442; Capt. Lewis Johnson, 24 US Infantry, December 4, 1877, in US Congress, House Committee on Military Affairs, *Testimony Taken by the Committee on Military Affairs in Relation to the Texas Border Troubles*, 45th Cong., 2nd Sess., 1877, H. Misc. Doc. 64, 142.

11. Dobak, *Freedom by the Sword*, 451–53.

12. Adam Arenson, "Fighting for the Legacy of Lincoln," *The New York Times*, December 13, 2013, http://opinionator.blogs.nytimes.com/2013/12/13/fighting-for-the-legacy-of-lincoln/?_r=0 (accessed February 17, 2015). See also Booker T. Washington, *Up from Slavery* (New York: Doubleday, 1901).

13. On Lincoln's views of blacks' military record, see James N. Leiker, "The Difficulties of Understanding Abe: Lincoln's Reconciliation of Natural Inequality and Natural Rights," in Brian R. Dirck, ed., *Lincoln Emancipated: The President and the Politics of Race* (Dekalb, IL: Northern Illinois University Press, 2007), 97. See also "An Act to Increase and Fix the Military Peace Establishment of the U.S.," *Congressional Globe*, 39th Cong., 1st Sess., July 28, 1866; Warren L. Young, *Minorities and the Military: A Cross-National Study in World Perspective* (Westport, CT: Greenwood Press, 1982); and Edward Coffman, *The Old Army: A Portrait of the American Army in Peacetime, 1794–1898* (New York: Oxford University Press, 1986), 365–71. The Sherman quote is addressed to the Secretary of War, February 6, 1877, cited in Thomas D. Phillips, "The Black Regulars: Negro Soldiers in the United States Army, 1866–1891" (PhD diss., University of Wisconsin, 1970), 282.

14. William Leckie's *The Buffalo Soldiers: A Narrative of the Negro Cavalry in the West* (Norman: University of Oklahoma Press, 1967) rescued black western soldiers from historical obscurity but popularized the myth of racial discrimination within army ranks. Revisionist scholarship posits that while individual officers certainly acted with racial prejudice, the "institutional racism" argument has little application to the frontier army. White regiments were also singled out for poor treatment, and the army as a whole constituted a system of institutional inequality. See William A. Dobak and Thomas D. Phillips, *The Black Regulars, 1866–1898* (Norman: University of Oklahoma Press, 2001). On black soldiers' relations with Hispanics and Indians, see James N. Leiker, *Racial Borders: Black Soldiers along the Rio Grande* (College Station: Texas A&M University Press, 2002).

15. On numbers of black soldiers along the border, see Leiker, *Racial Borders*, appendix 1, table 2, 184.

16. Marcus Cunliffe, *Soldiers and Civilians: The Martial Spirit in America, 1771–1865* (Boston: Little, Brown, 1968), 282–86; Adjutant General (AG) to Secretary of War, January 7, 1875, Selected Documents, Adjutant General's Office (AGO), Letters Received (LR), RG 94, NA; US Congress, House, *Report on the Relations of the United States with Mexico*, 45th Cong., 2nd Sess., 1877, H. Misc. Doc. 701, Vol. 3, 143.

17. Hatch to Assistant Adjutant General's Office (AAG), Department of Texas, May 17, 1875, in John MacGregor and Bernard C. Nalty, eds., *Blacks in the United States Armed Forces: Basic Documents* (Wilmington, DE: Scholarly Resources, 1977), 3: 108–11; Hatch to AG, April 4, 1876, Roll 198, and Solicitor General to Secretary of War, June 14, 1875, AGO-LR, M666, RG 94, National Archives Microfilm Publication (NAMP), Roll 196; and Reg. Returns, 9th Cavalry, May 1876, M744, NAMP, Roll 88.

18. US Congress, House, *Report on the Relations of the United States with Mexico*, Vol. 3, 120–22, 132–33, 135–37; "Affairs on the Rio Grande," Texas Adjutant General's Office (TX-AGO), Biennial Reports, 1875, Texas State Archives, 6–13, 31–32.

19. Ord, February 12, 1876, in US Congress, House, *Report on the Relations of the United States with Mexico*, Vol. 3, 174, 177; testimony of Lt. Col. John S. Mason, 4th Infantry, December 7, 1877, in US Congress, House, *Testimony Taken by the Committee on Military Affairs in Relation to the Texas Border Troubles*, 45h Cong., 2nd Sess., 1877, H. Misc. Doc. 64, 115.

20. On alcoholism in the frontier army, see Don Rickey Jr., *Forty Miles a Day on Beans and Hay: The Enlisted Soldier Fighting the Indian Wars* (Norman: University of Oklahoma Press, 1963), 156–71. On health at army bases in the Lower Valley, see "Medical History of Posts," Fort McIntosh (quote), April 1869; Fort Ringgold, Book 724, Entry 547, 1873–76, and Book 727; and Fort Brown, Book 734, RG 94, NA. "Mexican women" quote in Statement of Charles Best, May 22, 1875, AGO-LR, M666, RG 94, NA, Roll 197.

21. General Court-Martials, Ringgold Barracks, June 11–12, 1874, PP 4037, Judge Advocate General's Office (JAG), RG 153, NA; and Pension File of George Forniss, SO 1301070, Records of the Veterans Administration, RG 15, NA.

22. On comparative desertion rates, see Leiker, *Racial Borders*, 185.

23. "Texas Frontier Troubles," in US Congress, House, *Report on the Relations of the United States with Mexico*, Vol. 3, p. 246.

24. Ibid., 2–7, 250–53, newspaper quote on 246; and US Congress, House, *Mexican Border Troubles*, 45th Cong., 1st Sess., 1877–1878, H. Ex. Doc. 13, 13–15. On General Diaz's use of *federales* and his relations with the United States, see Clarence Clendenen, *Blood on the Border: The United States Army and the Mexican Irregulars* (New York: Macmillan, 1969) and Paul J. Vanderwood, *Disorder and Progress: Bandits, Police, and Mexican Development* (Lincoln: University of Nebraska Press, 1981).

25. Leiker, *Racial Borders*, 118–19, 124–29, 131–43, 184.

26. Albert Rodriguez, "Border Love on the Rio Grande: African American Men and Latinas in the Rio Grande Valley of South Texas (1850–1940)," BlackPast.org, http://www.blackpast.org/perspectives/border-love-rio-grande-african-american-men-and-latinas-rio-grande-valley-south-texas-1 (accessed November 27, 2015).

# 11

# *Discovering America's Forgotten War Front*

## The Rio Grande in the Era of the American Civil War

RUSSELL K. SKOWRONEK

*The past is never dead. It's not even past.*[1]
—WILLIAM FAULKNER

*What is history but fable agreed upon?*
—ATTRIBUTED TO NAPOLEON BONAPARTE

*History is written by the victors.*
—WINSTON CHURCHILL

—OR IS IT?

Anniversaries figure prominently in the lives of individuals. Woe upon the person who forgets a birthday or wedding anniversary, as each is a time to remember the past while looking to the future. Silver, golden, and diamond wedding anniversaries are celebrated with prescribed rituals on exact dates to honor the couple. With their passing, the exact dates of birth, marriage, and death fade for their surviving family members, whose lives are constantly adding new dates of current significance. What remains are stories, often apocryphal, of certain events that are retold down the generations.

Similarly, in nation states, dates that may be imbued with powerful meaning for one generation may fade for new generations. Fewer than fifty years ago every school-aged child in the United States knew that they would have two holidays in February marking Washington's

(February 22, 1732) and Lincoln's (February 12, 1809) birthdays. Now the generic "Presidents' Day" has wiped away this knowledge. The same may be said about the arrival of Columbus in the Bahamas (October 12, 1492) and the end of World War I on the eleventh hour of the eleventh day of the eleventh month of 1918—Armistice Day, known today as Veterans Day. Whether created as hagiography or to honor immigrants or those who fought in the "war to end all wars," their significance has changed or been rewritten within the context of time.

Other events have also served as generational watershed moments. We have been admonished to "Remember . . . the Alamo, Maine, Pearl Harbor, and 9/11." Individuals will say they remember where they were on D-Day, when Roosevelt died, when Kennedy was assassinated, or on VE or VJ Day. Now, seventy plus years on, "D-Day" is remembered on the History Channel and in reruns of Charles Schulz's comic strip "Peanuts," but as time passes, the exact dates are rapidly fading from common memory.

Just over half a century ago, in 1961, the United States observed the centennial of the American Civil War. At that time veterans of the Spanish-American, Korean, and World Wars had come of age surrounded by veterans and monuments dedicated to the memory of that earlier conflict sponsored by such organizations as the Sons of Union Veterans of the Civil War (1881), the United Daughters of the Confederacy (1894), and the Sons of Confederate Veterans (1896). They had watched those veterans winnowed until a scant five years earlier, in 1956, Albert Woolson, the last verified veteran of the war, passed away. It was an era when "white" and "colored" water fountains and restrooms were still the norm in the Florida Statehouse and Margaret Mitchell's *Gone with the Wind* was the quintessential story of the "Lost Cause," of a conflict over states' rights rather than slavery as a cause for the war.[2] There were commemorations and reenactments of battles featuring white people carrying or wearing historic accoutrements from the previous century. Over the next fifty years the narrative would change following the Civil Rights Act, the publication of Alex Haley's *Roots: The Saga of an American Family* (1976), the making of the film *Glory* (1989), Ken Burn's nine-part television mini-series *The Civil War* (1990), and ultimately, in July of 2015, more than 150 years after the end of the American Civil War, the removal of the Confederate battle flag from the grounds of the South Carolina State House.

Clearly the United States has changed. Anniversaries of specific battles are largely forgotten, but from that change a more nuanced and complicated story of the era has emerged based on previously unexplored lines of evidence viewed through different prisms than that of our grandfathers' generation.[3]

According to HistoryNet there were nearly "10,500 battles, engagements, . . . skirmishes, reconnaissances, naval engagements, sieges, [and] bombardments"[4] and other sites associated with the American Civil War. Of these, 380—including 5 sites in Texas—are recognized by the American Battlefield Protection Program of the National Park Service in 26 states.[5] Forgotten in this morass of sites were operations along the Rio Grande frontier with Mexico. As monumental battles raged across the American landscape east of the Mississippi and a Union naval blockade choked Confederate commerce, international law left one huge gap in the Union's war effort: the Rio Grande. Across this international boundary, tons of Confederate cotton poured into the global market and hundreds of millions of dollars and war materiel flooded into Confederate hands, extending the war and its cost in human misery. It is the story of this commerce and the human drama surrounding it that is encapsulated in this volume. Scholars are exploring a significant but largely unknown or underappreciated theatre in the history of the American Civil War. This information, told from a variety of perspectives, places the Rio Grande squarely in the midst of America's greatest conflict.

### *Avenues of Inquiry*

David Hurst Thomas suggests that our concept of the past is an idealized construction that reflects a distorted image of past reality.[6] Our idea of what constitutes "truth" changes through time and, as such, requires revision to reflect these changing perceptions of reality. For him, the most accurate reflection of the past is derived from an interdisciplinary and multisided "cubist" approach based on a combination of oral and documentary history, ethnographic analogy, and the archaeological record. Or as Robert L. Schuyler succinctly put it, "the spoken word, the written word, observed behavior, and preserved behavior."[7] These ideas have rattled around anthropology for nearly seventy years. In 1948, Walter Taylor advocated for a "conjunctive approach" that did not privilege one source of evidence over another, but rather combined them to help overcome their inherent biases.[8]

Aspects of the documentary and material records are contemporary creations representing forms of primary data that were once part of the systemic past. While both are biased in their own ways, from preservation to point of view, they are often complementary and nonexclusive data sets that can provide direct or indirect information on human behavior and may also provide information on the views and beliefs of individuals regarding their behaviors. Unlike the archaeological record, the documentary and oral history records do not directly preserve the remains of human behavior. When these various approaches are synthesized within an ethnographic framework, a "superior cultural reconstruction" can be formed.[9] More recently others have noted the false dichotomy between history and science, noting that a systematic and contextualized examination of diverse forms of evidence, including archaeological, documentary, cartographic, and geographical data, enriches our knowledge of the past, including the reconstruction of past lifeways for people who are otherwise mute in the historical record.[10]

Scholars studying history are often thwarted in their ability to find primary sources relating to a topic or issue. In the Rio Grande Valley this is especially true due to uneven preservation and a weak literary tradition. As the scholars in this volume demonstrate, by embracing the cubist or conjunctive approach, many of these shortcomings can be overcome through interpolation or triangulation using evidence from the archaeological, architectural, cartographic, geographic, documentary, and oral history records combined into a "superior cultural reconstruction" of the Civil War era along the Rio Grande, which considers the broader social and natural environment, the culture of the local populace, and larger national and international systemic concerns.

### *Geography, Environment, and Resources*

The story of the Rio Grande in the era of the American Civil War is further informed by geographical and environmental factors. People and livestock, including horses and cattle, require water, food or fodder, and salt. In the Nueces Strip these were limiting factors for the support of troops during their maneuvers. A multitude of Spanish colonial and Mexican Republican-era narrow land grants, known as *porciones*, line both shores of the river.[11] Of course, those who live near the Rio Grande had access to fresh water for irrigation, watering livestock, and the movement of people and materials across and up and down the river on ferries or on barges or other small watercraft.

Between the Nueces River and Rio Grande, a distance of 125 miles, there is no running water. Along the first terrace adjacent to the Rio Grande are oxbow lakes or *resacas*. Found in the low lying delta (Hidalgo, Cameron Counties) region, these were former channels of the river that were cut off through erosional processes associated with flooding. Long after they were formed, these resacas continued to hold water and fish from the regular flooding of the river. Of course fauna, flora, and people were drawn to them for their sustenance.

North of this were grasslands and brushlands known as the *brasada* country, or the "Wild Horse Desert." This included the South Texas Sand Sheet, a vast area of unconsolidated sand. An underground aquifer fed a few seeps or springs, including two in northern Hidalgo County near the modern community of Linn. Slightly saline and alkaline, one (San Juanito Springs) is located on the McAllen Ranch. Six miles (eight kilometers) northwest of Linn are the Santa Anita Springs.[12] It was in this area that salt, an important mineral resource, was found in Hidalgo and Willacy Counties at La Sal del Rey, La Sal Veja, and La Sal Blanca (East Lake). As Miller points out, salt was both an economic and strategic resource that was greatly valued by prehistoric Native peoples, Spanish colonial era settlers, and during the American Civil War.

In the early decades of the nineteenth century, ranches were established in the interior when cisterns were built and wells were dug.[13] Prior to this, the only other fresh water was found in ponds or waterholes (*charcos*) created when hurricanes and rainstorms filled a geological feature variably known as a deflation trough, a waterhole, or a *playa*, with water that could last for years before evaporating. Here, Native peoples had for millennia sought food and water when the Rio Grande was in flood.[14] For the Spanish-speaking pioneers of the area, when their contents were fresh, we see them termed *agua dulce*, but when stale and green, terms like *mala agua* or *agua verde* were used to describe them.[15]

This harsh and forbidding environment was traversed by runaway slaves, wagon trains filled with cotton, and cavalry patrols, all of which needed water.

### *"Aqui no estuvo Tejas" ("Texas was not here")*

For some 130 years from 1690 to 1821, the Spanish province of Tejas was bounded on the south by the Nueces River and the *Plano del Seno Mexicano* on the west by the headwaters of the Medina River, on the east by the Gulf of Mexico, and to the north and northeast by Louisiana. Spanish colonial Tejas (or Texas) was established to protect the northern borderlands from French and later English and American incursions. Some civilian settlers from the Canary Islands came to San Antonio, but it was largely a military and missionary frontier. After 1747, Texas was bounded on the south by the province of Nuevo Santander. Founded by José de Escandón, the province ran from the Nueces River south and was based solely on civilian farming and ranching settlements on both sides of the Rio Grande.

Following Mexican independence in 1821, the provinces were joined into the new state of Coahuila and Texas, which was subdivided into a number of departments based on the historic provinces. Twenty years later, in 1841, five years after the creation of the Republic of Texas, we find the first claim of the Rio Grande as the border between Mexico and the Republic.[16] Four years later, in December 1845, Texas joined the United States and promptly claimed its boundaries as being the Rio Grande. In January 1846, US armed forces under the command of Gen. Zachary Taylor entered the "Nueces Strip" north of the Rio Grande, starting the Mexican-American War. This would ultimately lead to the creation of the geographic Texas known today.[17]

### *Baptism Under Fire: The Legacy of the Mexican-American War*

In Winston-Salem, North Carolina, at the Reynolda House Museum of American Art, hangs the often reproduced 1848 painting *War News from Mexico* by Richard Caton Woodville. It centers on a man reading a newspaper report from the Mexican battlefields and illustrates the power of the printed word as the social media of its day. Education is a cornerstone of the United States. Building on the educational prescriptions of the Northwest Ordinance, the nascent republic became increasingly literate. In the first half of the nineteenth century, more than two hundred institutions of higher education were opened in the eastern United States.[18]

Americans eagerly consumed the news from the Mexican front. Led by heroes from the War of 1812, Generals Scott and Taylor, the articles made martyrs out of the fallen and celebrated victory after victory. The legacy of this notoriety can still be seen across the United States in the names of towns and counties named for battles and the fallen (e.g., Cerro Gordo, Ringgold—in California, Georgia, Illinois, Iowa, and North Carolina). Surviving junior officers like Jefferson Davis became famous in his native Mississippi and across the United States. The opening battles of the Mexican-American War took place along the northern banks of the Rio Grande. No fewer than fifty-four US Army junior officers who served at these battles would later become generals in the Confederate and Union armies a decade and a half later (see Tables

***Table 11.1. American commissioned officers who served at Palo Alto and Fort Brown in May of 1846, and later served as general officers in the Confederate army during the Civil War***

| Name | Killed in Action |
| --- | --- |
| Barnard Elliott Bee | Bull Run/Manassas, VA, July 21, 1861 |
| Braxton Bragg | |
| Arnold Elzey | |
| Franklin Gardner | |
| Robert Selden Garnett | Corricks Ford, WV, July 13, 1861 |
| Richard Caswell Gatlin | |
| William Joseph Hardee | |
| Theophilus Hunter Holmes | |
| Bushrod Rust Johnson | |
| Edmund Kirby Smith | |
| Lewis Henry Little | |
| James Longstreet | |
| John Porter McCown | |
| Lafayette McLaws | |
| John Bankhead MacGruder | |
| John Clifford Pemberton | |
| Gabriel James Rains | |
| Daniel Ruggles | |
| William Steele | |

| Name | Killed in Action |
|---|---|
| Carter Littlepage Stevenson | |
| David Emanuel Twiggs | |
| Lloyd Tilghman | |
| Earl Van Dorn | |

*Source: Francis E. Heitman,* Historical Register and Dictionary of the United States Army from Its Organization, *September 29, 1789, to March 27, 1903(Urbana, IL: University of Illinois, 1965).*

***Table 11.2. American commissioned officers who served at Palo Alto and Fort Brown in May of 1846, and later served as general officers in the Union army during the Civil War***

| Name | Killed in Action |
|---|---|
| Benjamin Alvord | |
| Christopher Columbus Augur | |
| Joseph K. Barnes | |
| William Thomas Harbaugh Brooks | |
| Robert Christie Buchanan | |
| Don Carlos Buell | |
| Napoleon Jackson Tecumseh Dana | |
| Lawrence Pike Graham | |
| Ulysses Simpson Grant | |
| John Porter Hatch | |
| Alexander Hays | Wilderness, VA, May 5–7, 1864 |
| William Hays | |
| Henry Moses Judah | |
| George Archibald McCall | |
| Joseph King Fenno Mansfield | |
| Randolph Barnes Marcy | |
| George Gordon Meade | |
| William Reading Montgomery | |
| Gabriel Rene Paul | |
| John James Peck | |
| Thomas Gamble Pitcher | |
| Alfred Pleasanton | |
| Joseph Haydn Potter | |

| Name | Killed in Action |
|---|---|
| John Fulton Reynolds | |
| Israel Bush Richardson | Antietam, MD, September 17, 1862 |
| John Cleveland Robinson | |
| Charles Ferguson Smith | |
| George Henry Thomas | |
| Seth Williams | |
| Thomas John Wood | |

*Source: Francis E. Heitman,* Historical Register and Dictionary of the United States Army from Its Organization, *September 29, 1789, to March 27, 1903(Urbana, IL: University of Illinois, 1965).*

11.1 and 11.2). These are a veritable "who's who" of the Civil War and include Bragg, Grant, Longstreet, and Meade.

As Douglas Murphy discusses in this volume, the victories of the Mexican-American War along the Rio Grande were very much in the forefront of the public's minds during the American Civil War. These were familiar names and places for the generation that served in the war with Mexico. Both sides looked upon those battles as touchstones during the American Civil War. Understandably though, at the end of the Civil War, interest in the Mexican War was greatly diminished. The hundreds of thousands of casualties and the destruction of cities and property were brought about under the direction of the then young heroes of this earlier war. The carnage and sectionalism meant there were no towns named for Civil War battles. National cemeteries and battlefields were marked, interpreted, and remain visible monuments for those who fought and died on both sides. An exception to this generalization was those battles that occurred along the Rio Grande. Today this is being remedied through the creation of the Rio Grande Valley Civil War Trail, which is educating a new generation, using the media of the twenty-first century, about the significance of the Rio Grande region in the era of the American Civil War.

### *New Populations on the Rio Grande:Anglo/African Americans*

Just as Mexico was gaining its independence from Spain, Moses Austin and his son and successor Stephen were given a contract to establish a colony on the Brazos River in Texas. Under Mexico, the contract was confirmed in 1822 and a proviso was added that an additional eighty acres would be given to the settlers for every slave they brought. Shortly thereafter, in 1829, slavery was outlawed. Texas did not comply, beginning the animosity with the central government in Mexico City. In 1836 there were five thousand enslaved African Americans in Texas and far fewer than a hundred in the villages that bordered the Rio Grande.[19]

With the annexation of the Nueces Strip following the Mexican-American War, there was an influx of civilian entrepreneurs, and military, from the eastern United States along the lower Rio Grande. While the majority who were of Western and Northern European ancestry clustered in and around Forts Brown and McIntosh and Ringgold Barracks, some like John Vale, Mifflin Kenedy, and John Young would marry into local Spanish-speaking families and settle in existing communities or ranches.

There was another group of immigrants who lived away from the main population centers in the nascent Hidalgo County. There, at ranches adjacent to government-licensed Rio Grande hand-drawn ferries, were families composed of "white" husbands (e.g., Abraham Rutledge, Nathaniel Jackson, John Webber) and their formerly enslaved "black" wives (e.g., Nancy Jackson, Matilda Hicks, Silvia Hector). As Leiker points out, by 1860 the number of African Americans in the counties bordering the Rio Grande had risen above three hundred, but a third of these were free men and women of color.

These Hidalgo County ranches became friendly way stations for runaway enslaved Africans traveling on the southbound Underground Railroad. These individuals had to traverse the nearly waterless South Texas Sand Sheet while dodging the then all-white military units or civilian slave catchers like Santos Benavides and John Salmon "Rip" Ford as they made their way to ferries that crossed the Rio Grande to the relative safety of Mexico. These families continued to provide succor to pro-Union forces during the Civil War.

It is not surprising that seventy years after the conflict, descriptions of this escape route were retold in WPA interviews. A century and a half later, their now Spanish-speaking descendants continue to relate family lore telling of their arrival by covered wagon from Alabama and other locales east of the Mississippi.[20]

## *One Piece at a Time: The Loss of the Historical Record*

Garza's discussion of the various interpretations of the Palmito Ranch battlefield epitomizes a central problem with the documentary record. As indicated by Rolando Garza in chapter 9, trouble lies in the fact that the "historical record fails to provide a consistent, objective, and accurate account of the battle." The contrasts and conflictions between the Union and Confederate recollection of events are telling. Was this the "fog of battle," the protection of one's honor at the end of the conflict, or the aggrandizement of the raconteur decades after the battle?

Military officers and historians are well acquainted with the nature of war. Defensive features from campsites to fortifications to trenches are tangible reminders of past sieges. In Germany, Turkey, and Canada there are still the walled cities of Rothenberg, Istanbul, and Quebec. In the United States the seaward approaches to Savannah and Charleston are still "defended" by the battered remnants of Forts Pulaski and Sumter. Foundations and such earthen features as trenches, redoubts, and earthworks are still visible features across Belgium and France from World War I and at sites from the American Revolution and Civil War such as Yorktown, Vicksburg, and Petersburg. At these, the easily lost detritus of everyday life from toothbrushes, buttons, buckles, shoes, food remains, and munitions are found in moats, latrines, bombproofs, and in the fields between the lines of antagonists.

But what of more mobile battles fought across open ground? These too leave evidence of a conflict, but that evidence is limited to portable artifacts such as buttons, badges, and bullets, which are easily lost in the heat of battle. Human or animal casualties were removed from the field by compatriots or nonhuman scavengers. Useable munitions were similarly retrieved. Yet, the small easily lost and later overlooked objects can, through their relative position to one another, reveal the movement of troops, providing a more nuanced and less biased picture of a battle. In the Rio Grande region, the two dozen battles fought over a two decade period (see Table 11.3) were of this ephemeral nature.

Modern battlefield archaeology was born in the 1980s at the Little Bighorn battlefield in Montana, the site of the 1876 defeat of Custer's 7th Cavalry.[21] Archaeologists wielding metal detectors and using standard forensic approaches, including ballistic study of spent ammunition, were able to trace the movement of the troopers and their Native

American foes across the battlefield. What emerged was a very different image of the battle then that told over the previous century.[22] What made their job easier was that the battlefield had been largely untouched since the summer of 1876. Portable artifacts by the thousand and some human remains were discovered where they had fallen a century earlier. Thirty years later these same techniques have been used to investigate other battlefield sites from the Mexican American and Civil Wars, their success tempered by the condition of the archeological record.

***Table 11.3. Battle sites in the Lower Rio Grande Valley, 1846–1865***

| Battle Site | Date |
|---|---|
| Rancho de Carricitos | April 25, 1846 |
| Fort Brown/Texas | May 3–9, 1846 |
| Palo Alto | May 8–9, 1846 |
| Resaca de la Palma | May 9, 1846 |
| Brownsville | September 28, 1859 |
| Rio Grande City | December 27, 1859 |
| La Bolsa | February 4, 1860 |
| Clareño, Zapata County | April 15, 1861 |
| Carrizo, Zapata County | May 22, 1861 |
| Supply Train (Roma) | December 4, 1862 |
| Rancho Soledad, Hidalgo County | December 26, 1862 |
| Mequital Lealeño, Mexico | January 1863 |
| Chaparral (Mier) Mexico | September 2, 1863 |
| Los Patricios, Duval County | March 13, 1864 |
| Santa Rosa, Cameron County | March 15, 1864 |
| Laredo, Webb County | March 19, 1864 |
| Las Rucias, Cameron County | June 25, 1864 |
| Brownsville, Cameron County | July 23, 26-27 |
| Clarksville, Cameron County | August 9, 1864 |
| Port Isabel, Cameron County | August 12, 1864 |
| White's Ranch, Cameron County | August 14, 1864 |
| Boca Chica Pass, Cameron County | October 14, 1864 |
| Palmito Hill, Cameron County | September 6, 1864 |
| Palmito Ranch, Cameron County | May 1, 1865 |

This objective source of information is diminished through the undocumented collection of artifacts. Some have compared this to the tearing of pages out of a history book and the resulting loss of knowledge. Leisure time has spawned a growing interest in the past. Television programs including *Antiques Roadshow* on PBS, *American Pickers* on the History Channel, and the now cancelled *Diggers* on National Geographic bring the significance of historic material culture into America's living rooms. In the desire to own a piece of the past, relic hunters collect those portable artifacts that are crucial to understanding battlefields and archaeological sites in general. During the twentieth century, the archeological records associated with the majority of unprotected mid-nineteenth century battlefields in the US have been highly compromised and often destroyed by modern land management practices and urban development. In addition, the development and availability of modern metal detector technology has allowed new generations of individuals to effectively collect artifacts from mid-nineteenth century battlefields. This activity, which often goes on for decades on unprotected sites, can devastate the integrity of the archeological record, sometimes to the point of rendering the record scientifically unserviceable. Since the 1960s, Palo Alto and Palmito Ranch battlefields and the sites of Bagdad, Clarksville, and the military camp at Brazos Santiago have been adversely affected through undocumented collecting at these sites.[23] Perhaps to assuage their conscience, some have donated their curios to local (e.g., Museum of Port Isabel, Port Isabel; the Ladd Hockey Collections at the Museum of South Texas History, Edinburg) and regional (e.g., Texas Civil War Museum, Fort Worth) museums. Others are proudly displayed in shadow boxes or are kept in shoeboxes pending the demise of their owners. Of course such activities are illegal on public property, but that does not stop dedicated collectors. This is why Garza's work at Palmito Ranch is so important for understanding this Civil War battle.

Historic structures dating from the nineteenth century are present from Brownsville to Laredo. Their existence is due to an arid physical climate and, until recently, a poor economic climate. Buildings on the military bases were constructed of a variety of materials, including adobe, fired brick, and wood. Many of these survived the closing of the bases in 1944 because they were turned over to local school districts

*Collectors have adversely affected the archaeological record. Top: Excavated relics from the Palmito Ranch, Texas Battlefield. The Ladd Hockey Collections from Bagdad. Courtesy of the Museum of South Texas History, Edinburg. Middle left: US breast plate from a cartridge box sling. Middle right: US belt buckle. Below: 1851 Colt Navy revolver with the hammer in the firing position and bullets still present in the cylinder. Courtesy of the Texas Civil War Museum, Fort Worth.*

who repurposed them for primary and secondary schools and community colleges. Ringgold Barracks in Rio Grande City has been identified by W. Stephen McBride as the "best example of a nineteenth century fort in the United States."[24] Other structures, like the Mifflin Kenedy warehouse, which dates to the 1850s, survive relatively intact as a public works facility in Rio Grande City. Upriver, and dating to the 1830s, are other similarly preserved structures such as Casa Ortiz in Laredo and Treviño Fort in San Ygnacio. In the National Historic Landmark District in Roma stands the shell of the John Vale/Noah Cox house. It also dates from the 1850s and, when a century old, the structure was used in the 1952 Marlon Brando film *Viva Zapata!* These buildings survived because of the economic downturn felt following the closing of military bases and the closing of the Rio Grande to commerce following the construction of Falcon Dam. Water impoundment projects developed for agricultural irrigation in Hidalgo and Cameron Counties led to the loss of many historic towns with structures dating from the eighteenth century under the waters of Falcon Reservoir.[25]

*A number of structures dating from before the American Civil War still stand along the Rio Grande, including (top to bottom) Casa Ortiz (1830) in Laredo; Treviño Fort in San Ignacio (1830); and the John Vale/Noah Cox house (1853) in Roma. Photos by the author.*

*Additional structures dating from before the American Civil War that still stand along the Rio Grande, including (top to bottom) the Mifflin Kenedy warehouse (1854), Rio Grande City; the Lee House (circa 1855) at Ringgold Barracks, Rio Grande City; and the Stillman House (1851) in Brownsville. Photos by the author.*

### *Mexico, the United States, and the Rio Grande: A Porous Border*

To understand the American Civil War in Texas requires understanding the history of Mexico. As Levinson points out, the two nations have been inexorably linked along the Rio Grande frontier. At the end of the Mexican-American War in 1848, the Rio Grande became the international boundary between the United States and Mexico. With the Treaty of Guadalupe Hidalgo, the international boundary crossed over the

Nueces to the Rio Grande, and with it families with land on both sides of the river. While it was militarized and regularly patrolled for nearly a century (from 1846 to 1944) by the US Army, it was, and remains to this day, a porous border where the US and Mexican economies are visibly linked due in part to the nature of the resident populace.

After a century in towns and ranches on both sides of the river, Spanish-speaking families living on the land where they were born and to which they had property rights were seen by newcomers from the eastern United States as foreigners. These new people, with a new language, laws, customs, and religions, formed new communities, including Brownsville, Edinburgh, Davis Landing / Rio Grande City, often surrounding military installations (e.g., Fort Brown, Ringgold Barracks, Fort McIntosh). The English-speaking "Anglo" newcomers were, and remain to this day, a minority in the region. Thus, for the Spanish-speaking "Natives," the river was not a boundary but simply a highway.

Familial and economic ties were maintained by the new "Mexican" Americans to their relatives south of the Rio Grande by way of a multitude of ferry crossings. Some of the recently arrived Anglos, such as John Young, John McAllen, and Mifflin Kenedy, joined them in these regular peregrinations back and forth across the Rio Grande following their marriages into the Ballí and Vela families. During the American Civil War, the porosity of the border combined with these familial ties helped men like Santiago Vidaurri and Richard King earn huge profits from the cross-border cotton trade.

Also underscoring the fluidity of the Rio Grande as a national boundary was, before the American Civil War, the pursuit of runaway slaves into Mexico by slave catchers Santos Benavides and John Salmon "Rip" Ford. Later, during that conflict, Benavides's and Ford's Confederate forces and pro-Union irregular partisans led by Octaviano Zapata, Antonio Ochoa, and Juan Cortina regularly forded the Rio Grande into Mexico to attack each other, to attack Mexican troops loyal to Maximilian, or to find succor among family and friends prior to crossing north of the Rio Grande to attack their enemies.

At the beginning of the second decade of the twenty-first century, "Operation Fast and Furious," under the direction of the Bureau of Alcohol, Tobacco, and Firearms, wanted to track the illegal movement of firearms into Mexico for use by drug cartels. While that "sting" operation failed, it was but the latest example of gun running across the Rio Grande. In 1866, tens of thousands of surplus small arms were passed to the forces of Benito Juárez. A decade later, an army provisioned in the United States and led by Porfirio Diaz invaded Mexico from Brownsville.

### *Commerce: The Rio Grande as a Highway*

Prior to 1846, movement across the Nueces Strip from Texas into Mexico was limited due to a lack of markets and the forbidding environment. Salt from Sal del Rey and other nearby salines had been collected in prehistory and during the Spanish colonial era. Much of it moved south to the Rio Grande and beyond. Later, during the Civil War, salt was redirected north for use in the Confederacy in the then empty wagons that had carried cotton to the Rio Grande.

This would change during the Mexican-American War. The Rio Grande was used to ferry troops and equipment into the interior. The river was navigable by steamboats as far as the Roma bluffs, more than a hundred miles from the mouth of the Rio Grande. After the war, surplus steamboats were purchased by Richard King, Mifflin Kenedy, and others to move materials up the Rio Grande to military posts and communities and produce downriver to the Gulf of Mexico.

Roads leading north from Brownsville, Edinburgh, Davis Landing, Roma, and Laredo to San Antonio, Corpus Christi, and beyond crossed the harsh interior environment. Runaway slaves and their pursuers, and others, traversed these roads in the years before the American Civil War. Within a year of the attack on Fort Sumter, it became clear that the Rio Grande, with its status as an international boundary, would serve as a direct line of supply for the South.

The previously little-used roads crossing the Nueces Strip witnessed the movement of 160 million pounds of cotton from Louisiana, Arkansas, "Indian Territory" (Oklahoma), and east Texas, with a value of $128,000,000, to the Rio Grande. Thus it was not hyperbole when, in 1864, St. Augustine Plaza was said to be stacked with five thousand bales or 2.5 million pounds of cotton in anticipation of the attack by the 2nd Texas Union Cavalry.

The five hundred pound bales were carried in both large four-wheeled wagons and smaller two-wheeled Mexican carts or *carretas*.

These must have been impressive vehicles. Geographical landmarks still mark this trade in Texas. Today in Nueces County, US Highway 77 crosses Carreta Creek between Bishop and Kingsville, Texas—one of the main routes of the Civil War era cotton trade. Oral histories, related a century after the war, said that the creek was named because cotton wagons would sometime mire and break down in its waters.[26]

When Union forces were present in the region, the Confederate cotton would be ferried across the Rio Grande to the safety of Mexico, where it would either be freighted to the mouth of the river or placed on steamboats and carried downstream. The paired communities with familial connections on both shores meant that the trade would usually be unmolested.

Once these bales reached the Mexican port of Bagdad, they were joined by cotton that had been carried in coastal vessels. There they were loaded on neutral vessels and carried across the Atlantic Ocean to the mills of Europe or, ironically, to mills in New England that profited from manufacturing uniforms for Union troops. The commerce prolonged the war and as a result cost thousands of casualties.

### *An African American Army of Occupation on the Rio Grande*

Few living along the lower reaches of the modern Rio Grande are aware of the prominent role of African American troops in the region during and after the Civil War. Beginning in 1865, with the lead up to the Battle of Palmito Ranch, and for the next forty-one years, these soldiers would defend the Rio Grande border.

While the majority operated out of pre–Civil War military installations like Forts Brown, McIntosh, and Ringgold, others occupied ranches and smaller communities such as Edinburgh and Roma. At the former they were employed constructing roads and buildings, many of which still stand. Those serving at the smaller more remote locales seemingly filled their time learning Spanish and finding marriage partners, with a few staying on in the region following their discharge. This was certainly true of the white officers. Lt. Col. George M. Dennett,[27] 9th Regiment of US Colored Troops, and Ireland-born 1st Lt. William Kelly[28] of the 8th US Colored Infantry stayed in Brownsville and are buried in the "Old City Cemetery."

As Leiker points out during the last third of the nineteenth century,

*Examples of buildings constructed by African American troops stationed in the Rio Grande Valley. Top: 1869 "Bakery," Fort McIntosh, Laredo. Middle: "Hospital," 1870, Ringgold Barracks, Rio Grande City. Bottom: 1868 "Cavalry Building," Fort Brown, Brownsville. Photos by the author.*

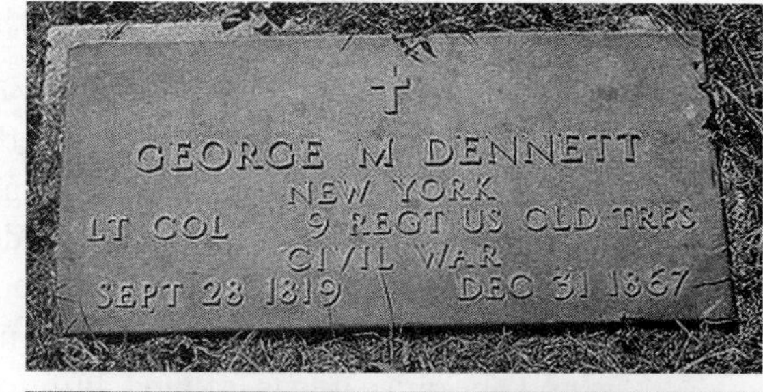

*Some USCT officers remained in Brownsville and surrounding communities following their discharge. Above: Lt. Col. George M. Dennett, 9th Regiment, USCT, 1819–67; Below: 1st Lt. William Kelly, 9th Regiment, USCT, 1840–21. Photos by the author.*

there seems to have been increasing acrimony between the black troops and the local populace at the main posts—a fact that is somewhat surprising given the amount of interracial marriage noted in the 1900 census. While historically this would culminate in the infamous 1906 "Brownsville affair," which led to the withdrawal of black regiments from along the Rio Grande, it does not negate four decades of service by African American soldiers in the Rio Grande Valley.

### *More Than a River: The Rio Grande Frontier in War and Peace*

*It was the destiny of this river from the first to be a frontier of rivalries, a boundary of kingdoms, a dividing line between opposing ambitions and qualities of life.*

—Paul Horgan

The Rio Grande has a unique but largely forgotten place in the history of the Civil War, and in American history in general. The Rio Grande region is best envisioned as an island surrounded a hostile environment. On this "island," which was bisected by the Rio Grande, were centuries-old communities based economically on animal husbandry, agriculture, and the collection of salt, whose focus had been across the Rio Grande in the Mexican heartland to the south.

Here in 1846, "Manifest Destiny" became tangible as the smoke cleared from the field at Palo Alto. New immigrants came to the "island" and turned the focus of the region north to Texas and the United States. In some cases, these newcomers became "cultural brokers" through their marriages to the original "islanders." With a foot on each bank and with economic and political connections beyond the "island," those mixed families would thrive. Other mixed-race families came to the "island" because it was isolated, but now part of their homeland. They too survived, but by assimilating and identifying as part of the original "island" ranch-based culture. We might reasonably ask if it was convenient for those descendants to forget that ancestry and embrace the dominant Spanish-speaking Mexican American identity that permeates the Rio Grande. Finally, there were the rest of the original Spanish-speaking "islanders" who followed their *caudillos*, whether they lived north or south of the river for traditional, familial, or economic reasons.

Out of the Mexican-American War came a generation of leaders whose vision of war was skewed through the lens of victory. These were men whose shared experiences at West Point and in the Mexican-American War would forever link them. Their tactics and weaponry, which was refined and tested across Mexico, would lead to battlefield casualties that would be unparalleled in the history of the world until World War I.

Cotton was the white gold that profited entrepreneurs, not only north and south of the Rio Grande but in Europe as well. It prolonged overall Confederate resistance and led to the invasion of the "island" by Union forces. The overland transport of cotton to steamboat landings or ferry crossings was predicated on the availability of water and land surfaces conducive to the movement of heavily laden wagons. This, in time, would serve as the basis of the modern highway system of South Texas.

Last, there are the African American soldiers who served on the "island" in the decades following emancipation. Of the four million who were held in bondage in 1860, there are very few oral histories. Of those interviewed as part of the Works Progress Administration during 1939, 43 percent were under the age of ten in 1865. Clearly these interviews, although valuable, are biased. Most of the men who served were emancipated. Their legacy is still visible from Laredo to Brownsville, and their story is still largely invisible in the history of Texas and beyond.

Why are these stories forgotten? For some in Texas, Faulkner's quote on history noted at the beginning of this chapter is accurate. The removal of the Jefferson Davis statue from the University of Texas South Mall[29] and a similar debate surrounding another monument in Brownsville's Washington Park[30] should make us pause to reflect. It might be better to place interpretive signs explaining why those monuments were originally erected and how they reflect a certain age and point of view. Did the legacy of the "Lost Cause" myth leave no room for Spanish-speaking Confederate and Union soldiers? Was it convenient for the descendants of both Confederate and Union veterans of the American Civil War to overlook the contributions of African American soldiers in the era of Jim Crow? And what became of those who profited during the war?

Now as the film *Free State of Jones* (2016) provides for the general public evidence of a lack of unity for the cause of the Confederacy, stories of the Rio Grande take on even greater importance. Revisionist historians and the descendants of the people who made the "island" their home will have much to ponder in the coming decades.

### *Parting Shots: The Significance of the Rio Grande in the Study of the American Civil War*

Was, as some have said, the Civil War in the Rio Grande a mere sideshow to the main act east of the Mississippi? Certainly the carnage and destruction witnessed there was and remains unparalleled in the history of the United States. Yet, we now can see that had the outward flow of cotton been stemmed, the conflict may have been shortened for lack of war materials. It may also be true that the outcome of the war could have been different had Maximilian prevailed over Juárez. Clearly the Rio Grande theatre of the American Civil War was anything but a sideshow.

Here we have considered the Rio Grande within its broader social and natural environment, in light of the culture of the local populace, and contextualized against larger national and international systemic concerns. We have seen how our knowledge of the past is lost incrementally. Documents are lost or destroyed. Memories of participants fade and ultimately are erased in death. Sites and their associated landscapes are altered or destroyed through natural and cultural processes, including hurricanes, erosion, and grazing, recycling, and urban development. Thus bias will always haunt our understanding of the past. Yet we can feel confident that the "cubist" approach, which has served as an underpinning of this volume, will continue to inform and shed light on the American Civil War era along the Rio Grande.

## *Notes*

1. William Faulkner, *Requiem for a Nun* (New York: Random House, 1951).

2. W. Stephen McBride, "Camp Nelson and Kentucky's Civil War Memory," *Historical Archaeology* 47, no. 3 (2013): 69–70; Helen Taylor, "Gone with the Wind and Its Influence," in *The History of Southern Women's Literature*, edited by Carolyn Perry and Mary Weaks-Baxter (Baton Rouge: Louisiana State University Press, 2002), 258–67; David W. Blight, *Race and Reunion: The Civil War in American Memory* (Cambridge, MA: Belknap Press, 2001), 283–84.

3. Kevin M. Levin, "Not Your Grandfather's Civil War Commemoration," *The Atlantic*, December 13, 2011, http://www.theatlantic.com/national/archive/2011/12/not-your-grandfathers-civil-war-commemoration/249920/ (accessed June 20, 2016).

4. "Civil War Battles: Major Battles from the American Civil War," http://www.historynet.com/civil-war-battles (accessed June 27, 2016).

5. "CWSAC Battle Summaries: Civil War Battle Summaries by State," The American Battlefield Protection Program (ABPP), https://www.nps.gov/abpp/battles/bystate.htm (accessed June 27, 2016).

6. David Hurst Thomas, "Columbian Consequences: The Spanish Borderlands in Cubist Perspective," *Columbian Consequences, Archaeological and Historical Perspectives on the Spanish Borderlands West* V01.1, edited by David H. Thomas (Washington, DC: Smithsonian Institution Press, 1989), 6–9.

7. Robert L. Schuyler, "The Spoken Word, the Written Word, Observed Behavior and Preserved Behavior: The Contexts Available to the Archaeologist," in *Historical Archaeology: A Guide to Substantive and Theoretical Contributions* (Farmingdale, NY: Baywood Publishing, 1978), 27–31.

8. Walter W. Taylor, "A Study of Archaeology." *American Anthropologist Memoir* 69, American Anthropological Association, 1948.

9. Schuyler, "The Spoken Word."

10. Kathleen Deagan, "Avenues of Inquiry in Historical Archaeology," in *Advances in Archaeological Method and Theory*, Vol. 5, edited by Michael B. Schiffer (New York: Academic Press, 1982), 158–62.

Kathleen A. Deagan "Neither History nor Prehistory: The Questions That Count in Historical Archaeology," *Historical Archaeology* 22, no. 1 (1988): 10; Gary M. Feinman, "Thoughts on New Approaches to Combining the Archaeological and Historical Records," *Journal of Archaeological Method and Theory* 4, no. 3/4 (1997): 367–77.

11. Galen D. Greaser, *New Guide to Spanish and Mexican Land Grants in South Texas* (Austin: Texas General Land Office, 2009), 86.

12. Gunner M. Bruce, *Springs of Texas*, Vol. 1, 2nd ed. (College Station: Texas A&M University Press, 2002), 228.

13. Greaser, *New Guide*, 86.

14. Juan L. González, Russell K. Skowronek, and Bobbie L. Lovett, "Deflation Troughs, Water and Prehistoric Occupation on the Margins of the South Texas Sand Sheet, Evidence from Hidalgo County, Texas," *Journal of Texas Archeology and History* (2014): 70–93.

15. Greaser, *New Guide*, 86, 90, 93, 121.

16. Mike Coppock, "The Republic of the Rio Grande," HistoryNet, http://www.historynet.com/the-republic-of-the-rio-grande.htm (accessed June 26, 2016).

17. Carol Christensen and Thomas Christensen, *The U.S.-Mexican War* (San Francisco: Bay Books, 1998).

18. Russell K. Skowronek, "Hail to Thee, O Alma Mater: Considering the Archaeology of Academia," in *Beneath the Ivory Tower: The Archaeology of Academia*, edited by Russell K. Skowronek and Kenneth Lewis (Gainesville: University Presses of Florida, 2010), 274–76.

19. Bacha-Garza, this volume; Randolph B. Campbell, "Slavery," *Handbook of Texas Online*, https://tshaonline.org/handbook/online/articles/yps01 (accessed June 28, 2016).

20. Personal communication between Guadalupe (Lupe) Flores and Roseann Bacha-Garza, University of Texas Rio Grande Valley, Border Studies Archive (June 15, 2016).

21. See Douglas D. Scott and Andrew P. McFeaters, "The Archaeology of Historic Battlefields: A History and Theoretical Development in Conflict Archaeology," *Journal of Archaeological Research* 19, no. 1 (March 1, 2011): 103–32.

22. Douglas D. Scott and Richard A. Fox Jr., *Archaeological Insights into the Custer Battle: An Assessment of the 1984 Field Season* (Norman: University of Oklahoma Press, 1987).

23. Robin L. Galloso, "Archaeological Potential of the Rio Grande Valley: A Look at Brazos Island with a Historical Focus on the Civil War" (master's thesis, Department of History, University of Texas Rio Grande Valley, Edinburg, TX, 2016).

24. Personal communication with Russell Skowronek, January 12, 2012.

25. W. Eugene George, *Lost Architecture of the Rio Grande Borderlands* (College Station: Texas A&M University Press, 2008).

26. Dr. Lisa Adam, Museum of South Texas History, personal communication with Russell Skowronek June 17, 2016.

27. Born on September 28, 1819, in Lyman, Maine, George M. Dennett enlisted as a sergeant major in the 38th Regiment of the New York Volunteers. The regiment formed in April of 1861 and saw service at the battles of Bull Run, Chantilly, Stone Bridge, Yorktown, and Williamsburg, where he was wounded in 1862. During this time, Dennett rose to the rank of captain, commanding Company D. The regiment was mustered out of service in June of 1863. Afflicted with malaria, Dennett went on leave until October 9, when he was appointed captain of the 7th USCI and mustered into Company D on October 14, 1863. Three weeks later, he mustered out of 7th USCI and was promoted to major, in the 9th USCI. On March 12, 1865, he was promoted for the final time to lieutenant colonel, in the 9th USCI. Personal

correspondence, W. Stephen McBride to Russell K. Skowronek, January 16, 2018.

On January 30, 1866, Dennett was given command of 1st Brigade, 1st Division, 25th Army Corps, and mustered out of the US Army on December 14, 1866. He lived in Hidalgo, Texas, and died on December 31, 1867. He was the author of *The History of the Ninth U.S.C. Troops from its Organization till Muster Out*, published in 1866.

28. Born in Ireland, William Kelly joined the 1st New York Mounted Rifles at the beginning of the Civil War and rose to the rank of sergeant. In the fall of 1863 he joined the 8th US Colored Infantry at Camp William Penn in Philadelphia as a second lieutenant, later rising to the rank of first lieutenant. He was stationed at Brazos Island and later Brownsville. While the 8th left Texas on November 10, 1865, Kelly remained. Personal correspondence, W. Stephen McBride to Russell K. Skowronek, January 16, 2018.

29. Jen Hayden, "Jefferson Davis Monument at the University of Texas Is Headed to a New Home," Daily Kos, August 13, 2015, http://www.dailykos.com/story/2015/8/13/1411770/-Jefferson-Davis-monument-at-the-University-of-Texas-is-headed-to-a-new-home (accessed July 16, 2016).

30. Christina R. Garza, "Petition Drive Seeks Removal of Jefferson Davis Monument," *The Brownsville Herald* (January 17, 2016), http://www.brownsville-herald.com/news/local/article_c04aa352-bd9b-11e5-b95a-8b48427ce181.html (accessed January 17, 2016).

# *References*


## *Primary Sources*

### Archival Centers

Archivo General del Estado de Nuevo Leon, Monterrey, Nuevo Len
Archivo General de la Nacion
Bexar County Historical Commission, San Antonio, TX
Briscoe Center for American History (BCAH)
Border Studies Archives, University of Texas Rio Grande Valley, Edinburg, TX
Center for the Study of American History (CAH), University of Texas at Austin
Charles Stillman Papers, Houghton Library, Harvard University
Hidalgo County Courthouse, Edinburg, TX
Houghton Library, Harvard University
Judge Advocate General's Office (JAG), National Archives, Washington, DC
Laredo Archives, St. Mary's University, San Antonio, TX
Margaret H. McAllen Memorial Archives, Museum of South Texas History, Edinburg, TX
Massachusetts Historical Society, Boston, MA
McAllen Ranch Archives (MRA)
National Archives (NA), Washington, DC
National Archives Microfilm Publication (NAMP)
National Archives and Records Administration (NARA)
Official Records of the Union and Confederate Navies in the War of the Rebellion (OR)
Texas State Archives (TSA), Austin, TX
University of Texas Rio Grande Valley Special Collections Library Archives, Edinburg, TX

## *Government Reports and Documents*

Congressional Series of United States Public Documents, Index to the Miscellaneous Documents of the House of Representatives for the Second Session of the Fifty-Third Congress 1893–94, Washington: Government Printing Office, vol. 3267, issue 4, 1895.

Drake, Ludlum C. "Recollections of the Civil War." Papers of the Military Order of the Loyal Legion of the United States, Michigan Commandery, Detroit, Bentley Historical Society, University of Michigan, Ann Arbor, 1891.

Haecker, Charles M. *A Thunder of Cannon*: *Archeology of the Mexican-American War Battlefield of Palo Alto*. National Park Service, Southwest Cultural Resource Centers, Professional Paper No. 52, Santa Fe, NM: National Park Service, 1994.

Heitman, Francis E. "Historical Register and Dictionary of the United States Army from Its Organization, September 29, 1789, to March 27, 1903." Act of Congress. Urbana: University of Illinois, 1965.

International Boundary and Water Commission, United States and Mexico, Anson Mills, and United States, eds. *Proceedings of the International (Water) Boundary Commission, United States and Mexico, Treaties of 1884 and 1889. Equitable Distribution of the Waters of the Rio Grande. United States Section.* 2 vols. Washington, DC: Government Printing Office, 1903.

Isbell, Francis W. "Jackson Ranch Church" (typescript, December 1982), Hidalgo County Historical Commission, Edinburg, TX.

México, Comisión Pesquisidora de la Frontera del Norte. *Reports of the Committee of Investigation Sent in 1873 by the Mexican Government to the Frontier of Texas.* New York: Baker and Godwin, 1875.

Myer, Terri. *Palmito Ranch Battlefield National Historic Landmark Nomination.* Washington, DC: National Park Service. 1994.

National Park Service. Palo Alto Battlefield National Historic Site: Boundary Study. Document on file at Palo Alto Battlefield National Historical Park. Brownsville, TX, 1982.

National Park Service American Battlefield Protection Program. "Palmito Ranch Battlefield National Historic Landmark Final Technical Report with Archaeological Survey Report." Report no. 2255-09-008. Washington, DC: Texas Historical Commission, 2011.

———. "Palo Alto Battlefield National Historic Site: Boundary Study." Document on file at Palo Alto Battlefield National Historical Park. Brownsville, TX: National Park Service, 1982.

Official Records, US Government. *The War of the Confederate Lion: A Compilation of the Official Records of the Union and Confederate Armies.* Series I, Vols. 41, 48. Washington, DC: US Government Printing Office, 1893; reprinted 1985.

US Bureau of the Census. *Population of the United States in 1860.* Washington, DC: Government Printing Office, 1864.

US Congress, US House of Representatives. *Testimony Taken by the Committee on Military Affairs in Relation to the Texas Border Trouble.* Washington, DC: Government Printing Office, 1878.

Warner, Theodore M. *Time Book of the Steamer Mustang*, 1864. Theodore M. Warner Collection, Margaret H. McAllen Memorial Archives, Museum of South Texas History, Edinburg, TX.

## Newspapers

*Ashtabula Weekly Telegraph* (Ohio)
*Baltimore Sun*
*Boston Daily Advertiser*
*Brownsville Daily Ranchero*

*The Brownsville Herald*
*The Brownsville Trade*
*The Caledonian* (St. Johnsbury, VT)
*Centinela del Rio Grande* (Brownsville, TX)
*Cincinnati Daily Gazette*
*Cleveland Morning Leader*
*Corpus Christi Ranchero*
*The Crisis* (Columbus)
*Daily Cleveland Herald*
*Daily Evening Bulletin* (San Francisco)
*Daily Morning News* (Savannah, GA)
*Daily National Intelligencer* (Washington, DC)
*Daily Ohio Statesman* (Columbus)
*Daily Picayune* (New Orleans)
*Daily Ranchero* (Matamoros)
*Daily True Delta* (New Orleans)
*The Farmers' Cabinet* (Philadelphia)
*Fayetteville Observer* (North Carolina)
*Galveston Weekly News*
*Houston Daily Telegraph*
*Houston Tri-Weekly Telegraph*
*Idaho Tri-Weekly Statesman* (Boise)
*Laredo Times*
*Lowell Daily Citizen and News* (Massachusetts)
*The Macon Daily Telegraph* (Georgia)
*New Haven Daily Palladium*
*New York Herald*
*New York Times*
*New York Tribune*
*Philadelphia Inquirer*
*Pittsfield Sun* (Massachusetts)
*Richmond Dispatch* (Virginia)
*The Ripley Bee* (Ohio)
*The Scioto Gazette* (Chillicothe, OH)
*Shreveport Weekly News*
*St. Cloud Democrat* (Minnesota)
*Texas State Gazette* (Austin)
*Trenton State Gazette* (New Jersey)
*Valley Morning Star* (Harlingen, TX)
*Virginia Free Press* (Charlestown, WV)
*Washington Evening Star* (Washington, DC)
*Wisconsin Daily Patriot* (Madison)
*The Wisconsin State Register* (Madison)

## *Oral History Interviews*

Baize, Santos Jackson, and William Baize. Interviewed by Roseann Bacha-Garza, Baeze Home, Edinburg, TX. Border Studies Archive: University of Texas Rio Grande Valley, January 13, 2016.

Ortiz, Flavia Webber. Interviewed by Roseann Bacha-Garza, Ortiz Home, Weslaco, TX. Border Studies Archive: University of Texas Rio Grande Valley, January 8, 2016.

## *Books*

Aleman, Lucas. *Historia de México*. Mexico City: Editorial Jus., 1942.

Allhands, J. L. *Gringo Builders*. Iowa City: privately printed, 1931.

Alonso, Ana María. *Thread of Blood: Colonialism, Revolution, and Gender on Mexico's Northern Frontier*. Tucson: University of Arizona Press, 1995.

Alonzo, Armando C. *Tejano Legacy: Rancheros and Settlers in South Texas 1734–1900*. Albuquerque: University of New Mexico Press, 1998.

Anna, Timothy E. *The Fall of the Royal Government in México City*. Lincoln: University of Nebraska Press, 1978.

Armitage, David. *The Ideological Origins of the British Empire*. Cambridge, New York: Cambridge University Press, 2000.

Bancroft, Hubert Howe. *History of the North Mexican States and Texas*. 2 vols. San Francisco: History Company Publishers, 1884–89.

Bannon, John Francis. *The Spanish Borderlands Frontier, 1513–1821*. New York: Holt, Rinehart, and Winston, 1970.

Bardon, Jonathan. *A History of Ulster*. Belfast: Blackstaff Press, 1992.

Basch, Samuel Siegfried Karl Ritter von. *Memories of México: A History of the Last Ten Months of Empire*, translated by Hugh McAden Oechler. San Antonio, TX: Trinity University Press, 1868.

Baum, Dale. *The Shattering of Texas Unionism: Politics in the Lone Star State during the Civil War Era*. Baton Rouge: Louisiana State University Press, 1999.

Berlandier, Jean Louis. *Journey to Mexico during the Years 1826 to 1834*. Austin: Texas State Historical Association in cooperation with the Center for Studies in Texas History, University of Texas at Austin, 1980.

Berlin, Ira, Joseph Riedy and Leslie S. Rowland, eds. *Freedom: A Documentary History of Emancipation, 1861–1867. Series II: The Black Military Experience*. New York: Cambridge University Press, 1982.

Blight, David W. *Race and Reunion: The Civil War in American Memory*. Cambridge, MA: Belknap Press, 2001.

Bolton, Herbert Eugene. *The Spanish Borderlands: A Chronicle of Old Florida and the Southwest*. New Haven, CT: Yale University Press, 1921.

———. *Texas in the Middle Eighteenth Century: Studies in Spanish Colonial History and Administration*. 1915; reprint, Austin: University of Texas Press, 1970.

Brune, Gunner M. *Springs of Texas*, vol. 1, 2nd ed. College Station: Texas A & M University Press, 2002.

Burgess, Andrea et al. *The Economist Pocket World in Figures 2015*. London: Profile Books, 2015.

Burian, Edward. *The Architecture and Cities of Northern Mexico from Independence to the Present*. Austin: University of Texas Press, 2015.

Cerruti, Mario and Miguel A. Gonzalez Quiroga. *El Norte de Mexico y Texas 1848–1880: Comerico, capitales, y trabajadores en una econmia de frontera*. Ciudad de Mexico: Instituto de Investigaciones Dr. Jose Maria Luis Mora, 1999.

Chapelle, Howard I. *American Small Sailing Craft: Their Design, Development, and Construction*. New York: W. W. Norton & Company, 1951.

Chartrand, René. *The Mexican Adventure 1861–67*. Men-At-Arms Series, no. 272. London: Osprey Publishing, 1994.

Christensen, Carol and Thomas Christensen. *The U.S.-Mexican War*. San Francisco: Bay Books, 1998.

Clendenen, Clarence. *Blood on the Border: The United States Army and the Mexican Irregulars*. New York: Macmillan, 1969.

Coddington, Ronald S. *African American Faces of the Civil War*. Baltimore: Johns Hopkins University Press, 2012.

Coffman, Edward. *The Old Army: A Portrait of the American Army in Peacetime, 1794–1898*. New York: Oxford University Press, 1986.

Cunliffe, Marcus. *Soldiers and Civilians: The Martial Spirit in America, 1771–1865*. Boston: Little, Brown and Company, 1968.

Daddysman, James W. *The Matamoros Trade: Confederate Commerce, Diplomacy, and Intrigue*. Newark: University of Delaware Press, 1984.

Daniell, L. E. *Types of Successful Men of Texas*. Austin: Nabu Press, 1890.

Davis, Thomas Brabson and Amado Ricon Virulegio. *The Political Plans of México*. Lanham, MD: University Press of America, 1987.

*Diccionario Porrúa de la Historia, Biografía, y Geografía de México*. Ciudad de México: Editorial Porrúa, S.A., 1995.

Dobak, William A. *Freedom by the Sword: The U.S. Colored Troops, 1862–1867*. Washington, DC: US Army Center of Military History, 2011.

Dobak, William A. and Thomas D. Phillips. *The Black Regulars, 1866–1898*. Norman: University of Oklahoma Press, 2001.

Dodd, Walter Fairleigh. *Modern Constitutions: A Collection of the Fundamental Laws of Twenty-Two of the Most Important Countries of the World, with Historical and Biographical Notes*. 2 vols. Chicago: University of Chicago Press, 1909.

Ely, Glen Sample. *The Texas Frontier and the Butterfield Overland Mail, 1858–1861*. Norman: University of Oklahoma Press, 2016.

———. *Where the West Begins*. Lubbock: Texas Tech University Press, 2011.

Evans, General Clement A., ed. *Confederate Military History, Vol. XI: A Library of Confederate States History. In Twelve Volumes, Written by Distinguished Men of the South*. Atlanta: Confederate Publishing, 1899.

Feherenbach, T. R. *Lone Star: A History of Texas and the Texans*. New York: Wings Books, 1991.

Fort, Karen. *A Feast of Reason: The Civil War Journal of James Madison Hall*. Forthcoming.

Fort, Karen G. B. *Bale o' Cotton: The Mechanical Art of Cotton Ginning*. College Station: Texas A&M University Press, 1992, 2015.

Fox-Genovese, Elizabeth. *Within the Plantation Household: Black and White Women of the Old South*. Chapel Hill: University of North Carolina Press, 1988.

Francaviglia, Richard V. *From Sail to Steam: Four Centuries of Texas Maritime History 1500–1900*. Austin: University of Texas Press, 1998.

Fremantle, Arthur James Lyon. *The Fremantle Diary: Being the Journal of Lt. Col. Fremantle, Coldstream Guards on His Three Months in the Southern States*. Boston: Little, Brown and Company, 1954.

———. *Three Months in the Southern States: April–June 1863*. 1864, reprint Lincoln: University of Nebraska Press, 1991.

Furber, George C. *The Twelve Months Volunteer; Or, Journal of a Private, in the Tennessee Regiment of Cavalry, in the Campaign, in Mexico, 1846–7*. Cincinnati: J. A. & U. P. James, 1849.

George, W. Eugene. *Lost Architecture of the Rio Grande Borderlands*. College Station: Texas A&M University Press, 2008.

Glasrud, Bruce A. *African Americans in South Texas History*. College Station: Texas A&M University Press, 2011.

Glatthaar, Joseph T. *Forged in Battle: The Civil War Alliance of Black Soldiers and White Officers*. New York: Free Press, 1990.

Grear, Charles David. *Why Texans Fought in the Civil War*. College Station: Texas A&M University Press, 2010.

Greaser, Galen D. *New Guide to Spanish and Mexican Land Grants in South Texas*. Austin: Texas General Land Office, 2009.

Harris, Charles III. *A Mexican Family Empire: The Latifundio of the Sanchez Navarros, 1765–1867*. Austin: University of Texas Press, 1975.

Hart, John Mason. *Empire and Revolution: The Americans in México since the Civil War*. Berkeley: University of California Press, 2002.

———. *Revolutionary México: The Coming and Process of the Mexican Revolution*. Stanford: Stanford University Press, 1997.

Hill, Lawrence F. *José De Escandón and the Founding of Nuevo Santander, a Study in Spanish Colonization*. Columbus: Ohio State University Press, 1926.

Horgan, Paul. *Great River: The Rio Grande in North American History*. 2 vols. New York: Rinehart & Co., 1954.

Hughes, William J., *Rebellious Ranger: Rip Ford and the Old Southwest*. Norman: University of Oklahoma Press, 1964.

Hunt, Jeffrey W. *The Last Battle of the Civil War: Palmetto Ranch*. Austin: University of Texas Press, 2002.

Hunter, Louis. *Steamboats on the Western Rivers: An Economic and Technological History*. Cambridge, MA: Harvard University Press, 1949.

Hurtado, Albert L. *Herbert Eugene Bolton: Historian of the American Borderlands*. Berkeley: University of California Press, 2012.

Irby, James A. *Backdoor at Bagdad: The Civil War on the Rio Grande*. El Paso: Texas Western Press, 1977.

Isbell, Frances. *Hidalgo County Ranch Histories*. Edinburg, TX: Hidalgo County Historical Commission and Hidalgo County Historical Society, 1994.

Jones, Oakah L. *Los Paisanos: Spanish Settlers on the Northern Frontier of New Spain*. Norman: University of Oklahoma Press, 1996.

Kearney, Milo and Anthony Knopp. *Boom and Bust: The Historical Cycles of Matamoros and Brownsville*. Austin: Eakin Press, 1991.

Kelly, Pat. *River of Lost Dreams: Navigation on the Rio Grande*. Lincoln: University of Nebraska Press, 1986.

Kireker, Charles. *History of the 116th Regiment U.S.C. Infantry*. Philadelphia: King and Baird, 1866.

Koselleck, Reinhart. *The Practice of Conceptual History, Timing History, Spacing Concepts*. Stanford, CA: Stanford University Press, 2002.

Lardas, Mark. *African American Soldier in the Civil War, USCT 1862–66*. Oxford, UK: Osprey Publishing, 2006.

Lea, Tom. *The King Ranch*, vol. 1. Boston: Little, Brown and Company, 1957.

Leckie, William. *The Buffalo Soldiers: A Narrative of the Negro Cavalry in the West*. Norman: University of Oklahoma Press, 1967.

Leiker, James N. *Racial Borders: Black Soldiers along the Rio Grande*. College Station: Texas A&M University Press, 2002.

Levinson, Irving. *Wars within Wars: Mexican Guerrillas, Domestic Elites, and the United States of America 1846–1848*. Fort Worth: Texas Christian University Press, 2005.

Lincoln, Abraham. *The Collected Works of Abraham Lincoln*. 9 vols. New Brunswick, NJ: Rutgers University Press, 1953.

Lonn, Ella. *Salt as a Factor in the Confederacy*. Tuscaloosa: University of Alabama Press, 1965.

Lott, Virgil N. and Mercurio Martinez. *The Kingdom of Zapata*. Austin: Eakin Press, 1983.

Lovett, Bobbie L., Juan L. Gonzalez, Roseann Bacha Garza, and Russell Skowronek. *Native American Peoples of South Texas*. Edinburg, TX: Community Historical Archaeology Project with Schools Program, 2014.

Lubbock, Francis Richard. *Six Decades in Texas: Or the Memoirs of Francis Richard Lubbock*, edited by C. W. Raines. Austin: Pemberton Press, 1968.

MacGregor, Morris J. and Bernard C. Nalty. *Blacks in the United States Armed Forces: Basic Documents*, vol. 3. Wilmington, DE: Scholarly Resources, 1977.

Marley, David F., ed. *Wars of the Americas: A Chronology of Armed Conflict in the Western Hemisphere, 1492 to the present*, vol. I. Santa Barbara, CA: ABC CLIO, 2008.

Martin, James Kirby, Randy J. Roberts, Steven Mintz, Linda O. McMurry, and James H. Jones. *America and Its Peoples*. New York: Pearson Longman, 2007.

McAllen Amberson, Mary Margaret, James A. McAllen, and Margaret H. McAllen. *I Would Rather Sleep in Texas: A History of the Lower Rio Grande Valley and the People of the Santa Anita Land Grant*. Austin: Texas State Historical Association, 2003.

McAllen, Mary Margaret. *Maximilian and Carlotta: Europe's Last Empire in México*. San Antonio, TX: Trinity University Press, 2014.

McFarland, Henry. *Sixty Years in Concord and Elsewhere: Personal Recollections of Henry McFarland 1831–1891*. Concord, NH: Rumford Press, 1899.

McPherson, James. *Battle Cry of Freedom: The Civil War Era*. New York: Oxford University Press, 1988.

Miller, Hubert J. *José de Escandón: Colonizer of Nuevo Santander*. Edinburg, TX: New Santander Press, 1980.

Morgan, M. J. *Border Sanctuary: The Conservation Legacy of the Santa Ana Land Grant*. College Station: Texas A&M University Press, 2015.

Murphy, Douglas. *Two Armies on the Rio Grande: The First Campaign of the U.S.-Mexican War*. College Station: Texas A&M University Press, 2015.

Nichols, James L. *The Confederate Quartermaster in the Trans-Mississippi*. Austin: University of Texas Press, 1964.

Pagden, Anthony. *Lords of All the World: Ideologies of Empire in Spain, Britain and France c. 1500–c. 1800*. New Haven, CT: Yale University Press, 1995.

Parisot, P. F. *Reminiscences of a Texas Missionary*. San Antonio, TX: Johnson Bros. Printing Co., 1899.

Perry, Laurens Ballard. *Júarez and Diaz: Machine Politics in México*. DeKalb: Northern Illinois University Press, 1978.

Pierce, Frank C. *A Brief History of the Lower Rio Grande Valley*. Menasha, WI: George Banta Publishing, 1917.

Pruneda, Pedro. *Historia de la Guerra de México desde 1861 a 1867, con Todos los Documentos Diplomáticos Justificativos*. Madrid: Elizade y Compañia, 1867.

Redkey, Edwin S., ed. *A Grand Army of Black Men: Letters from African-American Soldiers in the Union Army, 1861–1865*. New York: Cambridge University Press, 1992.

Richter, William L. *The Army in Texas during Reconstruction, 1865–1870*. College Station: Texas A&M University Press, 1987.

Rickey, Don, Jr. *Forty Miles a Day on Beans and Hay: The Enlisted Soldier Fighting the Indian Wars*. Norman: University of Oklahoma Press, 1963.

Ripley, Eliza M. *From Flag to Flag: A Woman's Adventures and Experiences in the South during the War, in Mexico, and in Cuba*. New York: D. Appleton and Company, 1889.

Roell, Craig H. *Matamoros and the Texas Revolution*. Denton: Texas State Historical Association, 2013.

Santleben, August. *A Texas Pioneer: Early Staging and Overland Freighting Days on the Frontiers of Texas and Mexico*, edited by I. D. Affleck. 1910, facsimile edition. Waco, TX: W. M. Morrison, 1967.

Schuler, L. J. *The Last Battle of the War between the States: May 13, 1865*. Brownsville, TX: Springman-King Company, 1960.

Schunior Ramírez, Emelia. *Ranch Life in Hidalgo County after 1850*. Edinburg, TX: New Santander Press, 1971.

Schwartz, Rosalie. *Across the Rio to Freedom: US Negroes in Mexico*. El Paso: Texas Western Press, 1975.

Scott, Douglas D. and Richard A. Fox Jr. *Archaeological Insights into the Custer Battle:*

*An Assessment of the 1984 Field Season*. Norman: University of Oklahoma Press, 1987.

Scott, Robert N, H. M. Lazelle, George B. Davis, Leslie J. Perry, Joseph W Kirkley, Fred C. Ainsworth, John S. Moodey, and Calvin D. Cowles. *The War of the Rebellion: A Compilation of the Official Records of the Union and Confederate Armies*. Washington, DC: Government Printing Office, 1880.

Sears, Richard D. *Camp Nelson, Kentucky: A Civil War History*. Lexington: University Press of Kentucky, 2002.

Sheridan, Philip H. *Personal Memoirs of P. H. Sheridan, General, United States Army in Two Volumes*. New York: Charles L. Webster and Company, 1888.

Smallwood, James M. *Time of Hope, Time of Despair: Black Texans during Reconstruction*. Port Washington, NY: Kennikat Press, 1981.

Smith, Reed William. *Samuel Medary and the Crisis: Testing the Limits of Press Freedom*. Columbus: Ohio State University Press, 1995.

Smithwick, Noah. *The Evolution of a State/Recollection of Old Texas Days*. Austin: University of Texas Press, 1983.

Steward, Theophilus G. *The Colored Regulars in the United States Army*. Philadelphia: AME Book Concern, 1904.

Stillman, Chauncey D. *Charles Stillman, 1810–1875*. New York: C.D. Stillman, 1956.

Stillman, Francis D. *The Stillman Family: Descendants of Mr. George Stillman of Wethersfield, Connecticut and Dr. George Stillman of Westerly, Rhode Island*. Greensburg, PA: F. D. Stillman, 1989.

Sumter, Jesse. *Paso del Aguila: A Chronicle of Frontier Days on the Texas Border*, edited by Ben E. Pingenot. Austin: Encino Press, 1969.

Thompson, Jerry D. *Cortina: Defending the Mexican Name in Texas*. College Station: Texas A&M University Press, 2007.

———. *Juan Cortina and the Texas Mexican Frontier, 1859–1877*. El Paso: Texas Western Press, 1994.

——— *Mexican Texans in the Union Army*. El Paso: Texas Western Press, 1986.

———. *Tejano Tiger: José de los Santos Benavides and the History of the Texas-Mexico Borderlands, 1823–1891*. Fort Worth, TX: Texas Christian University Press, forthcoming.

———. *Vaqueros in Blue and Gray*. Austin: State House Press, 2000.

Thompson, Jerry D. and Lawrence T. Jones III. *Civil War and Revolution on the Rio Grande Frontier: A Narrative and Photographic History*. Austin: Texas State Historical Association, 2004.

Thompson, Waddy. *Recollections of México*. New York: Wiley and Putnam, 1846.

Tilley, Nannie M., ed. *Federals on the Frontier: The Diary of Benjamin F. McIntyre 1862–1864*. Austin: University of Texas Press, 1963.

Toral, Brig. Gen. Jésus de Leon. *Historia Militar: La Intervencion Francesa en México*. Ciudad de México: Sociedad Mexicana de Geografia y Estadistica, 1962.

Townsend, Stephen A. *The Yankee Invasion of Texas*. College Station: Texas A&M University Press, 2006.

Tucker, Phillip T. *The Final Fury: The Last Battle of the Civil War*. Mechanicsburg, PA: Stackpole Books. 2001.

Tyler, Ronnie C. *Santiago Vidaurri and the Southern Confederacy*. Austin: Texas State Historical Association, 1973.

Underwood, Rodman L. *Waters of Discord: The Union Blockade of Texas in the Civil War*. Jefferson, NC: McFarland & Co., 2003.

Valerio-Jiménez, Omar S. *River of Hope: Forging Identity and Nation in the Rio Grande Borderlands*. Durham, NC: Duke University Press, 2013.

Vanderwood, Paul. *Disorder and Progress: Bandits, Police, and Mexican Development*. Lincoln: University of Nebraska Press, 1981.

Vasquez, Josefina Zoraida. *La supeusta republica del Rio Grande*. Victoria, Tamaulipas, Mexico: Instituto de Investigaciones Historia de la Universidad de Tamaulipas, 1995.

Wallace, Lew. *Lew Wallace: An Autobiography*. 2 vols. New York: Harper and Brothers, 1902.

Walraven, Bill. *Corpus Christi: The History of a Texas Seaport*. Woodland Hills, CA: Windsor, 1982.

Washington, Booker T. *Up from Slavery*. New York: Doubleday, 1901.

Watson, William. *The Civil War Adventures of a Blockade Runner*. College Station: Texas A&M University Press, 2001.

Weber, David J. *The Spanish Frontier in North America*. New Haven, CT: Yale University Press, 1992.

West, Elliot. *The Last Indian War: The Nez Perce Story*. New York: Oxford University Press, 2009.

Wilson, Keith P. *Campfire of Freedom: The Camp Life of Black Soldiers during the Civil War*. Kent, OH: Kent State University Press, 2002.

Winsor, Bill. *Texas in the Confederacy: Military Installations, Economy and People*. Hillsboro, TX: Hill Junior College Press, 1978.

Woodman, Lyman L. *Cortina: Rogue of the Rio Grande*. San Antonio, TX: Naylor Company, 1950.

Wood, Robert D., trans., Death and Taxes. San Antonio, TX: San Mary's University Duplication Services, 2001.

Wooster. Ralph A., ed. *Texas in the Civil War*. Austin: Texas State Historical Association, 1995.

Ybarra, Samuel Handy and Delia Handy Ybarra. *Handy Anthology: Handy Family Genealogy: History, Documents, and Photos*. Blurb, 2008.

Young, Warren L. *Minorities and the Military: A Cross-National Study in World Perspective*. Westport, CT: Greenwood Press, 1982.

## *Theses and Dissertations*

Downing de Juana, Ana Cristina. "Intermarriage in Hidalgo County 1860–1900." Master's thesis, University of Texas–Pan American, July 1998.

Galindo, Mary Jo. "Con Un Pie En Cada Lado: Ethnicities and the Archaeology of Spanish Colonial Ranching Communities along the Lower Rio Grande Valley." PhD diss., University of Texas at Austin, 2003.

Graf, LeRoy P. "The Economic History of the Lower Rio Grande Valley, 1820–1875." 2 Vols. PhD diss., Harvard University, 1942.

Marcum, Richard T. "Fort Brown, Texas: The History of a Border Post." Master's thesis, Texas Technical College, 1964.

Petrovich, Margaret W. "The Civil War Career of Colonel John Salmon 'Rip' Ford." Master's thesis, Stephen F. Austin College, 1961.

Phillips, Thomas D. "The Black Regulars: Negro Soldiers in the United States Army, 1866–1891." PhD diss., University of Wisconsin, 1970.

Thompson, James H. "A Nineteenth Century History of Cameron County, Texas." Master's thesis, University of Texas at Austin, 1965.

Zeitlin, Richard. "Brass Buttons and Iron Rails: The United States Army and American Involvement in México, 1861–1865." PhD diss., University of Wisconsin, 1973.

## *Journal Articles and Book Chapters*

Adelman, Jeremy and Stephen Aron. "From Borderlands to Borders: Empires, Nation-States, and the Peoples in between in North American History." *American Historical Review* 104, no. 3 (1999): 814–41.

Brown, Marley. "The Use of Oral and Documentary Sources in Historical Archaeology: Ethnohistory at the Mott Farm." In *Historical Archaeology: A Guide to Substantive and Theoretical Contributions*, edited by Robert Schuyler. Farmingdale, NY: Baywood Publishing, 1978.

Cheeseman, Bruce S. "'Let Us Have 500 Good Determined Texans': Richard King's Account of the Union Invasion of South Texas, November 12, 1863, to January 20, 1864." *The Southwestern Historical Quarterly* 101, no. 1 (1997): 76–95.

Cunningham, Debbie S. "Friar Simón Del Hierro's Diary of the Preliminary Colonization of Nuevo Santander, 1749: An Annotated Translation." *Catholic Southwest* 23 (2012): 36–55.

———. "The Natives of the Seno Mexicano." *Southern Quarterly* 51, no. 4 (2014): 55–71.

Davenport, Harbert. "Notes on Early Steamboating on the Rio Grande." *Southwestern Historical Quarterly* 49, no. 2 (1945): 286–89.

Deagan, Kathleen. "Avenues of Inquiry in Historical Archaeology." In *Advances in Archaeological Method and Theory*, vol. 5. Edited by Michael B. Schiffer. New York: Academic Press (1982): 151–77.

———. "Neither History nor Prehistory: The Questions That Count in Historical Archaeology." *Historical Archaeology* 22, no. 1 (1988): 7–12.

Delaney, Robert W. "Matamoros, Port for Texas during the Civil War," *Southwestern Historical Quarterly*, 58, no. 4 (1955): 473–87.

Feinman, Gary M. "Thoughts on New Approaches to Combining the Archaeological and Historical Records." *Journal of Archaeological Method and Theory*, 4, no. 3/4 (1997): 367–77.

Finkelman, Paul. "Story Telling on the Supreme Court: *Prigg v. Pennsylvania* and Justice Joseph Story's Judicial Nationalism." *The Supreme Court Review 1994* (1995): 247–94.

Gonzalez, Juan L., Russell K. Skowronek, and Bobbie L. Lovett. "Deflation Troughs, Water and Prehistoric Occupation on the Margins of the South Texas Sand Sheet, Evidence from Hidalgo County, Texas." *Journal of Texas Archaeology and History* 1, no. 1 (2014): 70–93.

Haecker, Charles M. "A Historical Archaeological Study of the Battlefield of Palmito Ranch, 'The Last Conflict of the Great Rebellion.'" In *From These Honored Dead: Historical Archaeology of the Civil War*, edited by Clarence R. Geier. Douglas D. Scott, and Lawrence E. Babits. Gainesville: University Presses of Florida, 2014, 57–71.

Hart, John Mason. "The 1840s Southwestern México Peasants' War: Conflict in a Transitional Society." In *Riot, Rebellion, and Revolution*, edited by Friedrich Katz. Princeton, NJ: Princeton University Press, 1988.

Heidler, Jeanne T. "'Embarrassing Situation': David E. Twiggs and Surrender of United States Forces in Texas, 1861." In Ralph A. Wooster, ed., *Lone Star Blue and Grey: Essays on Texas and the Civil War*. Austin: Texas Historical Association, 1996, 29–46.

Henderson, Mary Virginia. "Minor Empresario Contracts for the Colonization of Texas, 1825–1834." *The Southwestern Historical Quarterly* 31, no. 4 (1928): 295–324.

Hester, Thomas R. "The Prehistory of South Texas." In *The Prehistory of Texas*, edited by Timothy K. Perttula. College Station: Texas A&M University Press, 2004, 127–52.

Knight, Larry. "United States Colored Troops in Texas during Reconstruction, 1865–1867." *Southwestern Historical Quarterly* 109, no. 3 (2006): 336–57.

Leiker, James N. "The Difficulties of Understanding Abe: Lincoln's Reconciliation of Natural Inequality and Natural Rights." In *Lincoln Emancipated: The President and the Politics of Race*, edited by Brian R. Dirck. Dekalb: Northern Illinois University Press, 2007, 73–98.

Mayer, Jean. "Las Oposiciones Francesas a Expédition du Mexique." In *El Poder y la Sangre: Guerra, Estado y Nación en la Decada de 1860*, edited by Guillermo Palacios and Erika Pani. Ciudad de México: El Colegio de México, 2014, 451–80.

McBride, W. Stephen. "Camp Nelson and Kentucky's Civil War Memory." *Historical Archaeology* 47, no. 3 (2013): 69–80.

Mecham, J. Lloyd. "The Origins of Federalism in Mexico." *The Hispanic American Historical Review* 18, no. 2 (1938): 164–82.

Miller, Christopher L. "Prelude to Rivalry: The Frontier Foundations of Two Global Empires." In *The Soviet Union and the United States: Rivals of the Twentieth-Century: Coexistence and Competition*, edited by Eva-Maria Stolberg. Frankfurt am Main: Peter Lang, 2013, 11–31.

Myers, Marshall, and Chris Propes, eds. "'I Don't Fear Nothing in the Shape of Man': The Civil War and Texas Border Letters of Edward Francis, United States Colored Troops." *The Register of the Kentucky Historical Society* 101, no. 4 (2003): 247–49.

Nichols, James David, "The Line of Liberty: Runaway Slaves and Fugitive Peons in the Texas-Mexico Borderlands." *Western Historical Quarterly* 44, no. 4 (2013): 413–33.

Printz, Andrew Jackson. "The del Norte Goes to Texas." *S&D Reflector* (December 2006): 35–38.

Rippy, J. Fred, "Border Troubles along the Rio Grande, 1848–1860." *Southwestern Historical Quarterly* 23, no. 2 (1919): 91–111.

Sandos, James A. "From 'Boltonlands' to 'Weberlands': The Borderlands Enter American History." *American Quarterly* 46, no. 4 (1994): 595–604.

Schuyler, Robert L. "The Spoken Word, the Written Word, Observed Behavior and Preserved Behavior: The Contexts Available to the Archaeologist." In *Historical Archaeology: A Guide to Substantive and Theoretical Contributions*. Farmingdale, NY: Baywood Publishing, 1978, 278–83.

Scott, Douglas D., and Andrew P. McFeaters. "The Archaeology of Historic Battlefields: A History and Theoretical Development in Conflict Archaeology." *Journal of Archaeological Research* 19, no. 1 (March 2011): 103–32.

Sibley, Marilyn McAdams. "Charles Stillman: A Case Study of Entrepreneurship on the Rio Grande, 1861–1865." *Southwestern Historical Quarterly* 77 (1973): 227–40.

Skowronek, Russell K. "Hail to Thee, O Alma Mater: Considering the Archaeology of Academia." In *Beneath the Ivory Tower: The Archaeology of Academia*, edited by Russell K. Skowronek and Kenneth Lewis. Gainesville, FL: University Presses of Florida, 2010, 274–76.

Skowronek, Russell K., and Bobbie L. Lovett. "Coahuiltecans of the Rio Grande Region." In *Native American Peoples of South Texas*. Edinburg, TX: Community Historical Archaeology Project with Schools Program, 2014, 13–22.

Taylor, Helen. "Gone with the Wind and Its Influence." In *The History of Southern Women's Literature*, edited by Carolyn Perry and Mary Weaks-Baxter. Baton Rouge: Louisiana State University Press, 2002, 258–67.

Taylor, Walter W. "A Study of Archaeology." *American Anthropologist* Memoir 69, American Anthropological Association (1948): 5–263.

Thomas, David Hurst. "Columbian Consequences: The Spanish Borderlands in Cubist Perspective." In *Columbian Consequences, Archaeological and Historical Perspectives on the Spanish Borderlands West*, V01.1. Edited by David H. Thomas. Washington, DC: Smithsonian Institution Press, 1989: 1–14.

Turner, Frederick Jackson. "The Significance of the Frontier in American History." *The Annual Report of the American Historical Association* (1894): 119–227.

Tyler, Ronnie C. "Cotton on the Border." *Southwestern Historical Quarterly* 73, no. 4 (1970): 456–77.

———. "Cotton on the Border, 1861–1865." In *Lone Star Blue and Gray: Essays on*

*Texas in the Civil War*, edited by Ralph A. Wooster. Austin: Texas State Historical Association, 1995, 211–34.

———. "Fugitive Slaves in Mexico." *Journal of Negro History* 57 (1972): 1–12.

Vanderwood, Paul. "Betterment for Whom? The Reform Period: 1855–75." In *The Oxford History of Mexico*, edited by Michael C. Meyer and William H. Beezley. Oxford: Oxford University Press, 2000, 349–72.

Zavaleta, Antonio N. "Colored Death: The Tragedy of Black Troops in the Lower Rio Grande, 1864–1906." *Studies in Rio Grande Valley History* 6 (2005): 343–60.

Zorrilla, Juan Fidel, Maribel Miró Flaquer, and Octavio Herrera Pérez. *Tamaulipas: Una Historia Compartida I, 1810–1921*. 2 vols. San Juan Mixcoac, Mexico: Universidad Autónoma de Tamaulipas, Instituto Investigaciones Históricas, 1993.

## *Encyclopedia and Internet Entries*

Alonzo, Armando C. "Mexican-American Land Grant Adjudication." *Handbook of Texas Online*, https://tshaonline.org/handbook/online/articles/pqmck (accessed April 15, 2016).

Arenson, Adam. "Fighting for the Legacy of Lincoln." *The New York Times*, December 13, 2013, http://opinionator.blogs.nytimes.com/2013/12/13/fighting-for-the-legacy-of-lincoln/?_r=0 (accessed February 17, 2015).

Arkowitz, Hal, and Scott O. Lilienfeld. "Why Science Tells Us Not to Rely On Eyewitness Accounts." *Scientific American* (January 1, 2010), http://www.scientificamerican.com/article/do-the-eyes-have-it/. (accessed August 29, 2016).

Avalon Project, Documents in Law, History, and Diplomacy. "Treaty of Guadalupe-Hidalgo." Lillian Goldman Law Library, Yale Law School, http://avalon.law.yale.edu/19th_century/guadhida.asp (accessed January 16, 2016).

Barker, Eugene C., and James W. Pohl. "Texas Revolution." *Handbook of Texas Online*, http://www.tshaonline.org/handbook/online/articles/qdt01 (accessed July 30, 2016).

Campbell, Randolph B. "Slavery." *Handbook of Texas Online*, https://tshaonline.org/handbook/online/articles/yps01 (accessed June 28, 2016).

Carroll, H. Bailey. "Texan Santa Fe Expedition." *Handbook of Texas Online*, http://www.tshaonline.org/handbook/online/articles/qyt03 (accessed July 30, 2016).

"Civil War Battles: Major Battles from the American Civil War." HistoryNet, *http://* www.historynet.com/civil-war-battles (accessed June 27, 2016).

Coole, Ruth Musgrave. "La Sal Vieja." *Handbook of Texas Online*, https://tshaonline.org/handbook/online/articles/r0101 (accessed January 12, 2016).

Coppock, Mike. "The Republic of the Rio Grande." HistoryNet, http://www.historynet.com/the-republic-of-the-rio-grande.htm (accessed June 26, 2016).

Cote, Joseph W. "Pathways of Freedom: Rethinking the Underground Railroad 1810–1865." Dr. Martin Luther King Task Force, http://freedomexhibit.org/virtual/ (accessed June 20, 2015).

CWSAC Battle Summaries. "Civil War Battle Summaries by State." The American

Battlefield Protection Program (ABPP), https://www.nps.gov/abpp/battles/bystate.htm (accessed June 27, 2016).

"Empresario." *Handbook of Texas Online*, http://www.tshaonline.org/handbook/online/articles/pfe01 (accessed July 30, 2016).

García, Clotilde P. "Escandon, Jose De." *Handbook of Texas Online*, http://www.tshaonline.org/handbook/online/articles/fes01 (accessed July 25, 2016).

Garza, Christina R. "Petition Drive Seeks Removal of Jefferson Davis Monument." *The Brownsville Herald* (January 17, 2016), http://www.brownsvilleherald.com/news/local/article_c04aa352-bd9b-11e5-b95a-8b48427ce181.html (accessed January 17, 2016).

Hart, John Mason. "Stillman, Charles." *Handbook of Texas Online*, http://www.tshaonline.org/handbook/online/articles/fst57 (accessed July 30, 2016).

Hayden, Jen. "Jefferson Davis Monument at the University of Texas Is Headed to a New Home." *Daily Kos* (August 13, 2015), http://www.dailykos.com/story/2015/8/13/1411770/-Jefferson-Davis-monument-at-the-University-of-Texas-is-headed-to-a-new-home(accessed July 16, 2016).

Isbell, Frances. "Brewster Ranch Cemetery," Hidalgo County Historical Society, Cemeteries of Texas, January 1980, http://www.cemeteries-of-tx.com/Etx/Hidalgo/Cemetery/brewster.htm (accessed October 27, 2017).

———. "Relampago Cemetery." Hidalgo County Historical Society, Hidalgo County Cemeteries of Texas, (accessed December 2, 2010).

Kelly, Patrick J. "Lincoln Looks South of the Border." *The New York Times*, November 22, 2013, http://opinionator.blogs.nytimes.com/2013/11/22/lincoln-looks-south-of-the-border/?_r=0 (accessed January 18, 2016).

Levin, Kevin M. "Not Your Grandfather's Civil War Commemoration." *The Atlantic*, 2011, http://www.theatlantic.com/national/archive/2011/12/not-your-grandfathers-civil-war-commemoration/249920/ (accessed June 20, 2016).

Long, Christopher. "Old Three Hundred." *Handbook of Texas Online*, http://www.tshaonline.org/handbook/online/articles/um001 (accessed July 4, 2016).

"Major Elihu Dwight Smith: 1796–1868." SFAA Genealogy, http://strongfamilyofamerica.org/genealogy/getperson.php?personID=I06665&tree=dwight_2012_01_01 (accessed July 25, 2015).

McAllen, Margaret, and Mary Margaret McAllen. "McAllen Ranch." *Handbook of Texas Online*, http://www.tshaonline.org/handbook/online/articles/apm05 (accessed August 1, 2016).

Muir, Andrew Forest. "Webber, John Ferdinand." *Handbook of Texas Online*, (accessed June 20, 2015).

Neu, C. T. "Annexation." *Handbook of Texas Online*, http://www.tshaonline.org/handbook/online/articles/mga02 (accessed July 30, 2016).

Rodriguez, Albert. "Border Love on the Rio Grande: African American Men and Latinas in the Rio Grande Valley of South Texas (1850–1940)." *BlackPast.org*, http://www.blackpast.org/perspectives/border-love-rio-grande-african-american-men-and-latinas-rio-grande-valley-south-texas-1 (accessed November 27, 2015).

"Texas Slave Narrative Sally Wroe." *Roots Web*, http://freepages.genealogy.rootsweb.

ancestry.com/~ewyatt/_borders/Texas%20Slave%20Narratives/Texas%20W/Wroe,%20Sallie.html (accessed June 20, 2015).

Vigness, David M. "Republic of the Rio Grande." *Handbook of Texas Online*, http://www.tshaonline.org/handbook/online/articles/ngr01 (accessed July 31, 2016).

Weddle, Robert S. "La Salle Expedition." *Handbook of Texas Online*, http://www.tshaonline.org/handbook/online/articles/up101 (accessed July 24, 2016).

———. "La Salle's Texas Settlement." *Handbook of Texas Online*, http://www.tshaonline.org/handbook/online/articles/ue107 (accessed July 24, 2016).

"What Kind of Historical Source Are Letters and Diaries?" History Matters: The U.S. Survey Course on the Web, http://historymatters.gmu.edu/mse/letters/whatkind.html (accessed April 19, 2016).

# About the Authors

ROSEANN BACHA-GARZA (MA, University of Texas–Pan American) is the Program Manager of the Community Historical Archaeology Project with Schools (CHAPS) Program at the University of Texas Rio Grande Valley in Edinburg, Texas. Outlined in her thesis, "San Juan and Its Role in the Transformation of the Rio Grande Valley," is the succession of Spanish land grantees, displaced Civil War families, Anglo entrepreneurs, and Mexican Revolution refugees and their migration to San Juan at various stages of municipal development. She coedited several books, including *Blue and Gray on the Border: The Rio Grande Valley Civil War Trail* and *The Civil War on the Rio Grande, 1846–1876* (with Russell Skowronek and Christopher Miller 2018), *The Native American Peoples of South Texas*, and *From Porciones to Colonias: The Power of Place and Community-Based Learning in K-12 Education*, as part of a grant-sponsored project for Rio Grande Valley K–12 educators. The book *Images of America: San Juan* (Arcadia, 2010) was authored by Roseann Bacha-Garza and the San Juan Economic Development Corporation, which won Preservation Texas's Heritage Education Award.

ROLANDO L. GARZA (MA, University of Texas at Brownsville) is the Archeologist and Chief of Resource Management at Palo Alto Battlefield National Historical Park in Brownsville, Texas. After receiving a BA in Anthropology from the University of Texas in 1990, he worked on various Cultural Resource Management projects throughout Texas and New Mexico, including a stint serving as Field Director for the Texas Department of Transportation on the Freedman's Cemetery project in Dallas. In 1998 Garza joined the National Park Service at the Southeast Archeological Center, gaining invaluable experience investigating battlefields from the American Revolution, the War of 1812, and the US Civil War, as well a variety of other historic and prehistoric sites in the southeast region. He returned to his hometown in 2001 to work at the recently established Palo Alto Battlefield National Historical Park. He is an active steward of the archeological resources in Cameron County and serves on Brownsville's Heritage Council.

KAREN GERHARDT FORT (MA, Baylor University, 1997) is the author of *Bale O' Cotton: The Mechanical Art of Cotton Ginning* (Texas A&M University Press, 1992; reprint, 2015), as well as five books for Arcadia Publishing about towns in the Rio Grande Valley. She has had two articles published by *North and South* magazine regarding the Civil War in Texas, and has conducted background research for a documentary film, *The Home Front: Life in Texas during the Civil War* (1998). *A Feast of Reason* (State House Press, 2017) is a biography based upon the Civil War journal kept by East Texas planter/merchant James Madison Hall. She has contributed to the Civil War Trail project by the CHAPS program through her podcast segment about Fort Ringgold. A retired museum director, she created exhibits at the Robert E. Lee House Museum at Fort Ringgold for the Rio Grande City C.I.S.D. She continues to write books about the cotton industry.

THOMAS A. FORT (MA, University of Arizona, 1978) is Senior Historian at the Museum of South Texas History in Edinburg, Texas. He has studied and written about Lower Rio Grande history for forty years, including several podcast segments for the Civil War Trail project by the CHAPS Program, University of Texas Rio Grande Valley. Fort also has created numerous museum exhibits about regional history, including the Rio Grande steamboat era and the Civil War in South Texas. Publications include *Borderlands, The Heritage of the Lower Rio Grande through the Art of José Cisneros*, Hidalgo County Historical Museum (Museum of South Texas History), 1998; "Los Algodones: The 'Cotton Times' of the Rio Grande Valley's Civil War Era," *Texas Highways* magazine, Texas Department of Transportation, December 2013; and "Rio Grande Steamboats," *Texas Heritage* magazine, Texas Historical Foundation, fall 2004.

JAMES N. LEIKER (PhD, University of Kansas) is a professor of history and Chair of the Department of History and Political Science at Johnson County Community College in Overland Park, Kansas. His published articles on race relations in the American West have appeared in *Western Historical Quarterly*, *Army History*, *Great Plains Quarterly*, and *Kansas History*, among others. Dr. Leiker's books include *Racial Borders: Black Soldiers along the Rio Grande* (Texas A&M University Press, 2002), and with Ramon Powers, *The Northern Cheyenne Exodus in History and Memory* (Norman: University of Oklahoma Press, 2011), which won the distinguished book prize from the Center for Great Plains Studies.

IRVING W. LEVINSON (PhD with honors, University of Houston) is a Fulbright Garcia-Robles Scholar and an associate professor of history at the University of Texas Rio Grande Valley. He is the author of *Wars within Wars: Mexican Guerrillas, Domestic Elites, and the United States of America 1846–1848* (Texas Christian University Press, 2005) and the coeditor and a contributor to *Latin American Positivism* (Lexington Books, 2013). A recipient of the Society for Military History's Moncado Prize (2010), he also is the author of six published articles.

MARY MARGARET MCALLEN was raised on a storied South Texas ranch and writes about the history of the Southwest and Mexico. Her three books include the award-winning and best-selling *I Would Rather Sleep in Texas* (Austin: Texas State Historical Association, 2003), *A Brave Boy and a Good Soldier: John C. C. Hill and the Texas Expedition to Mier* (Austin: Texas State Historical Association, 2006), and *Maximilian and Carlota: Europe's Last Empire in Mexico* (San Antonio, TX: Trinity University Press, 2015). She has written book introductions and contributed to anthologies, and has appeared on the PBS series *History Detectives* and contributed to *Faces of America*. She lives in San Antonio and serves after earning her MA in history as an adjunct professor of history at the University of Texas at San Antonio. She currently serves as Director of Special Projects at the Witte Museum.

DR. W. STEPHEN MCBRIDE is the Director of Interpretation and Archaeology at Camp Nelson Civil War Heritage Park, Jessamine County, Kentucky. Dr. McBride received his bachelor's degree in anthropology from Beloit College, Wisconsin, and his master's and doctorate degrees in anthropology from Michigan State University. He specializes in historical archaeology of eighteenth and nineteenth century United States. Dr. McBride has directed many excavations and has authored or coauthored numerous articles on Camp Nelson and other sites for professional journals and edited volumes. He has coauthored the books/booklets *Frontier Forts of West Virginia: Historical and Archaeological Explorations* (2003;

with Kim McBride and Greg Adamson); *Seizing Freedom: Archaeology of Escaped Slaves at Camp Nelson, Kentucky* (2010; with Kim McBride); and *Frontier Defense: Colonizing Contested Areas in the Greenbrier Valley of West Virginia* (2014; with Kim McBride). Dr. McBride also coedited (with Kim McBride and David Pollack) *Historic Archaeology in Kentucky* (1995).

CHRISTOPHER L. MILLER was born and raised in Portland, Oregon, and received his bachelor of science from Lewis and Clark College and his PhD from the University of California, Santa Barbara. He is currently professor of history at the University of Texas Rio Grande Valley. He is the author of *Prophetic Worlds: Indians and Whites on the Columbia Plateau* (Rutgers University Press, 1985); coauthor of *Making America: A History of the United States*, now in its seventh edition (Cengage, 2015); coeditor with Tamer Balcı of *The Gülen Hizmet Movement: Circumspect Activism in Faith-Based Reform* (Cambridge Scholars, 2012); and coeditor with Roseann Bacha-Garza and Russell K. Skowronek of *Blue and Gray on the Border: The Rio Grande Valley Civil War Trail* (Texas A&M University Press, 2018). His articles and reviews have appeared in numerous scholarly journals and anthologies, as well as standard reference works. He has been a research fellow at the Charles Warren Center for Studies in American History at Harvard University and was the Nikolay V. Sivachev Distinguished Chair in American History at Lomonsov Moscow State University (Russian Federation).

DOUGLAS MURPHY (PhD, University of North Carolina–Chapel Hill) is Chief of Operations at Palo Alto Battlefield National Historical Park. He has contributed articles to *Hemisphere* and *Military History of the West*, and served as a writer for the National Park Service booklet *Hispanics in the Civil War: From Battlefield to Homefront* (National Park Service, 2011), which won awards from the National Association of Interpretation and the American Association of State and Local History. His book *Two Armies on the Rio Grande: The First Campaign of the US-Mexican War* (Texas A&M University Press, 2015) was awarded both the Clotilde P. Garcia Tejano Book Prize and the Brigadier General James R. Collins Jr. Book Prize for Military History.

# ABOUT THE AUTHORS

RUSSELL K. SKOWRONEK (PhD, Michigan State University), is Associate Dean, School of Interdisciplinary Programs and Community Engagement, College of Liberal Arts, and a professor of anthropology and history at the University of Texas Rio Grande Valley, where he serves as the director of the Community Historical Archaeology Project with Schools and he holds the Houston Endowment Chair for Civic Engagement. He is the author or editor of *X Marks the Spot: The Archaeology of Piracy* (with Charles R. Ewen, University Press of Florida, 2006); *Situating Mission Santa Clara de Asís* (Academy of American Franciscan History, 2006); *HMS Fowey, Lost . . . and Found* (with George Fischer, University Press of Florida, 2009); *Beneath the Ivory Tower: The Archaeology of Academia* (with Kenneth Lewis, University Press of Florida, 2010); *Ceramic Production in Early Hispanic California: Craft, Economy, and Trade on the Frontier of New Spain* (with M. James Blackman and Ronald L. Bishop, University Press of Florida, 2014); and *Pieces of Eight, More Archaeology of Piracy* (with Charles R. Ewen, University Press of Florida, 2016).

JERRY THOMPSON is Regents Professor of History at Texas A&M International University in Laredo. Thompson is the recipient of numerous awards and honors from the Arizona Historical Society, Historical Society of New Mexico, and the Texas State Historical Association. He has twice received the Best Scholarly Book Award from the Texas Institute of Letters, first for his *Civil War to the Bitter End: The Life and Times of Major General Samuel Peter Heintzelman* and his biography of Juan Nepomuceno Cortina, entitled *Cortina: Defending the Mexican Name in Texas*. He received the Kate Broocks Bates Award from the Texas State Historical Association for *Civil War and Revolution on the Rio Grande Frontier*, which he coauthored with Larry Jones. He has twice received the Tejano Book Award, first for his biography of Cortina and in 2012 for his *Tejanos in Gray: The Civil War Letters of Captains Manuel Yturria and Rafael de la Garza*. Thompson has also received the Senator Judity Zaffarini Medal for his teaching excellence and academic accomplishments, as well as the Texas A&M University System Teaching Excellence Award. Thompson received his BA in history from Western New Mexico University, his MA in history from the University of New Mexico, and his doctorate in history from Carnegie Mellon University. He is past president of the Texas State Historical Association, and in 2018 received the TSHA Mary Jon and J. P. Bryan Award for his contributions to Texas history. His *A Civil War History of the New Mexico Volunteers and Militia* (Albuquerque: University of New Mexico Press, 2015) is considered a groundbreaking study of the subject. His most recent book is *Tejano Tiger: José de los Santos Benavides and the Texas-Mexico Borderlands, 1823–1891* (Fort Worth, TX: Texas Christian University Press, 2017), which was awarded the Texas Institute of Letters' Most Significant Scholarly Book Award in 2018.

# Index

Page numbers in *italics* refer to figures and tables.

## *Other Books in the Elma Dill Russell Spencer Series in the West and Southwest*

*Aspects of the American West Three Essays*
Joe B. Frantz and W. E. Hollon

*Trader on the American Frontier: Myth's Victim*
Howard R. Lamar and Kristin E. Parsons

*America's Frontier Culture: Three Essays*
Ray A. Billington and W. T. Jackson

*How Did Davy Die?*
Dan Kilgore

*Grave of John W. Hardin: Three Essays on Grassroots History*
C. L. Sonnichsen

*Juan Davis Bradburn: A Reappraisal of the Mexican Commander of Anahuac*
Margaret S. Henson

*Civil War Recollections of James Lemuel Clark*
L. D. Clark

*Texas Longhorn: Relic of the Past, Asset for the Future*
Donald E. Worcester

*Red Hole in Time*
Muriel Marshall

*Travels in Mexico and California*
A. B. Clarke

*Mexican War Journal and Letters of Ralph K. Kirkham*
Robert R. Miller

*Regional Studies: The Interplay of Land and People*
Glen E. Lich

*Immigrant Soldier in the Mexican War*
Frederick Zeh and William J. Orr

*Where Rivers Meet: Lore from the Colorado Frontier*
Muriel Marshall

*Massacre on the Lordsburg Road: A Tragedy of the Apache Wars*
Marc Simmons

*Geronimo's Kids: A Teacher's Lessons on the Apache Reservation*
Robert S. Ove and H. Henrietta Stockel

*Defiant Peacemaker: Nicholas Trist in the Mexican War*
Wallace L. Ohrt

*Life among the Texas Indians: The WPA Narratives*
David La Vere

*Plains Indians*
Paul H. Carlson

*Conquest of the Karankawas and the Tonkawas, 1821-1859*
Kelly F. Himmel

*Chiricahua Apache Women and Children: Safekeepers of the Heritage*
H. H. Stockel

*Hispanics in the Mormon Zion, 1912-1999*
Jorge Iber

*Comanche Society: Before the Reservation*
Gerald Betty

*True Women and Westward Expansion*
Adrienne Caughfield

*Robertsons, the Sutherlands, and the Making of Texas*
Anne H. Sutherland

*Life Along the Border: A Landmark Tejana Thesis*
Jovita González and Maria E. Cotera

*Lone Star Pasts: Memory and History in Texas*
Gregg Cantrell and Elizabeth H. Turner

*Secret War for Texas*
Stuart Reid

*Colonial Natchitoches: A Creole Community on the Louisiana-Texas Frontier*
H. S. Burton and F. Todd Smith

*Yeomen, Sharecroppers, and Socialists: Plain Folk Protest in Texas, 1870-1914*
Kyle G. Wilkison

*More Zeal Than Discretion: The Westward Adventures of Walter P. Lane*
Jimmy L. Bryan

*On the Move: A Black Family's Western Saga*
S. R. Martin

*Texas That Might Have Been: Sam Houston's Foes Write to Albert Sidney Johnston*
Margaret S. Henson

*Tejano Leadership in Mexican and Revolutionary Texas*
Jesús F. De la Teja

*Texas Left: The Radical Roots of Lone Star Liberalism*
David O. Cullen

*How Did Davy Die? And Why Do We Care So Much?*
James E. Crisp and Dan Kilgore

*Drumbeats from Mescalero: Conversations with Apache Elders, Warriors, and Horseholders*
H. H. Stockel

*Turmoil on the Rio Grande: History of the Mesilla Valley, 1846-1865*
William S. Kiser

*Texas Right: The Radical Roots of Lone Star Conservatism*
David O' Donald Cullen and Kyle G. Wilkison

*We Never Retreat: Filibustering Expeditions into Spanish Texas, 1812–1822*
Ed Bradley

*General Alonso de León's Expeditions into Texas, 1686–1690*
Lola Orellana Norris

*Comanches and Germans on the Texas Frontier: The Ethnology of Heinrich Berghaus*
Daniel J. Gelo and Christopher J. Wickham, with contributions by Heide Castañeda

*Murder and Intrigue on the Mexican Border: Governor Colquitt, President Wilson, and the Vergara Affair*
John A. Adams

*Woolly West: Colorado's Hidden History of Sheepscapes*
Andrew Gulliford

*Preserving German Texan Identity: Reminiscences of William A. Trenckmann, 1859–1935*
Walter L. Buenger